FREE TRADE AND ITS ENEMIES IN FRANCE, 1814–1851

In the aftermath of the French Revolution, advocates of protection against foreign competition prevailed in a fierce controversy over international trade. This ground-breaking study is the first to examine this 'protectionist turn' in full. Faced with a reaffirmation of mercantile jealousy under the Bourbon Restoration, Benjamin Constant, Jean-Baptiste Say and regional publicists advocated the adoption of the liberty of commerce in order to consolidate the new liberal order. But after the Revolution of 1830 a new generation of liberal thinkers endeavoured to reconcile the jealousy of trade with the discourse of commercial society and political liberty. New justifications for protection oscillated between an industrialist reinvention of jealousy and an aspiration to self-sufficiency as a means of attenuating the rise of urban pauperism. A strident denunciation of British power and social imbalances served to defuse the internal tensions of the protectionist discourse and facilitated its dissemination across the French political spectrum.

DAVID TODD is a Lecturer in World History in the History Department at King's College London.

IDEAS IN CONTEXT

Edited by David Armitage, Richard Bourke, Jennifer Pitts and John Robertson

The books in this series will discuss the emergence of intellectual traditions and of related new disciplines. The procedures, aims and vocabularies that were generated will be set in the context of the alternatives available within the contemporary frameworks of ideas and institutions. Through detailed studies of the evolution of such traditions, and their modification by different audiences, it is hoped that a new picture will form of the development of ideas in their concrete contexts. By this means, artificial distinctions between the history of philosophy, of the various sciences, of society and politics, and of literature may be seen to dissolve.

The series is published with the support of the Exxon Foundation.

A list of books in the series will be found at the end of the volume.

FREE TRADE AND ITS ENEMIES IN FRANCE, 1814–1851

DAVID TODD
King's College London

CAMBRIDGE
UNIVERSITY PRESS

CAMBRIDGE
UNIVERSITY PRESS

University Printing House, Cambridge CB2 8BS, United Kingdom

Cambridge University Press is part of the University of Cambridge.

It furthers the University's mission by disseminating knowledge in the pursuit of education, learning and research at the highest international levels of excellence.

www.cambridge.org
Information on this title: www.cambridge.org/9781107036932

Derives from a book originally published in French as *L'Identité économique de la France: libre-échange et protectionnisme (1814–1851)* by Éditions Grasset & Fasquelle, 2008 © Éditions Grasset & Fasquelle, 2008

First published 2015

Printed in the United Kingdom by Clays, St Ives plc

A catalogue record for this publication is available from the British Library

Library of Congress Cataloguing in Publication data
Todd, David, 1978–
[Identité économique de la France. English]
Free trade and its enemies in France, 1814–1851 / David Todd, King's College London.
pages cm
Translation of the author's L'identité économique de la France.
Includes bibliographical references and index.
ISBN 978-1-107-03693-2 (hbk.)
1. France–Economic conditions–19th century. 2. France–Commerce–History–19th century. 3. International trade–19th century. I. Title.
HF3556.T6313 2015
382'.71094409034–dc23
2014045609

ISBN 978-1-107-03693-2 Hardback

Contents

Acknowledgements — *page* vi
List of abbreviations — ix

Introduction — 1
1 The reactionary political economy of the Bourbon Restoration — 20
2 Economists, winegrowers and the dissemination of commercial liberalism — 55
3 Completing the Revolution: political and commercial liberty after 1830 — 89
4 Inventing economic nationalism — 123
5 The contours of the national economy — 155
6 The Englishness of free trade and the consolidation of protectionist dominance — 190
Conclusion — 229

Bibliography — 238
Index — 267

Acknowledgements

Free Trade and its Enemies in France, 1814–1851 is an extensively revised version of a book published in French, *L'Identité économique de la France, 1814–1851* (Paris: Éditions Bernard Grasset, 2008). Most of the material under consideration in the French and English versions is the same. But while the French book was chiefly intended as a contribution to the social history of ideas and *mentalités*, the English version primarily engages with the more vibrant field, in the English-speaking world, of intellectual history. Both versions are equally committed to the promotion of what I believe can be a fruitful dialogue between historians of ideas and economic historians.

I am very grateful to David Armitage for encouraging me to write this English version and for his insightful comments on various aspects of the project. I also wish to thank Elizabeth Friend-Smith for her editorial work at Cambridge University Press, and Christophe Bataille and Patrick Weil, general editor and series editor at Éditions Bernard Grasset, for their support with the completion of the earlier French version.

By far the largest of my intellectual debts goes to Emma Rothschild, who supervised the PhD thesis on which this book is based. Her vision of what intellectual and economic history should seek to achieve has been a constant source of inspiration. Her suggestions and comments have helped to fashion a great many specific aspects as well as the broader thrust of the book.

Several conversations with the late François Crouzet helped to awaken my curiosity in divergent British and French attitudes towards free trade. I am grateful to the examiners of the thesis, Pierre Rosanvallon and Robert Tombs, who made many useful suggestions on the significance of protectionism for nineteenth-century French political culture. The book also owes a great deal to the comments of three anonymous referees, in particular a constructive critic of the relationship between eighteenth- and nineteenth-century French debates about commerce by 'Reader A'.

Additional thanks are due to many members of my family, friends and colleagues, for numerous stimulating discussions and answers to specific queries. A far from exhaustive list includes Sunil Amrith, Christopher Bayly, Fabrice Bensimon, Hélène Blais, Angus Burgin, Edward Castleton, Christophe Charle, Carole Christen, Christopher Clark, Guillaume Daudin, Martin Daunton, Nicolas Delalande, Quentin Deluermoz, Richard Drayton, Michael Drolet, Olivier Dufau, Marcel Gauchet, Perry Gauci, Boyd Hilton, Jean-Pierre Hirsch, Étienne Hofmann, Istvan Hont, Julian Hoppit, Jeff Horn, Antony Howe, Lynn Hunt, Joanna Ines, Maurizio Isabella, François Jarrige, Colin Jones, Shruti Kapila, Laure Kodratoff, Fabien Knittel, Michael Kwass, Michael Ledger-Lomas, Claire Lemercier, Georges Liébert, Dominique Margairaz, Philippe Minard, Renaud Morieux, William O'Reilly, William Nelson, Gabriel Paquette, Jennifer Pitts, Pedro Ramos Pinto, Paul Readman, Pernille Røge, François-Joseph Ruggiu, Florian Schui, Pierre Singaravélou, John Shovlin, Michael Sonenscher, Gareth Stedman Jones, Frank Trentmann, Nicolas Todd, Richard Tuck, François Vatin and Julien Vincent.

As one of the book's themes is the attention to the material context that permitted the formulation and dissemination of certain ideas, I am very glad to have an opportunity to thank the institutions that provided me with financial support at various stages of the making of this book: the British Council, Trinity College (Cambridge), Trinity Hall, the Centre for History and Economics, the Andrew W. Mellon Foundation, King's College London and the Philip Leverhulme Trust. I also wish to express my gratitude for the assistance, patience and kindness of the staff of numerous libraries, archives and research centres. Special thanks are due to Martine Hilaire, at the Section du XIXe siècle of the Archives Nationales, and to Inga Huld Markan, the executive officer at the Centre for History and Economics in Cambridge.

I am grateful to Lord Clarendon and the Chambre de Commerce et d'Industrie de Mulhouse for their permission to cite material from, respectively, the Clarendon Papers at the Bodleian Library (Oxford) and the archives of the Mulhouse Chamber of Commerce at the Centre Rhénan d'Archives et de Recherches Economique (Mulhouse). Parts of Chapters 3 and 4 draw from the first section of my article, 'John Bowring and the Global Dissemination of Free Trade', already published by Cambridge University Press in the *Historical Journal*, 51 (2) (2008): 373–97.

Translations of quotations from texts in French are my own, although I have consulted and often followed existing published translations. French words and phrases in quotations from texts in English have not been translated. Unless otherwise stated, emphases in quotations are original.

By communicating his enthusiasm about life and making sure that I could never oversleep in the morning, my two-year-old son, Joseph, has contributed in his own way to the completion of the manuscript, although not as much as his mother, Victoria, to whom this book is dedicated.

Abbreviations

AASMP	Archives de l'Académie des Sciences Morales et Politiques
ACCM	Archives de la Chambre de Commerce de Mulhouse
ADBR	Archives Départementales du Bas-Rhin
ADCO	Archives Départementales de la Côte d'Or
ADG	Archives Départementales de la Gironde
ADM	Archives Départementales de la Moselle
ADN	Archives Départementales du Nord
ADTN	Association pour la Défense du Travail National
ALE	Association pour la Liberté des Echanges
AMB	Archives Municipales de Bordeaux
AMM	Archives Municipales de Mulhouse
AN	Archives Nationales
AP	Archives parlementaires
ASIM	Archives de la Société Industrielle de Mulhouse
AUP	Auckland Papers
BJL	Brynmore Jones Library, University of Hull
BL	British Library
BMB	Bibliothèque Municipale de Bordeaux
BNF	Bibliothèque Nationale de France
BODL	Bodleian Library, University of Oxford
CERARE	Centre Rhénan d'Archives et de Recherches Economiques
CICE	Comité des Industries Cotonières de l'Est
MS Clar.	Clarendon Papers
NAF	Nouvelles Acquisitions Françaises
SR	Stadtarchiv Reutlingen
TNA	The National Archives

Introduction

The impact of commerce on international and domestic politics emerged as a major concern of European thinkers and statesmen in the context of 'archaic globalization', a process powered by an increase in the inter-continental exchange of commodities between 1600 and 1800.[1] After the Napoleonic wars, British hegemony aided and abetted an unprecedented acceleration in the growth of international trade, marking the onset of 'modern globalization'.[2] As a result, the controversy on commerce not only increased in intensity but also changed in nature. First, between the 1820s and the 1840s, Britain became the first European country to dismantle its arsenal of mercantilist restrictions. It also began to use its naval and economic clout to promote the lowering of trade barriers throughout the world. The absolute freedom of trade, still dismissed as 'an Oceana or Utopia' by Adam Smith in 1776, now appeared as a concrete possibility, although one tinged with fear that it might entrench British supremacy.[3] Second, the growing industrial specialization of Europe resulting from the acceleration of international trade had unforeseen and troubling social consequences, especially the spread of a new form of urban poverty exemplified by the destitution of British factory workers.[4] The controversy on commerce became a debate over British poverty as well as British power, and, outside Britain, the means of escaping both. It was to denote the intensification of the concern with commerce and the emergence of new sets of beliefs that terms such as 'free trade', *libre-échange* and *Freihandel*

1 Christopher A. Bayly, '"Archaic" and "Modern" Globalization in the Eurasian and African Arena, c. 1750–1850', in Anthony G. Hopkins (ed.), *Globalization in World History* (London, 2002), pp. 47–73; on early modern debates about archaic globalization, see Istvan Hont, *The Jealousy of Trade: International Competition and the Nation-State in Historical Perspective* (Cambridge, Mass., 2005).

2 On nineteenth-century globalization, see Christopher A. Bayly, *The Birth of the Modern World, 1780–1914: Global Connections and Comparisons* (Oxford, 2004) and Jürgen Osterhammel, *The Transformation of the World: A Global History of the Nineteenth Century*, trans. Patrick Camiller (Princeton, NJ, 2014).

3 Adam Smith, *The Wealth of Nations: Books IV–V*, ed. Andrew Skinner (London, 1999), p. 48.

4 Gareth Stedman Jones, *An End to Poverty? A Historical Debate* (London, 2004), esp. pp. 133–62.

or 'protectionism', *protectionnisme* and *Protektionismus* were forged in the early decades of the nineteenth century.

I

The book retraces the beginnings of this controversy on modern globalization and the rejection of 'British' free trade in France, from the fall of the first Napoleonic Empire in 1814–15 until the advent of the second in 1851. Intellectual arguments for free trade dated back to the second half of the eighteenth century and were not exclusively British. Rather, they were elaborated by French (François Quesnay, Turgot, Abbé Raynal) and Scottish (David Hume, Adam Smith) Enlightenment philosophers.[5] The single most influential text calling for the constitution of a global market was probably Raynal's *Histoire des deux Indes*, a European best-seller which went through fifty French-language editions and countless translations between 1772 and 1790.[6] Yet, after 1815, it was in Britain that free trade gradually became a dominant ideology and official policy, a transformation often symbolized by the successful campaign of the Anti-Corn Law League for the repeal of agricultural protection in the 1840s. Historians have shown that the British enthusiasm for free trade was not only rooted in the persuasive powers of classical political economy but owed at least as much to a complex set of moral, religious and geopolitical considerations.[7] It proved an enduring feature of British intellectual and political life, lasting at least until the Edwardian era.[8]

[5] Emma Rothschild, *Economic Sentiments: Adam Smith, Condorcet, and the Enlightenment* (Cambridge, Mass., 2001); on liberal ideas about trade in eighteenth-century France, see also Catherine Larrère, *L'Invention de l'économie au XVIIIe siècle: du droit naturel à la physiocratie* (Paris, 1992) and Simone Meyssonnier, *La Balance et l'horloge: la genèse de la pensée libérale en France au XVIIIe siècle* (Paris, 1989).

[6] Anthony Strugnell, Andrew Brown, Cecil Courtney et al., 'Introduction générale', in Guillaume-Thomas Raynal, *Histoire philosophique et politique des établissements et du commerce des Européens, Tome 1: livres I à V*, ed. Anthony Strugnell, Andrew Brown, Cecil Courtney et al. (Paris, 2010), pp. xxvii–lii; Robert Darnton, *The Forbidden Best-Sellers of Pre-Revolutionary France* (New York, 1996), p. 63.

[7] Boyd Hilton, *Corn, Cash and Commerce: The Economic Policies of the Tory Governments, 1815–1830* (Oxford, 1977) and *The Age of Atonement: The Influence of Evangelicalism on Social and Economic Thought* (Oxford, 1988); on the entanglement of economic with political and moral concerns in nineteenth-century British political economy, see Donald Winch, *Riches and Poverty: An Intellectual History of Political Economy in Britain, 1750–1834* (Cambridge, 1996) and *Wealth and Life: Essays on the Intellectual History of Political Economy in Britain, 1848–1914* (Cambridge, 2009).

[8] Anthony Howe, *Free Trade and Liberal England* (Oxford, 1997) and 'Free Trade and Global Order: The Rise and Fall of a Victorian Vision', in Duncan Bell (ed.), *Victorian Visions of Global Order* (Cambridge, 2007), pp. 26–46; Lars Magnusson, *The Tradition of Free Trade* (London, 2004), esp. pp. 46–69; Frank Trentmann, *Free Trade Nation: Commerce, Consumption and Civil Society in Modern Britain* (Oxford, 2008).

Semantic and linguistic innovations marked the novelty and Britishness of free trade as an ideology. Whereas in English 'free trade' previously referred to a specific 'trade or business which may be pursued without restrictions' as in 'a free trade in corn', in the 1820s it acquired the more general sense of 'trade or commerce conducted without the interference of customs duties designed to restrict imports' from the rest of the world, as in 'a system of free trade'.[9] For example, in an entry of his *Rural Rides* dated November 1825, William Cobbett, the conservative turned radical critic of industrialization, derided 'this new project of "free trade" and "mutual gain"' as 'humbug'.[10] In the 1830s and 1840s, this new meaning of 'free trade' inspired the forging of neologisms in foreign languages, such as *libre-échange* in French. Searching Google Books, I found no occurrence of 'libre échange' in reference to the circulation of commodities in French-language publications before 1829 and six occurrences between 1830 and 1833, four of which appear in translations of English writings.[11] It was Frédéric Bastiat, an avid reader of British periodicals and admirer of the Anti-Corn Law League, who gave a hyphenated version of the expression wider currency when he launched the newspaper *Le Libre-échange* in 1846. *Freihandel* was also calqued from English into German at the same period.[12]

While nineteenth-century free trade was British, France soon came to embody its 'other', protectionism. The earliest occurrence of 'protectionist' I could identify in existing databases was part of a speech delivered on 5 June 1834 by the Hull MP and free-trader, Thomas Perronet Thompson, on the reciprocity of shipping duties between Britain and France.[13] The speech alluded to the extreme agitation of French public opinion over trade policy, and it is noteworthy that Thompson was at the

[9] 'Free trade', *Oxford English Dictionary*, 3rd edn, June 2007 (www.oed.com, accessed 19 March 2014).

[10] William Cobbett, *Rural Rides*, 3rd edn, 2 vols. (London, 1885), vol. I, pp. 400–3.

[11] Search for 'libre échange', 1820–1833, in Google Books, works in French (http://books.google.fr, accessed 19 March 2014). The four translations were: James S. Buckingham, *Discours préliminaire prononcé à l'Athénée à l'occasion d'un cours sur les Indes orientales*, trans. Benjamin Laroche (Paris, 1830), p. 40; 'Note sur l'agriculture de la France', translated from the *Morning Chronicle*, in *Journal d'Agriculture et des Manufactures des Pays-Bas*, 12 (1830): 212–17, at p. 213; 'Progrès constitutionnels de la Prusse', translated from *Blackwoods*, in *Revue Britannique*, 3rd series, 4 (1833): 193–214, at p. 205; and 'De la fabrication et du commerce des soieries en France et en Angleterre', translated from the *Westminster Review*, in *Revue Britannique*, 3rd series, 6 (1833): 53–76, at p. 72. The other two occurrences were in two Saint-Simonian publications: *L'Européen, Journal des Sciences Morales et Économiques*, 1 (1830), p. 66, and Emile Barrault (ed.), *Religion saint-simonienne: recueil des prédications*, 2 vols (Paris, 1832), vol. II, p. 7.

[12] Lutz Mackensen (ed.), *Ursprung der Wörter* (Wiesbaden, 1998), p. 140; and Friedrich Kluge (ed.), *Etymologisches Wörterbuch der deutschen Sprache* (Berlin, 1967), p. 217.

[13] For Thompson, 'to attempt to play the protectionist or prohibitionist in places where we had no power, appeared to him an impossibility, not to say an absurdity', quoted in *The Times*, 6 June 1834.

time in close correspondence with John Bowring, who was engaged in a campaign to reduce the influence of the 'anti-free-traders' in France.[14] Yet the word only took hold in English in the 1840s. After the account of Thompson's speech in 1834, the next two occurrences of 'protectionist' in *The Times* date from 1843, followed by five occurrences in 1844 and fifteen in 1845.[15] These occurrences mostly referred to the British supporters of the Corn Laws, who founded the Society for the Protection of Agriculture in February 1844.[16] A letter from Lord Fitzwilliam, a Whig politician, to George Pryme, Professor of Political Economy at Cambridge, dated 28 February 1844, stressed the term's novelty: 'I am glad to see that you have been giving your mind to the *protectionists*, as they are now called.'[17] In France, opponents of free trade after 1830 preferred to style themselves the defenders of *travail national* (national labour) or of the *système protecteur* (protective system). *Protectionnisme* and its derivatives in French were probably imported from English. The earliest occurrence of *protectionniste* I could identify, in a work extolling the Anti-Corn Law League's crusade for free trade published in 1845 by Bastiat, also referred to British defenders of the Corn Laws.[18] *Protectionnisme* retained a pejorative connotation and was not widely used until the end of the century. Similarly, *Protektionismus* was introduced in German in the 1840s, but it only gained wide currency in the 1880s.[19]

After 1850, and the collapse of support for protection in Britain, France came to be seen, in Britain and elsewhere, as the incarnation of protectionism. 'Two systems', free trade and protection, the American economist and adversary of British free trade, Henry Carey, wrote in 1858, 'are before the world … Leader in the advocacy of the first has been, and is, Great Britain. Leader in the establishment of the second, and most consistent in its maintenance, is France.'[20] So ingrained did the perception of France as the land of protectionism become that in 1876 increases in the tariffs of the United States and Canada led *The Times* to exclaim, with melancholy surprise: 'It is not the French population alone or chiefly

[14] Thomas Perronet Thompson to John Bowring, 28 October 1834, Hull, Brynmore Jones Library (hereafter BJL), Thompson MSS, 4/5.

[15] Search for 'protectionist', 1830–45, in The Times Digital Archive, 1785–2008 (http://gale.cengage.co.uk/times.aspx, accessed 19 March 2014).

[16] On the defence of the Corn Laws, see Anna Gambles, *Protection and Politics: Conservative Economic Discourse* (London, 1999), esp. pp. 56–85.

[17] George Pryme, *Autobiographic Recollections*, ed. Alicia Bayne (Cambridge, 1870), p. 306.

[18] Frédéric Bastiat, *Cobden et la ligue* (Paris, 1845), p. 394.

[19] Wolfgang Pfeifer (ed.), *Etymologisches Wörterbuch des Deutschen*, 2 vols. (Berlin, 1993), vol. II, p. 57.

[20] Henry Carey, *Letters to the President on the Foreign and Domestic Policy of the Union* (Philadelphia, Pa., 1858), p. 133.

which is protectionist.'[21] At the turn of the twentieth century, Germany sometimes rivaled France as Britain's economic other and symbol of protectionist policies.[22] But the image of France as intrinsically hostile to free trade has remained influential to this day. *The Economist*, a periodical which has consistently advocated free trade since its foundation in 1843, still lambasts the protectionism of 'Fortress France' as fervently as in the nineteenth century.[23]

The coinage of new words or phrases tends to mark ideological crystallization rather than intellectual innovation. Free trade and protectionism, or *libre-échange* and *travail national*, were not coherent doctrines, but slogans. Yet their very nature of slogan, evoking a variety of economic, political and moral considerations, makes them useful keys to interrogate contemporary ideas about the early stage of what is now construed as nineteenth-century globalization. Adopting a simultaneously comparative and connective perspective, the book examines the reception, attempts at reinterpretation and eventual rejection of British free trade in France. As such, it is a contribution to both the history of the transformations of liberalism in France after 1815 and to a transnational history of political and economic ideas.

II

The book analyses the elaboration and dissemination of a politico-economic discourse that was neither hostile to capitalism nor political liberalism, but rejected the cosmopolitan project of a global market as destructive of social stability as well as national independence. Although the premises of this discourse can be found in the attacks of counter-revolutionary thinkers on the political economy of the Physiocrats and Adam Smith before 1820, it was the adoption of free trade by Britain and the fear of British-style pauperism that led a majority of French liberals to endorse the protection of 'national labour' and stress its compatibility with market economics and representative institutions. In the 1840s, just as free trade achieved ascendancy in Britain, it was relegated to the margins of French intellectual and political life. The national political economy of

[21] *The Times*, 22 January 1876, quoted in Henry Carey, *Commerce, Christianity and Civilization versus British Free Trade* (Philadelphia, Pa., 1876), pp. 3–4.

[22] Trentmann, *Free Trade Nation*, pp. 93–100.

[23] Compare, for instance, 'Protectionism in France', *The Economist*, 26 May 1894, with 'Protectionism in France: Fair Is Foul', *The Economist*, 26 June 1993, or 'French Protectionism: Fearful Fortress France', *The Economist*, 29 October 2005.

the French protectionists drove an enduring wedge between French liberalism and classical economics and contributed to the divergence between French and British liberalism after 1830.

The outcome of the controversy on international trade in France can only appear predictable with the benefit of hindsight. Before the early nineteenth century, France was home to a vibrant and influential tradition of *laissez-faire* ideas. Under the influence of Physiocratic thinkers, the Bourbon monarchy proved keen to introduce free-market reforms in the grain and colonial trades.[24] The treaty that liberalized exchanges between Britain and France in 1786 resulted from a French initiative.[25] Until the 1790s, Adam Smith, often viewed as a successor of Quesnay and Turgot, was widely praised or disparaged, throughout Europe, as an advocate of 'French' ideas of political and economic liberty.[26] In France, *The Wealth of Nations* went through four translations and ten editions by 1802.[27] In the early years of Napoleon Bonaparte's rule, French debates about Smith set advocates of different interpretations against one another rather than his followers against his opponents.[28]

Only the imperatives of economic warfare against Britain, with the advent of the Continental Blockade, temporarily silenced advocates of a liberal trade policy after 1805. The first three chapters of this book highlight the resurgence of support for a radical conception of economic liberty after the fall of Napoleon. In Chapter 1, I examine how the reactionary political economy of the Bourbon Restoration revived liberal

[24] On economic reforms in France after the Seven Years' War, see Steven L. Kaplan, *Bread, Politics and Political Economy in the Reign of Louis XV*, 2 vols. (The Hague, 1976), esp. vol. 1, pp. 97–163; Jean Tarrade, *Le Commerce colonial de la France à la fin de l'Ancien Régime: l'évolution du régime de 'l'exclusif' de 1763 à 1789*, 2 vols. (Paris, 1972), esp. vol. 1, pp. 167–285; on Physiocracy, see Liana Vardi, *The Physiocrats and the World of Enlightenment* (Cambridge, 2012) and Pernille Røge, 'Political Economy and the Reinvention of France's Colonial System, 1756–1802' (unpublished Ph.D. thesis, University of Cambridge, 2010).

[25] Orville T. Murphy, 'Du Pont de Nemours and the Anglo-French Commercial Treaty of 1786', *Economic History Review*, new series, 19 (3) (1966): 569–80; and Marie Donaghay, 'Exchange of Products of the Soil and Industrial Goods in the Anglo-French Commercial Treaty of 1786', *Journal of European Economic History*, 19 (2) (1990): 377–401.

[26] Emma Rothschild, 'Political Economy', in Gareth Stedman Jones and Gregory Claeys (eds.), *The Cambridge History of Nineteenth-Century Political Thought* (Cambridge, 2011), pp. 748–79, at pp. 751–3; and Rothschild, *Economic Sentiments*, pp. 52–71.

[27] Kenneth Carpenter, *The Dissemination of the Wealth of Nations in French and in France, 1776–1843* (New York, 2002), pp. xxi–lxiii; on the popularity of Smithian political economy in France in the 1790s, see also Gilbert Faccarello and Philippe Steiner (eds.), *La Pensée économique pendant la Révolution française, 1789–1799* (Grenoble, 1990); and James Livesey, 'Agrarian Ideology and Commercial Republicanism in the French Revolution', *Past and Present*, 157 (1997): 94–121.

[28] Richard Whatmore, *Republicanism and the French Revolution: An Intellectual History of Jean-Baptiste Say's Political Economy* (Oxford, 2000), pp. 171–3.

frustrations about commercial prohibitions and the regulation of colonial trade. Chapter 2 considers the emergence of a militant discourse in favour of *liberté commerciale*, an early translation of free trade, in the 1820s, while Chapter 3 looks at the intensification and dissemination, with the active encouragement of the British government, of protests for trade liberalization in the wake of the 1830 Revolution.

The endorsement of protection by a majority of liberals after the mid 1830s did not therefore result from a French Colbertian atavism. Historians of Old Regime France have in any case demonstrated that the legacy of Jean-Baptiste Colbert was not one of unmitigated interventionism and, more broadly, that eighteenth-century economic debates were not structured around the opposition between mercantilism and *laissez-faire*.[29] Much more important were the contests between advocates and adversaries of luxury and divergent appreciations of the danger posed by the rapid growth in the public debt.[30] To the extent that contemporaries debated the implications of 'archaic globalization' before the French Revolution, they can more helpfully be divided between defenders of a moderately reformist 'science of commerce' epitomized by Montesquieu and the supporters of a more radical Physiocratic agrarianism, rather than between liberals and *dirigistes*.[31] Even for the early decades of the nineteenth century, the modern dualism between liberalism and interventionism fails to account adequately for the complex and changing views of contemporaries on the international circulation of commodities.[32]

Yet, by comparison with the abundance of works on British free trade or even German responses to the later stages of nineteenth-century globalization, historians have paid scant attention to the protectionist turn of French liberalism after 1830.[33] Historians of economic thought pursuing

[29] Philippe Minard, *État et industrie: la fortune du colbertisme dans la France des lumières* (Paris, 1998), esp. pp. 292–314; see also Jean-Claude Perrot, *Une histoire intellectuelle de l'économie politique, XVIIe–XVIIIe siècles* (Paris, 1992).

[30] John Shovlin, *The Political Economy of Virtue: Luxury, Patriotism, and the Origins of the French Revolution* (Ithaca, NY, 2006); Michael Sonenscher, *Before the Deluge: Public Debt, Inequality, and the Intellectual Origins of the French Revolution* (Princeton, NJ, 2007); Anoush F. Terjanian, *Commerce and Its Discontents in Eighteenth-Century French Political Thought* (Cambridge, 2013).

[31] Paul Cheney, *Revolutionary Commerce: Globalization and the French Monarchy* (Cambridge, Mass., 2010), pp. 21, 168–94.

[32] William M. Reddy, *The Rise of a Market Culture: The Textile Trade and French Society* (Cambridge and Paris, 1984); Jean-Pierre Hirsch, *Les Deux rêves du commerce: entreprise et institution dans la région lilloise (1780–1860)* (Paris, 1991); Nicolas Bourguinat, *Les Grains du désordre: l'État face aux violences frumentaires dans la première moitié du XIXe siècle* (Paris, 2002), pp. 53–111.

[33] Sebastian Conrad, *Globalisation and the Nation in Imperial Germany* (Cambridge, 2010); Cornelius Torp, *Die Herausforderung der Globalisierung: Wirtschaft und Politik in Deutschland, 1860–1914* (Göttingen, 2005).

a doctrinal approach, mainly concerned with the elaboration of modern economic analysis, have usually dismissed nineteenth-century French debates as of limited intellectual significance.[34] The handful of works dealing with support for free trade in France have dated its emergence to the 1840s and attributed it to diffusion from Britain.[35] The even scarcer works that have seriously examined the views of French adversaries of free trade tend to describe them in the anachronistic language of modernization theory and development economics.[36] Interest in the nineteenth-century controversy over free trade in France has also suffered from the long prevalence of a materialist interpretation, which attributed the dominance of protectionism to the influence of rent-seeking industries. The multi-volume reference work, *Histoire économique et sociale de la France*, edited by Ernest Labrousse and Fernand Braudel, brushed aside nineteenth-century debates about free trade in four pages, reaching the conclusion that 'the pressure of opinion [in favour of protection] did not rest on a precise ideology' but 'merely corresponded to the influence of dominant interests'.[37] This influential view has often confined works on the French debates over free trade and protection to a history of industrial lobbying.[38]

The last three chapters of *Free Trade and its Enemies* analyse instead the elaboration, dissemination and triumph of a new anti-free-trade ideology after 1835. In response to the clamour for free trade, Chapter 4 argues, several liberal publicists invented new justifications for protection that either stressed the need to meet the British industrial challenge or called for autarky in order to prevent the spread of British-style pauperism. In Chapter 5, I study the dissemination of this nationalist economist

[34] See, for example, Joël Ravix, 'Le Libre-échange et le protectionnisme en France', in Yves Breton and Michel Lutfalla (eds.), *L'Économie politique en France au XIXe siècle* (Paris, 1991), pp. 485–523; on the limits of the doctrinal approach, see Winch, *Riches and Poverty*, esp. pp. 15–16.

[35] See, for example, Alex Tyrrell, '"La Ligue Française", the Anti-Corn Law League and the Campaign for Economic Liberalism in France during the Last Days of the July Monarchy', in Anthony Howe and Simon Morgan (eds.), *Rethinking Nineteenth-Century Liberalism: Richard Cobden Bicentenary Essays* (Aldershot, 2006), pp. 99–116.

[36] Francis Démier, 'Nation, marché et développement dans la France de la Restauration' (unpublished doctoral dissertation, University of Paris X, 1991), esp. pp. 2–11; another, older but equally presentist exception, concerned with tracing the origins of the 'doctrine of national economics', is René Maunier, 'Les Économistes protectionnistes en France de 1815 à 1848', *Revue Internationale de Sociologie*, 19 (3) (1911): 485–514.

[37] Fernand Braudel and Ernest Labrousse (eds.), *Histoire économique et sociale de la France*, 4 vols. (Paris, 1977–93), vol. III.1, pp. 155–9.

[38] See, for example, Jürgen Hilsheimer, *Interessengruppen und Zollpolitik in Frankreich: die Auseinandersetzungen um die Aufstellung des Zollstarifs von 1892* (Heidelberg, 1973), and Michael S. Smith, *Tariff Reform in France, 1860–1900: The Politics of Economic Interests* (Ithaca, NY, 1980).

discourse through the influence of new pressure groups and the debates between protectionists about the limits of national solidarity at the turn of the 1840s. Finally, Chapter 6 shows how the Association pour la Défense du Travail National, founded in the wake of the Anti-Corn Law League's victory in Britain, successfully defended the protection of national labour by portraying free trade as an 'English' doctrine and its French supporters as traitors.

The book examines the protectionist turn of French liberalism not only in the intellectual context created by earlier debates about archaic globalization but also in the economic context of modern globalization and the political context of post-Revolutionary reconstruction. The difference between archaic and modern globalization was qualitative as well as quantitative, with the latter form of globalization reaching more deeply into domestic economic structures and daily lives. In the eighteenth century, international trade grew 10 per cent per decade and remained limited to goods with a high value-to-weight ratio. Between 1820 and 1914, it surged 40 per cent per decade and extended to all commodities. The advent of a global market, as measured by the convergence of commodity prices and resulting in a much higher level of national or regional specialization, only began in the 1820s.[39] For France, the new global division of labour implied a gradual specialization in *demi-luxe* (semi-luxury) industries such as Lyonnais silk products, *articles de Paris* (marquetry, knick-knacks, furniture, glove-making, etc.) and the production of wine.[40] Such a specialization was unappealing to the French ruling class. On the one hand, it implied a form of economic growth that seemed more difficult to translate into political power than Britain's textile manufacturing, metal-working or coal-mining. On the other, it encouraged the growth of sectors with a workforce that enjoyed a deserved reputation for political restlessness, be it Parisian artisans, Lyonnais silk-workers or southern winegrowers.

French protectionism was therefore a response to the pressures of the new global market. To some extent, it helped to shape what some economic historians, rejecting Anglocentric accounts of industrialization, have described as the French path of economic growth in the nineteenth century, less spectacular but more balanced than Britain's, and which achieved

[39] Kevin H. O'Rourke and Jeffrey G. Williamson, 'When Did Globalization Begin?', *European Review of Economic History*, 6 (1) (2002): 23–50; see also Kevin H. O'Rourke and Jeffrey G. Williamson, *Globalization and History: The Evolution of a Nineteenth-Century Atlantic Economy* (Cambridge, Mass., 1999), pp. 29–55, and Ronald Findlay and Kevin H. O'Rourke, *Power and Plenty: Trade, War, and the World Economy in the Second Millennium* (Princeton, NJ, 2009), pp. 378–87, 395–407.

[40] Patrick Verley, 'Essor et déclin des industries du luxe et du demi-luxe au XIXe siècle', in Jacques Marseille (ed.), *Le Luxe en France: du siècle des 'Lumières' à nos jours* (Paris, 1999), pp. 107–23.

a similar rate of per-capita income growth over the years 1815 to 1914.[41] However, French protectionism is better construed as an ideology than as an economic policy. France after 1815 did not withdraw from international trade, remaining instead the second largest commercial power after Britain until the 1880s.[42] Overall, it is not clear that the level of protection from foreign competition was higher in France than in Britain, at least until the 1870s. But, as even economic historians mostly interested in quantitative data could not help noticing, although British and French statesmen reduced tariffs at a similar pace after 1820, 'the British talked of free trade, while the French … always spoke of going no further than moderate protection'.[43] It is this contrast in the political language about international trade that the book seeks to explain.

French hostility to British free trade was closely linked with what François Furet identified as the main imperative of French politics after 1814: 'terminer' (ending or completing) the Revolution.[44] While historians of political ideas used to treat the years 1814–60 as an awkward parenthesis between the Revolution and the emergence of modern republicanism, recent scholarship has highlighted the ideological creativity of the period and of liberal thinkers in particular. In a context of constitutional convergence with Britain, French liberals adapted the legacy of the Enlightenment to offer compelling theories of representative government that eschewed republican Jacobinism as an aberration and stressed the need for intermediate bodies and a restricted franchise.[45] In *Free Trade and its Enemies*, I try to nuance this picture by

[41] Patrick O'Brien and Cağlar Keyder, *Economic Growth in Britain and France, 1780–1914: Two Paths to the Twentieth Century* (London, 1978); Patrick O'Brien, 'Path Dependency, or Why Britain Became an Industrialized and Urbanized Economy Long before France', *Economic History Review*, new series, 49 (2) (1996): 213–49; François Crouzet, 'The Historiography of French Economic Growth in the Nineteenth Century', *Economic History Review*, new series, 56 (2) (2003): 215–42; Jeff Horn, *The Path Not Taken: French Industrialization in the Age of Revolution, 1750–1830* (Cambridge, Mass., 2006).

[42] Paul Bairoch, *Commerce extérieur et développement économique de l'Europe au XIXe siècle* (Paris, 1976), pp. 219–38; Jean-Claude Toutain, 'Les Structures du commerce extérieur de la France, 1789–1970', in Maurice Lévy-Leboyer (ed.), *La Position internationale de la France: aspects économiques et financiers, XIXe–XXe siècles* (Paris, 1977), pp. 53–74.

[43] John V. Nye, *War, Wine, and Taxes: The Political Economy of Anglo-French Trade, 1689–1900* (Princeton, NJ, 2007), p. 12; see also Nye's articles, 'The Myth of Free-Trade Britain and Fortress France: Tariffs and Trade in the Nineteenth Century', *Journal of Economic History*, 51 (1) (1991): 23–46; and 'Guerre, commerce, guerre commerciale', *Annales ESC*, 47 (3) (1992): 613–32. On the limits of Nye's methodology, see my review, in *H-France Review*, 9 (2009): 422–5.

[44] François Furet, *La Révolution de Turgot à Jules Ferry, 1770–1880*, 2 vols. (Paris, 1988), vol. II: *Terminer la Révolution: de Louis XVIII à Jules Ferry*.

[45] For overviews, see Jeremy Jennings, 'Constitutional Liberalism in France: From Benjamin Constant to Alexis de Tocqueville', in Gareth Stedman Jones and Gregory Claeys (eds.), *The Cambridge History of Nineteenth-Century Political Thought* (Cambridge, 2011), pp. 349–73, and Jeremy Jennings, *Revolution and the Republic: A History of Political Thought in France since the Eighteeenth Century* (Oxford, 2011). Important contributions to this reappraisal include: Pierre

showing that convergence with Britain did not extend to attitudes towards international trade and that the distrust of nineteenth-century globalization helped defeat aspirations to emulate the British liberal model in France.

Just as recent scholarship has shown that economic concerns played a significant part in French politics before and during the Revolution, the book seeks to show that the intensification of international trade was a major preoccupation in French political life after 1814. Louis de Bonald and other royalist writers were the first to denounce the potentially corrosive effects of free trade on French power and stability, while Benjamin Constant and other liberals railed against the countless violations of individual freedoms by the customs administration. After the 1830 Revolution consecrated a liberal interpretation of the 1814 constitutional Charter, a wide range of prominent figures, from the Romantic novelist Stendhal to the utopian socialist Etienne Cabet, clamoured for a parallel liberal revolution in commercial policy. Yet the 1830s and 1840s witnessed a gradual *volte-face* of French liberalism. Led by Adolphe Thiers, the future founder of the French Third Republic, a slew of liberal publicists lambasted free trade as an 'English' invention designed to overturn the French Revolutionary legacy because it would spread the twin British evils of aristocracy and pauperism. By the mid 1840s, even the anarchist Pierre-Joseph Proudhon, who considered every form of state intervention with extreme suspicion, conceded the need of trade barriers to contain 'the mercantile feudality that was born in England and now threatens, like the cholera, to invade Europe'.[46]

III

As well as an examination of the protectionist turn of French liberalism, this book offers a new, transnational account of the dissemination of nationalist political economy after the Napoleonic wars. The roots of modern economic nationalism lay in what early advocates of free trade condemned as 'mercantile jealousy', a phrase denoting a zero-sum-game conception of international trade determined by the logic of war. Jealousy inspired the policies described by later historians as 'mercantilist', which aimed at

Rosanvallon, *Le Moment Guizot* (Paris, 1985) and *La Monarchie impossible: les chartes de 1814 et 1830* (Paris, 1994); Lucien Jaume, *L'Individu effacé; ou, Le Paradoxe du libéralisme français* (Paris, 1997); and Annelien de Dijn, *French Political Thought from Montesquieu to Tocqueville: Liberty in a Levelled Society?* (Cambridge, 2008).

46 Pierre-Joseph Proudhon, *Système des contradictions économiques ou philosophie de la misère*, 2 vols. (Paris, 1846), vol. II, pp. 5–77.

obtaining a surplus in the 'balance of trade' thanks to the regulation of foreign and colonial exchanges.[47] The nineteenth-century protectionists, the book argues, elaborated a new language, simultaneously designed to adjust mercantilist concerns to the new challenge of British industrialization and to spread jealous sentiments beyond the narrow circles of princes and their ministers. Yet this new protectionist language was riven by a major contradiction between an industrialist response to the threat of British economic supremacy – best represented by Friedrich List, the author of *The National System of Political Economy* (1841) – on the one hand and a temptation to withdraw from the global market in order to achieve self-sufficiency – a project reminiscent of Johann Gottlieb Fichte's *The Closed Commercial State* (1800) – on the other. A shared economic Anglophobia helped to mask the tensions between these conflicting aspirations, while the resulting ambiguity broadened the appeal of protectionism.

The use of German intellectual figures to illustrate the two main poles of French protectionism is intended to denote the role of transnational exchanges – especially between France and Germany – in the formulation of protectionist ideas rather than to make a genealogical claim. List and Fichte had little impact on early French debates about modern globalization: the former's *National System* was translated into French in 1851 and the latter's *Closed Commercial State* in 1940.[48] In these two cases, influence went rather the other way, since List and Fichte's divergent critiques of free trade both resulted from a direct engagement with contemporary French political and economic thought.[49] A more important point is the way in which the growth of international trade after 1815 gave rise to an intensely transnational debate, with the forging of mutually reinforcing commercial and intellectual connections. Contemporaries were well aware of these interactions. In an early use of the German translation of 'free trade' in 1829, Johann Wolfgang von Goethe praised 'der Freihandel der Begriffe und Gefühle' (the free trade of ideas and sentiments) that prevailed since 1815 and contributed, 'as much as the circulation of manufactured and agricultural products', to an increase in 'the wealth and general welfare of mankind'.[50] In the conclusions of the *Mémoires d'outre-tombe*,

[47] Hont, *The Jealousy of Trade*, pp. 5–6, 111–56; Lars Magnusson, *Mercantilism: The Shaping of an Economic Language* (London, 1994).

[48] Friedrich List, *Le Système national d'économie politique*, trans. Henri Richelot (Paris, 1851), and Johann Gottlieb Fichte, *L'État commercial fermé*, trans. Jean Gibelin (Paris, 1940).

[49] Isaac Nakhimovsky, *The Closed Commercial State: Perpetual Peace and Commercial Society from Rousseau to Fichte* (Princeton, NJ, 2011), Chapters 1 and 2; William O. Henderson, 'Friedrich List and the French Protectionists', *Zeitschrift für die gesamte Staatswissenschaft*, 138 (2) (1982): 262–75.

[50] 'Gespräch mit A. E. Odyniec, 25 August 1829', in Johann Wolfgang Goethe, *Gedenkausgabe der Werke, Briefe und Gespräche*, ed. Ernst Beutler, 27 vols. (Zurich, 1949–77), vol. XXIII, p. 625.

François-René de Chateaubriand expressed more disquiet when considering how the reduction of 'fiscal and commercial barriers' between nations, concurrently with new technologies, enabled 'ideas' to travel as fast as 'commodities' and rendered inevitable the abolition of 'old forms of separation' between peoples.[51]

The debate on international trade at the dawn of nineteenth-century globalization is therefore a privileged terrain for exploring the possibilities of a new transnational form of intellectual history.[52] While works examining the transnational dimension of British free trade have mostly underlined its diffusion from Britain to the rest of the world, focusing on France demonstrates the importance of the reinterpretation of ideas as they crossed borders and the reciprocal nature of intellectual exchanges.[53] Until the mid nineteenth century, the legacy of the early modern 'Republic of Letters' helped to maintain the status of French as the principal medium of intellectual exchange in Europe and the French arena as a major ideological battleground.[54] List wished to publish his *National System of Political Economy* simultaneously in German and in French, and the manuscript of an incomplete French version can be found in his personal papers.[55] When Richard Cobden, the 'apostle of free trade', embarked on his tour to promote commercial liberalism across Europe in 1846, he took some lessons to improve his French and was often frustrated at his inability to harangue his interlocutors in the Continent's *lingua franca*.[56]

Conversely, and contrary to the widespread image of politics in post-Napoleonic France as introverted, the French elites were attentive to the intensification of global exchanges of commodities and its consequences. This concern was most apparent in the debates about the sources and fragilities of British commercial prosperity, but it extended to the rest

[51] François-René de Chateaubriand, *Mémoires d'outre-tombe*, 12 vols. (Paris, 1849–50), vol. XI, p. 459; the passage is dated 1841.

[52] David Armitage, *Foundations of Modern International Thought* (Cambridge, 2013), pp. 17–32; on the transnational circulation of economic and social ideas, at a later stage of nineteenth-century globalization, see Daniel T. Rodgers, *Atlantic Crossings: Social Politics in a Progressive Age* (Cambridge, Mass., 1998).

[53] Charles P. Kindleberger, 'The Rise of Free Trade in Western Europe, 1820–75', *Journal of Economic History*, 35 (1) (1975): 20–55; on the need to eschew a diffusionist approach, see Wolfram Kaiser, 'Cultural Transfers of Free Trade at the World Exhibitions, 1851–1862', *Journal of Modern History*, 77 (3) (2005): 563–90; and David Todd, 'John Bowring and the Global Dissemination of Free Trade', *Historical Journal*, 51 (2) (2008): 373–97.

[54] Hans Bots and Françoise Waquet, *La République des lettres* (Paris, 1997), pp. 34–44; on the global dimension of French literary dominance, see Pascale Casanova, *La République mondiale des lettres* (Paris, 1999), esp. Chapters 2 and 3.

[55] Reutlingen, Stadtarchiv Reutlingen (SR), List MSS, Fasc. 23.3.

[56] Richard Cobden, *The European Diaries of Richard Cobden, 1846–1849*, ed. Miles Taylor (Aldershot, 1994), p. 51.

of Europe and the world.[57] According to Alexis de Tocqueville, who visited the USA at the time of the 'nullification crisis', when South Carolina refused to implement the so-called 'tariff of abominations' in 1828–33, 'the tariff question gave rise to the only political passions disturbing the Union'.[58] So enthralled was German public opinion by the creation of the *Zollverein* or customs union in 1834, the historian Edgar Quinet reported from the country of philosophy *par excellence*, that even there 'the customs question [had] replaced for all the question of categorical imperatives'.[59] Nor was this attention confined to European countries or the prerogative of the elite. At the turn of the 1840s, the pamphlets and petitions of rural flax spinners from French Flanders, Normandy and Brittany frequently cited the destitution of Indian cotton spinners as a result of British competition to justify their demand for a rise in the French tariff on imports of linen yarns. 'The insatiable avidity of England', a pamphlet asserted, 'is about to cause the same results on the European continent as in India'.[60]

A mixture of fascination and revulsion for the British economic model remained the most potent foreign influence on French debates about international trade after 1815. Yet the adoption of free trade and the progress of industrialization in Britain after 1820 radically altered what this model represented: from the epitome of mercantile jealousy, it became a symbol of commercial liberalism.[61] French advocates of free trade consequently adopted a more Anglophile tone, although they retained misgivings about the social consequences of industrialization and pointed out that the abolition of trade barriers need not result in the replication of the British emphasis on large-scale manufacturing. In response, French opponents of free trade elaborated a protectionist language that used Anglophobia

[57] Gareth Stedman Jones, 'National Bankruptcy and Social Revolution: European Observers on Britain, 1813–1844', in Patrick O'Brien and Donald Winch (eds.), *The Political Economy of British Historical Experience, 1688–1914* (Oxford, 2002), pp. 61–92; Roberto Romani, 'Political Economy and Other Idioms: French Views on English Development, 1815–1848', *European Journal of the History of Economic Thought*, 9 (3) (2002): 359–83.

[58] Alexis de Tocqueville, *De la démocratie en Amérique*, 14th edn, 2 vols. (Paris, 1864), p. 35; on the nullification crisis, see William S. Belko, *The Triumph of the Antebellum Free Trade Movement* (Gainesville, Fla., 2012).

[59] Edgar Quinet, *Allemagne et Italie* (Paris, 1836), p. 114.

[60] Louis Estancelin, *De l'importation en France des fils et tissus de lin et de chanvre d'Angleterre* (Paris, 1842), p. 39.

[61] Sophus Reinert, *Translating Empire: Emulation and the Origins of Political Economy* (Cambridge, Mass., 2011), pp. 70–2; on the jealous nature of Britain's traditional commercial policies, see Ralph Davis, 'The Rise of Protection in England, 1689–1786', *Economic History Review*, 19 (2) (1966): 306–17; and Kenneth Morgan, 'Mercantilism and the British Empire, 1688–1815', in Patrick O'Brien and Donald Winch (eds.), *The Political Economy of British Historical Experience, 1688–1914* (Oxford, 2002), pp. 165–92.

to conceal divergent goals. While some denounced British attempts to export free trade as a Machiavellian ploy to deprive other countries of the means of acquiring modern industries, others propounded the defence of national labour as a means of preserving a balanced and self-sufficient economy. As the latter discourse proved the more popular, French protectionists increasingly resorted to a Fichtean rhetoric, even when they pursued Listian goals.

The French protectionists occasionally referred to the constitution of the *Zollverein* as an instance of national economic solidarity, or, after the advent of the Second Republic in 1848, to the USA as a model of protectionist republicanism. The use of such alternative models helped to consolidate the legitimacy of the French protective system. But this book pays more attention to the ways in which the French experience served to inspire protectionist ideas abroad. The most important example is the case of Friedrich List, whose work was used to justify protectionist policies from Hungary to Japan in the second half of the nineteenth century. Since 1945, scholarship has highlighted the impact of List's American exile on the shaping of his ideas.[62] I show in Chapter 4 that List's hostility to free trade pre-dated his stay in the USA and was decisively influenced by his views on the French economy and by the effervescence of protectionist ideas in France after 1830. It was in Paris, where List served as the correspondent of the *Allgemeine Zeitung* between 1837 and 1840, that he wrote the manuscript of his *National System*.

Free Trade and its Enemies in France, 1814–51 further seeks to undermine the nation-centric perspective that dominates scholarship on the history of political economy by stressing the regional dimension of French debates and the role of direct interactions between certain regions and the rest of the world. In particular, it highlights the contrast between the Atlantic south-west, where memories of maritime prosperity in the eighteenth century and strong ties to Britain would facilitate the spread of free-trade ideas, and the north-east, rendered more receptive to protectionist ideas by the development of manufacturing during the Continental Blockade.[63] This regional focus also permits close study of the transformation of contemporary views about international trade. While the failure to revive France's highly regulated colonial and Atlantic trade led Bordeaux and its winegrowing hinterland to embrace free trade after 1825, the fear of British

[62] Keith Tribe, *Strategies of Economic Order: German Economic Discourse, 1750–1950* (Cambridge, 1995), pp. 32–65.

[63] On the tension between maritime and Continental aspirations in French history, see Edward W. Fox, *History in Geographic Perspective: The Other France* (New York, 1972).

competition made the liberal Alsatian manufacturers adopt increasingly protectionist views after 1835. Of course, the pursuit of their material interests determined the stances of the Bordelais merchants and Alsatian industrialists. But it was new political and economic ideas that modified how they perceived their interests.

Another transnational dimension of the French debate over free trade was a series of intersections with the issues of empire and colonization. There are some similarities between the protectionist turn and the imperialist turn of French liberals after 1830, not least a common origin in the twin fears of national decline and social dislocation.[64] Yet the relationship between protectionism and imperial liberalism was complex. Early advocates of free trade were hostile to the *exclusif*, a set of restrictions on colonial trade which the Restoration enforced with renewed vigour in France's remaining colonies after 1814. But several prominent supporters of free trade were tempted by the possibility of a new form of colonization that would encourage the expansion of global trade and civilization. Jean-Baptiste Say made an early appeal to the creation of European settlements in North Africa, while Tocqueville, the most illustrious supporter of French colonization in Algeria, was an admirer of Cobden and favoured the repeal of restrictions on France's external trade. This French version of 'free-trade imperialism' helped to inspire France's global expansion between 1840 and 1880.[65]

Examining attitudes towards empire also highlights a crucial difference between the traditional jealousy of trade and modern protectionism. Before 1830, the royalist adversaries of free trade were strident defenders of the *exclusif*. After the advent of the July Monarchy, several protectionists, especially those with a Listian preoccupation with industrial development, also supported the colonization of Algeria, but they were indifferent or hostile to the interests of France's remaining plantation islands. Fichtean protectionists were even more wary about the costs of colonial expansion. They sometimes favoured withdrawal from North Africa and loudly supported the development of new domestic industries that would reduce French dependency on imports of colonial goods. The widespread

[64] Jennifer Pitts, *A Turn to Empire: The Rise of Imperial Liberalism in Britain and France* (Princeton, NJ, 2005), Chapters 6 and 7; see also Jean-Louis Marçot, *Comment est née l'Algérie française (1830–1850): la Belle utopie* (Paris, 2012).

[65] David Todd, 'A French Imperial Meridian, 1814–1870', *Past and Present*, 210 (2011): 155–86; and 'Transnational Projects of Empire in France, c. 1815–c.1870', forthcoming in *Modern Intellectual History*; on free-trade imperialism in Britain, see Bernard Semmel, *The Rise of Free Trade Imperialism: Classical Political Economy, the Empire of Free Trade and Imperialism, 1750–1850* (Cambridge, 1970).

enthusiasm for 'indigenous' beet sugar as a substitute for imported cane sugar after 1840, examined in Chapter 5, illustrates the predominance, among protectionists, of an attitude of malignant neglect towards empire.

IV

In order to analyse the political utilization of economic ideas, this book pays close attention to processes of reinterpretation, locating them in the relevant international, national or regional political context. It is also concerned with the issues of impact and reception, presenting evidence, when it could be found, on the intended or actual audiences of texts on political economy. Besides helping to elucidate the meaning and significance of specific texts, such information highlights the reach of the controversy on free trade beyond the intellectual and political elite.

This concern with reception has led me to adopt a broad definition of political context that includes emotions as well as abstract theory.[66] Taking emotions into consideration is vital, for instance, to understand the free-traders' insistence on the arbitrary or vexatious aspects of the practical implications of trade restrictions for tradesmen, travellers or inhabitants of border regions. Far from being a superficial aspect of pleas for free trade, such denunciations resonated with a widespread fear – at least until the definitive fall of the Bourbons in 1830 – of a return to the erratic ways of the Old Regime. The use of Anglophobia by the protectionists was another form of appeal to economic emotions. Recent scholarship has warned us against misconstruing the Anglophobic rhetoric of some sections of the French elite as the reflection of popular feelings, at least in the pre-Revolutionary era.[67] However, Michelet's denunciation of materialist England as an 'anti-France' in his best-selling work *Le Peuple* (1846) cannot be reduced to a rhetorical ploy.[68] As shown in Chapter 6, the lambasting of free trade by the protectionists as an 'English' concept that threatened the legacy of the French Revolution proved remarkably effective.

Together with their political and sometimes religious reinterpretation, the dissemination of free-trade or protectionist ideas relied on their

[66] On economic sentiments and emotions, see Emma Rothschild, 'An Alarming Commercial Crisis in Eighteenth-Century Angoulême: Sentiments in Economic History', *Economic History Review*, new series, 51 (2) (1998): 268–93, and *Economic Sentiments*.

[67] Renaud Morieux, 'Diplomacy from Below and Belonging: Fishermen and Cross-Channel Relations in the Eighteenth Century', *Past and Present*, 202 (2009): 83–125; Fabrice Bensimon, 'British Workers in France, 1815–1848', *Past and Present*, 213 (2011): 147–89.

[68] Jules Michelet, *Le Peuple*, 3rd edn (Paris, 1846), p. 319.

application to concrete issues. The French *économistes* – a word which from 1820 denoted an intellectual specialization in political economy rather than adherence to the narrower principles of Physiocracy – fervently wished to render their ideas accessible to large numbers. Jean-Baptiste Say's *Cours complet d'économie politique pratique* was designed to 'place these [economic] abstractions within the reach of everyone' and teemed with practical illustrations of how trade restrictions increased the cost of items such as Jamaican rum, ploughs, bed sheets or curtains.[69] As well as highlighting the efforts of prominent intellectuals such as Say to spread their ideas about international trade, the book pays close attention to the role of lesser known publicists, representing an intermediate form of economic thought, in shaping new arguments for and against free trade.[70] These include Henri Fonfrède, a Bordelais journalist and winegrower who castigated protection as a means for northern manufacturers to capture the riches of the agricultural south, and Christophe-Joseph-Alexandre Mathieu de Dombasle, a Lorraine agronomist who championed a balanced and self-sufficient form of economic development. These pamphleteers shaped contemporary opinions on international trade in the course of a succession of debates that often focused on very concrete issues, such as warehousing privileges (the right to store imported goods without paying duties), transit (the duty-free importation of goods destined to be re-exported), the future of the French wine industry, or the respective merits of colonial cane sugar and indigenous beet sugar, rather than the more abstract concepts of national labour and free trade.

To what extent did the ideas of economists and publicists about international trade percolate through post-Napoleonic French society? Say himself thought that he was writing for an audience of 50,000, or what he described as the 'classes mitoyennes', a larger audience than early modern controversies on the balance of trade.[71] Throughout the book, I offer data based on the declarations of the Paris printers to the Librairie, an administration established by Napoleon to supervise publishing, which confirm the order of magnitude of Say's figure: print runs of expensive economic

[69] Jean-Baptiste Say, *Cours complet d'économie politique pratique*, 6 vols. (Paris, 1828–9), vol. I, p. 126, and vol. III, pp. 291, 360.

[70] On the high, intermediate and low forms of economic thought, see Rothschild, 'Political Economy', p. 749; see also the distinction between theoretical, practical and popular knowledge in Mary O. Furner and Barry Supple (eds.), *The State and Economic Knowledge* (Cambridge, 1990), pp. 3–39.

[71] Philippe Steiner, 'French Political Economy, Industrialism and Social Change', in George Stathakis and Gianni Vaggi (eds.), *Economic Development and Social Change: Historical Roots and Modern Perspectives* (London, 2006), pp. 232–56, at p. 243.

treatises were usually between 1,000 and 2,000, while the total circulation of the most successful and cheaper pamphlets could exceed 5,000. Each copy had several readers and different types of publications reached different audiences, making 50,000 a conservative estimate.[72]

Ideas for and against free trade were also disseminated in press organs, from daily national and regional newspapers, which dedicated an increasing share of their columns to debates about international trade, to new specialized sheets in the 1840s, such as the protectionist biweekly *Le Moniteur Industriel* or the pro-free trade weekly *Le Libre-échange*. Petitions offer valuable examples of how ordinary producers and consumers used new ideas to formulate their claims, while the contemporary testimonies of state officials and other observers shed light on the state of national or local public opinion. These sources suggest that the concern about commerce often spread beyond the enfranchised middle class. It affected the thousands of Parisian seamstresses who worried about the ban on the importation of British cotton yarns in 1816, the tens of thousands of Gironde winegrowers who petitioned for free trade in the late 1820s and the 214 artisans and manufacturers in the small town of Roubaix (Nord) who made a donation to support the defence of national labour in 1846. The intensification of globalization after 1815 not only increased the stakes but also considerably enlarged the audience of the controversy over free trade.

[72] On these data and their reliability, see Martyn Lyons, 'Les Best-sellers', in Roger Chartier and Henri-Jean Martin (eds.), *Histoire de l'édition française*, 2nd edn, 4 vols. (Paris, 1989–91), vol. III, pp. 409–37; Frédéric Barbier, 'The Publishing Industry and Printed Output in Nineteenth-Century France', in Kenneth Carpenter (ed.), *Books and Society in History* (New York, 1983), pp. 199–230; David Bellos, 'Le Marché du livre à l'époque romantique: recherches et problèmes', *Revue Française d'Histoire du Livre*, 20 (3) (1978): 647–59. On the French publishing industry after 1815, see Christine Haynes, *Lost Illusions: The Politics of Publishing in Nineteenth-Century France* (Cambridge, Mass., 2010). On the role of printed text in the dissemination of ideas, see Darnton, *Forbidden Best-Sellers*, esp. pp. 169–80, and Roger Chartier, *Les Origines culturelles de la révolution française*, 2nd edn (Paris, 2000), esp. pp. 99–133.

CHAPTER I

The reactionary political economy of the Bourbon Restoration

The debate about international trade in the decade after the fall of Napoleon remained firmly anchored in the language and representations of the eighteenth century. Such continuity reflected, in part, the natural persistence of earlier ideas about the importance of commerce and, sometimes, the survival or revival of pre-Revolutionary flows of commodities across Europe, the Mediterranean and the Atlantic. This stress on ideological continuity fits awkwardly with the still prevalent view of the Revolutionary era as a major economic rupture, a perception grounded in the old debate between proponents and adversaries of a Marxist interpretation, who highlighted, respectively, the crucial or catastrophic effects of the Revolution on the development of capitalism in France. Opponents of the Marxist interpretation insisted in particular on the collapse of French overseas trade, as a result of more than two decades of maritime warfare with Britain.[1] More recently, however, economic historians have begun to reappraise the resilience of French commercial activities during this period, thanks to the use of neutral flags and other indirect channels.[2] From the standpoint of the history of ideas, it should also be noted that contemporaries could not know whether this major disruption would become a permanent rupture. For many of them, it seemed more likely that French overseas trade, as after each previous maritime war with Britain for over

[1] The classical statement of the Marxist interpretation is Ernest Labrousse, *La Crise de l'économie française à la fin de l'Ancien Régime* (Paris, 1943); pessimistic accounts that highlight the negative consequences of the Revolution on foreign trade include François Crouzet, 'Les Conséquences économiques de la Révolution: à propos d'un inédit de Sir Francis d'Ivernois', *Annales Historiques de la Révolution Française*, 168 (1962): 182–217 and 169 (1962): 336–62; and François Crouzet, 'Wars, Blockade and Economic Change in Europe, 1792–1815', *Journal of Economic History*, 24 (4) (1964): 567–88.

[2] Paul Butel, 'Succès et déclin du commerce colonial français de la Révolution à la Restauration', *Revue Économique*, 40 (6) (1989): 1079–96; Silvia Marzagalli, 'Le Négoce maritime et la rupture révolutionnaire: un ancien débat revisité', *Annales Historiques de la Révolution Française*, 352 (2008): 184–207.

a century and as recently as during the Peace of Amiens in 1802–3, would experience a formidable resurgence.[3]

Commercial reconstruction was one of the most pressing issues facing the restored Bourbon monarchy: during the first parliamentary session of 1814–15, legislative chambers dedicated over a fifth of their debates to the regulation of commerce.[4] As in the eighteenth century, the Bourbon regime turned towards the pursuit of an agressive mercantile strategy, modelled on what remained widely perceived as the source of Britain's commercial success.[5] This strategy was also inspired by nostalgia for two recently lost commercial empires: France's prosperous colonial demesne in the Caribbean, in particular Saint-Domingue, declared independent under the name of Haiti by slave insurgents in 1804 but over which the peace settlement of 1815 reaffirmed French sovereignty, and the Continental System, which ensured French pre-eminence on European markets under Napoleon. Yet it gradually became clear that traditional policies such as the ban on imports of cotton textiles or the revival of the *exclusif* with France's remaining colonies would not suffice to permit a spontaneous return to commercial prosperity. In order to overcome these difficulties, the Bourbon Restoration adopted policies that were much more restrictive than the regulation of trade under the Old Regime, including new commercial privileges for colonial planters and metropolitan seaports and new corn laws – inspired by Britain's 1815 ban on grain imports – for landowners.[6] Continuity with eighteenth-century patterns of thought about commerce was not only a product of natural persistence. It also stemmed from a deliberate and sustained effort to bring the economic past back to life.[7]

3 Guillaume Daudin, *Commerce et prospérité: la France au XVIIIe siècle* (Paris, 2005), pp. 213–16; François Crouzet, *La Guerre économique franco-anglaise au XVIIIe siècle* (Paris, 2008), pp. 341–66.

4 Out of 1,823 pages in the reproduction of the session's debates, 374 bore on the regulation of foreign trade; my calculation, based on Jérôme Mavidal and Émile Colombey (eds.), *Archives parlementaires*, 126 vols. (Paris, 1862–1912), vols. XII, XIII and XIV; the *Archives parlementaires* will henceforth be referred to as AP.

5 On earlier debates about France's adequate response to Britain's commercial success, see Whatmore, *Republicanism and the French Revolution*, pp. 37–60; Istvan Hont, 'The 'Rich Country-Poor Country' Debate Revisited: The Irish Origin and French Reception of the Hume Paradox', in Carl Wennerlind and Margaret Schabas (eds.), *David Hume's Political Economy* (London, 2008), pp. 243–323.

6 For detailed descriptions of the Restoration's commercial legislation, see Ernest Levasseur, *Histoire du commerce de la France*, 2 vols. (Paris, 1911–12), vol. II, pp. 107–36; and Léon Amé, *Études sur les tarifs de douanes et sur les traités de commerce*, 2 vols. (Paris, 1876), vol. I, pp. 65–156.

7 On nostalgia for the pre-Revolutionary commercial order under the Bourbon Restoration, see David Todd, 'Before Free Trade: Commercial Discourse and Politics in Early Nineteenth-Century France', in Martin Daunton and Frank Trentmann (eds.), *Worlds of Political Economy: Knowledge and Power in the Nineteenth and Twentieth Centuries* (Basingstoke, 2004), pp. 47–68; and David Todd, 'Remembering and Restoring the Economic Old Regime: France and Its Colonies, 1815–1830', in

The commercial prohibitive system of the Bourbon Restoration was reactionary in a political as well as in an economic sense. The Revolution had amplified the concern with the social disturbance caused by the spread of commerce and luxury. As early as 1800, Alexandre d'Hauterive, a protégé of Charles Maurice de Talleyrand-Périgord at the Ministry of External Relations, attributed the Revolutionary upheaval to the formidable growth of trade before 1789 in *De l'état de la France à la fin de l'an VIII*: 'The first, the most ancient, and most essential cause of the Revolution has arisen from the action of the commercial system and the spirit of industry on the social system of all the nations in Europe.' Commerce affected France more than other European countries, he added, because 'the sensibility of the nation' was 'more active and more mobile'.[8] Charles Francoville, the *rapporteur* of the law that rendered permanent the wartime prohibitions on most manufactured products in November 1814, echoed this concern: banning foreign imports, he contended, would 'ennoble' professions and render them 'more fixed', so that 'everyone will then renounce this mobility that constantly displaces the condition of men'. 'When the Revolution no longer exists in facts', he concluded, 'make sure that it no longer exists in minds'.[9]

This chapter explores several facets of this entanglement of political with economic concerns in the prohibitive commercial policies of the Bourbon Restoration. It first examines the intellectual reaffirmation of a jealous conception of trade as a zero-sum game to show that it was directed at the perceived Revolutionary tendencies of Physiocratic and Smithian political economy as much as at their liberal economics. The chapter then highlights the reactionary undertones of two specific sets of prohibitive policies: the harsh implementation of a ban on imports of cotton textiles, which continued the severe repression of smuggling during Napoleon's Continental Blockade, and the regime's extraordinary determination to revive France's colonial trade by means of new commercial privileges. Sporadic but strident protests against these policies, I argue, remained couched in a political language of individual rights rather than support for free-market economics and expressed a construction of the regulation of commerce as an attack on the post-Revolutionary liberal order. Liberal writers on political economy condemned prohibitive policies only timidly or even conceded the need for prohibitions as long as

Michael Rowe et al. (eds.), *War, Demobilization and Memory: The Legacy of War in the Era of Atlantic Revolutions* (Basingstoke, forthcoming); parts of this chapter draw on elements of these essays.

8 Alexandre d'Hauterive, *De l'état de la France à la fin de l'an VIII* (Paris, [1800]), pp. 256–8.

9 AP, vol. XIII, p. 540 (12 November 1814).

Britain maintained its own. Instead, the end of the chapter shows, it was Benjamin Constant, a political thinker rather than an economic theorist, who, in response to the aggravation of prohibitive policies, mounted a stalwart defence of *laissez-faire* in foreign trade as an essential component of modern liberty.

I

The reaffirmation of mercantile jealousy began under Napoleon, as part of a broader rejection of philosophical abstractions and Revolutionary utopianism. France's Revolution had dismantled most aspects of the Old Regime's mercantile system, from urban guilds to chartered companies and even, under the pressure of slave insurgents in Saint-Domingue, slavery. The customs law of 15 March 1791 reduced restrictions on imports and confirmed the liberal 1786 treaty with Britain.[10] Yet war suspended normal commercial relations after 1792, and the Consulate (1799–1804) reversed the course of liberal reforms, reinstating some regulations in domestic industries, reaffirming the *exclusif* for colonial trade and restoring slavery in France's colonies.[11] After Haitian independence and the battle of Trafalgar dispelled hopes of reviving the colonial trade, Napoleon also sought to implement a strict ban on the importation of British manufactured and colonial goods into Europe. This Continental System or Blockade failed to ruin Britain but severely curtailed the Continent's exchanges with the rest of the world and encouraged the growth of manufacturing industries in France and annexed Belgian, German and Italian territories.[12]

For liberal opponents of Napoleon, the Continental System appeared as mercantile jealousy *à outrance*, demonstrating its damaging effects on the

[10] Jeremy J. Whiteman, 'Trade and the Regeneration of France, 1789–1791: Liberalism, Protectionism and the Commercial Policy of the Constituent Assembly', *European History Quarterly*, 31 (2) (2001): 171–204; Jean Tarrade, 'La Révolution et le commerce colonial: le régime de l'exclusif de 1789 à 1800', in Comité pour l'Histoire Économique et Financière de la France, *État, finances et économie pendant la Révolution francaise* (Paris, 1991), pp. 553–64; Cheney, *Revolutionary Commerce*, pp. 195–228; Laurent Dubois, *Avengers of the New World: The Story of the Haitian Revolution* (Cambridge, Mass., 2004), pp. 152–70.

[11] Michael D. Sibalis, 'Corporatism after the Corporations: The Debate on Restoring the Guilds under Napoleon I and the Restoration', *French Historical Studies*, 15 (4) (1988): 718–30; Claire Lemercier, *Un si discret pouvoir: aux origines de la chambre de commerce de Paris, 1803–1853* (Paris, 2003), pp. 22–30; Yves Benot, *La Démence coloniale sous Napoléon* (Paris, 1992).

[12] Stuart J. Woolf, *Napoleon's Integration of Europe* (London, 1991), pp. 134–56; François Crouzet, *L'Économie britannique et le blocus continental, 1806–1813*, 2nd edn (Paris, 1987); Kevin H. O'Rourke, 'The Worldwide Economic Impact of the French Revolutionary and Napoleonic Wars', *Journal of Global History*, 1 (1) (2006): 123–49.

moral fabric of the nation as well as its limited economic effectiveness.[13] Germaine de Staël, the daughter of Jacques Necker and symbol of liberal resistance to Napoleon, argued in her posthumous *Considérations on the French Revolution*: 'Nothing rendered Napoleon more unpopular than that increase in the price of sugar and coffee which affected the daily habits of all classes.' The burning of British merchandise on the public squares of European cities, she added, was 'the living picture of tyrannical absurdity'. Citing the works of Friedrich Gentz and of her friend August von Schlegel, two publicists hostile to Napoleonic imperialism, she thought that the failure of the Blockade to prevent the growth of British power proved the futility of jealousy in matters of trade: 'As a woman does not procure more homage to herself by being angry at that which is offered to her rival; so a nation can carry off the palm in commerce and industry only by finding means of attracting voluntary tributes, and not by proscribing competition.'[14]

Staël's reference to Gentz, combined with her jibe at the 'official gazette writers … ordered to insult the English nation and government', was perhaps a veiled attack on Hauterive, whose *De l'état de la France* was a semi-official response to Gentz's effusive writings on British economic supremacy.[15] Hauterive's diatribe against England's 'commercial invasions' and his call for a 'federal act of navigation' that would ban British trade from the European continent have sometimes been interpreted as prefiguring the Continental System.[16] His arguments and rhetoric certainly inspired Napoleonic propaganda in favour of the System after 1805. But in *De l'état de la France*, Hauterive described himself as a staunch adversary of bellicose commercial policies. It was Oliver Cromwell's Navigation Act, he contended, that marked the advent of commercial 'hostility' and 'jealousy' between European nations. Placing his own analysis in the continuity

[13] The Continental Blockade continued to horrify notable liberal thinkers well into the twentieth century; see Eli Heckscher, *The Continental System: An Economic Interpretation* (Oxford, 1922), and Bertrand de Jouvenel, *Napoléon et l'économie dirigée* (Brussels and Paris, 1942).

[14] Germaine de Staël, *Considérations sur la révolution française* (Paris, 1983), pp. 405–6. The reference to Schlegel was probably an allusion to his pamphlet, *Sur le système continental et ses rapports avec la Suède* (Hamburg, 1813), an English translation of which was published under the name of Madame de Staël-Holstein, as *Appeal to the Nations of Europe against the Continental System* (London, 1813).

[15] Staël, *Considérations*, p. 406; on the Gentz–Hauterive controversy, see Murray Forsyth, 'The Old European States-System: Gentz Versus Hauterive', *Historical Journal*, 23 (3) (1980): 521–38; and Emma Rothschild, 'Language and Empire, c. 1800', *Historical Research*, 78 (200) (2005): 208–29; on comparisons between the goals of British and French imperialism around 1800, see also Richard Whatmore, *Against Empire: Geneva, Britain and France in the Eighteenth Century* (New Haven, Conn., 2012), pp. 228–70.

[16] Hauterive, *De l'état de la France*, pp. 138, 167–8.

of the Abbé Fénelon's critique of the mercantile system in *Les Aventures de Télémaque* (1699), Hauterive asserted that the true 'principles' of political economy 'proscribe as political scourges, all commercial restraints, privileges, and prohibitions. No person sooner than myself would break those fatal chains which the greedy genius of revenue has in all times imposed on the communication of general industry'. He only supported a Continental act of navigation as a temporary retaliatory measure, after which 'prohibitive laws [would] be abolished for ever'.[17]

Hauterive's denunciation of jealousy was probably sincere. He played no part in the creation of the Continental System, even falling into semi-disgrace in 1805 (he was relegated from the Bureau Politique to the archives of the Ministry of Foreign Affairs) because he opposed the expansionist turn of the Napoleonic regime. After the fall of Napoleon, he retained his position at the foreign ministry and remained an acerbic critique of British policy. For example, in an 1816 analysis of a project of colonization of Madagascar submitted to the French government by a Dutch Physiocrat, Dirk van Hogendorp, Hauterive thought that the project was bound to fail due to the opposition of Britain, which its recent victories had 'rendered more demanding, more imperious and more avid of exclusive advantages'. Invoking the writings of Jeremy Bentham against colonization, he even condemned all colonial undertakings, because tropical goods could be obtained peacefully and at a lower cost by trade.[18] In 1817, Hauterive also published an abstruse work on political economy, intended for his fellow administrators rather than the general public, in which he castigated 'the theory of prohibitive laws' as the cause of 'the colonial system, slavery, the cupid hatreds which are called national hatreds, the cupid wars which are called trade wars', and which in turn engendered 'excessive, corrupting and unfairly distributed riches, destitution, servitude, ignorance and crimes'.[19]

The intellectual rehabilitation of jealousy may be more equitably attributed to François Ferrier, later dubbed the 'Pindar of Customs' and, in a comparison with the Greek poet who denigrated Homer's work, the 'Zoilus of Adam Smith' by Adolphe Blanqui, a disciple of Jean-Baptiste Say.[20] Ferrier's successful career in the customs administration was

[17] Hauterive, *De l'état de la France*, pp. 19, 129, 164–6; on the critique of jealousy by Fénelon, see Paul Schurman, 'Fénelon on Luxury, War and Trade', *History of European Ideas*, 38 (2) (2012): 179–99.

[18] Alexandre d'Hauterive, 'Note sur l'ouvrage du Comte de Hogendorp', Archives des Affaires Etrangères, Fonds divers, Ameriques, vol. XVII, fols. 286–7.

[19] Alexandre d'Hauterive, *Eléments d'économie politique* (Paris, 1817), p. 200.

[20] Jean-Baptiste Say, 'Théorie de M. Ferrier', in *Œuvres diverses de Jean-Baptiste Say*, ed. Charles Comte, Eugène Daire and Horace Say (Paris, 1848), pp. 355–7, at p. 355.

intertwined with the expansion of the Continental Blockade: a customs sub-inspector in Bayonne in 1804, he became Inspector in Worms (Rhineland) in 1805, Inspector in Genoa (Liguria) in 1808, Director in Rome in 1810, and Director General of the customs administration across the Empire between 1812 and 1814, and again during the Hundred Days in 1815. The publication of *Du gouvernement considéré dans ses rapports avec le commerce* (1805), a treatise that advocated the close supervision of foreign trade by the government, aided his administrative ascent. The book made a powerful and lasting impression as one of the first systematic attacks on Smithian political economy. In 1845, Karl Marx accused Friedrich List, in his *National System of Political Economy* (1841), of having plagiarised Ferrier.[21]

Ferrier's book explicitly sought to stem and reverse the dissemination of liberal political economy, which he associated closely with other Revolutionary ideas: 'When we read Smith and the economists [Physiocrats], we must defend ourselves against the seduction of their idyllic descriptions, and the lure of an imaginary best which is the enemy of the good and of which we have experienced the terrible consequences for ten years.' Ferrier agreed with Smith that the expansion of commerce since the sixteenth century had considerably enriched Europe, but he warned against literal and simplistic interpretations of the *Wealth of Nations*: 'there are two men within Smith and two works within his work'. The one who should not be trusted was his French incarnation, 'Smith the economist, who lived in France amidst the leaders of the [Physiocratic] sect'. The one who could be admired, Ferrier contended, was his English incarnation, or rather the interpretation of his book that prevailed in England. Since its publication in 1776, 'the principles of [commercial] administration' had remained unchanged across the Channel, 'despite his book, which [the English] consider, save for a few chapters, as a novel'. The 'extreme disorder' and numerous 'contradictions' of the *Wealth of Nations* made it 'a maze without any exit', deliberately designed to deceive European readers: 'everything suggests that Smith pursued the secret goal of spreading in Europe principles, the implementation of which, as he very well knew, would hand over the market of the universe to his country'.[22]

Rather than follow the prescriptions of Smith, Ferrier argued, France should abide by the wiser advice of the eighteenth-century defenders of an

[21] Roman Szporluk, *Communism and Nationalism: Karl Marx versus Friedrich List* (Oxford, 1988), p. 39.

[22] François Ferrier, *Du gouvernement considéré dans ses rapports avec le commerce* (Paris, 1805), pp. 217, 385–9.

aggressive mercantile policy such as Jean-François Melon in his *Essai politique sur le commerce* (1734), Nicolas Dutot in his *Réflexions politiques sur les finances et le commerce* (1738), or François Véron de Forbonnais in his *Éléments du commerce* (1754). He praised the wisdom of Charles Secondat de Montesquieu and quoted lengthy extracts from books 20 and 21 of the *Spirit of the Laws*, on the regulation of foreign and colonial trade.[23] This section of the *Spirit of the Laws* encapsulated the principles of what Paul Cheney has described as a 'science of commerce' in the eighteenth century, and it is possible to view Ferrier's *Du gouvernement* as an attempt to revive this pre-Revolutionary paradigm.[24] In practice, Ferrier propounded a return to the customs policies of Colbert, including severe restrictions on imports of manufactured products and the strict implementation of the *exclusif* with the colonies, together with a ban on the unprofitable trade with Asia and perhaps the restoration of guilds. Although he conceded that bullion should not be confused with wealth, he still considered that it could help to stimulate production and endorsed the 'balance of trade' as 'one of the best economic institutions of modern nations'.[25]

Ferrier's rehabilitation of the science of commerce should be viewed as a contribution to the effervescence of counter-revolutionary ideas on politics, society and religion after 1800.[26] In *Du gouvernement*, Ferrier condemned the Revolution as a 'terrible catastrophe'.[27] His mentor was Joseph Fiévée, a royalist journalist and adviser of Napoleon who encouraged the monarchical drift of the regime. Fiévée pushed Ferrier to write a book hostile to Adam Smith's political economy, before correcting in person the manuscript of *Du gouvernement* and arranging for its publication.[28] Ferrier himself described the anti-Revolutionary writer Edmund Burke as his 'favourite author' about 'the politics born out the Revolution'. After the collapse of the Napoleonic Empire, Ferrier remained in the customs administration but fell back to the rank of Director at Dunkirk, facing the English coastline across the Channel. Although he expressed no qualms about the change in dynasty, the progressive and authoritarian Napoleonic regime remained his political ideal. He disliked 'reactionary royalists' but

[23] Ferrier, *Du gouvernement*, pp. 217–23. [24] Cheney, *Revolutionary Commerce*, pp. 52–86.

[25] Ferrier, *Du gouvernement*, p. 225.

[26] Bee Wilson, 'Counter-revolutionary Thought', in Gareth Stedman Jones and Gregory Claeys (eds.), *The Cambridge History of Nineteenth-Century Political Thought* (Cambridge, 2011), pp. 9–38.

[27] Ferrier, *Du gouvernement*, p. 26.

[28] Joseph Fiévée and François Ferrier, *Correspondance de Joseph Fiévée et de François Ferrier (1803–1837)*, ed. Etienne Hofmann (Bern and Paris, 1994), pp. 19–24, 42–4; on Fiévée's career and ideas, see John A. W. Gunn, *When the French Tried to Be British: Party, Opposition and the Quest for Civil Disagreement, 1814–1848* (Montreal, 2009), pp. 193–256.

disapproved of the concessions to liberal ideas in the 1814 Charter: 'I cannot reconcile myself with the idea of France under a representative government.' The country's political and geopolitical disasters, he believed, stemmed from 'the mobility of ideas in France', and '[t]he only remedy to this malady lay with a strong, harsh if need be, government'.[29]

Examining the recent history of commercial relations in two new editions of his treatise, published in 1821 and 1822, Ferrier found new evidence in support of the mercantile system. He admitted that the Continental System was excessively 'fiscal' and 'hostile' but insisted that it caused 'immense' harm to British trade and marvelled at the 'universal movement' of industry it fostered across Continental Europe. Since the peace, as European states maintained the wartime restrictions on British imports, 'a multitude of special blockades' had succeeded the former 'general blockade'. Such policies did not produce as potent an impression as Napoleon's grand design but would prove more effective because they relied on the free will of nations. Britain, he believed, was 'only beginning to suffer' from 'the system adopted by Bonaparte', even though it might be another fifty to sixty years before Continental manufacturers could beat British competition and bring about Britain's 'decadence'.[30] The new editions of *Du gouvernement* also redirected Ferrier's earlier criticisms of Smith against Jean-Baptiste Say and his disciples, who he dismissed, in a parallel with the the Physiocrats, as the 'economists of the nineteenth century'. The foreword of the third edition compared them to alchemists and equated their obsession with 'the unlimited liberty of commerce' with the pursuit of the 'philosopher's stone'.[31]

Despite their divergent appreciations of the value of Adam Smith's political economy, Hauterive and Ferrier shared the conviction that British policy embodied mercantile jealousy. They even agreed that the best remedy lay in retaliation, but Hauterive regretted the need for temporary retaliatory measures, while Ferrier advocated a permanent return to a system of commercial warfare. This French perception of Britain as pursuing a selfish and aggressive trade policy remained widespread after the fall of Napoleon, from the far left to the far right of the intellectual and political spectrum. For example, it was prominent in two analyses of the British economic system in the aftermath of the Napoleonic

[29] Ferrier to Fiévée, 5 and 20 June 1816, in *Correspondance*, pp. 137–8, 142.

[30] François Ferrier, *Du gouvernement dans ses rapports avec le commerce*, 2nd edn (Paris, 1821), pp. 392–6.

[31] François Ferrier, *Du gouvernement dans ses rapports avec le commerce*, 3rd edn (Paris, 1822), new subtitle 'de l'administration commerciale opposée aux économistes du 19e siècle', and pp. v–vi.

wars, Say's *De l'Angleterre et des Anglais* (1815) and Maurice Rubichon's *De l'Angleterre* (1816–19). Say, a republican who refused to collaborate with the Napoleonic regime after 1803, held ambivalent views about Britain. On the one hand, he respected British representative institutions and admired the industriousness of the British people. On the other, *De l'Angleterre et des Anglais* condemned the British high taxes, high tariffs and colonial expansion as a 'bad economic system' and was pessimistic about Britain's commercial prospects: the enormous public debt and endemic aristocratic corruption required an ever higher level of taxation, which was 'making it impossible to sell at as cheap a rate as other nations less borne down by public burdens' and would soon deprive its producers from 'maintaining a competition with foreigners'.[32]

Rubichon was a merchant and fervent royalist, who spent most of the Revolutionary and Napoleonic era as an *émigré* in England. The first volume (1816) of his *De l'Angleterre* denounced 'representative government' as a cause of permanent disorder and British efforts to encourage its adoption as an attack on 'civilization's foundations'.[33] The second volume (1819), by contrast, sang the praises of British economic organization, which Rubichon viewed as a reinvigorated 'feudal system'. The concentration of land property in England enabled the rapid rise of agricultural productivity and released workers and capital for the development of manufacturing and commerce. Rubichon ridiculed the belief 'of the economists [the Physiocrats] and their follower, Adam Smith' that 'the World's happiness depended on the liberty of commerce'. It was the delusion of the primacy of external trade, he argued, that led Napoleon to the excesses of the Continental Blockade: 'When this phantasmagorical hero issued the Berlin decree', which extended the ban on British imports to the entire continent in 1806, 'the joyous roars of our revolutionaries matched those of the demons when Satan announces that he will set them free from their woes to wage war on the Everlasting.'[34]

Rubichon conceded that Britain had fought numerous wars to extend its trade and colonial possessions around the globe but argued that its successes had reduced rather than increased its riches. He made an exception for Britain's new Indian empire, 'one of the truly superb parts of this monarchy', because the East India Company governed it without 'public assemblies' and could impose a beneficial trade thanks to its 'exclusive

[32] Jean-Baptiste Say, *De l'Angleterre et des Anglais*, 2nd edn (Paris, 1816), pp. 27, 35.
[33] Maurice Rubichon, *De l'Angleterre*, 2nd edn, 2 vols. (Paris, 1817–19), vol. I, p. vii.
[34] Rubichon, *De l'Angleterre*, vol. II, pp. 306, 325–6.

privilege'. France, however, needed neither a large external trade nor colonies to become as prosperous as Britain. It should instead restore feudal institutions, encourage the growth of its agriculture and confine the development of its manufactures to those that employed indigenous raw materials. The decline of France's trade relative to England's had been seen as a 'cause for jealousy' when it should be celebrated as a 'cause for triumph', for it would enable France to achieve much greater self-sufficiency than its rival.[35] Starting from radically opposed ideological premises, Say and Rubichon similarly concluded that Britain's prosperity should not be attributed to its continued pursuit of jealous policies.

Some liberal writers on political economy even invoked British policy to justify France's adherence to prohibitions. This was true, in particular, of Jean-Antoine Chaptal, the Girondin chemist turned Minister of the Interior under the Consulate and an influential advocate of economic growth during the Restoration.[36] In *De l'industrie française* (1819), Chaptal conceded that 'sound political economy' recommended only moderate customs duties on imports, for a system of prohibitions 'isolates nations and breaks off commercial relations'. However, prohibitions in Continental Europe derived from 'a just right of retaliation' in the face of the exclusive policy pursued by Britain for over a century. France should only repeal its prohibitions when Britain 'ceases to ban our lace products, our silk products etc. and to impose enormous duties on our other manufactured products' and 'admits our wines in the same conditions as Portuguese wines'.[37] *De l'industrie française* was an influential book, with a print run of 3,000 according to the records of the Librairie administration. This was a high figure, especially for a work of political economy, surpassing the second volume of Rubichon's *De l'Angleterre* (1,000 copies) or even Jean-Charles Simonde de Sismondi's well known *Nouveaux principes d'économie politique* (2,000), both also published in 1819.[38] A separate edition of the forty-page section of *De l'industrie française* on trade policy was even published in the USA, under the auspices of Matthew Carey, the father of the protectionist Henry Carey.[39] Charles Ganilh, a liberal lawyer who was imprisoned during the Terror, also drew on the example of British prosperity to call into question the Revolutionary enthusiasm

[35] Rubichon, *De l'Angleterre*, vol. II, pp. 367–8, 425–6.

[36] Elsa Bolado and Lluis Argemi, 'Jean-Antoine Chaptal: From Chemistry to Political Economy', *The European Journal of the History of Economic Thought*, 12 (2) (2005): 215–39.

[37] Jean-Antoine Chaptal, *De l'industrie française* (Paris, 1819), pp. 445–9, 455.

[38] Impressions 6776 (24 November 1818) and 7605 (18 January 1819), Paris, Archives Nationales (hereafter AN), F18*II 5; impression 9738 (29 July 1819), AN, F18*II 6.

[39] Jean-Antoine Chaptal, *Des douanes et des prohibitions* (Philadelphia, Pa., 1819).

for Adam Smith's ideas in his *Théorie de l'économie politique*, published in 1815. Accusing the unregulated circulation of commodities of fostering 'envy, hatred and all the anti-social passions', he defended a system of 'limited liberty' for foreign trade.[40]

Jean-Baptiste Say's own prudence offers another significant example of liberal timidity about the regulation of international trade. The second edition of his *Traité d'économie politique*, published in 1814, included a new section, 'On the Balance of Trade', which firmly condemned mercantile jealousy in principle. 'Products', he asserted, were 'always exchanged for products', making the search for trade surpluses futile. Yet Say made several substantial concessions to the partisans of restrictions. Citing Adam Smith's views in the *Wealth of Nations*, he agreed that prohibitions for national defence purposes were sometimes necessary. Going further than Smith, he put forward an early version of the infant industry argument, supporting temporary protection for new industries in countries less advanced than Britain. In addition, Say argued that when producers were faced with heavy direct taxes at home (as was the case, he claimed, in France), compensatory duties were justified to restore fair competition.[41] In his less theoretical *Catéchisme d'économie politique* (1815), Say merely condemned 'absolute prohibitions', implicitly leaving much room for moderate restrictions on commercial exchanges.[42]

Say's case is important because his reservations about free trade would gradually disappear from later editions of the *Traité* and *Catéchisme*. It is also significant because his works already enjoyed a wide audience in the aftermath of the Napoleonic wars: no figure is available for the 1814 edition of the *Traité*, but the print runs of the third (1816) and fourth (1819) editions of the *Traité* were, respectively, 2,000 and 3,000, while the print run of the 1815 *Catéchisme* was 1,500.[43] No figure is available for the successive editions of Ferrier's *Du gouvernement*, but the book's circulation is likely to have been more modest. In 1805, Fiévée informed his protégé that the first edition 'did not sell like a novel, but like a work on administration'.[44] Ferrier's work, however, represented the influential views of

[40] Charles Ganilh, *Théorie de l'économie politique fondée sur les faits résultant des statistiques de la France et de l'Angleterre*, 2 vols. (Paris, 1815), vol. I, p. 22 and vol. II, pp. 219–20. In 1821, Ganilh published a second, nearly identical, edition of his *Théorie*, of which 1,000 copies were printed; see impression 2864 (12 September 1821), AN, F18*II 7.

[41] Jean-Baptiste Say, *Traité d'économie politique*, 2nd edn, 2 vols. (Paris, 1814), vol. I, pp. 210–30.

[42] Jean-Baptiste Say, *Catéchisme d'économie politique* (Paris, 1815), pp. 130–6.

[43] Impression 762 (17 June 1815), AN, F18*II 1; impression 5822 (30 September 1816), AN, F18*II 3; and impression 9673 (22 July 1819), AN, F18*II 6.

[44] Fiévée to Ferrier, 8 January 1805, in *Correspondance*, p. 54.

the customs administration, while liberal timidity facilitated the practical reaffirmation of mercantile jealousy in the early years of the Bourbon Restoration.

II

The revived form of jealousy that inspired the Restoration's commercial policy did not only correspond with an economic strategy. It was also designed to repress the disorders inherited from the Revolutionary era and consolidate the restoration of monarchical power. To understand the connection made by Ferrier and others between the freedom of trade and revolutionary tendencies, it is necessary to examine briefly the practical workings of the prohibitive system and how it served to contain liberal aspirations within France as well as foreign commodities outside it. The very phrase 'prohibitive system' conveyed distinct repressive and counter-revolutionary undertones: it recalled the concept of 'prohibitive regime' used to describe not only commercial but also civil and religious restrictions in the eighteenth century, at the same time as it suggested continuity with Napoleon's 'Continental System'. Smuggling, already rife in the last decades of the Old Regime, was widely seen as a subversive activity.[45] The political dimension of prohibitive policies was manifest in the case of the ban on imports of cotton textiles, enforced with extreme vigour after its confirmation in 1814.[46] This prohibition demonstrated a desire to emulate the British commercial model, while the exceptional measures of surveillance and control required for its implementation alarmed liberal adversaries of the regime.

In the wake of the foreign invasion and the delineation of new borders in the spring of 1814, the regulation of foreign trade by the customs administration fell into disarray. Six months later, the Prefect of the Haut-Rhin in Alsace still complained that 'smuggling … is carried out with such audacity in my department, that it renders illusory the prohibitive system wisely established by our laws'. In Basel across the Swiss border, he added, the *prime d'assurance* (rate charged by smugglers for the illicit introduction of merchandise) on British cotton textiles had declined

[45] On the similarities between economic and other forms of regulation under the old regime, see Paolo Napoli, *Naissance de la police moderne* (Paris, 2003); on the politics of the fear of smuggling, see Michael Kwass, 'The Global Underground: Smuggling, Rebellion, and the Origins of the French Revolution', in Suzanne Desan, Lynn Hunt and William M. Nelson (eds.), *The French Revolution in Global Perspective* (Ithaca, NY, 2013), pp. 15–31.

[46] On the emergence of the French cotton industry, see Serge Chassagne, *Le Coton et ses patrons. France, 1760–1840* (Paris, 1991).

from between 30 and 40 per cent in the autumn of 1813 to between 10 and 12 per cent.[47] Rumours that a commercial treaty would soon complement the peace treaty with Britain further alarmed French manufacturers. Several chambers of commerce from cotton-manufacturing regions issued petitions warning the government that England 'may by this means [of a treaty] pump our bullion and annihilate our industry', as 'was the result of the 1786 treaty' (Troyes), and demanding that France preserve the 'prohibitive system', which had brought such immense 'wealth and prosperity' to England (Amiens).[48] The Rouen Chamber of Commerce, which led the protests against the 1786 treaty before the Revolution, publicly denounced the rumoured treaty as a violation of the 'political and social right' to the prohibition of foreign manufactured goods. The government should instead focus on the repression of smuggling: 'let us treat smugglers as rigorously as in England, and then contraband in our country will considerably diminish'.[49]

The Restoration soon eschewed the proposed treaty, and the government instructed prefects to employ 'severe regulations and harsh punishments' against smugglers.[50] But following the Hundred Days and a second foreign invasion in June 1815, complaints against the disorganization of the customs service and the proliferation of smuggling intensified.[51] In the repressive context of the White Terror, cotton manufacturers also learnt to couch their demands in the language of reactionary royalism.[52] For instance, an anonymous pamphlet in favour of the prohibitive system narrated the implausible tale of a former *émigré*, ruined by the sale of his estates during the Revolution. Upon his return under Napoleon,

47 Draft of a letter from the Prefect of the Haut-Rhin to the Director General of Agriculture, Commerce and Manufactures, [December 1814], Colmar, Archives Départementales du Haut-Rhin, 5P 66.

48 The Troyes Chamber of Commerce to the Ministry of the Interior, 28 July 1814, and Memorandum from Amiens Chamber of Commerce, [summer 1814], AN, F12 1941.

49 Chambre de Commerce de Rouen, *Mémoire sur la nécessité de maintenir le système prohibitif et sur les inconvénients d'un traité de commerce avec l'Angleterre* (Rouen, 1814), pp. 4, 7. See also [Anon.] ('L.N.D.'), *Observations sur le traité de commerce projeté entre la France et l'Angleterre* (Paris, 1814); Adam Frères et al., *Prohibition des produits des fabriques étrangères, répression de la fraude* (Paris, 1814); and [Anon.] ('G.'), *De l'influence du système maritime de l'Angleterre sur le repos de l'Europe, son commerce et son industrie* (Paris, 1815).

50 The Minister of the Interior to the Prefect of the Meurthe, 28 January 1815, Nancy, Archives Départementales de la Meurthe-et-Moselle, P8.

51 [Anon.], 'Mémoire des manufacturiers de coton de la ville de Paris', 15 September 1815; Lille Chamber of Commerce to the Minister of the Interior, 6 March 1816; 'Réflexions sur la fraude et sur les moyens de la réprimer', 31 March 1816, AN, F12 2502.

52 Emmanuel de Waresquiel and Benoit Yvert, *Histoire de la Restauration, 1814–1830: naissance de la France moderne* (Paris, 1996), pp. 149–96; Daniel P. Resnick, *The White Terror and the Political Reaction after Waterloo* (Cambridge, Mass., 1966).

he founded a cotton factory to provide his former farmers, also impoverished by the Revolution, with a living. But now that 'foreign products have flooded French territory', he risked being ruined again, unless the government adopted 'repressive measures' against smuggling and discouraged the 'frivolity' of Frenchwomen, who suffered from a 'blind frenzy' for foreign textiles.[53] The pamphlet only had a limited circulation, with 500 copies printed in March 1816.[54] But the way in which it combined an exacerbated form of jealousy with a language of political and moral purification captured the *Zeitgeist.*

In April 1816, the *ultra-royaliste* majority of the *chambre introuvable*, elected in August 1815, adopted a battery of repressive measures against smuggling, amid a concert of laments on the material and moral decline of French commerce. According to Antoine Dussumier-Fonbrune, a former *émigré* and *ultra* deputy for the Gironde, France owed the transformation of smuggling into 'an entire system of commerce' to its 'disastrous Revolution': 'It was natural that, in drying up all the sources of loyal industry, the Revolution opened up other ones, of an impure nature.' Charles Cornet d'Incourt, an *ultra* deputy for the Somme, also attributed the proliferation of smuggling to the 'fatal discords' of the Revolution, which had 'altered the public spirit'.[55] To remedy the situation, the customs law of 28 April 1816 increased the powers of the customs administration to search travellers, tradesmen and residents in an area extended to 25 kilometres inland from the borders. The law also augmented penalties against smuggling, with a minimum fine of 500 francs and up to three years' imprisonment for ordinary offences, while smuggling cases were transferred from justices of the peace and *tribunaux d'instance* to the *cours correctionnelles* and, when they involved six or more individuals, the *cours prévôtales*, the exceptional and summary courts established to punish disloyalty to the Bourbons during the Hundred Days. Finally, the law provided for the search and seizure of foreign cotton and woollen textiles by the customs administration, the police and the *gendarmerie*, throughout French territory. This provision empowered officials to search any building, including private houses, while a permanent commission of experts (*jury assermenté*) would examine samples and determine whether seized textiles were French or foreign.

[53] [Anon.] ('A.G. and A.P.'), *De l'influence désastreuse de la fraude sur l'industrie française et sur les finances de l'État* (Paris, 1816), pp. 8, 16–17.
[54] Impression 4221 (13 March 1816), AN, F18*II 2.
[55] AP, vol. XVII, p. 164 (9 April 1816) and p. 262 (16 April 1816).

The legislation was a partial return to the Continental Blockade, when a vast customs administration (35,000 officials) enjoyed exorbitant powers across the Empire and a special order of jurisdiction (*tribunaux des douanes* and *cours prévôtales*, already, as courts of appeal) dealt with customs offences. As a result, the customs administration remained, under the Restoration, a powerful branch of the state apparatus and, with 25,000 officials, the second largest after the army. Its functions were not confined to the regulation of foreign trade. Not only did it inherit the collection of the hated salt tax (the former *gabelle*) from the defunct Ferme Générale, but it was also charged with the political control of the country's borders.[56] Instructions to customs houses included lists of undesirable aliens to be turned away, usually for political reasons, such as Spanish liberal refugees, and the titles of foreign periodicals to be seized, such as radical British or Belgian newspapers.[57] As under the Old Regime, customs officials were also supposed to inspect all imported books to check that 'they contained nothing contrary to the government or the interest of the state'.[58]

This powerful, highly centralized and hierarchical administration elicited much apprehension among liberals. The Director General from 1814 to 1824 was Pierre de Saint-Cricq, a royalist who had served as a customs official since 1801.[59] Ferrier described his successor as a 'friend', who shared his views on commercial policy.[60] By contrast, Benjamin Constant, in a speech delivered at the Chamber of Deputies in 1819, denounced Saint-Cricq as 'a kind of minister who has two thousand employees of his nomination under him, is free of all responsibility [before the parliamentary chambers], surrounded by an innumerable clientele and vested with powers of influence' exceeding those of real ministers.[61] After 1824, Saint-Cricq retained his influence on commercial legislation as President of a new Bureau du Commerce et des Colonies from 1825 and as the first holder of a new ministerial portfolio of Commerce in 1828–9. Elevated

56 Jean Clinquart, *L'Administration des douanes sous le Consulat et l'Empire* (Neuilly-sur-Seine, 1979) and *L'Administration des douanes sous la Restauration et la Monarchie de Juillet* (Neuilly-sur-Seine, 1981).

57 The archives of the customs administration before 1870 disappeared in the fire of the Ministry of Finances during the Commune of 1871, but collections of instructions from the years 1815–30 can be found in other archives, e.g., 'Registre d'Ordre du Bureau de Bordeaux', Bordeaux, Archives des Douanes, 3B 21, and 'Registre d'Ordres du Bureau de Montpellier', Montpellier, Archives Départementales de l'Hérault, 5P 86.

58 See minutes of verifications of book imports for the years 1817–25, AN, F18 176 to F18 182; on this practice under the Old Regime, see Darnton, *Forbidden Best-Sellers*, p. 5.

59 Jean Bordas, *Les Directeurs généraux des douanes: l'administration et la politique douanière, 1801–1939* (Paris, 2004), pp. 481–502.

60 Ferrier to Fiévée, 5 June 1816, in *Correspondance*, p. 139.

61 AP, vol. xxv, pp. 156–8 (16 June 1819).

to the peerage after the 1830 Revolution, he remained the incarnation of prohibitive policies in the eyes of free-traders, who referred to him as a 'child ... of the Continental System' or 'the supreme director of prohibitive economics'.[62]

Of all the measures adopted to curtail smuggling in April 1816, the most controversial was the search for prohibited textiles. Between March 1816 and March 1817, at least seven anonymous pamphlets attacking the measure appeared in Paris.[63] The combined print runs of the seven publications was 4,500, a large figure given that their circulation seems to have been mostly confined to the capital.[64] All the pamphlets condemned the retroactive character of the law, which applied to foreign textiles introduced before its adoption, and the menace of domiciliary visits, which jeopardized the individual freedoms guaranteed by the 1814 Charter. The pamphlet that attracted the most attention was a *Mémoire sur la prohibition des mousselines* (1,000 copies). The author drew on 'enlightened writers' to condemn policies inspired by the theory of the balance of trade, stressing in the manner of Say that commerce always consisted 'in the exchange of products from one country with the products of another country'. But he focused his criticisms on the insufficient domestic production of thin cotton yarns. Parisian women who sewed muslins were forced to purchase smuggled British textiles and would now find themselves unemployed. The new law was therefore not only 'immoral' and 'impolitic' but also 'tyrannical', because it threatened to reduce French workers to the same abject poverty as in England: 'for of the thousand causes that contributed to this scourge [of the poverty of workers in England], can anyone doubt that the prohibitive system, which has increased the price of everything, is one of the most important?'[65]

Two responses to this *Mémoire* testify to its impact. The author of an anonymous *Réfutation* (500 copies) felt compelled to respond because

[62] *L'Écho de la Fabrique*, 19 August 1832, quoted in Jacques Canton-Debat, 'Un homme d'affaire lyonnais: Arlès-Dufour (1797–1872)' (unpublished Ph.D. dissertation, University of Lyon II, 2000), p. 238; *Le Mémorial Bordelais*, 6 March 1834.

[63] [Anon.], *Réflexions sur les articles 58, 59, 61, 62 et 63 du projet de loi sur le budget de 1816* (Paris, 1816); [Anon.], *Réflexions sur l'article 61 du projet de loi de budget de 1816* (Paris, 1816); [Anon.], *Mémoire sur la prohibition des mousselines* (Paris, 1816); [Anon.], *Observations à messieurs les députés contre les articles 59 et suivants du titre 6 de la loi sur les douanes* (Paris, 1816); [Xavier Audouin], *Quelques idées sur les prohibitions commerciales* (Paris, 1816); [Anon.], *Le Pour et le contre* (Paris, 1817); [Anon.], *Questions sur les prohibitions* (Paris, 1817).

[64] Impressions 4289 (21 March 1816), 4666 (8 May 1816) and 5465 (19 August 1816), AN, F18*II 2; impressions 6367 (4 December 1816), 6467 (13 December 1816), 374 (8 February 1817) and 598 (4 March 1817), AN, F18*II 3.

[65] [Anon.], *Mémoire sur la prohibition des mousselines*, pp. 3–6, 16–18.

the *Mémoire* was 'spread with such profusion' and its 'specious sophisms' seemed to have persuaded so many readers. A more official response by fourteen Paris cotton manufacturers (1,500 copies) accused the liberal pamphlet of having caused undue alarm among the thousands of Parisian 'seamstresses' and 'embroideresses'.[66] The two responses insinuated that the author of the *Mémoire* was himself a speculator in smuggled British goods. The latter issued a rejoinder, *Le Pour et le contre* (1,000 copies), in which he maintained that the law breached the Code Civil inherited from the Revolution as well as the principles established by 'writers on political economy'.[67] The rejoinder's title was certainly an allusion to a well known pamphlet against the colonial *exclusif* before the Revolution.[68] The pamphlet war prompted the *ultra* deputy for the Loire-Inférieure, Charles Richard, a former Vendéen insurgent, to complain that pamphlets against the law of 28 April 1816 were 'extensively disseminated' in the capital. Such public criticisms of commercial policy, he contended, were 'unconventional' and 'dangerous'.[69]

An annotation in the margins of the Librairie registers makes it possible to identify the author of another contribution to the controversy, *Quelques idées sur les prohibitions* (800 copies), as Xavier Audouin, a Jacobin, friend of the extremist Jacques Hébert and advocate of the Terror in 1793–4.[70] An official at the Ministry of the Marine in the late 1790s, he authored a work that echoed Hauterive's attack on British jealous policies and castigated the theory of the balance of trade in 1800.[71] In *Quelques idées*, Audouin drew on Smith and Say to condemn the mercantile system and urged his countrymen not to follow the British model of commercial policy, which enriched a few at the expense of all the subjects of the British Empire: 'Are we willing to sacrifice, like [the English], our tastes, our fortunes, our liberties in order to uphold our prohibitions?' Somewhat ironically for a former advocate of Terrorist measures, Audouin's chief concern was the political and moral repercussions of the nationwide search for prohibited cotton textiles – the encouragement

66 [Anon.] ('A.G.'), *Réfutation du mémoire intitulé: mémoire sur la prohibition des mousselines* (Paris, 1816), p. 21; [Anon.], *Mémoire des manufacturiers de coton de Paris* (Paris, 1817), pp. 10–11. For the number of printed copies, see impressions 5847 (2 October 1816) and 81 (8 January 1817), AN, F18*II 3.

67 [Anon.], *Le Pour et le contre*, pp. iii–iv.

68 Jean-Baptiste Dubuc, *Le Pour et le contre sur un objet de grande discorde et d'importance majeure* (London, 1784); on the controversy surrounding this pamphlet, see Tarrade, *Le Commerce colonial*, vol. II, pp. 555–62.

69 AP, vol. XIX, p. 411 (8 March 1817).

70 Impression 6467 (13 December 1816), AN, F18*II 3.

71 Xavier Audouin, *Du commerce maritime, de son influence sur la richesse et la force des états* (Paris, [1800]).

of 'denunciation' and 'slander', the multiplication of 'inquisitions' and 'domiciliary visits', the probable creation of a 'special police force' and the proliferation of 'political suspicion' as well as 'commercial suspicion'. The measure was therefore reminiscent of 'these days when the errors of the laws prepared the crimes of its enforcers' and when France was 'covered with prisons, and full of victims'.[72]

Anti-Bonapartist and anti-Jacobin repression no doubt contributed to the fears of Audouin and the other pamphleteers who attacked the law of 28 April 1816. The search for prohibited textiles throughout French territory nonetheless outlasted the White Terror and was only repealed, together with the ban on foreign textiles, in 1860. Yet the archives of the commission charged with determining whether seized textiles were French or not, which contain registers indicating the results of 5,458 seizures between 1816 and 1844, suggest that liberal fears were not absolutely unfounded. Repression peaked immediately after the adoption of the law, with approximately 400 seizures per year in 1816–18, before falling to 200 annual seizures in 1825–9 and fewer than 100 in 1843–4.[73] Even more telling is the geography of repression in its early years. Out of 532 seizures made over 16 months in 1818–19, 184 (35 per cent) took place in or near Paris (Seine department) and 65 (12 per cent) in or near Lyon (Rhône), two cities that deserved their reputation as liberal strongholds. By contrast, there were only two seizures in or near Marseille (Bouches-du-Rhône) and none in the Nantes or Bordeaux regions (Loire-Inférieure and Gironde), other major commercial centres where royalist opinions prevailed.[74] Anecdotal evidence from Mulhouse (Haut-Rhin) suggests that prefects used the threat of searches to pressure merchants and manufacturers hostile to the regime during elections.[75]

Moreover, for the merchants and shopkeepers who were subjected to the procedure, searches, often conducted in broad daylight to edify the public, were frightening and humiliating experiences. Alongside the minutes of seizures, countless justificatory receipts and a few well preserved textile samples, the records contain numerous moving protests. Jean-Baptiste Bourgogne, for example, a shopkeeper in the small town of Condé (Nord), complained in July 1816 that customs officials had treated his wife and daughters 'in an improper fashion', planted false receipts in

[72] [Audouin], *Quelques idées*, pp. 17, 69–71.
[73] My calculations, based on the registers of decisions by the *jury assermenté*, AN, F12* 5694–704.
[74] My calculations, based on seizures recorded from 19 May 1818 to 9 November 1819, AN, F12*5696 and 5697.
[75] Paul Leuilliot, *L'Alsace au début du XIXe siècle*, 3 vols. (Paris, 1959), vol. 1, p. 436.

his papers and forged his signature on the minutes that he refused to sign. The local *commissaire de police* endorsed his petition, confirming that the Bourgogne family 'were terror-stricken by such drastic measures'.[76] In March 1818, the seizure of 256 pieces of 'percale, muslin and other cotton fabrics' plunged Lazare Dockès, a Colmar (Haut-Rhin) merchant, and his family 'into a state of anxiety and despair'. It was because he was 'an Israelite', Dockès contended, that customs officials had searched his shop and had chosen to do so 'on a Friday afternoon', knowing that the Sabbath would prevent him from lodging a complaint immediately.[77] Records from the *cours prévôtales* suggest that their action against smuggling networks placed a similar emphasis on spectacular proceedings and punishment. In the winter of 1817, Gaspard Giacomini, an army officer who resigned his commission in 1789 and now *prévôt* (president) of the Var *cour prévôtale* in Provence, spent several weeks personally investigating the seizure of several bales of cotton goods and barrels of rum at a beach near Antibes. Giacomini obtained the conviction of a perfume-seller in the village of Le Cannet and his main accomplice to five-year jail terms preceded by a one-hour defamatory exposition on the market square of Draguignan in November 1817. But he could do nothing against the alleged commissioner of the smuggling operation, an unnamed 'Englishman' based in Nice (then in Piedmont).[78]

In February 1818, Saint-Cricq claimed victory for his administration's 'war' against smuggling, declaring to the Chamber of Deputies that the *prime d'assurance* had risen in less than two years from 10 per cent 'to an average rate of 30 per cent'. The following year, he confirmed that the fare required by smugglers varied between 25 and 40 per cent, depending on the section of the border and the type of goods.[79] Confidential documents from the customs administration cite comparable figures, with, for instance, an increase of the insurance rate on the Belgian border, by September 1817, to 25 per cent on cotton yarns and 30–5 per cent on cotton textiles.[80] Mercantile jealousy was restored in practice as well as in theory. But the reinforcement of repression against smuggling revived a sense that restrictions on the liberty of commerce also endangered political and individual freedoms.

76 'Affaire Jean-Baptiste Bourgogne', AN, F12 1973–4.
77 'Affaire Lazare Dockès', AN, F12 1977.
78 'Affaire d'Antibes', Draguignan, Archives Départementales du Var, 2U 180.
79 AP, vol. xx, p. 726 (14 February 1818) and vol. xxv, p. 154 (16 June 1819).
80 A customs inspector in the Nord department to Saint-Cricq, 27 September 1817, AN, F12 2503.

III

The practical reaffirmation of jealousy was not limited to the partial continuation of the Continental System or confined to the protection of domestic manufacturing industries. On the contrary, it extended to the regulation of the colonial trade, regarded by Raynal, Smith and their disciples as the foulest aspect of mercantile jealousy, due to its association with slavery and the slave trade. After 1814, the Restoration made a formidable endeavour to revive exchanges with France's remaining colonies within the regulatory framework of a resuscitated *exclusif*. These efforts confirm that the Revolution did not constitute an immediate and complete rupture with eighteenth-century patterns of thought about international trade. In order to compensate for the territorial and economic decline of France's overseas empire, the revamped *exclusif* was even more restrictive than under the Old Regime, with new privileges granted to planters and seaports. Yet these new restrictions elicited considerable protests in regions such as Alsace that had benefited from the expansion of Continental exchanges under Napoleon.

The reactionary colonial strategy of the Restoration achieved some significant successes. In order to prop up the economic recovery of Martinique, Guadeloupe and Bourbon (Réunion), the Bourbon regime introduced, in the autumn of 1814, a *surtaxe* or additional tax on colonial goods originating from the rest of the world. Such a preferential tariff had not been needed before 1789, because French colonial producers then easily undercut their competitors on the metropolitan as well as other European markets. The new tariffs facilitated the rapid development of a French colonial production increasingly specialized in cane sugar and destined to the metropolitan market. Between 1815 and 1820, France's annual imports from its colonies rose from 2.5 to 90 million francs and the share of these imports in total French imports from 1 to 20 per cent. Such figures did not match the 200 million francs, making over 35 per cent of total imports, of the 1780s. But the contribution of colonies to total French imports, after a steep decline in the 1830s, would not reach the 20 per cent threshold again until the 1930s.[81] This growth of the colonial trade after 1815 resulted in a last bout of prosperity for slave plantations in Martinique, Guadeloupe and Bourbon.[82]

[81] Todd, 'A French Imperial Meridian', p. 167.

[82] Paul Butel, *Histoire des Antilles françaises, XVIIe–XXe siècles* (Paris, 2002), pp. 246–59; Hai Qang Ho, *Contribution à l'histoire économique de l'île de La Réunion, 1642–1848* (Paris, 1998), pp. 162–7.

In the colonies, administrators were instructed to restore and enforce the regulations of '24 March 1763', '25 January 1765', '20 December 1783' and '30 August 1784' – in other words the *exclusif* legislation, which reserved most trade for metropolitan merchants.[83] The late 1810s also witnessed an illicit but spectacular resurgence of the French slave trade. The Bourbon regime was too dependent on British support to rescind the abolition of the trade decreed by Napoleon, in a vain attempt to gain British sympathies, during the Hundred Days. But after 1815, the Restoration turned a blind eye to the activities of French slave traders. According to available estimates, the number of slaves embarked on French ships across the Atlantic rose from fewer than 1,000 in 1814 to a yearly average of 17,000 in 1820–5, a figure matching the numbers of the 1770s and making France the largest slave-trading nation of post-Napoleonic Europe after Portugal.[84] The Restoration also made sustained efforts to try and restore effective French sovereignty over Saint-Domingue. In March 1816, hoping to reassert French commercial influence, it authorized the resumption of trade with the breakaway colony, subjecting imports from Haiti to only half the *surtaxe* on foreign colonial goods. Imports from Haiti rose from 2.5 to 15 million francs.[85] The latter figure represented only a tenth of the pre-Revolutionary trade with the colony. But given the adverse political conditions, it confirms that the disruptions of the years 1792–1815 weakened rather than annihilated the French Atlantic trade.

This commercial revival explains why Say and Constant launched forceful attacks on the colonial system, slavery and the slave trade during the Restoration.[86] Yet it was another aspect of colonial reaction, a piece of legislation reserving the re-exportation of colonial goods to seaports, that proved the most controversial in metropolitan opinion. Re-exports of colonial goods from French ports to Continental Europe had been a significant

[83] The Minister of the Marine to the *Gouverneur* and the *Intendant* of Martinique, 16 August 1814, Centre des Archives d'Outre-Mer, Aix-en-Provence, 11COL 61, xi.

[84] Due to the absence of official records after the abolition of the trade, the figure is probably an underestimate, and it does not take into account French slave trading in the Indian Ocean; The Transatlantic Slave Trade Database (www.slavevoyages.org, accessed 11 April 2013). On the illegal French slave trade after 1815, see Serge Daget, *Répertoire des expéditions négrières françaises à la traite illégale: 1814–1850* (Nantes, 1988).

[85] Todd, 'Remembering and Restoring'; Jean-François Brière, *Haïti et la France, 1804–1848: le rêve brisé* (Paris, 2008), pp. 47–105.

[86] Philippe Steiner, 'J.-B. Say et les colonies ou comment se débarrasser d'un héritage intempestif', *Cahiers d'Économie Politique*, 27 (1996): 153–73; Jennifer Pitts, 'Constant's Thought on Slavery and Empire', in Helena Rosenblatt (ed.), *The Cambridge Companion to Constant* (Cambridge, 2009), pp. 115–45, esp. pp. 125–38; see also Lawrence C. Jennings, *French Anti-Slavery: The Movement for the Abolition of Slavery in France, 1802–1848* (Cambridge, 2000), pp. 1–23.

feature of the pre-Revolutionary Atlantic trade.[87] In order to facilitate a resurgence, the same law of 18 April 1816 that increased repression against the smuggling of foreign textiles also banned the introduction of colonial goods, even when destined to be re-exported, by land borders. Moreover, the law limited to maritime cities the privilege of *entrepôt réel* – the right to store goods in customs warehouses without paying duties for up to a year, before introducing them on the domestic market or re-exporting them.[88] The legislation effectively excluded inland and usually liberal cities from the re-export trade to the benefit of royalist ports such as Bordeaux, Nantes and Marseille. Ferrier, among others, justified such a privilege as due compensation for the damage caused to seaports by the Revolution and as a means of reviving France's long-distance trade and naval power.[89]

These privileges answered the wishes of seaports' merchants, led by the Bordelais. It is worth underlining the support of Bordeaux merchants for jealous policies in the aftermath of the Napoleonic wars because after 1830 they became ardent partisans of free trade. In the late 1810s, nostalgia for the prosperity of the Atlantic trade, of which Bordeaux had been a major beneficiary, still prevailed.[90] Between 1815 and 1820, the Bordeaux Chamber of Commerce repeatedly demanded increases in the preferential tariff for the importation of goods by French ships and even proposed the implementation of the Revolutionary 'law of 3 September 1793', a lapsed ban on imports by foreign ships modelled on Britain's Navigation Acts. The Bordelais merchants supported the legislation limiting *entrepôt* rights to seaports, in the hope that their city would become again 'a warehouse for the products of the East and West Indies, which from here can be re-expedited to the rest of Europe'. They also endorsed the ban on imports of colonial goods by land borders as the sole effective means of preventing the fraudulent introduction, via Amsterdam and Antwerp, of foreign colonial goods on the French market: 'Only thanks to an absolute, complete prohibition can the customs effectively monitor the borders and can maritime trade enjoy the guarantees necessary to its prosperity.'[91] The construction, between 1821 and 1824, of the Entrepôt des Denrées Coloniales,

[87] Tarrade, *Commerce colonial*, vol. II, pp. 749–57.

[88] *Entrepôt fictif*, by contrast, designated the right for merchants to keep in their own stores certain imported goods for up to a year without paying duties, but it was limited to a handful of bulky products, for which illicit operations were deemed impossible or unprofitable.

[89] François Ferrier, *Mémoire sur la demande d'un entrepôt de denrées coloniales à Paris* (Paris and Lille, 1819), pp. 28–32.

[90] Paul Butel, 'Crise et mutation de l'activité économique à Bordeaux sous le Consulat et l'Empire', *Revue d'Histoire Moderne et Contemporaine*, 17 (3) (1970): 540–58.

[91] The Bordeaux Chamber of Commerce to the President of the Chamber of Deputies, 23 December 1815, and the Chamber of Commerce to Saint-Cricq, 2 February 1818, Bordeaux, Archives

at a substantial cost of 1.2 million francs, testified to the Bordelais faith in the revival of re-exports of tropical goods.[92]

But the new legislation angered Continental merchants and gave rise, in 1818, to one of the bitterest commercial controversies after the fall of Napoleon, on the seemingly trivial issue of the 'transit' (re-exportation) of colonial goods across Alsace. Alsatian protests against the restrictions drew on memories of the province's privileges under the Old Regime, when it remained beyond the reach of French customs (*à l'instar de l'étranger effectif*). They were also suffused with more recent memories of the region's flourishing if not always licit trade with Continental Europe during the Blockade.[93] The protests aimed at recapturing the trade in colonial goods along the Rhine valley, from Antwerp or Amsterdam to southern Germany and Switzerland. Before 1789, such goods were hauled until Strasbourg and then, as the Rhine ceased to be navigable, by carriages along the left (French) bank of the river. This trade survived until the abolition of Alsace's commercial privileges in July 1793, before a drastic decline during the war years. It resumed after 1815. Yet, as a result of the ban on the introduction of colonial goods by land borders, merchandise from the Netherlands was now transported along a slightly longer itinerary on the right (German) bank of the Rhine.

In order to overcome the opposition of seaports to a lifting of the ban – even one limited to the Bas-Rhin and Haut-Rhin departments – the Alsatian merchants launched an unusual campaign to enlist the support of public opinion. 'Publicity', wrote a delegate of the Strasbourg Chamber of Commerce in Paris, was their 'main means of attack'.[94] In 1817, the Chamber of Commerce issued a first pamphlet that combined a defence of 'exchanges' as 'the true principle of commerce' with patriotic considerations: 'Is it for France or for a foreign country that we wish to guarantee, along a route of 150, 250 leagues, the subsistence of countless coachmen, farmers, wheelwrights, saddlers, farriers and all sorts of workers?'[95] In 1818, the Chamber of Commerce financed the impression of supplements to

Départementales de la Gironde (hereafter ADG), 02/081/276, register 1815–18, fols. 26, 136–8; the Chamber of Commerce to Saint-Cricq, 16 June 1818, ADG, 02/081/277, register 1818–22, fols. 7–8.

92 The Chamber of Commerce to the Mayor of Bordeaux, 7 August 1821, ADG, 02/081/277, register 1818–22, fols. 135–6; minutes of the Chamber of Commerce, 19 July 1824, ADG, 02/081/305, register 1823–5, fol. 46.

93 John F. Boscher, *The Single Duty Project* (London, 1964), pp. 5–7; Geoffrey J. Ellis, *Napoleon's Continental Blockade: The Case of Alsace* (Oxford, 1981), pp. 149–97.

94 Charles Schattenmann to the Strasbourg Chamber of Commerce, 20 March 1818, Strasbourg, Archives Départementales du Bas-Rhin (hereafter ADBR), 79J 70.

95 Chambre de Commerce de Strasbourg, *Pétition aux fins de l'établissement du transit général par la France et subsidiairement du transit de l'Allemagne en Suisse* (Strasbourg, 1817), pp. 7, 12.

several national newspapers, including the influential *Le Journal des Débats*, which called for the relaxation of the ban on re-exportation by land borders. It also issued three new pamphlets, with an extraordinary combined print run of 11,000 copies: *Du transit d'Alsace* (1,000 copies), *Quelques observations en faveur du transit d'Alsace* (8,000) and *Encore un mot du transit d'Alsace* (2,000).[96] Despite their politically liberal undertones, the texts invoked the traditional liberties of commerce and the influx of bullion that would result from recapturing the transit trade rather than the political economy of Smith and Say. They also dismissed the seaports' fears of a resurgence of smuggling as 'chimerical' given the meticulous customs controls to which transit was subjected.[97] A delegate of the Strasbourg Chamber of Commerce rejoiced that, thanks to their propaganda, 'transit across Alsace has become a popular issue in Paris': 'everyone is talking about it, in the salons and in the antechambers, in trading firms as well as in small shops'.[98]

Despite the relative moderation of Alsatian demands, the campaign's success alarmed royalists, both because they did not wish to relax the repression of smuggling and because they considered the regulation of commerce a matter for the state rather than the public. The *ultra* deputy Baron Morgan de Belloy, Chair of the Customs Legislation Commission and staunch defender of prohibitions, denounced the proliferation of publications in favour of transit across Alsace as an 'extraordinary phenomenon' inspired by 'political motives'.[99] In the Chamber of Deputies, the seaports' representatives, almost all royalists, staunchly opposed a formal proposal to authorize transit across Alsatian departments. They underlined the opportunities for smuggling that even a partial exemption from the prohibition would generate. Above all, they defended the ban as a compensation for the unjust transfer of riches that had taken place, since 1789, from maritime areas to inland regions. In the words of Charles Richard, the *ultra* defender of Nantes' interests:

> For twenty-five years, [our] ships remained idle and rotted in the harbours. Trade was redirected to the [land] borders, where the proximity of armies attracted the riches and the gold of Europe, while in the ports, the ruin of our colonies, the vain attempts to re-conquer them, the lack of activity resulting from protracted wars, the perfidious illusions of ephemeral peace altered – nay, annihilated commercial wealth.[100]

[96] Impressions 3933 (23 February 1818), 4247 (18 March 1818), 4334 (24 March 1818), AN, F18*II 4.

[97] [Jean-Georges Humann, Saum l'Aîné and Charles-Henri Schattenmann], *Quelques observations présentées à la chambre des députés en faveur du transit d'Alsace* (Paris, 1818), p. 5.

[98] Charles Schattenmann to the Strasbourg Chamber of Commerce, 5 April 1818, ADBR, 79J 70.

[99] AP, vol. XXI, p. 464 (24 March 1818).

[100] AP, vol. XXI, p. 488 (26 March 1818).

Prohibitive legislation was intended to reverse the reorientation of French commerce in the Revolutionary era.

Deputies rejected transit across Alsace by 101 to 96 votes.[101] According to a delegate of the Strasbourg Chamber of Commerce, the main cause of their parliamentary defeat lay in the solidarity of royalist deputies with the seaports: when the Chamber divided, 'the entire right side of the assembly stood up in order to reject transit'. A second factor, another delegate reported, was the opposition of Saint-Cricq, the Director General of Customs, who 'loves us, we merchants of the land borders, in the same way as Saturn loved his children' and opposed any measure that might hinder the repression of smuggling. Since he had 'twenty-six thousand positions at his disposal', Saint-Cricq enjoyed 'considerable ascendancy' among deputies.[102] The following year, the Chamber of Deputies finally authorized the transit of colonial goods across Alsace, but with so many precautions against the risks of smuggling that the Strasbourg merchants were unable to recapture the trade along the Rhine valley.[103] Also in 1819, the seaports saw off demands from liberal merchants for the extension of *entrepôt réel* rights to Paris and other inland cities.[104]

The controversy over Alsatian transit shows that the Restoration's strategy of colonial reaction did not leave opinion indifferent, although indignation focused on the dispensation of new commercial privileges inside metropolitan France rather than the revival of the slave trade. It also further highlights how the regulation of commerce after 1815 became perceived as a political as well as an economic issue. The royalists suspected demands for a greater liberty of commerce of seeking to undermine the restored monarchy's legitimacy. Conversely, jealousy increasingly appeared as the commercial facet of reactionary royalism.

IV

The conflation of jealousy and political reaction reached its apex when the *ultra-royalistes*, in the wake of the Duc de Berry's assassination in February 1820, regained the reins of government. Comte Joseph de Villèle emerged

[101] AP, vol. XXI, p. 495 (27 March 1818); according to the stenographer, the vote was followed by 'a protracted and intense agitation'.

[102] Charles Schattenmann to the Strasbourg Chamber of Commerce, 27 March 1818, ADBR, 79J 70; Georges Humann to the Strasbourg Chamber of Commerce, 13 February 1818, ADBR, 79J 71.

[103] AP, vol. XXIV, pp. 193–6, 239–52 and 268–83 (4, 7 and 8 May 1819).

[104] Démier, 'Nation, marché et développement', pp. 893–924.

as the principal *ultra* leader and became Premier in the autumn of 1821. While he was a planter in Bourbon in the 1790s, Villèle had helped defeat the implementation, in the Indian Ocean colony, of the Revolutionary law that abolished slavery. In the 1820s, he championed the adoption of stringent prohibitive laws for agricultural and colonial producers. His defence of landowners' commercial interests formed part of a broader effort to reconstitute the economic power of the aristocracy, symbolized by the granting of a 650 million francs indemnity (derided by the liberal opposition as 'le milliard des émigrés') to families whose property was sold as *biens nationaux* during the Revolution in April 1825 and the imposition of a 150 million francs indemnity for expropriated planters in return for the recognition of Haitian independence in July 1825. Villèle even attempted, in vain, to reintroduce primogeniture in 1826.[105]

The exacerbation of jealousy after 1820 was also a response to the early stirrings of nineteenth-century globalization, in particular the emergence of new producers of foodstuffs and raw materials in eastern Europe, the Americas and Asia. The adoption of a sliding scale of import duties on grain at the turn of the 1820s aimed at checking the rise of cheap grain imports from southern Ukraine and resulted in a de-facto ban until 1830. It was aggressively reactionary, since it did not revive but upended the Old Regime's system of restrictions on grain exchanges, which limited exports in order to protect consumers. According to its defenders, the first corn law adopted in July 1819 simultaneously sought to contain 'the agricultural revolution of Russian provinces' and compensate French grain producers for the measures taken against *accapareurs* (grain hoarders) by 'the awful regime of 1793'.[106] The 1819 law having failed to stymie the influx of Russian grain, *ultra* deputies obtained the adoption of more severe restrictions in July 1821. Villèle, in a speech that caused a 'general sensation' among deputies and consolidated his leadership of the *ultra* party, compared the rise of Russian exports to the discovery of a 'wheat mine' that might disrupt European societies as much as Spanish gold and silver mines had transformed them in the sixteenth century. Villèle admitted that grain imports still represented only a small fraction of French consumption (about $\frac{1}{160}$), but foreign trade had, in his opinion, a disproportionate impact on 'imagination' and 'minds', with 'disastrous' effects on prices.[107]

[105] Waresquiel and Yvert, *Histoire de la Restauration*, pp. 295–363.
[106] AP, vol. xxv, pp. 289, 598 (22 June and 7 July 1819).
[107] AP, vol. xxxi, pp. 130–5 (23 April 1821) and pp. 196–8 (27 April 1821).

The 1819 and 1821 corn laws divided the left. Jacques-Antoine Manuel, a figurehead of the opposition with Bonapartist sympathies, condemned 'philanthropic reflexions on the universal liberty of commerce' and applauded to the protection of French grain producers. In contrast, Benjamin Constant denounced the law as a blatantly self-interested measure given the predominance of large landowners among deputies: 'you increase the price of the foodstuff produced by your properties and of which your granaries are full', an accusation that elicited 'violent murmurs on the right and the centre' of the chamber. In Constant's view, the new corn legislation set France on the same disastrous economic course as Britain, 'where the high price of grain, aristocratic elections and guilds have rendered necessary the tax for the poor'. Constant even compared the greed of French royalists to the cupidity of Roman patricians, whose efforts to increase the price of necessities had precipitated the collapse of the Republic. 'It is to this cause', he concluded, 'that one must attribute the fall of almost all states'.[108]

In 1822, the Villèle government pushed through the chambers a customs law that steeply increased tariffs on foreign sugar, iron and cattle. The doubling of the *surtaxe* on foreign sugar was intended to shelter planters from Brazilian, Cuban and Indian competition, while the increase in duties on iron and cattle to levels near or above 100 per cent *ad valorem* chiefly benefited forest proprietors (most French iron was still made with charcoal rather than coke) and cattle owners. Defenders of the law employed a language of exacerbated mercantilism. Louis Bourienne, Napoleon's former private secretary and Chair of the Customs Committee, asserted that 'the richest nation [was] always the one that exports the most and imports the least' and lambasted 'these preachers of independence, these speculators of nations, who advocate the destruction of what time has consecrated and replace it with theories, suppositions, and dreams'. The Comte de Montbron praised 'the excellent book of Monsieur Ferrier' (a recent re-edition of *Du gouvernement*) and attacked modern philosophy, 'which has questioned the necessity of customs just as it questioned the necessity of colonies, the navy, monarchy, religion'.[109] Unless the prohibitive system was consolidated, Villèle argued, commodities from around the globe would annihilate French wealth:

> Let us imagine for a moment the system of prohibition abolished. Odessa will flood you with its grain, England with its iron, hardware, textiles and almost all the objects of common usage and comfort ... Bengal and Brazil will send their sugar at prices far lower than the sugar of your colonies.

[108] AP, vol. XXXI, p. 253 (4 May 1821).

[109] AP, vol. XXXVI, pp. 123–5 (8 April 1822).

> The Americans will send you their tobacco, their cotton, their cod. I will say more, you will lose your commerce: because if you annihilate all these productions, there will no longer exist any means of exchange.[110]

Liberal deputies condemned the law as 'feudal' and '*privilégiaire*' (privilegiary), while Constant attacked the 'principles' expounded by Villèle as 'destructive' of 'commercial transactions'.[111] The acrimonious tone of the debates stirred up interest in the press. In 1814, the main national newspapers only mentioned parliamentary debates about customs legislation to regret they were 'barely noticed' by the public.[112] In 1822, the *Courrier Français*, organ of the radical left, complained that 'the majority of the chamber [was] alien to true economic knowledge'. The royalist *Gazette de France* did not comment on the tariff increases but denounced the protests it elicited in France, Switzerland and Germany as the fruit of 'ill-intentioned rumours' spread by 'the faction that [was] stirring throughout Europe' in order to overthrow monarchical governments.[113] Attitudes towards international trade were increasingly polarized according to political allegiances.

Such political determination of ideas about commerce should not be regarded as self-evident. In particular, the conflation of royalism with mercantilism was still recent. In an essay on 'the wealth of nations' published in 1810, Louis de Bonald, the influential counter-revolutionary thinker, dismissed with equal contempt the admirers of Adam Smith and the advocates of the balance of trade, because both subscribed to the materialistic conception of wealth embodied by England and its immense commerce. Although Bonald expressed a preference for the more 'noble' pursuit of agriculture over manufactures and commerce, he chiefly advocated the adoption of a broader conception of wealth, which would consist in the cultivation of the 'moral forces' of nations and the restoration of traditional 'Christian manners'.[114] Similarly, Rubichon, the reactionary author of *De l'Angleterre*, poured as much scorn on the 'thousands of French writers and administrators' who worried about the balance of trade as on the Revolutionary admirers of Smith, because they equally exaggerated the contribution of foreign trade to national wealth.[115]

By contrast, after 1820, royalist writers on political economy tended to embrace an aggressive version of the mercantile system. They continued to

[110] AP, vol. XXXVII, p. 59 (27 June 1822).
[111] AP, vol. XXXVI, p. 733 (24 June 1822); vol. XXXVII, p. 94 (28 June and 29 June 1822).
[112] *Le Journal de Paris*, 1 October 1814; see also *Le Journal des Débats*, 16 November 1814.
[113] 'De la loi de douanes', *Le Courrier Français*, 3 July 1822; *La Gazette de France*, 31 July 1822.
[114] Louis de Bonald, 'De la richesse des nations', 23 December 1810, in *Œuvres complètes de M. de Bonald*, ed. Abbé Migne, 3 vols. (Paris, 1864), vol. II, pp. 307–18.
[115] Rubichon, *De l'Angleterre*, vol. II, pp. 350–7.

praise the virtues of self-sufficiency but also stressed the need to encourage exports and the colonial trade. In *Du Système d'impôt fondé sur les principes de l'économie politique* (1820), Auguste de Saint-Chamans, a fervent *ultra*, provocatively endorsed Adam Smith's epithet by describing himself as an advocate of the '*mercantile system*'. His hostility to the liberty of commerce was grounded in political memories as well as intellectual considerations: 'I know', he wrote, 'how much so many general principles about such or such complete liberty have cost us and still cost us today.'[116] In 1823, Saint-Chamans reiterated his views more playfully in a dialogue, *Le Petit-Fils de l'homme aux quarante écus*, a title inspired by Voltaire's sarcastic attack on the Physiocrats in 1768 (although Saint-Chamans distanced himself from Voltaire's subversive religious views in the preface). In the dialogue, Monsieur André, a grandson as naive as the character invented by Voltaire, ruined the village where he owned an estate by encouraging the inhabitants to implement 'Adam Smith's system' of virtuous economy. André's friend, 'Monsieur Trueman', presumably an Englishman, then restored the village's prosperity by promoting luxury, the consumption of locally made goods and the circulation of bullion. Trueman conceded that foreign trade was beneficial as long as imports did not threaten domestic industries, but his preference went to exchanges with colonies, because they combined the advantages of 'internal commerce' with an encouragement to naval power.[117] The following year, in a more theoretical *Nouvel essai sur la richesse des nations*, Saint-Chamans defended prohibitions, luxury, high public expenditure and even war as the best means to enrich a nation, as demonstrated by the British example.[118]

Saint-Chamans' works were probably not widely disseminated. Only 500 copies were printed of *Du système d'impôt*.[119] Yet his acerbic attacks on the Physiocrats, Smith and Say make him a good representative of *ultra* economics. Ferrier recorded the concurrence of Saint-Chamans' views with his own and considered *Du système d'impôt* a 'remarkable' work.[120] Saint-Chamans' treatise also earned the endorsement of Bonald, who thought it 'successfully combated the various systems of political economy of Adam Smith and his disciples'. Bonald remained more apprehensive than Saint-Chamans about luxury, underlining its disruptive social and political impact on Europe in the eighteenth century. He was particularly

[116] Auguste de Saint-Chamans, *Du système d'impôt fondé sur les principes de l'économie politique* (Paris, 1820), pp. 180–93, 243–4.
[117] Auguste de Saint-Chamans, *Le Petit-Fils de l'homme aux quarante écus* (Paris, 1823), pp. 19, 110–11.
[118] Auguste de Saint-Chamans, *Nouvel essai sur la richesse des nations* (Paris, 1824), pp. 75–6.
[119] Impression 1420 (18 May 1820), AN, F18*II 7.
[120] Ferrier, *Du gouvernement*, 2nd edn, p. xxxix.

worried about the consequences of the new 'luxury of machines', which 'piles up men in cities and corrupts them'. But, overall, he felt in sympathy with Saint-Chamans' attack against political economy, a 'science ... all the more useless ... in that it leads to a result, *laissez-faire* and *laissez-passer*, which can be achieved without studies and books'.[121]

Another advocate of an exacerbated form of jealousy after 1820 was Vincent Viénot de Vaublanc, born in Saint-Domingue and a stalwart defender of colonial slavery at the Legislative Assembly in 1791–2.[122] A royalist conspirator in the 1790s, he rallied to the Napoleonic regime and supported its efforts to prevent England from becoming 'the sovereign dominator of commerce all over the world'.[123] He served as Minister of the Interior during the White Terror in 1816 and became, after 1820, a vocal defender of colonial planters' interests. His *Du Commerce de la France* (1822) extolled the mercantile, naval and colonial strategy pursued by England since the seventeenth century. Colonies, he contended, remained one of France's most valuable assets for they reduced its dependence on imports from the rest of the world: 'The more different from each other the components of an empire, the more this empire can satisfy its own needs.' Vaublanc's support for the mercantile system and colonial trade was also inspired by political considerations. In a later work, he conceded that Adam Smith's ideas about the liberty of commerce were superficially 'attractive' but warned that 'the famous declaration of rights [in 1789], beguiled us too, and yielded dreadful results'.[124]

It is in this context of an effusion of reactionary mercantilism that one must locate Benjamin Constant's influential eulogy of commerce under the Restoration. Constant was an early defender of the necessity and benefits of foreign trade. An entry in his journal dated 1804 derided Fichte's *Der geschlossene Handelstaat* as the 'masterpiece' of the school of German 'madmen' who did not know 'real life' and ignored 'modern civilization'. 'God bless their Spartan ideas', he added, but 'if they could govern, they would start Robespierre again'. The draft of Constant's *Principes de politique*, written during Napoleon's reign, also contained a vibrant defence of the liberty of commerce and industry. This section was omitted from the book published in 1815, because Constant feared linking 'commercial'

121 Louis de Bonald, 'Sur l'économie politique', [1820 or 1821] in *Œuvres complètes*, vol. II, pp. 298–307, inaccurately dated 1810 in this edition.

122 On Vaublanc's political ideas, see Gunn, *When the French Tried to Be British*, pp. 130–92.

123 Vincent Viénot de Vaublanc, *Rivalité de la France et de l'Angleterre* (Paris, [1803]), p. 378.

124 Vincent Viénot de Vaublanc, *Du commerce de la France* (Paris, 1822), pp. 112; *Du commerce maritime* (Paris, 1828), p. 14; see also *Du commerce de la France: examen des états de M. le directeur général des douanes* (Paris, 1824).

and 'civil liberty' might weaken support for the latter, which he held as more important.[125] Gradually, however, and probably in reaction to the aggravation of prohibitive policies, the philosopher declared his support for economic liberty and underlined its connections with political liberty.

In *De l'esprit de conquête* (1814), Constant had asserted that the 'epoch of war' was coming to an end and that Europe was entering the 'epoch of commerce'.[126] In the second edition of his *Réflexions sur les constitutions* (1818), he included part of the material left out of the *Principes* as an appendix, in which he lambasted commercial prohibitions as 'privileges'. Such measures, he contended, were not only an 'injustice' in favour of a few producers but also caused 'a relative loss [of wealth] for the nation as a whole' and, above all, 'a loss of liberty' due to the 'harassing and oppressive means' used for their implementation. The scale of state intervention required by the repression of smuggling made commercial prohibitions the most dangerous type of restriction on freedom because 'more than any other' they rendered 'individuals hostile to the government'.[127] In his famous discussion of the relative merits of ancient and modern liberty in 1819, Constant located the origins of the latter in the inexorable rise of commerce. Yet he noted that the progress of commerce rendered 'the action of arbitrary power more oppressive than in the past, because, as our speculations are more varied, arbitrary power must multiply itself in order to reach them'. The growth of commerce therefore made ever more pressing 'the need for the representative system'.[128] Instead of setting aside the liberty of commerce lest it frighten supporters of liberal institutions, Constant now used it as a cornerstone of his system.

The aggravation of commercial restrictions under Villèle confirmed *a contrario* the connection between political and economic liberty. But it also suggested that representative institutions, at least under the limited conditions of the 1814 Charter, were not sufficient to protect commerce and modern liberty. Abandoning his reflection on constitutional forms, Constant addressed the issue of the substance of legislation – on commerce, but also on education and the judicial administration – required to promote a liberal order in his *Commentaire sur l'ouvrage de Filangieri* of which the first

[125] Benjamin Constant, *Écrits politiques*, ed. Marcel Gauchet (Paris, 1997), pp. 543–5, 777.

[126] Benjamin Constant, *De l'esprit de conquête et de l'usurpation* (Paris, 1814), repr. in Constant, *Écrits politiques*, pp. 117–302, quotation at p. 130.

[127] Benjamin Constant, 'De la liberté d'industrie', extract from *Réflexions sur les constitutions*, 2nd edn (Paris, 1818) repr. in Constant, *Écrits politiques*, pp. 545–62, quotation at pp. 546–7.

[128] Benjamin Constant, 'De la liberté des anciens comparée à celle des modernes', (Paris, 1819) repr. in *Écrits politiques*, pp. 589–619, quotation at pp. 614–15.

part came out in 1822 and the second in 1824.[129] A commentary on *The Science of Legislation*, a work by the Neapolitan Enlightenment philosopher Gaetano Filangieri first published in the 1780s, may at first appear disconnected from contemporary struggles over commerce, since it did not directly confront the defence of mercantile jealousy by Villèle, Saint-Chamans or Vaublanc. But the *Commentaire* can be interpreted as an indirect attack on the willingness of numerous liberals to compromise with royalist jealousy when it seemed to favour material prosperity. In the parliamentary debates on prohibitive legislation between 1819 and 1822, Constant jousted with fellow liberals such as Manuel as often as with *ultras*. Moreover, royalist advocates of prohibitions frequently and maliciously invoked works written by liberal writers on political economy that conceded the need for restrictions on foreign trade such as Chaptal's *De l'industrie* (1819).[130]

In the *Commentaire*, Constant located the origins of liberal timidity about commerce in a lingering belief that the government rather than citizens themselves should carry out material and moral improvement, a belief which Filangieri's work served to illustrate despite its intellectual 'mediocrity'. Beyond Filangieri, the *Commentaire* attacked many other figures of the Enlightenment, including Necker, 'the most virtuous and most respectable defenders of the prohibitive system' (the deferential tone was perhaps inspired by Constant's close friendship with Germaine de Staël, Necker's daughter), and the Abbé Galiani, 'the first and most formidable adversary of the system of liberty'. Constant even expressed strong reservations about the Physiocrats, Necker and Galiani's adversaries during the controversy on grain legislation, because although 'the economists' [Physiocrats] shunned 'prohibitions', they attributed to the government a function of 'encouragement' that also undermined liberty. The view inherited from the Physiocrats that the government ought to sustain high grain prices, he contended, helped to spawn the recent 'extraordinary terror' of 'abundance' and the adoption of British-style corn laws in France. Similarly, laws protecting industry from foreign competition were, if 'not always injurious, … at least always useless'.[131]

In addition to the controversy on the circulation of grain, the *Commentaire* reappraised the significance of another eighteenth-century debate, on the causes and fragility of British prosperity. Constant concurred with Filangieri's condemnation of 'the absurdity and the cruelty

[129] Clorinda Donato, 'Benjamin Constant and the *Commentaire sur l'ouvrage de Filangieri*: Notes for an Intercultural Reading', *Historical Reflections/Réflexions Historiques*, 28 (3) (2002): 439–54.

[130] AP, vol. xxxi, p. 118 (23 April 1821); vol. xxxvi, p. 751 (24 June 1822).

[131] Benjamin Constant, *Commentaire sur l'ouvrage de Filangieri*, 2 vols. (Paris, 1822–4), vol. i, pp. 6, 14; vol. ii, pp. 88–100, 108.

of commercial prohibitions' in Britain. He, too, hoped for 'the decadence of England', because it conditioned 'the commercial, industrial and even political independence of Europe'. Yet, unlike Filangieri and so many other writers on political economy, Constant did not believe that either Britain's enormous public debt or the miserable condition of its workers would cause its downfall, because both factors served to reinforce the solidarity of property owners with the state. Instead, it was the economic strain of the struggle against Revolutionary France and the relinquishing of their patronage obligations by British aristocrats – illustrated by the selfishness of the Corn Laws – that would bring down oligarchical rule in Britain and British commercial tyranny over the world. Only the repeal of prohibitive laws and a greater division of property through the abolition of primogeniture could perhaps prevent the danger of 'violent and sudden innovations'. 'I say perhaps', Constant added, 'because I don't know whether it is not already too late.'[132]

Contrary to what has been claimed, Constant after 1815 therefore did not consider Britain as 'a model modern republic', unlike the more critical Say.[133] His appreciation of Britain's political economy closely resembled Say's ambivalence. More significant was Constant's novel and growing insistence on the importance of commerce as both the main pursuit of individuals in a modern liberal order and as the means of establishing such an order. His defence of free commerce was still directed at Jean-Jacques Rousseau's critique of luxury, which he would have recognized as a source of inspiration of Fichte's closed commercial state. But it was also addressed to those who used the promotion of commerce to justify an extension of state power, from the Physiocrats to reactionary advocates of jealousy under the Restoration. Emphatic praise of Turgot, Smith and Say in the *Commentaire* demonstrated Constant's reappraisal of Smithian political economy as indispensable to the advent of a liberal order, even if he would later express reservations about the excessive materialism of some of its advocates.[134] The conclusion of the *Commentaire* called for a radical simplification of the tortuous 'political vocabulary' inherited from the eighteenth century: 'for industry, the motto of governments ought to be: *laissez-faire et laissez-passer*'.[135] In response to the reaffirmation of

[132] Constant, *Commentaire*, vol. I, pp. 88–111.

[133] Richard Whatmore, 'The Politics of Political Economy in France from Rousseau to Constant', in Mark Bevir and Frank Trentmann (eds.), *Markets in Historical Context: Ideas and Politics in the Modern World* (Cambridge, 2004), pp. 46–69, at p. 68.

[134] Robert Alexander, 'Benjamin Constant as a Second Restoration Politician', in Helena Rosenblatt (ed.), *The Cambridge Companion to Constant* (Cambridge, 2009), pp. 146–71, at pp. 158–62.

[135] Constant, *Commentaire*, vol. II, p. 301.

jealousy, Constant sought to expurgate progressive thought from its reservations about industrial and commercial freedoms and reasserted the existence of a strong connection between economic and political liberty.

The language and concerns of the eighteenth century about commerce and the risks of British supremacy did more than survive in the early years of the Bourbon Restoration. They were revived and given a more radical political meaning, first on the right and then on the left of the political spectrum. For sceptics and adversaries of the liberal order such as Ferrier or Bonald, *laissez-faire* in foreign trade not only endangered French wealth but also risked resuscitating the threat of domestic revolution: the ideas of the économistes, as the Physiocrats continued to be called, and of Adam Smith were subversive as well as erroneous. On the left, by contrast, the exacerbation and reactionary accents of jealous policies led to a rehabilitation of the liberty of commerce as inseparable from other political or individual freedoms and the Revolutionary legacy. This reappraisal, the next chapter shows, became a major and effective theme of liberal propaganda during the political and economic crisis that engulfed the Restoration after 1825. But it also gave rise to new disputes, among adversaries of reactionary royalism, on the respective importance of the moral and material components of liberty and the economic meaning of what contemporaries were beginning to describe as *libéralisme*.

CHAPTER 2

Economists, winegrowers and the dissemination of commercial liberalism

The early stirrings of nineteenth-century globalization encouraged the dissemination of radical ideas on the liberty of commerce in late Restoration France. According to the economist Adolphe Blanqui, it was now evident that 'the freeing of the seas' since the fall of Napoleon and the progress of 'universal competition' would result in a 'commercial revolution' that would sweep away France's 'prohibitive system'.[1] As the global age of political revolutions came to an end, the 1820s witnessed an abrupt acceleration and modification of international trade flows. The lifting of mercantilist restrictions on trade with the newly independent states of Latin America and colonies in South and South-East Asia boosted intercontinental exchanges, but at the expense of traditional patterns of trade between Europe and the West Indies or the Levant.[2] These transformations thwarted the reactionary commercial policies pursued by the Bourbon Restoration. The financial panic of 1825 in Britain and America, caused by the bankruptcy of several Latin American republics and followed by a decline in Anglo-American imports of French semi-luxury goods, compounded France's commercial difficulties.[3] While the value of French imports grew by approximately 50 per cent under the Restoration, French exports stagnated. The country's trade surplus, which the royalist mercantilists hoped to increase, was slashed by 80 per cent.[4] Following a series of

[1] Adolphe Blanqui, 'Essai sur la révolution commerciale qui se prépare en France', *Revue Encyclopédique*, 42 (1829): 34–49.

[2] Findlay and O'Rourke, *Power and Plenty*, pp. 371–8; O'Rourke and Williamson, 'When Did Globalization Begin?', pp. 36–9; on the global political context, see David Armitage and Sanjay Subrahmanyam (eds.), *The Age of Global Revolutions in Global Context* (Basingstoke, 2009) and Jeremy Adelman, 'An Age of Imperial Revolutions', *American Historical Review*, 113 (2) (2008): 319–40.

[3] Maurice Lévy-Leboyer, *Les Banques européennes et l'industrialisation internationale dans la première moitié du XIXe siècle* (Paris, 1964), pp. 464–88; Albert Broder, *L'Économie française au XIXe siècle* (Paris, 1993), pp. 24–7.

[4] Imports rose from an annual average of 308 million francs in 1816–20 to 455 million in 1826–30, while exports slightly declined from 503 million francs to 487 million over the same years; my

poor grain harvests from 1827, difficulties developed into a fully-fledged economic crisis, which has sometimes been cited as the underlying cause of the 1830 Revolution.[5]

Another factor stimulating the growing popularity of liberal ideas about trade was the new course of British commercial policy in the 1820s.[6] As early as 1822, the Comte de Vaublanc, a stalwart advocate of prohibitive laws, complained that 'as soon as the topic of commerce is touched upon in a *salon*, one hears assurances that this great change [of the adoption of a new commercial system by Britain] is accomplished or imminent, and that France must not lag behind'.[7] The prevailing perception of Britain as a formidable example of mercantile jealousy ensured that reductions in the British tariff on manufactured imports and the relaxation of restrictions on colonial navigation made a powerful impression on French observers. Recanting their earlier criticisms of British commercial policies, Jean-Baptiste Say and other liberal writers on political economy now hailed Britain as an economic model that should be emulated. The British example also emboldened Say and his disciples to demand the complete repeal of restrictions on foreign trade and affirm the primacy of citizens' welfare over geopolitical calculations. In response, defenders of the prohibitive system, including Saint-Cricq and Ferrier, derided British reforms as meaningless concessions given the extent of British commercial hegemony and maintained that Britain could only afford them because it had pursued jealous policies so relentlessly for so long.

The chapter examines how a new language of radical commercial liberalism was forged and spread in late Restoration France. Support for free trade became a defining feature of the *économistes*, a word which now referred to Say and his disciples rather than the Physiocrats. As well as earlier protests against the prohibitive system, this commercial liberalism remained firmly ensconced in the broader-based political hostility to the perceived reactionary tendencies of the regime. It even played an often

calculations, based on Ministère du Commerce, *Statistique de la France*, 10 vols. (Paris, 1838), vol. VII, pp. 8–9.

[5] Paul Gonnet, 'Esquisse de la crise économique en France de 1827 à 1832', *Revue d'Histoire Économique et Sociale*, 33 (3) (1955): 249–91; Ernest Labrousse, 'How Revolutions Are Born, 1789–1830–1848', in François Crouzet, William H. Chaloner and Walter M. Stern (eds.), *Essays in European Economic History, 1789–1914* (London, 1969), pp. 1–14; Pamela Pilbeam, 'The Economic Crisis of 1827–1832 and the 1830 Revolution in Provincial France', *Historical Journal*, 32 (2) (1989): 319–38; on the political tensions that erupted in revolution in 1830, see David Pinkney, *The French Revolution of 1830* (Princeton, NJ, 1972) and Robert Alexander, *Rewriting the French Revolutionary Tradition: Liberal Opposition and the Fall of the Bourbon Monarchy* (Cambridge, 2003).

[6] Hilton, *Corn, Cash and Commerce*, pp. 173–201.

[7] Vincent Viénot de Vaublanc, *Du commerce de la France*, p. 135.

neglected role in the revival of the liberals' electoral fortunes after 1825, especially in maritime and export-oriented regions such as Bordeaux and its winegrowing hinterland. However, as liberal ideas about trade reached new sections of society, they were reinterpreted according to regional economic and political circumstances. In order to illustrate this process, the chapter pays close attention to the efforts of a Bordelais publicist, Henri Fonfrède, to promote a version of commercial liberty that remained compatible with the defence of local privileges and rejected the materialistic tendencies of political economy. Despite or thanks to such ambiguities, calls for commercial liberty resounded throughout regions where winegrowing, one of France's largest industries, predominated. These debates pitted against each other various economic and regional interests, but they were also concerned with the nature of what Fonfrède termed, in an early usage of the new -ism, 'veritable liberalism' and the relationship between its material and moral component in post-Revolutionary France.

I

In the 1820s, Jean-Baptiste Say confirmed his status as the leading representative of political economy in France. Shunning earlier accounts that reduced Say to a popularizer of Adam Smith and an early advocate of free-market economics, Richard Whatmore has persuasively shown that Say's economic convictions were intimately connected with his republican moral and political beliefs.[8] However, under the Bourbon Restoration, Say's ideas underwent some notable evolutions. First, his determination to make political economy accessible led him to adopt a more polemical tone and to emphasize the material benefits of a liberal economic order, even if his ultimate goal remained to encourage the spread of republican values. Second, commercial reforms in the 1820s led him to reappraise the merits of the British model. New disciples such as Adolphe Blanqui and Charles Dupin accentuated this Anglophile turn of French political economy.

In the first edition of his *Traité d'économie politique* in 1803, Say already insisted that the primary purpose of his book was the diffusion of correct principles of political economy. The book, he explained in the preface, was intended not for statesmen or other writers but for the 'middling classes of society', from which 'knowledge originates' and 'is disseminated amongst

[8] Whatmore, *Republicanism and the French Revolution*, pp. 5–6; on Say's life and career, see also Evert Schoorl, *Jean-Baptiste Say: Revolutionary, Entrepreneur, Economist* (London, 2013).

the highest and lowest orders of the people'.[9] Say's conviction that writers on political economy should concentrate their efforts on diffusion rather than theoretical debates intensified under the Restoration. In a manuscript probably dating from the 1820s, he maintained that political economy was now a science with foundations as solid as physics or chemistry. 'All that therefore remains to be done', he concluded, was 'to spread, to vulgarize so to speak this kind of knowledge, to draw from [its diffusion] very happy consequences, and among others a positive tendency towards friendly communications between men and between nations'. In another unpublished piece looking back over his career and probably dating from the late 1820s, he contended that his commitment to the dissemination of economic principles was what distinguished him from British writers on political economy such as James Mill, David Ricardo or Thomas Malthus, who wrote only 'for one another': 'I pursued a different approach. I concerned myself with the public only.'[10]

Under the Restoration, Say published four more editions of the *Traité* (1814, 1816, 1819, 1826) as well as three editions of his *Catéchisme d'économie politique* (1815, 1821, 1826) that explained the principles of production, distribution and consumption under the form of simple questions and answers. A review of the fifth edition of the *Traité* by Charles Dunoyer, a close friend of Say's son-in-law Charles Comte, asserted in 1827 that 12,000 copies of the *Traité*'s five editions and 6,000 copies of the *Catéchisme*'s three editions had been sold in France and elsewhere: 'it is to M. Say', he concluded 'that we owe the popularization of political economy in Europe'.[11] The registers of the Librairie and Say's personal correspondence confirm the order of magnitude of the figures given by Dunoyer.[12] These were extremely high by contemporary standards. In his *Autobiography*, John Stuart Mill expressed his satisfaction at the 'rapid success' of his *Principles of Political Economy* (1848), the classical textbook

[9] Jean-Baptiste Say, *Traité d'économie politique*, 2 vols. (Paris, 1803), vol. 1, pp. xxvii–xxviii.

[10] 'De l'état actuel de nos connaissances en économie politique', [1825?], and untitled manuscript, [late 1820s?], Bibliothèque Nationale de France (hereafter BNF), Nouvelles Acquisitions Françaises (hereafter NAF), MS 26237, fols. 68–75, 150.

[11] Charles Dunoyer, 'Traité d'économie politique', *Revue Encyclopédique*, 34 (1827): 63–90.

[12] According to the Librairie registers, there were in total 3,500 copies printed of the first and second editions of the *Catéchisme*, impressions 762 (17 June 1815), AN, F18*II 1, and impression 3673 (14 November 1821), AN, F18*II 7; according to the same source, there were in total 5,000 copies printed of the third and fourth editions of the *Traité*: impression 5822 (30 September 1816), AN, F18*II 3, and impression 9673 (22 July 1819), AN, F18*II 6; and, in a letter to Rapilly, Say mentioned that 3,000 copies were printed of the fifth edition of the *Traité*, 5 May 1826, BNF, NAF, MS 26253, fol. 113.

of economics in the Victorian era, of which there were three editions and 3,250 copies printed between 1848 and 1852.[13]

The elegant lucidity of Say's writings is widely acknowledged, but his business acumen also contributed to the commercial success of his works. Say supervised in person the dispatching of dozens of copies to specific bookshops in Paris, Geneva, London and New York. He sometimes enclosed 'a model advertisement for newspapers', or a few complimentary copies to be given to influential people, 'which [would] not reduce sales, and on the contrary [would] increase them by making people talk [about the book]'.[14] Say checked on the pace of sales with his booksellers and remonstrated with them, for instance Jean-Jacques Paschoud in Geneva, when he was disappointed with the figures: 'Let me express some doubts about the efforts that you have made to spread my *Traité d'économie politique* in [Switzerland and Italy].'[15] Say's desire to reach foreign as well as French readers is noteworthy, and numerous translations, including five German editions of the *Traité* between 1807 and 1831 and seven English editions in the USA between 1821 and 1836, testify to the international scope of his writings' popularity.[16]

Yet his efforts focused on the dissemination of political economy in France. When the second edition of the *Catéchisme* came out in 1821, he had advertisements inserted in the main liberal newspapers and periodicals, '*Le Courrier [Français], Le Journal du Commerce, La Revue Encyclopédique,* and ... *Le Constitutionnel*', in return for two complimentary copies given to the editor of each publication. Say used the services of four different publishers for the five editions of the *Traité*, always seeking to obtain a more advantageous contract and to increase the pace of sales. In 1826, he apologized to his friend Deterville, the publisher of the fourth edition, for having granted the diffusion of the fifth to Rapilly: not only had the latter made him a more interesting financial offer, Say explained, but 'relocating sales in the neighbourhood of the stock exchange and bankers, will make them, I believe, more rapid'.[17] Say also gave eight lectures on political economy every year at the Athénée Institute between

[13] John Stuart Mill, *Autobiography* (London, 1989), p. 178.

[14] Say to Paschoud, 31 May and 1 June 1814; Say to Delaunay, 12 July 1814; Say to Murray, 4 August 1815; and Say to Derham, 4 August 1815, BNF, NAF, MS 26253, fols. 88–9, 94–6.

[15] Say to Paschoud, 25 July 1815, BNF, NAF, MS 26253, fol. 95.

[16] Philippe Steiner, 'Introduction: l'économie politique comme science de la modernité', in Jean-Baptiste Say, *Cours d'économie politique et autres essais*, ed. Philippe Steiner (Paris, 1996), 9–46, at p. 17.

[17] Say to Bossange, 9 November 1821; Say to Deterville, 8 April 1826, BNF, NAF, MS 26253, fols. 104–5, 112.

1816 and 1819 and thirty lectures every year at the Conservatoire des Arts et Métiers from 1820.[18] His unpublished papers contain considerations on the desirability of teaching political economy in *lycées* as well as short essays contending that 'Poets must know Political Economy' or that even *littérateurs* should possess at least 'a tincture' of this science.[19] In 1820, he envisaged writing a very small octodecimo volume of 'Political Economy for the instruction of ladies' but went no further than the outline of an advertisement on the need for 'people of the sex' to have 'correct notions' of political economy if they wanted to be 'fully educated'.[20]

As Say intensified his efforts to spread the principles of political economy across French society, he laid increasing emphasis on the need to remove obstacles on foreign trade. The substantial concessions made to the advocates of trade barriers in the 1814 edition of the *Traité* gradually disappeared from later editions. For instance, Say expunged from the fourth and fifth edition his earlier contention that countries with a relatively high level of direct taxation (such as France) should impose a compensatory duty on imports from countries relying more heavily on indirect taxation (such as Britain). A new footnote even called into question Adam Smith's exception in favour of protection for products essential to national security on the grounds that suppliers could always be found in times of war.[21] This rejection of one of the most venerable justifications for jealousy manifested a new radicalism that shunned geopolitical considerations as obsolete and would be an important feature of free-trade propaganda in Britain as well as in France after 1830. A similar radicalization can be detected in changes to the text of the *Catéchisme*, with an additional chapter in the 1821 and 1826 editions that ridiculed the theory of the balance of trade and called for the establishment of 'a system that would reduce as much as possible the obstacles and costs that impede trade with foreign countries'.[22] Say's (incomplete) notes for his lectures at the Athénée before 1820 suggest that they did not broach the issue of commercial policy. By contrast, from 1824, three of his annual lectures at the

[18] Philippe Steiner, 'Jean-Baptiste Say et l'enseignement de l'économie politique en France, 1816–1832', *Économies et Sociétés: Cahiers de l'ISMÉA, Série PE*, 20 (1986): 63–95; Lucette Le Van-Lemesle, *Le Juste ou le riche: l'enseigement de la l'économie politique, 1815–1950* (Paris, 2004), pp. 54–77.

[19] 'Pour prouver que l'économie politique devrait entrer dans l'enseignement public', n.d., 'Qu'un poète doit savoir l'économie politique', n.d.; and 'Qu'une teinture, tout au moins, des sciences, est nécessaire aux simples littérateurs', n.d., BNF, NAF, MS 26238, fols. 28, 35, 37.

[20] Say to Audot, 20 December 1820, BNF, NAF, MS 26253, fols. 101–2.

[21] Compare *Traité* (1814), vol. 1, pp. 213–25, with *Traité* (1817), vol. 1, pp. 209–21 and *Traité* (1819), vol. 1, pp. 223–36 and *Traité* (1826), vol. 1, pp. 266–81.

[22] Compare *Catéchisme* (1815), pp. 130–6 with *Catéchisme* (1821), pp. 97–111 and *Catéchisme* (1826), pp. 92–106.

Conservatoire dealt with international trade. A marginal annotation by Say on the course programme for 1826–7 indicates that the lecture on the balance of trade 'pleased' his audience, 'perhaps because of the animadversions that [he] proffered'.[23]

Say's efforts to disseminate political economy culminated with the publication of his *Cours complet d'économie politique pratique* (1828–9). Even though the work comprised six volumes, it was destined, according to the subtitle, to 'all citizens'. Say drafted an advert describing the book as 'political economy, not systematic in the manner of this good Dupont de Nemours, not metaphysical in the manner of Ricardo, but practical in the manner of M. J.-B. Say'. 'There are few readings more profitable than this one', the advertisement added, and 'less tiresome'.[24] The text of the *Cours complet*, based on Say's lectures, was indeed very accessible – Say's audience at the Conservatoire, police informants reported, included 'large groups of artisans' as well as 'merchants', 'petty writers' and the sort of people 'who daily frequent the capital's most disreputable public reading rooms'.[25] Yet the price of each volume was 6.50 francs, and Say's advice to his publisher on how to pitch the book shows that he more realistically expected buyers to be established or aspiring members of the middle classes, such as 'all those engaged in administrative or industrial activities', and also 'landowners', 'merchants', 'those who wish to become mayors' or 'those who wish to become deputies'.[26]

The critique of restrictions on international trade featured prominently in the *Cours complet*. In the introduction, Say used the example of the nefarious influence of the system of the balance of trade, which resulted in 'we nations being cooped up, each of us in a pen, by armies of customs and police officers', to illustrate the need for widespread 'instruction' in the true principles of political economy. In the fourth part on the role of 'institutions in the economics of societies', he invoked the influence of 'Messieurs Ferrier, Vaublanc, Saint-Chamans … the champions of the balance of trade' on the government and the public to justify his lengthy refutation of mercantilist principles. Say resorted to very concrete examples in order to convey the costs of protection to lay readers, for example arguing that Frenchmen, 'as consumers', were

[23] 'Programme des cours', 1826, BNF, NAF, MS 26249. [24] BNF, NAF, MS 26236, fols. 115–17.

[25] Paris Prefect of Police to Minister of the Interior, 28 December 1824, quoted in André Liesse, 'Un professeur d'économie politique sous la Restauration: Jean-Baptiste Say, au Conservatoire des Arts et Métiers', *Journal des Économistes*, 5th series, 44 (1901): 3–22, 161–74.

[26] Say to Rapilly, 26 June 1828, BNF, NAF, MS 26253, fol. 115.

> sacrificed in their most constant capacity, every day of the year, every hour of the day and even during our sleep; since the bedclothes in which we sleep, our mattresses, the bed frame, our curtains, our furniture, our apartment and the slates or the tiles around us are all items that we consume while we are asleep.[27]

Another notable feature of the *Cours complet* was the confirmation of Say's reappraisal of the British model since his condemnation of Britain's colonial and economic policies in *De l'Angleterre et des Anglais* (1815). The book reproduced nearly *in extenso* Say's 1824 article in defence of British rule in India, while another section defended settlement colonization as 'favourable to the progress of the human species and its happiness'. Say's only reservation was his preference for colonization by settlers of British descent, while nations 'distinguished by their social talents rather than by talents useful to societies', an allusion to the contemporary perception of the French national character, 'were not fit to found colonies'.[28] Say's new enthusiasm for the expansion of British rule derived in part from the recent reforms of Britain's commercial policies. He rejoiced that the House of Commons had finally taken heed of Adam Smith's counsels and that the British 'prohibitive system … [would] soon be if not totally abandoned, at least considerably mitigated'. In his view, Britain's liberal turn would consolidate its prosperity, and he ridiculed the claims of those who attributed 'the success of British industry' to jealous policies.[29]

The print run of the first four volumes of the *Cours complet* was 2,300, and the first volume sold 700 copies in three months. These figures were respectable. But Say was disappointed, and it is noteworthy that a second edition had to wait until 1840.[30] Despite the lucidity of Say's prose, the price – nearly 40 francs for the six volumes – and the length – nearly 3,000 pages – limited its impact as an instrument of popularization. Of possibly greater significance in the dissemination of liberal political economy was Say's role in launching the career of several younger economists under the Restoration. These included Charles Comte and Charles Dunoyer, the advocates of *industrialisme*, a doctrine that extolled the merits of productive work in a manner consonant with Say's concern with industriousness as a foundation of republican morality, in the late 1810s.[31] After 1820, Say also

[27] Say, *Cours complet*, vol. I, pp. 42–3, vol. III, pp. 285–6, 360.

[28] Say, *Cours complet*, vol. IV, pp. 12–54, 453–60; see also Jean-Baptiste Say, 'Essai historique sur les origines, les progrès et les résultats probables de la souveraineté des Anglais aux Indes', *Revue Encyclopédique*, 23 (1824): 281–99.

[29] Say, *Cours complet*, vol. III, pp. 362–3.

[30] Impression 262 (16 January 1828), AN, F18*II 15; Say to Deterville, [June] 1828, BNF, NAF, MS 26253, fols. 115–16.

[31] Edgar Allix, 'Jean-Baptiste Say et les origines de l'industrialisme', *Revue d'Économie Politique*, 24 (4) (1910): 303–13 and 24 (5) (1910): 341–63; Ephraïm Harpaz, 'Le Censeur européen: histoire

became close with two of his successors as lecturers on political economy at the Athénée, Charles Dupin and Adolphe Blanqui. Born in 1784, Dupin was a naval engineer who undertook six journeys in Britain to study its naval shipyards and served as Say's courier with Jeremy Bentham between 1816 and 1824.[32] Born in 1798, Blanqui attributed his interest in political economy to his encounter with Say in the early 1820s and soon became his main disciple, succeeding him as Professor of Political Economy at the Conservatoire in 1830.[33]

Dupin and Blanqui shared Say's concern with *industrie*.[34] They also both played a significant part in the reappraisal of the virtues of the British model by French political economists after 1820.[35] In a multi-volume account of British military, naval and commercial forces that relied on the information gathered during his travels across the Channel, Dupin praised the way in which Britain succeeded in preserving its liberal institutions while increasing its military power and industrial advance over the Continent since the beginning of the century. The book also hailed the decline of the 'narrow jealousy' of British commercial policy and the recent realization that 'it is useful for one's buyers to become richer, if one wants to become a prosperous seller'.[36] In a shorter relation of his own tour of Britain, from Southampton to Glasgow in 1823, Blanqui also eulogized the material and moral achievements of the country. Although he expressed some misgivings on the extent of urban poverty in London and industrial areas, Blanqui's tone was less critical than Say's in *De l'Angleterre*, and the lesson he drew from his sojourn simpler: 'nothing in the world, I think, more thoroughly demonstrates the advantages of liberty than the brilliant situation of this country'.[37] In 1829, Blanqui also paid homage to William Huskisson, the President of the British Board of Trade, as the first statesman who applied 'the sound doctrines of political economy' to 'public administration'.[38]

d'un journal industrialiste', *Revue d'Histoire Économique et Sociale*, 37 (2) (1959): 185–219 and 37 (3) (1959): 328–57.

32 Say to Bentham, 8 July 1820, University College London, Ogden Papers, MS 62, fol. 25.

33 Martin S. Staum, 'French Lecturers in Political Economy, 1815–1848: Varieties of Liberalism', *History of Political Economy*, 30 (1) (1998): 95–120.

34 Roberto Romani, *National Character and Public Spirit in Britain and France* (Cambridge, 2002), pp. 99–106, 110–15.

35 Margaret Bradley and Fernand Perrin, 'Charles Dupin's Visits to the British Isles, 1816–1824', *Technology and Culture*, 32 (1) (1991): 47–68; Francis Démier, 'Adolphe Blanqui: la leçon anglaise d'un économiste libéral français', in Sylvie Aprile and Fabrice Bensimon (eds.), *La France et l'Angleterre au XIXe siècle* (Paris, 2006), pp. 49–67; see also Lucette Le Van-Lemesle, 'Les Économistes français et l'usage des modèles étrangers', *Revue d'Histoire du XIXe siècle*, 23 (2001): 73–86.

36 Charles Dupin, *Voyages dans la Grande-Bretagne*, 5 vols. (Paris, 1821–4), vol. 1, p. xiv.

37 Adolphe Blanqui, *Voyage d'un jeune français en Angleterre et en Ecosse* (Paris, 1824), p. vii.

38 Adolphe Blanqui, 'Considérations sur la réforme commerciale opérée en Angleterre sous les auspices de M. Huskisson', *Revue Encyclopédique*, 41 (1829): 31–45, at p. 38.

After 1825, Dupin and Blanqui made significant and original contributions to the popularization of political economy. Although the genre in France owed a lot to Say's *Catéchisme*, it was possibly invigorated by the translation, in French, of Jane Marcet's *Conversations on Political Economy* (1816), in 1825.[39] The following year, Blanqui published a *Précis d'économie politique*, which aimed at 'representing in a simple, lucid and precise manner the principles established' by Adam Smith, Jean-Baptiste Say and David Ricardo. There remained no significant controversy of political economy, the author argued, making it possible for him to expound the new science in 'a very small space'.[40] Blanqui meant this literally: the *Précis* was a trigesimo-secundo volume (approximately 5 inches by 3 inches) and part of a 'portative' encyclopedia series, which had a circulation of approximately 2,000 copies per volume.[41] The *Précis* was written simply and teemed with concrete examples. To prove that the prohibitive system had done 'more harm to mankind than the Inquisition to Spain', Blanqui gave examples of the reciprocal nature of commercial exchanges, such as a Bayonne merchant who sold dyed cloth in return for logwood from South America via a tradesman from Alvarado in Spain, or a Bordeaux merchant who traded 6,000 bottles of Château Lafite for 100 kilograms of Swedish iron. In an 'analytical vocabulary of political economy' appended to the *Précis*, Blanqui gave, for 'smuggling', the laconic definition: 'Punishment inflicted upon prohibitive governments.'[42] On the eve of the 1830 Revolution, Blanqui also founded an ephemeral *Revue Nationale*, whose goal was to 'popularize the science of economics' and show its relevance 'to our immediate needs, to our everyday business'.[43] Another instance of this vogue for the popularization of economics was Joseph Droz's *Économie politique*, a work of which 1,500 copies were printed in 1829.[44] The book aimed 'to go always from what is known to what is unknown, in a volume which would not be long enough to wear out concentration'.[45]

Dupin felt even less attraction for abstract theory than other economists and used instead statistical analysis to demonstrate the benefits of industriousness. His *Forces productives et commerciales de la France* (1827)

[39] Jane Marcet, *Entretiens sur l'économie politique dégagée de ses abstractions* (Paris, 1825).
[40] Adolphe Blanqui, *Précis d'économie politique* (Paris, 1826), pp. i–ii.
[41] Impressions 405 and 406 (29 January 1829), AN, F18*II 17.
[42] Blanqui, *Précis*, pp. 92–113, 246.
[43] *Revue Nationale: Recueil d'Économie Politique*, 1 (1830), 20.
[44] Impression 5344 (3 November 1828), AN, F18*II 16.
[45] Joseph Droz, *Économie politique, ou principes de la science des richesses* (Paris, 1829), p. ix.

celebrated the increase in France's output of agricultural and manufactured goods since the fall of Napoleon. The book also sought to establish a link between material and moral improvement. In Dupin's view, it was the application of 'the virtues of the citizen' to productive activities that accounted for the rapid recovery of the French economy after the turmoil of the Revolutionary and Napoleonic era. Conversely, material progress discouraged frivolity and immorality, as shown by the growing proportion of printed works concerned with useful subjects such as legislation or science and by the decline in the number of illegitimate births. Dupin also drew attention to the faster pace of material and moral improvement in the north and the east, which he attributed to higher rates of enrolment in primary schools than in the rest of the country.[46]

Les Forces productives, of which 2,000 copies were printed, established Dupin's reputation as an expert on economic issues. Yet each of the work's two quarto volumes cost 25 francs, limiting the number of potential readers.[47] To make his main conclusions more widely available, Dupin published the introduction separately – the publication enjoyed three editions and a combined print run of 1,200 in just two months.[48] To disseminate his ideas even further, Dupin also published, over the next twelve months a series of six sextodecimo (seven inches by four inches) volumes entitled *Le Petit Producteur* and costing only 75 centimes per volume. Each volume praised the benefits of industriousness and technological progress in relation to different sections of the population, *Le Petit Fabricant* offering practical recommendations to manufacturers and artisans, *Le Petit Propriétaire* to farmers, *L'Ouvrier français* to workers, etc. The print run of each volume was between 3,000 and 4,000 copies, making a very large total of approximately 20,000 copies for the entire series.[49]

Dupin's eulogy of productive work in *Le Petit Producteur* remained closely linked with liberal ideas about trade and politics, as shown by the fourth volume, *Le Petit Commerçant*, which sought to ridicule the reactionary defenders of the prohibitive system. This volume consisted in a dialogue between the enthusiastic Lefranc, a twenty-two-year-old merchant apprentice, and his absurd mentor, 'Monsieur Prohibant', a former employee of the Ferme Générale, aged sixty-seven. As the two men toured France's richest industrial provinces, from Abbeville to Lille

[46] Charles Dupin, *Forces commerciales et productives de la France*, 2 vols. (Paris, 1827), p. v.
[47] Impressions 801 (10 February 1827) and 3486 (5 July 1827), AN, F18*II 14.
[48] Impressions 2526 (10 May 1827), 2896 (1 June 1827) and 3437 (3 July 1827), AN, F18*II 14.
[49] Impression 4517 (7 September 1827), 5063 (17 October 1827) and 6115 (22 November 1827), AN, F18*II 14; impression 1512 (24 March 1828), AN, F18*II 15.

and from Strasbourg to Besançon, Prohibant dismissed Lefranc's scepticism about the impact of prohibitions as youthful sentimentality: 'Do you not wish to protect French manufactures, imprudent and cosmopolitan young man?' The narrator, however, interjected a different conclusion: the plight of border inhabitants subjected to customs vexations and of destitute workers reduced to smuggling in order to survive 'demonstrated the uselessness, the immorality and the barbarity of absolute prohibitions or excessive restrictions to the young Lefranc'. Prohibant's faults were not confined to economic policy. He was a fanatical reactionary, hostile to every innovation, from steam engines to religious tolerance. One of his heroes was the Spanish inquisitor Tomás de Torquemada, who 'burnt heretics like English merchandise during the good old times of the Continental Blockade' and whose 'holy order', the Dominicans, 'prohibited human liberties'.[50] Commercial liberty, such parallels suggested, should be defended alongside other freedoms against the reactionary political and religious tendencies of the restored monarchy.

II

The large circulation figures of the works of economists suggest that their promotion of liberal ideas about trade did not leave opinion indifferent. Between 1825 and 1830, for example, the Bordelais *notables* relinquished the phraseology of mercantile jealousy and learnt to defend their interests in the language of commercial liberty. However, the case of Bordeaux shows that the dissemination of liberal ideas about trade was not a process of diffusion by replication. Instead, it required a considerable work of critical reinterpretation that took into consideration the region's specific political and economic circumstances. The principal author of this work of reinterpretation in Bordeaux was the liberal publicist Henri Fonfrède, whose conception of commercial liberty subordinated material to moral concerns and left some room for local economic privileges as a means of countervailing the dangers of excessive centralization. Fonfrède's eloquent defence of true liberty helped transform not only the economic ideas but also the political leaning of the Bordelais *notables*: while all the Gironde's eight deputies elected in March 1824 were royalists, Bordeaux's department returned seven liberals and only one royalist at the November 1827 election, a much more pronounced swing to the left than in the rest of the country.[51]

[50] Charles Dupin, *Le Petit Commerçant* (Paris, 1828), pp. 64–7, 70–2.

[51] Robert Dupuch, 'Le Parti libéral à Bordeaux et dans la Gironde sous la deuxième restauration', *Revue Philomathique de Bordeaux*, 5 (1902): 21–31, 77–86, 172–88; André-Jean Tudesq

Born in 1788, Henri Fonfrède was the son of Jean-Baptiste Boyer-Fonfrède, a Gironde deputy at the National Convention who was executed in October 1793. Under the Restoration, he was the liberal party's foremost publicist in the Gironde. In the late 1810s, he edited the *Tribune de Bordeaux*, an advanced liberal news-sheet placed under the patronage of Benjamin Constant. After a succession of heavy fines forced the *Tribune* to cease publication in 1820, he regularly contributed to *L'Indicateur Bordelais*, a liberal daily. Fonfrède enjoyed modest independent wealth as the owner of a small vineyard in Saint-Louis de Montferrand, near the Gironde estuary. Yet in 1827 he suffered heavy financial losses as the partner of a minor Bordelais commercial firm, a misfortune which might have contributed to his ire against the Restoration's commercial policies.[52] In a report on the state of public opinion in the Gironde in 1827, the Prefect described Fonfrède, the 'son of a regicide' (his father voted for the death of Louis XVI), as 'the leader' of the department's liberals and a 'highly talented orator and writer'. According to the Prefect, although Fonfrède had 'a rather gentle manner in his social interactions', he was 'a boundless fanatic' in politics and 'one of the most dangerous men in the [liberal] party'.[53] The word 'fanatic' was only a slight exaggeration. Fonfrède's sole passions in addition to politics appear to have been fishing and hunting. He never married, and there are no traces of any relationship other than friendship in his (probably expurgated) correspondence. In his own words, he was 'the most insipid of old bachelors and hermits'.[54]

Yet Fonfrède cut a large figure in his region's public life. He kept up an abundant correspondence with fellow liberals throughout the country and became the head of Aide-Toi, the liberal electoral committee, for the Gironde in 1829.[55] Although not a theoretician, he was an eloquent writer and a skilful political operator, who knew how to use ideas in order to destabilize his adversaries or bolster support for his cause. His passionate style electrified his audience, while his rhetorical instinct led him to forge interesting neologisms such as *financiariser*, *industrialiser* and

'La Restauration: renaissance et déceptions', in Louis Desgraves and Georges Dupeux (eds.), *Bordeaux au XIXe siècle* (Bordeaux, 1969), pp. 35–59; Sherman Kent, *The Election of 1827 in France* (Cambridge, Mass., 1975), pp. 157–83.

[52] Jean-Jacques Hémardinquer, 'Henri Fonfrède ou l'homme du midi révolté (1827–1838)', *Annales du Midi*, 88 (1976): 451–64; Edouard Feret, *Statistique de la Gironde*, 3 vols. (Bordeaux, 1874–89), vol. III, p. 253; Jean Cavignac, *Les Vingt-Cinq Familles: les négociants à Bordeaux sous Louis-Philippe* (Bordeaux, 1985), pp. 182–7.

[53] The Prefect of the Gironde to the Minister of the Interior, 2 July 1827, AN, F7 6769, folder 7.

[54] Fonfrède to Campan, 17 February 1832, Bordeaux, Bibliothèque Municipale de Bordeaux (hereafter BMB), MS 1087.

[55] The National Secretary of Aide-Toi to Fonfrède, 18 October 1829, BMB, MS 1095, vol. I, fols. 21–2.

décolonisation, or to pioneer the use of *nationalisme* in an economic context. Fonfrède established his reputation as a writer on economic affairs with a series of articles attacking Charles Dupin's statistical method and, in particular, his contention that the relative backwardness of France's south should be attributed to its lower educational or moral attainments.[56] In the series entitled 'Des départements du Nord et du Midi', Fonfrède insisted that the Midi's relative poverty was instead due to the 'restrictive system of customs' established under the Terror. Whereas the Girondins only sought to achieve 'relative equality', their dream of 'absolute equality' led the Montagnards to try and abolish the foreign and colonial trade on which southern prosperity relied. Terrorist republicans wished to stamp out not just 'fédéralisme' and 'modérantisme' but also 'négociantisme'. The Continental Blockade aggravated the relative decline of France's Midi: 'the manufacturing industry of the north underwent an immense development', while 'the decay of the agricultural departments of the south was fully completed'. Their economic distress detached southerners from Napoleon and explained their support for the return of the Bourbons in 1814. Yet the Restoration granted northern manufacturers 'the absolute monopoly of French consumption' and foreign retaliatory tariffs against French prohibitions further reduced the export markets of southern agriculturalists.[57]

In addition to stressing the influence of history on economic development, Fonfrède took issue with Dupin's materialistic conception of liberty and his excessive reliance on statistics. This aspect of Fonfrède's critique echoed the reservations recently expressed by Constant about the economic reductionism of the industrialists and anticipated Say's own objections to a statistical approach.[58] According to Fonfrède, Dupin's conclusion that 'the Chaussée d'Antin and the rue Vivienne', the strongholds of the corrupt Parisian bourgeoisie, were more moral than 'the plains of the Gironde, Agenais and Languedoc' demonstrated the vacuity of his method. The 'illegal union of the two sexes', used by Dupin to measure morality, was the 'least serious' degree of corruption. This measure failed to take into account a wide range of vices, from 'hardness of the heart' to

[56] Dupin exposed these views in *Effets de l'enseignement populaire sur les prospérités de la France* (Paris, 1826), before the publication of *Les Forces Productives*, and his lectures were reviewed in *Le Globe*, which enabled Fonfrède to start his response in December 1826.

[57] 'Des départements', 1st, 2nd, 3rd and 4th articles, *L'Indicateur Bordelais*, 31 December 1826 and 4, 11 and 20 January 1827.

[58] Benjamin Constant, 'Compte rendu de l'industrie et la morale considérées dans leurs rapport avec la liberté', *Revue Encyclopédique*, 29 (1826): 416–35; Jean-Baptiste Say, 'De l'objet et de l'utilité des statistiques' *Revue Encyclopédique*, 35 (1827): 529–53.

'thirst for power', and of virtues, from 'devoted friendship' to 'patriotism'. If a comprehensive evaluation of morality were possible, it would show the greater prevalence of 'degenerate individuals' in northern France as a result of financial speculation among the rich and of the 'servile mechanism' imposed on the workers of manufactures. 'Gauging the morality of men with the use of figures' was, in any case, 'a veritable mockery', typical of 'the fanaticism of the new school, which ha[d] written on its banners: *Without industry, no salvation!*'. Fonfrède conceded that material wealth was 'a good and useful thing' but denied that it could be held as 'the vital principle of society'. Morality and liberty stemmed neither from abundance, as claimed by the industrialists, nor poverty, as claimed by Rousseau, but from an even distribution of riches between provinces and between citizens. It was 'inequality' that, by putting 'in direct and immediate contact extreme opulence with extreme poverty', fostered 'the passions and vices' of the poor and rich alike.[59]

Forced to suspend his series of articles by the reinforcement of censorship on the eve of the 1827 election, Fonfrède pursued his analysis of the industrial perversion of liberalism in several letters to his friend Charles-Alcée Campan, another Bordelais liberal exiled in Brussels. 'Have the liberal leaders', Fonfrède wondered, 'decided to extinguish all the moral strengths of society? To materialize, financialize [*financiariser*] and industrialize [*industrialiser*] it so that it has no other recourse but to be handed over to the callousness of power?' Industry could prosper under a despotic regime. If liberals replaced 'the noblest sentiments of human nature' with 'these three sacred words: *produce*, *sell* and *earn*', Parisian liberals would be left 'in their opposition to despotism, with a mercantile herd of rich and corrupt slaves'.[60] Fonfrède conceded that in the past industry helped sap the foundations of feudal power. But he feared that the 'devouring strength' of private interests now endangered the very foundations of good citizenry: '*political virtue, selflessness, patriotism*'. Fonfrède wished to demonstrate this truth 'to its very core', but this required freedom of the press. Otherwise, 'the censors, like setters, would point [him] out and detect in [his] writings such a smell of true liberty that they would not grant [him] even one sentence'.[61]

Fonfrède claimed that his attack on Dupin was 'a resounding success' with Bordelais opinion, 'especially among royalists'. Several

[59] 'Des départements', 5th and 6th articles, *L'Indicateur*, 20 February and 27 June 1827.

[60] Fonfrède to Campan, 31 July 1827, BMB, MS 1089, fol. 50; *financiariser* and *industrialiser* were neologisms that Fonfrède used again in later articles.

[61] Fonfrède to Campan, 26 August 1827, BMB, MS 1089, fols. 59–60, 62.

royalist *notables* offered to support his election as deputy for the Gironde. Fonfrède refused but congratulated himself on having sown confusion in the ranks of his opponents.[62] The Bordelais royalist merchants and vineyard owners were increasingly concerned by the stagnation of foreign trade. A more specific anxiety was the renewal of demands for the creation of warehouses in Paris and other Continental cities, which threatened the privileges of seaports for the storage of colonial goods. Demands for new warehouses were commonly perceived as emanating from the same liberal publicists and periodicals that praised Say's political economy and the industrialists: Fonfrède's attack on Dupin therefore appeared as directed against the enemies of Bordeaux's commercial interests and seemed all the more effective that it was couched in a liberal rather than a mercantilist language.

In 1824–5, the Bordeaux Chamber of Commerce already saw off a campaign by the Parisian *Journal du Commerce* and several publicists for the abolition of the seaports' warehousing privileges.[63] The campaign, the Chamber of Commerce reported to its delegate in Paris, alarmed everyone in Bordeaux, 'from the merchant house … to the smallest tradesman's shop or artisan's workshop'. In December 1824, a memorandum by the Chamber of Commerce dismissed the demands for the creation of new warehouses as a manifestation of Parisian 'greed', affirmed the traditional rights of seaports and stressed the dangers of making Paris the 'sole market' of colonial goods. In breach of the regulations that banned chambers of commerce from publishing their communications with the government, the Bordelais merchants had 900 copies of the memorandum printed in order to fight the 'highly publicized arguments' and 'slander' of the Parisians. In June 1825, Villèle promised the Bordelais that he would not give in to demands for new warehouses.[64] But the Chamber of Commerce's public defence of Bordeaux's privileges had little effect on public opinion, and their preservation seemed dangerously dependent on the survival of the royalist government.

During the electoral campaign for the November 1827 election, the liberal opposition revived the issue of warehouses in order to galvanize support from the commercial middle classes in Paris and other Continental

[62] Fonfrède to Campan, 4 September 1827, BMB, MS 1089, fol. 72.

[63] Démier, 'Nation, marché, développement', pp. 1434–57.

[64] The Bordeaux Chamber of Commerce to the Minister of the Interior, 7 December 1824, ADG, 02/081/277, register 1822–5, fols. 102–5; the Bordeaux Chamber of Commerce to Élie Gautier, 20 May 1825, ADG, 02/081/278, register 1825–8, fol. 1; and minutes of the Bordeaux Chamber of Commerce, 29 June 1825, ADG, 02/081/305, register 1823–5, fol. 92.

cities. In October, a petition signed by a large number of Parisian 'manufacturers, bankers, merchants and tradesmen' demanded the immediate abolition of commercial privileges that violated the 'equal rights' guaranteed by the Charter.[65] These protests drew extensively on the language of political economy. For example, a pamphlet by Pierre-Joseph Chedeaux, the liberal Mayor of Metz, opened with a quotation from Jean-Baptiste Say ('Commerce is the transport of merchandises from one location to another'). Castigating the 'privileges' conceded by the government to seaports, the pamphlet argued that only the lifting of restrictions on exchanges with Continental Europe would revive France's Atlantic trade by enlarging the scope of products that could be sold in return for American commodities to include 'silks from Kreveld, haberdashery from Elberfeld, cloths from Westphalia, ironmongery from Remscheid, knick-knacks from Nuremberg etc.' as well as French manufactured goods. In conclusion, Chedeaux cited the liberalization of British commercial legislation as evidence that all European governments were about to adopt 'a liberal system' of commerce and affirmed that 'laisser passer, laisser faire' was the 'universal cry' of Europe.[66]

In the face of such rhetoric and as a result of the relative success of the liberal opposition at the 1827 election, the commercial privileges of seaports seemed at greater risk than ever since the beginning of the Restoration. The danger prompted François Ferrier, the advocate of mercantile jealousy, to publish a staunch defence of prohibitive legislation on the storage of colonial goods. For Ferrier, the question of warehouses was 'vital' because a new warehouse in Paris threatened to annihilate French shipping and complete 'the ruin of our colonies'. He dismissed the Parisian merchants' hopes of turning the capital into a major market for the re-exportation of colonial goods as inspired by nostalgia for the Continental Blockade, when maritime communications were nearly abolished and Paris served as Europe's main commercial centre for the redistribution of merchandise. Yet this commercial prosperity was dependent on political circumstances that could not be recreated and a new warehouse in Paris would only benefit the shipping of France's maritime rivals. Ferrier also dismissed the liberalization of British regulations

[65] [Anon.], *Pétition des manufacturiers, banquiers, négociants et commerçants de la place de Paris* (Paris, 1827). See also F. Pochard, *Exposé de la situation critique du commerce à Paris* (Paris, 1827); D.-L. Rodet, *Questions commerciales* (Paris, 1828); and François Larréguy, *Des entrepôts intérieurs d'après le droit commun et l'intérêt général* (Paris, 1829).

[66] Pierre-Joseph Chedeaux, *Lettre sur le transit et l'entrepôt* (Paris, 1828), pp. 7–8, 11–14; the print run of the pamphlet was 1,000, see impression 2330 (5 May 1828), AN, F18*II 15.

on the storage of colonial goods as irrelevant, because, unlike in France, in Britain the measure would benefit national shipping. Finally, and this seems to have been Ferrier's greatest fear, the abolition of the seaports' privileges, by rescinding their stake in the prohibitive system, would render maritime merchants vulnerable to the economists' propaganda for the liberty of commerce.[67]

After the removal of censorship in November 1827, Fonfrède resumed his series of articles and explicitly connected his attack on Dupin's work with the defence of Bordeaux's commercial privileges. The creation of a warehouse in Paris, he warned, would complete the 'continual absorption of all social vitality by the centre of the state', a process primarily originating from the regime's authoritarian and reactionary politics: 'one must be totally blind not to perceive the intimate connection between political reaction and the material decay of the provinces'. But the Restoration's centralizing aspirations now benefited from the complicity of the 'industrial party'. The growth of the public debt since 1815 had drained financial capital from the provinces to Paris, and the industrialists similarly hoped to concentrate commercial affairs thanks to the creation of a warehouse in the capital. Yet, in 'truly free and happy countries', Fonfrède argued, 'happiness stems precisely from the division of social forces between several locations'. Such decentralization was indispensable to the advent of 'un véritable libéralisme', conforming to the noble views of Madame de Staël rather than Dupin's base materialism.[68] It was an early usage of *libéralisme*, a word first recorded in 1818 but little used before 1830.[69]

The debasement of liberty by the industrialists, Fonfrède continued, ultimately derived from an erroneous interpretation of the causes of British prosperity. Contrary to the assertions of Comte, Dunoyer and Dupin, the flourishing of liberty across the Channel owed little to the prosperity of industry: it derived from the institutional compromises between Normans and Saxons in the Middle Ages, a view probably inspired by Augustin Thierry's *Histoire de la conquête de l'Angleterre par les Normands* (1825). Only later 'did liberty foster the growth of industry [in England], and yet industry only prospered and developed to maintain the most shocking inequalities of wealth within the country and to create a system of exclusion and despotism over the entire world'. Liberty in

[67] François Ferrier, *De l'entrepôt de Paris: second mémoire* (Paris and Lille, 1828), pp. 11–26, 57–60.

[68] 'Des départements', 7th article, *L'Indicateur*, 7 December 1827.

[69] Alain Rey (ed.), *Dictionnaire historique de la langue française*, 2 vols. (Paris, 1993), vol. 1, p. 1124; and Guillaume Bertier de Sauvigny, 'Liberalism, Nationalism and Socialism: The Birth of Three Words', *Review of Politics*, 32 (2) (1970): 147–66, at p. 150–5.

England was 'a national treasure, which it [was] forbidden to export', as proved by the political and commercial enslavement of India. Fonfrède dismissed Britain's recent commercial reforms as posturing intended to stave off an impending crisis of overproduction caused by excessive reliance on manufacturing.[70]

The industrialists' excessive admiration for Britain, Fonfrède added, was combined with an exaggerated view of the benefits of manufacturing, illustrated by their ambivalent use of the word *industrie*: this term 'rapidly [changed] meaning on the lips of current economists', who conceded in theory that it designated 'every productive activity, physical or moral' and yet in practice showed themselves exclusively concerned with the prosperity of 'manufacturing works or, so to speak, industrial industry'. In Fonfrède's view, the growth of manufacturing, a stultifying activity, endangered liberty, while agriculture constituted 'the most essential link between citizens and their homeland': it 'improve[d] moral standards and never corrupt[ed] them' and was 'therefore eminently liberal'. The industrialists should therefore not be trusted when they 'clamoured for the liberty of commerce' because they would never support the repeal of protection for cotton, iron, steel and hardware manufacturers. As long as the 'industrial system' did not 'tend towards the liberty of commerce', Fonfrède maintained, the commercial privileges of seaports should be left untouched.[71]

Fonfrède's series of articles was noticed beyond the Gironde. According to Fonfrède, the foreword of Dupin's *Forces productives*, which called on southerners to emulate rather than lament their northern countrymen's achievements, was 'a ridiculous palinode intended as an indirect response'.[72] *Le Précurseur*, a liberal newspaper in Lyon, accused Fonfrède's articles of 'violating the most undisputed principles of political economy'. In a response to the Lyonnais daily, the Bordelais publicist denied that he harboured 'disdain' for the 'science of economics'. But he disapproved of 'the sect-like enthusiasm that makes some people blindly adopt the opinions of the school's leaders' and rejected claims that it should rank among 'exact sciences'.[73] At the same time, Fonfrède had no sympathy for the advocates of the mercantile system, describing them as 'senseless

[70] 'Des départements', 8th and 9th articles, *L'Indicateur*, 12 and 18 December 1827.
[71] 'Des départements', 9th, 10th, 11th and 12th articles, *L'Indicateur*, 18 December 1827, 22 December 1827, 30 January 1828 and 9 February 1828.
[72] Fonfrède to Campan, 17 June 1828, BMB, MS 1087; see 'Hommage aux habitants de la France méridionale', in Dupin, *Forces productives*, vol. 1, pp. i–viii.
[73] *L'Indicateur*, 21 and 22 February 1828.

writers' and 'stubborn defenders of old errors' and 'monarchical' opinions.[74] Fonfrède might be said to have upheld a republican conception of the liberty of commerce, primarily concerned with the promotion of virtue, against the economists' defence of the liberty of commerce, which placed an increasing emphasis on material prosperity. It is telling that Fonfrède tended to discriminate between Say, a republican whom he respectfully described as 'the most talented economist of our times', and the industrialists, deriding the latter as the 'doctrinaires' of 'commercial economics'.[75] The *doctrinaires* in politics were partisans of a constitutional monarchy with a strong executive power, such as François Guizot. Fonfrède's pejorative analogy suggested that the industrialists, too, were enemies of republican ideals.

Fonfrède's republican critique of industrialism also had a powerful impact on local public opinion. The circulation of major provincial dailies such as *L'Indicateur* stood at approximately 1,000 copies, and every copy had several, sometimes dozens, of readers.[76] In 1829, the Prefect of Bordeaux complained that 'even workers' read *L'Indicateur*, in inns or at their workplace.[77] Moreover, Fonfrède's audience now extended beyond traditional liberal readers to include the royalist *notables*. His articles on warehouses 'earned him, from the *ultras*, appreciations, compliments, correspondence etc. These good people are delighted that a liberal does for them, what no doubt they don't know how to do themselves'.[78] As protests for commercial liberty intensified in 1828–9, these royalists would formally join the liberal opposition. This about-face should not be reduced to an instance of the determination of political opinions by material interests, since it also illustrated the capacity of ideas, in this case Fonfrède's diatribe against the industrialist economists, to modify political allegiances.

Similarly, it would be a mistake to dismiss Fonfrède's defence of warehousing privileges on behalf of 'veritable liberalism' as sophistry. The concept of liberalism in the 1820s was new and its content vague. Fonfrède's distrust of centralization chimed well with the French liberal tradition since Montesquieu's emphasis on the need for intermediate bodies. His discomfort with the double-edged use of *industrie* by the economists pointed to a genuine lexical ambivalence, which had been underlying debates

[74] 'Des départements', 8th article, *L'Indicateur*, 12 December 1827.

[75] 'Des départements', *L'Indicateur*, 3rd and 11th articles, 11 January 1827 and 30 January 1828.

[76] Claude Bellanger, Jacques Godechot, Pierre Guiral and Fernand Terrou (eds.), *Histoire générale de la presse française*, 5 vols. (Paris, 1969–76), vol. II, p. 150.

[77] The Prefect of the Gironde to the Minister of the Interior, 5 February 1829, AN, F7 6769, folder 7.

[78] Fonfrède to Campan, 18 March 1828, BMB, MS 1087.

about economic change since the late eighteenth century.[79] Fonfrède was also right to distrust the commitment to economic liberty of Dupin, who went on to become an advocate of protection after 1830. It would be fairer to view his polemic articles as evidence of the extreme ideological fluidity of the late 1820s, a period when the meaning of economic liberty and its relationship with political liberty were the objects of an intense controversy, in the provinces as well as on the Parisian intellectual stage.

III

Anxieties about the stagnation of foreign trade contributed to the disappointing results of the November 1827 election for the royalists. Out of 450 deputies in the lower chamber, the number of opposition liberals increased from fewer than 40 to around 180.[80] In January 1828, the moderate royalist Jean-Baptiste de Martignac replaced Villèle as Premier, and, in order to address concerns with the economy, a portfolio of commerce and public works was created. Yet the appointment of Saint-Cricq, the architect of the prohibitive system, as the first holder of the new ministerial position made radical reforms unlikely. Debates at the Chamber of Deputies soon confirmed the extent of liberal expectations with regard to trade policy and the controversial potential of the word *liberté* in relation to commerce. The original text of the new chamber's first *adresse* (yearly motion to the King) asserted that the 'real good' of commerce, industry and agriculture lay 'in liberty'. 'Anything that hinders our commercial relations', the text added, 'has damaging effects, and repercussions which are felt by the most distant interests'. Saint-Cricq protested against the use of the word *liberté*, which might result in 'serious abuses'. Amendments tending to suppress the word were rejected, but deputies consented to assuage Saint-Cricq's concerns by modifying the second sentence, so that in the final version of the *adresse* it began with 'Anything that *unnecessarily* hinders our commercial relations'.[81] Still, in Bordeaux, *L'Indicateur* applauded the Chamber's declaration 'in favour of the liberty of commerce' and argued that it heralded 'more than anything else' the change that its new composition 'must impart on public affairs'.[82]

[79] Gareth Stedman Jones, '*Industrie*, Pauperism, and the Hanoverian State: The Genesis and Political Context of the Original Debate about the "Industrial Revolution" in England and France, 1815–1840', Centre for History and Economics, working paper (Cambridge, 1997); Florian Schui, *Early Debates about Industry: Voltaire and His Contemporaries* (London, 2007), pp. 26–34.

[80] Kent, *The Election of 1827*, pp. 169–72.

[81] AP, vol. LII, pp. 750–1 (5 March 1828); my emphasis.

[82] *L'Indicateur*, 11 March 1828.

In the subsequent twelve months, protests against prohibitive policies spread and intensified, especially in winegrowing regions. In the late 1820s, with 2 million workers producing 40 to 50 per cent of the world's wine, winegrowing was one of France's largest industries and its second largest source of exports after the fabrication of silk textiles. Yet the stagnation of trade and a series of abundant vine harvests resulted in a significant fall in the price of wine after 1825.[83] The extent and causes of the wine industry's crisis were controversial. Saint-Cricq and other officials maintained that wine exports had not diminished and attributed the crisis to overproduction. According to official statistics, French wine exports slightly rose in value, from 40 million francs per year in 1815–16 to 45 million in 1828–9.[84] But in export-oriented regions specialized in the production of fine wines such as the Gironde and Burgundy, liberal publicists dismissed the figures as unreliable or complained that French policy prevented a more significant growth of exports. An unprecedented movement of mass protests in favour of commercial liberty ensued.

As noticed earlier, the liberal success at the 1827 election was particularly resounding in the Gironde. The department's Prefect attributed this result to 'the reading of newspapers', perhaps an allusion to Fonfrède's attacks on the regime, but also to 'the difficulties encountered in selling this region's commodities', especially wines.[85] In March 1828, a dozen vineyard owners, all 'ultras' according to Fonfrède, set up a committee 'in order to address protests to the government' on trade policy. When two members of the committee visited Fonfrède and asked him to write a petition on their behalf, he refused, stressing that the advent of commercial liberty was not possible under a royalist government: 'our sufferings', he told the royalist *notables*, 'will not be alleviated by changes to our administration as you are suggesting. It is within the political framework of the state that the radical vice lies. As long as that framework remains in place, we shall be ruined.' Since the *notables* would not be able to sign a text that underscored '*the source of evil*' (reactionary royalism), Fonfrède preferred to remain silent.[86]

[83] Michel Lachiver, *Vins, vignes et vignerons français*, 2nd edn (Paris, 1997), pp. 393–5; Noelle Plack, *Common Land, Wine and the French Revolution: Rural Society and Economy in Southern France, c. 1789–1820* (Farnham, 2009), pp. 105–29; James Simpson, *Creating Wine: The Emergence of a World Industry, 1840–1914* (Princeton, NJ, 2011), pp. 8–22. On the economic difficulties of the Gironde winegrowers at the end of the 1820s, see Tudesq, 'La Restauration', pp. 53–5, and Paul Butel, *Les Dynasties bordelaises* (Paris, 1991), pp. 186–91.

[84] Ministère du Commerce, *Statistique de la France*, vol. VII, pp. 8–9, 515.

[85] The Prefect of the Gironde to the Minister of the Interior, 30 June 1828, Paris, AN, F7 6769, folder 7.

[86] Fonfrède to Campan, 18 March 1828, BMB, MS 1087.

The royalist vineyard owners eventually recruited Etienne Hervé, a Bordeaux lawyer of moderate political opinions, to draft the petition. The document was signed by 12,563 winegrowers – over five times the number of enfranchised voters in the department – and forwarded to the legislative chambers in May. The petition did not abide by the canons of liberal political economy. Instead, it combined elements of Montesquieu's science of commerce with Fonfrède's critique of the excessive importance given to manufacturing industries. The petitioners lambasted the 'prohibitive system' as 'the most lamentable of errors' and praised the moral and material advantages of commerce:

> Nature, in its infinite variety, has conferred upon each land specific attributes; it has marked out the true purpose of every soil, and through the diversity of products and needs, it has sought to unite men with a universal bond and foster those ties which have brought about commerce and civilization.

Using Fonfrède's language, the petitioners denounced the 'manufacturing fury' that was impoverishing 'the most fertile land in Europe' and transferring riches from the south to the north of the country. The petition did not mention the names of Adam Smith or Say. But it invoked Chaptal and Dupin, using the their quantitative estimates in *De l'industrie française* and *Des forces productives* to contend that agriculture employed six times as many Frenchmen as manufacturing, and winegrowing 3 million workers against only 70,000 in iron forges. The petition also borrowed from the language of jealousy, underlining the potential contribution of wine exports, which amounted to more than 80 million francs before 1789, to France's 'balance of exchanges'.[87]

The example of the Gironde inspired winegrowers from seventeen other departments to send petitions to the legislative chambers in the spring of 1828.[88] The new petitioners willingly acknowledged the influence of the Gironde winegrowers. Those of the Indre-et-Loire paid homage to 'one of France's most celebrated provinces, for its wealth and for the genius of its inhabitants' and described the Gironde petition as 'a model to which all

[87] [Etienne Hervé], *Pétition des propriétaires de vignes du département de la Gironde et mémoire à l'appui* (Bordeaux, 1828), pp. 5–6, 10–12, 59–70; the names of the fifteen members of the Comité des Propriétaires de Vignes de la Gironde confirm that they belonged to the department's royalist elite: ten of them were nobles, including a former *ultra* representative of the Gironde at the Chamber of Deputies, Bernard-Henri de Pontet, and the *ultra* Deputy-Mayor of Bordeaux during the White Terror, Pierre-Romain Blanc-Dutrouil.

[88] Ten departments in the south-west, four in Alsace and Lorraine, two in the Loire valley and one in Burgundy; AP, vol. LV, p. 579 (1 July 1828).

regions … should refer'.[89] The wave of petitions caused a sensation in the legislative chambers. In the Chamber of Peers, the Comte Molé, future Premier under the July Monarchy, called on France to follow the example of 'enlightened, liberal moderation' given by British commercial reforms.[90] In the lower chamber, a dozen liberal deputies demanded an immediate reform of France's commercial 'system of rejection' or 'overly exclusive system of customs'. These included Benjamin Constant, by then a deputy for the Bas-Rhin, who argued that the government should 'return the Charter to Alsace, and indeed to the whole of France, by abolishing monopoly' and 'return the liberty of commerce to the border provinces by freeing them from scandalously exaggerated measures of exception and prohibitions'.[91]

Royalist defenders of the prohibitive system rejected the winegrowers' demands and attributed their difficulties to an excessive cultivation of the vine. In the Chamber of Peers, Villèle pointed to the example of another winegrowing country, Portugal, which had opted for liberal commercial intercourse with Britain since the Methuen treaty of 1703 and suffered prolonged economic decline as a result.[92] In the Chamber of Deputies, Saint-Cricq echoed Villèle's apocalyptic warnings of 1821 and 1822 should France opt for commercial liberty:

> Which country will buy our grain in the face of competition from Poland and Crimea, our hemp in the face of competition from Russia, our wool in the face of competition from Spain, Prussia and Moravia, our cattle in the face of competition from Germany and the Netherlands, our woollen clothes in the face of competition from England, the Netherlands and Germany, our linen clothes in the face of competition from Ireland and the Netherlands, or our cotton fabrics in the face of competition from England and Switzerland?[93]

Without the prohibitive system, Saint-Cricq concluded, France would be left with only two industries, wine and silk. Yet, in order to assuage protests, the Minister of Commerce agreed to convene a special commission of inquiry that would examine the possibility of relaxing restrictions on the storage of colonial goods and reducing the sugar and iron tariffs.

In October, Saint-Cricq issued a report confirming that a commercial inquiry would be held in the early months of 1829. However, the report damped down expectations of an ambitious reform by rejecting 'absolute'

89 [Anon.], *Pétition par les propriétaires du vignoble blanc des coteaux de la Loire* (Paris, 1828), p. 3.
90 AP, vol. LV, pp. 453–4 (1 July 1828).
91 AP, vol. LV, pp. 579–607 (5 July 1828) and vol. LVI, pp. 417–21 (25 July 1828).
92 AP, vol. LV, pp. 468–70 (1 July 1828). 93 AP, vol. LVI, pp. 150–6 (16 July 1828).

doctrines in commercial policy and insisting that 'a protective tariff' remained 'indispensable'. The commission of inquiry included several *ultras*, moderate royalists and moderate liberals but excluded representatives of the left.[94] Extensive coverage of Saint-Cricq's report in the press confirmed a growing interest on the part of the public for the debate on international trade and the persistence of a strong correlation between political and economic opinions. *Le Courrier Français* (circulation: 6,000 copies), a radical sheet, accused Saint-Cricq's report of 'lingering with love on the history of the system' that he had created, and despaired of any improvement. The liberal *Journal du Commerce* (2,500) regretted the absence of Jean-Baptiste Say in the commission but hoped that the 'publicity' surrounding the inquiry would help to spread 'sound doctrines' of political economy. The moderate *Journal des Débats* (11,000) and the liberal *Constitutionnel* (20,000) also hoped that it would spread 'knowledge' (*lumières*) or 'torrents of knowledge' on the potential benefits of freer trade. By contrast, the right-wing press was hostile or indifferent. The royalist *Gazette de France* (11,000) considered an inquiry useless at a time when writings on political economy had become 'so numerous'. It also feared that 'by calling into question the entire commercial legislation', the inquiry would cause anxiety among producers and the 'complete stagnation' of industry: such matters were better decided upon 'in the secrecy of the cabinet'. The *ultra Quotidienne* (6,000) reproduced Saint-Cricq's report but did not comment on it.[95]

In the early months of 1829, a second wave of seventy-two petitions by winegrowers from thirty-six departments kept up the pressure for a reform of commercial policy.[96] A new petition from the Gironde threatened the government with the organization of further protests if the inquiry did not result in 'the modification of our tariffs'.[97] 'Let France adopt a system less prohibitive towards foreigners', vineyard owners from the Bouches-du-Rhône asserted, 'and foreigners [would] hasten to consume our products'.[98] The Gironde remained the epicentre of the protests, with approximately 20,000 out of 50,000 to 60,000 petitioners

[94] *Le Moniteur Universel*, 8 October 1828.

[95] *Le Courrier Français*, 9 October 1828; *Le Journal du Commerce*, 9 October 1828; *Le Constitutionnel*, 9 October 1828; *Le Journal des Débats*, 9 October 1828; *La Gazette de France*, 9 October 1828; *La Quotidienne*, 9 October 1828. For the political leaning and circulation of each newspaper, see Daniel L. Rader, *The Journalists and the July Revolution: The Role of the Political Press in the Overthrow of the Bourbon Restoration* (The Hague, 1973), pp. 17–35, and Bellanger et al., *Histoire générale de la Presse*, vol. II, pp. 76, 100.

[96] AP, vol. LVIII, pp. 145–7 (4 April 1829), and pp. 409–10 (18 April 1829).

[97] 'Propriétaires de vignes de la Gironde', 10 February 1829, AN, C 2097.

[98] [Anon.], *Pétition des propriétaires de vignes et des négociants en vins du département des Bouches du Rhône* (Marseille, 1829), p. 25.

across France.[99] The regions the most inclined to follow the lead of the Bordelais, who actively sought to coordinate protests, were areas producing high-quality wines, the most likely to be exported.

Burgundy, where protests against the prohibitive system flourished in 1829, is a case in point. It is noteworthy that in Burgundy as in the Gironde, demands for commercial liberty were combined with hostility towards Parisian centralization. Burgundy's wine exports to central Europe had increased under Napoleon and declined under the Restoration, especially as a result of foreign retaliatory measures against the 1822 French tariff.[100] In January 1829, the Romantic poet Alphonse de Lamartine, himself the owner of a large vineyard in Saône-et-Loire, drafted a petition for his department's winegrowers. Lamartine's economics were as melodramatic as his poetry. Lamenting the impoverishment of France's '6 million' winegrowers, he decried the prohibitive system as a 'sort of national suicide' and demanded 'the complete adoption' of the system of 'the liberty of commerce'.[101]

The example of the Saône-et-Loire inspired vineyard owners of the Beaune arrondissement in the neighbouring department of Côte d'Or to issue a petition signed by 3,355 winegrowers. The drafter of the Beaune petition was Théophile Foisset, a publicist who played, on a smaller scale than Fonfrède, the same role of local mediator of liberal economic ideas. Born in 1800, Foisset had recently returned to Beaune, his hometown, as judge at the Tribunal Civil of Beaune, after a few years spent in Paris where he read law and became influenced by liberal Catholic ideas. He owned a vineyard and edited a small periodical, *Le Provincial*, dedicated to the study of Burgundy's history and the defence of provincial liberties. In December 1828, Foisset agreed to become Secretary of the Beaune Comité des Proprietaires de Vignes, founded in July 1828 to ensure 'publicity' about the sufferings of the local wine industry.[102] Foisset's appointment seems to have been prompted by a communication from the Gironde committee, in which the Bordelais exhorted the Beaune winegrowers to redouble their efforts in order to defeat the 'sly influences', 'powerful alliances' and 'discreet machinations' of the defenders of 'monopolies'.[103]

[99] My estimate, based on lists of signatories in AN, C 2097.

[100] Pierre Lévêque, *Une société provinciale: la Bourgogne sous la Monarchie de Juillet* (Paris, 1983), pp. 130–7.

[101] Text of the petition in Cargill Sprietsma, *Lamartine et Théophile Foisset* (Paris, 1936), pp. 12–18; the original petition is missing from AN, C 2097 and the number of signatories unknown.

[102] 'Comité des propriétaires de vignes et négociants de l'arrondissement de Beaune', 5 July 1828, Dijon, Archives Départementales de la Côte d'Or (hereafter ADCO), 34J 41.

[103] The Gironde Committee to the Beaune Committee, 19 December 1828, ADCO, 34J 41.

Foisset was charged with drafting a petition and a memorandum, a task which he fulfilled earnestly but without passion. He was pleased to have become Secretary of the Beaune Committee because his appointment proved 'that [he was] not considered a new arrival here' after his long stay in Paris, and he hoped that the position would serve his ambition of being 'elected a deputy' for his hometown. After spending his days at the courthouse, he dedicated his evenings 'and the nights if necessary' to drafting the Committee's minutes, correspondence and memorandum. But his sarcastic tone betrayed his lack of enthusiasm: 'I am deep into tables, figures and political economy. It is marvellous!'[104] This absence of personal interest in economics paradoxically confirms that international trade was becoming a widespread concern: even in a small provincial town such as Beaune, the capacity to write in a well informed manner about commerce was perceived as a useful asset by the ambitious young man. For his memorandum, Foisset was able to use the Gironde 1828 petition, from which he quoted, and Lamartine's petition, a copy of which he secured from the poet.[105] He also reproduced nearly verbatim several passages from an article in *Le Globe*, a leading liberal weekly.[106] In addition, he probably consulted the handful of works on political economy that he owned, according to a catalogue of his books drawn up in 1830: two volumes by Say (most likely the *Traité*), one volume by Ferrier (certainly *Du gouvernement*) and one volume by Saint-Chamans (perhaps *Du système de l'impôt*, or the *Nouvel essai sur la richesse des nations*).[107]

Foisset's memorandum competently summarized Say's attacks on the doctrine of the balance of trade, arguing that curtailing imports amounted to 'banning our exports in a similar proportion'. It also contested Saint-Cricq's figure on wine exports, accusing him of having chosen some dates that concealed an actual decline and insisting that even if French exports had only stagnated, they had failed to keep pace with the overall rise of consumption in Europe since 1815. However, unlike petitions from Bordeaux and the south-west, which often expressed nostalgia for the scale of maritime exports at the end of the Old Regime, the Beaune memorandum preferred to recall commercial prosperity under Napoleon: 'Nothing is better remembered among tradesmen than the vast number of shipments then made by vineyards in Burgundy, Champagne and Lorraine

104 Foisset to Boucley, 29 December 1828, ADCO, 34 J 103; Foisset to Brugnot, 21 February 1829, ADCO, 34J 94.
105 Sprietsma, *Lamartine et Foisset*, pp. 11–12.
106 'Du système prohibitif', *Le Globe*, 22 October 1828.
107 Catalogue, 21 December 1830, ADCO, 34J 101.

beyond France's current borders!' At that time, 'there were no barriers on our products, because Europe was under our sway and France had 150 [sic, for 130] departments, with a population of 50,000,000 consumers!'[108]

In January 1829, the winegrowers' protest movement culminated with the creation of a central committee in Paris. The national committee issued a pamphlet, the *Mémoire sur le système actuel des douanes*, of which 6,000 copies were printed in April, making it one of the most widely circulated writings on international trade under the Restoration.[109] Although the pamphlet was signed by all the twenty-one regional delegates who made up the Central Committee, its real author was known to be the delegate for the Charente-Inférieure, Tanneguy Duchâtel. Say, for instance, acknowledging receipt of a copy, congratulated Duchâtel on the 'good principles' that the pamphlet contained.[110] Born in 1803, Duchâtel was the author of a recent treatise that praised Thomas Robert Malthus' work on the links between fertility and poverty, although it was more optimistic than the *Essay on Population* on the possibility of alleviating poverty thanks to a combination of 'hard work, economy and prudence within marriage'. Unlike Malthus, who defended the necessity of protection, Duchâtel's treatise attacked the 'prohibitive system', asserting that 'it has created more poverty than a large number of charitable institutions can hope to relieve'.[111] Duchâtel was also the main contributor of articles on political economy in *Le Globe*, the high-quality liberal periodical.[112] He went on to become a close ally of Guizot under the July Monarchy, serving as his Minister of the Interior from 1840 until the Revolution of 1848.

Duchâtel's *Mémoire* on behalf of the winegrowers was devoid of the regionalist undertones of local protests and paid scant attention to the specific problems faced by the wine industry. Instead, it consisted in a lucid exposition of the potential benefits of freer trade for the whole of France that conformed to the political economy of Say: 'exchanges will fertilize the industry of all nations and universal prosperity will be the happy result of these peaceful relations'. Rather than lamenting the decay of the wine trade, the *Mémoire* pointed to the overall decline of French exports since the 1780s and contrasted it with the trebling of British

[108] 'Mémoire à l'appui de la pétition des propriétaires de vignes de la Côte d'Or', ADCO, 34J 41.
[109] Impression 1780 (15 April 1829), AN, F18*II 17.
[110] Jean-Baptiste Say, *Mélanges et correspondance d'économie politique*, ed. Charles Comte (Paris, 1833), p. 173.
[111] Tanneguy Duchâtel, *La Charité dans ses rapports avec l'état moral et le bien-être des classes inférieures* (Paris, 1829), pp. 145–6, 154.
[112] On Duchâtel's writings in *Le Globe*, see Jean-Jacques Goblot, *La Jeune France libérale: Le Globe et son groupe littéraire, 1824–1830* (Paris, 1995), pp. 309–25.

exports over the same period. Throughout, the text was adamant that the prohibitive system impoverished not only wine producers but all French consumers.[113] This widely disseminated *Mémoire* may therefore be construed as an attempt to forge an alliance between the liberal economists and the protesting winegrowers. Yet its abstract tone somewhat bowdlerized the appeal of commercial liberty, which was anchored in specific regional grievances.

IV

As the political crisis intensified, efforts to obtain a reform of France's commercial system floundered. Contrary to initial promises, the sessions of Saint-Cricq's commercial inquiry were held in secret, reducing its impact on public debates. Moreover, the inquiry commission abstained from making recommendations on the question of warehouses and only proposed very modest reductions in the sugar and iron tariffs.[114] Saint-Cricq and Ferrier also launched an ideological counter-offensive, describing British commercial reforms as a trap designed to consolidate Britain's economic supremacy. After the appointment of a new government led by the *ultra* Jules de Polignac in July 1829, protests in favour of commercial liberty merged with an increasingly radical opposition to the regime.

Since 1824, Saint-Cricq, no longer Director General of Customs, had retained his influence over commercial policy as the President of the Bureau du Commerce et des Colonies. In a report approved by the King and his ministers in July 1825, Saint-Cricq already considered that British tariff reductions merely 'recorded a *fait accompli*', namely the uselessness of Britain's restrictions on foreign manufactured products given the superiority of British manufacturers. Saint-Cricq noted that the protection of British agriculture was undiminished because 'as long as England has rivals to fear, it will keep its market closed'. Britain's commercial reforms nonetheless constituted a danger, he contended, because they might be falsely construed as a change of commercial system and lead Continental Europe astray: 'having exhausted the benefits of the prohibitive regime, [England] will praise the advantages of commercial liberty, it will feign to recognize these doctrines as the only ones favourable to the wealth of nations'. But Europe should eschew 'the bait of nominal reciprocity' that was only intended to gain British manufacturers 'a few million external

[113] [Tanneguy Duchâtel], *Mémoire sur le système actuel des douanes* (Paris, 1829), pp. 8, 16–17.
[114] Ministère du Commerce, *Enquête sur les fers* (Paris, 1829) and *Enquête sur les sucres* (Paris, 1829).

consumers' at the expense of their Continental rivals.[115] The same year, another report by Saint-Cricq similarly dismissed the relaxation of restrictions on British colonies' exchanges as a manifestation of Britain's global commercial hegemony and warned against the temptation of emulating a policy that would ruin France's colonies and navy. In a third report, also dated from 1825, Saint-Cricq even envisaged the extension of the French colonial demesne to North Africa, where France's commercial privileges in the regency of Algiers should, in his view, be treated as 'the possible seed of a French colony'.[116]

As the prohibitive legislation seemed under threat after 1828, defenders of mercantile jealousy publicly rebutted the notion that Britain had embraced commercial liberty. The main object of the Comte de Vaublanc's *Du commerce maritime* (1828) was to prevent 'a false imitation of what has been done in England'.[117] In May 1829, defending a customs law proposal based on the recommendations of the inquiry commission before the Chamber of Deputies, Saint-Cricq reiterated his opposition to 'the theories that want … infinite commercial liberty' and insisted that the 'new economic course' pursued by England had been the object of 'false interpretations'. England's new commercial policy remained as 'ingenious' as in the past because it merely consisted in 'ceasing to forbid what it no longer needs to prevent'. In order to make the real meaning of British reforms 'palpable' to French deputies, Saint-Cricq had copies of a work by a 'distinguished administrator' and 'one of our most vigorous writers' on political economy distributed to all of them.[118]

Saint-Cricq did not name the author, but the work in question was certainly François Ferrier's *Du système maritime et commercial de l'Angleterre*, published in May 1829. The former enforcer of the Continental Blockade was worried by the progress of liberal ideas about trade in French opinion. In a first pamphlet on the commercial inquiry published in January 1829, he attributed the popularity of the Anglophile 'school of economics' to the 'mobility' of ideas in France and drew a parallel with the contemporary French craze for English Elizabethan drama: 'This mobility … extends to literature. The English are faithful to Shakespeare, while we

[115] Report by Saint-Cricq to the Conseil Supérieur du Commerce et des Colonies, 10 July 1825, AN, F12*193/4.

[116] Reports by Saint-Cricq to the Conseil Supérieur du Commerce et des Colonies, 18 October 1825 and 23 November 1825, AN, F12*193/4; on early proposals to establish a French colony on the territory of the regency of Algiers, see David Todd, 'Resituer l'expédition d'Alger dans l'histoire de l'impérialisme français: problèmes de périodisation et perspectives trans-impériales', forthcoming in *Revue d'Histoire Moderne et Contemporaine*.

[117] Viénot de Vaublanc, *Du commerce maritime*, p. i.

[118] AP, vol. LIX, pp. 374–87 (21 May 1829).

shall soon betray Racine for Shakespeare.'[119] In his private correspondence with Fiévée, Ferrier's tone was anguished. Comparing the excitement generated by the inquiry in many French towns to the disorders in the French countryside on the eve of 1789, he viewed the agitation in favour of commercial liberty as the forerunning sign of 'an imminent ... revolution'.[120]

Du système maritime focused on Britain's commercial reforms, the misinterpretation of which constituted in Ferrier's view the immediate cause of agitation against the prohibitive system: 'Books, memoranda, pamphlets, articles in newspapers' all cited the example of Britain in defence of commercial liberty. In response, Ferrier examined in detail British official documents to show that Britain only repealed protection when it was no longer needed. Echoing the warnings of Villèle and Saint-Cricq, he contended that the abolition of prohibitions would hand over the sceptre of 'universal monarchy' to Britain and transform Continental Europe into an industrial 'desert'. Should France renew the experience of the treaty of 1786, he asserted, it would only be left with 'luxury' industries such as 'silk, gilding, fashion'. But, striking a more optimistic note, Ferrier also viewed Britain's reforms as a symptom of its vulnerability. Britain's commercial success and excessive population made it overly dependent on 'external consumers' and subjected its industrial activity to 'continuous vicissitudes': 'few events around the globe do not have an impact on its manufactures, and most of them are not favourable'. Rather than merely defending Britain's traditional mercantile system, Ferrier sketched out a new justification of protection that underlined the benefits of self-sufficiency: France was 'less powerful outside' than England, but it had 'more riches inside' and needed not envy its neighbour. This novel argument would become central to the defence of the protective system under the July Monarchy.[121]

A few petitions discussed by deputies in June 1829 echoed the diatribes of Saint-Cricq and Ferrier against commercial liberty. Approximately 300 manufacturers from Rouen in Normandy insisted that the winegrowers represented only a fraction of French agriculture, while most farmers could not face 'the competition of Russian, Polish and African grain' or 'that of Spanish, Saxon and English wools'. The abolition of 'the prohibitive and conservative principle' that determined French commercial

[119] François Ferrier, *De l'enquête commerciale* (Paris and Lille, 1829), pp. 8–9.

[120] 'Note pour M. F.', enclosed in a letter from Ferrier to Fiévée, 7 May 1829, in *Correspondance*, p. 184.

[121] François Ferrier, *Du système maritime et commercial de l'Angleterre au XIXe siècle* (Paris, 1829), pp. 3, 110–17.

legislation would result, they claimed, in 'frightening catastrophes': 'The English would reap our gold so necessary to the redemption of their [public] debt and would plot with greater ease the complete ruin of France.' More than 500 'proprietors, manufacturers and tradesmen' of the Saint-Quentin arrondissement in Picardy also attributed 'these ideas that threaten to subvert our internal prosperity' to the 'encouragements' of British statesmen.[122] To the dismay of supporters of commercial liberty, the chamber voted that the government should take the two petitions into consideration.[123]

Just as opponents of commercial reform were gaining in confidence, political and constitutional issues took precedence over debates about international trade with the provocative appointment of an *ultra* ministry by the King in July 1829 – the new government no longer included a minister of commerce. The following months witnessed a rapid aggravation of political tensions, and, throughout the country, local liberal committees called for the non-payment of taxes. It is noteworthy that in winegrowing regions, committees of vineyard owners were at the forefront of the anti-government agitation. In the Gironde, the Prefect reported that winegrowers' protests, from 'individual complaints', were turning into 'collective demands, meetings and affiliations', at first in his department and increasingly in neighbouring ones. 'These demands', he added, 'have rapidly become menacing: they have led to the examination of political issues and the elaboration of a general scheme to resist authorities.'[124]

A few weeks later, the Gironde Prefect noticed a formal rapprochement between the liberals, led by 'a sombre, passionate and remarkably talented man, who made a sort of religion out of his hatred for the monarchy', undoubtedly Fonfrède, and 'several landowners', who 'until now … had been renowned for the fervour of their royalist opinions', and most of whom belonged to the vineyard owners' committee.[125] In a new series of articles entitled 'Des vignobles et du ministère', Fonfrède sealed his alliance with the royalist *notables*. The articles consisted in a systematic refutation of the arguments of Saint-Cricq and the other adversaries of the winegrowers. The journalist noted an inflexion in the rhetoric of Saint-Cricq, who now defended a 'protective' rather than 'prohibitive' system of legislation. Yet

[122] Petition by 'les manufacturiers, fabricants, négociants et commerçants de la Seine-Inférieure', [winter 1829], and petition by 'les propriétaires, manufacturiers et négociants de l'arrondissement de Saint-Quentin', 9 February 1829, AN, F12 2506.

[123] AP, vol. LX, pp. 313–14, 516–27 (13 and 20 June 1829).

[124] Prefect of the Gironde to the Minister of the Interior, 24 June 1829, AN, F7 6769, folder 7.

[125] Prefect of the Gironde to the Minister of the Interior, 13 July 1829, AN, F7 6769, folder 7.

Fonfrède maintained that Saint-Cricq's goal remained the establishment of 'industrial slavery' in France. Parrying accusations that the winegrowers merely pursued their narrow material interest, Fonfrède also underlined the moral and political costs of restrictions on international trade: 'the system of protection implies', he wrote, 'necessarily and for ever, the destruction of commercial links between peoples; a highly immoral conception, for in teaching nations how to do without one another's help and industries, it destroys original connections and breaks up the peaceful obstacles that a thousand commercial relations set up against the ambition of conquerors.' As Fonfrède turned his attention to the appointment of the Polignac ministry, he did not keep to his initial promise of also refuting the arguments of Ferrier, 'the most constant, and one must admit one of the most intelligent supporters of Monsieur de Saint-Cricq's system'.[126]

Liberal discontent and winegrowers' protests also merged in other parts of the country. In Burgundy, a member of the Dijon vineyard owners' committee later reminisced, the two movements were so intertwined that anyone who cultivated the vine was 'suspected of republicanism' by the authorities.[127] In Alsace, the Prefect of the Bas-Rhin also noted a strong connection between winegrowers' protests and the growth of hostility to the government: 'if wines could be sold, not a single farmer would know whether or not there [had] been a change of ministry. … the difficulties encountered by winegrowers … make them more receptive to mischievous ideas'.[128] In February 1830, the winegrowers prepared new petitions in Burgundy and the Gironde.[129] The plan came to nothing, probably because the political crisis submerged other concerns after deputies voted for an *adresse* hostile to the government in March and a new royalist electoral defeat in June. A Parisian insurrection on 27, 28 and 29 July forced Charles X to abdicate, and Louis-Philippe d'Orléans succeeded him as sovereign of a parliamentary monarchy. Bordeaux was one of the few provincial cities to experience its own revolution, with Fonfrède calling for armed resistance to the regime and insurgents storming most public buildings – the hated customs house was the last to surrender and hoist down the white Bourbon flag.[130] In Alsace, too, hostility to the regime and

[126] 'Des vignobles et du ministère', 2nd, 3rd and 5th articles, *L'Indicateur*, 20, 22 and 28 July 1829.

[127] Jean-Baptiste Guillemot, *Esquisse au sujet de l'association des propriétaires de vignes* (Dijon, 1833), p. 32.

[128] Prefect of the Bas-Rhin to the Minister of the Interior, 5 September 1829, AN, F 7 6771, folder 9.

[129] Foisset to Lamartine, 14 February 1830, ADCO, 34J 101; the Prefect of the Gironde to the Minister of the Interior, 17 February 1830, AN, F7 6769, folder 7.

[130] Dupuch, 'Le Parti libéral', p. 187; Michel Boyé, *La Douane de Bordeaux: un lieu, des hommes* (Bordeaux, 1999), pp. 155–9.

resentment against trade restrictions were closely associated, as bands of smugglers put to flight customs brigades, waving the formerly banned tricolour flag and chanting 'Vive la liberté'.[131]

Never had the connection between commercial and political liberty seemed stronger than in the dying days of the Bourbon monarchy. Say and his disciples' relentless propaganda ensured that the prohibitive system should be viewed as an important dimension of the Bourbon despotism. Even though they sometimes rejected what they perceived as the excessive materialism of political economy, local publicists such as Fonfrède in Bordeaux helped to disseminate liberal ideas about trade and insisted that a change in commercial policy required a liberal political order. Winegrowers' protests against the prohibitive system were one of the sources of the liberal tide that swept away the Bourbon dynasty in 1830. Yet 'commercial liberty' remained a slogan rather than a well defined doctrine or policy. It meant different things to Parisian economists and regionalist publicists and to northern manufacturers and southern winegrowers. By bringing these ambiguities to the fore, the liberal triumph of 1830 would gradually result in a split between those who wished the adoption of complete free trade and those who only wanted to attenuate the rigours of the prohibitive system.

[131] Leuilliot, *L'Alsace*, vol. II, p. 275.

CHAPTER 3

Completing the Revolution

Political and commercial liberty after 1830

The early years of the July Monarchy were an era of extraordinary liberal convergence between France and Britain. Following the fashion for diachronic comparisons between the Stuarts and the Bourbons in the 1820s, the relatively peaceful Revolution of 1830 was soon dubbed, by analogy with England's Glorious Revolution, the *Trois Glorieuses* (Three Glorious Days).[1] The British constitutional model inspired a revision of France's Charter that reinforced guarantees for individual freedoms and the powers of legislative chambers at the expense of the Crown, while a lowering of the franchise doubled the size of the French electorate, from 100,000 to 200,000.[2] The July Monarchy also made immediate and earnest efforts to suppress France's illicit slave trade, which collapsed after 1831.[3] The return of the Whigs to power in Britain and the passage of the Reform Act in 1832 further galvanized hopes of a lasting rapprochement between Europe's two great progressive powers. In both countries, 'reform', understood as a liberal alternative to the violence of revolution or counter-revolution, became the watchword of the 1830s.[4] In 1834, a treaty of alliance was even concluded between the two former rivals, in order to protect recently established liberal constitutional orders in Belgium, Spain and Portugal.[5]

Of course, in reality, diplomatic tensions between Britain and France revived in the 1840s, and the July Monarchy gave way after 1848 to a

[1] Geoffrey Cubitt, 'The Political Uses of Seventeenth-Century English History in Restoration France', *Historical Journal*, 50 (1) (2007): 73–95.

[2] Rosanvallon, *La Monarchie impossible*, pp. 105–48; Alain Laquièze, *Les Origines du régime parlementaire en France (1814–1848)* (Paris, 2002), pp. 77–124.

[3] Paul Kiestra, *The Politics of Slave Trade Suppression in Britain and France, 1814–1848* (Basingstoke, 2000), pp. 148–62.

[4] Patrick Harismendy (ed.), *La France des années 1830 et l'esprit de réforme* (Rennes, 2006); Arthur Burns and Joanna Innes (eds.), *Rethinking the Age of Reform: Britain, 1780–1850* (Cambridge, 2003).

[5] Raymond Guyot, *La Première Entente Cordiale* (Paris, 1926), pp. 15–125; Roger Bullen, *Palmerston, Guizot and the Collapse of the Entente Cordiale* (London, 1974), pp. 1–24; Robert Tombs and Isabelle Tombs, *That Sweet Enemy: The French and the British from the Sun King to the Present* (London, 2006), pp. 332–4.

democratic republic and Bonapartist Caesarism. Together with the harsh judgements passed by some contemporary opponents such as Karl Marx, who derided Louis-Philippe's regime as 'a stock company for the exploitation of the French national wealth', this retrospective knowledge has done much to obscure the intensity of liberal excitement and optimism in the wake of the 1830 Revolution.[6] Yet, several decades after the *Trois Glorieuses* and despite subsequent disappointments, John Stuart Mill still recalled how the event 'roused [his] utmost enthusiasm' and 'gave [him], as it were, a new existence'.[7] Only more recently have historians begun to reappraise the significance of the 1830 Revolution as the intellectual and political apex of French liberalism. But with the notable exception of the thought of Alexis de Tocqueville, the subsequent evolution of liberal ideas in France has often been treated as an instance of stagnation and stultification.[8]

By contrast, this chapter explores a little known aspect of liberal effervescence in the aftermath of the 1830 Revolution: the flourishing of liberal ideas about trade and, in particular, the radicalization of free-trade opinions in Bordeaux. It is also a contribution to the analysis of the process of realignment that took place among liberals in the wake of victory over reactionary royalism. Historians of the July Monarchy are familiar with the split between supporters of *Mouvement*, who favoured further reform in France and support for liberal revolutionaries abroad, and advocates of *Résistance*, who stressed the necessity to restore internal order and preserve external peace. *Résistance* quickly gained the upper hand and dominated parliamentary politics until the regime's downfall in 1848.[9] Here I would like to highlight another rift, between liberals who demanded the complete abolition of restrictions on foreign trade and those who viewed some degree of commercial protection as compatible with political liberty. This realignment of commercial opinions only imperfectly mirrored the split between *Mouvement* and *Résistance*, sowing the seed of a potential division between what would later be described as economic and political liberalism.

This chapter first highlights the significance of commercial reforms in the early years of the July Monarchy. Economic historians have neglected

[6] Karl Marx, *The Class Struggles in France, 1848–1850*, trans. Henry Kuhn (New York, 1924), p. 37.
[7] Mill, *Autobiography*, p. 137.
[8] Jennings, 'Constitutional Liberalism', pp. 365–72; and *Revolution and the Republic*, Chapter 4; Rosanvallon, *Le Moment Guizot*, pp. 305–19.
[9] Hugh A. C. Collingham, *The July Monarchy: A Political History of France, 1830–1848* (London, 1988), pp. 55–83; Bertrand Goujon, *Monarchies post-révolutionnaires* (Paris, 2012), pp. 239–56.

these legislative changes because they did not significantly alter the level of tariffs.[10] But the advent of a politically neutral commercial administration and the abolition of privileges on the storage of goods addressed major liberal concerns under the Restoration. The chapter then examines the dismay of some advocates of commercial liberty, the Bordelais merchants, who gained nothing in return for the loss of their commercial privileges. Their disappointment led them to redefine commercial liberty as consisting primarily in the reduction of tariffs and accuse the liberal 1830 Revolution of being only half-completed. The chapter also points to the role of interactions with Britain in these debates about the limits of commercial liberty in France. As part of an effort to obtain an agreement on mutual tariffs reductions between Britain and France, John Bowring, an agent of the British Board of Trade, toured the French provinces in order to dispel anti-British feelings. His efforts acted as a catalyst for the emergence of radical demands for free trade. Liberal convergence with Britain was the product not only of intellectual admiration for the British model but also of an original and practical experiment in the transnational dissemination of ideas.

I

The effervescence of liberal ideas about trade in the aftermath of the 1830 Revolution reflected a certain sensibility as much as the material interests of some branches of industry. *Liberté* was the watchword of the 1830 Revolution. Three-quarters of the insurgents who applied for the 'medal of July', a reward for those who distinguished themselves on the barricades, said that they fought 'for liberty'.[11] Liberty also 'guided the people' in Eugène Delacroix's well-known painting about the success of the Parisian insurrection (1831). Romanticism, then at its height in French literary and artistic life, best captured this liberal mood – in 1828, Victor Hugo defined it as 'liberalism in literature'.[12] The liberty celebrated by the Romantics was not confined to abstract literary or constitutional ideas. Looking back on the heyday of the 'Romantic school', Gustave Flaubert contended in 1852 that it 'only demanded, as one would now put it, *le libre-échange*'. Conversely, in his *National System of Political Economy*

[10] An exception is Barrie M. Ratcliffe, 'The Tariff Reform Campaign in France, 1831–1836', *Journal of European Economic History*, 7 (1) (1978): 61–138.

[11] Edgar L. Newman, 'What the Crowd Wanted in the French Revolution of 1830', in John Merriman (ed.), *1830 in France* (New York, 1975), pp. 17–40.

[12] Victor Hugo, *Œuvres complètes*, 18 vols. (Paris, 1967–71), vol. III.2, p. 922.

(1841), the protectionist Friedrich List argued that 'sentimentality and Romanticism played … no little part' in the diffusion of free-trade ideas.[13]

Not only Germaine de Staël, Benjamin Constant and Alphonse de Lamartine, as seen in previous chapters, but also other figureheads of French Romanticism such as Honoré de Balzac, Stendhal and Jules Michelet expressed their preference for the free circulation of commodities and the abolition of customs controls.[14] A similar congruence of economic opinions and artistic tastes can be observed among advocates of free trade, down to local publicists in Bordeaux and Burgundy. At the same time as Fonfrède combated the *industrialisme* of Comte, Dunoyer and Dupin, he fought 'the partisans of classicism' in the columns of *L'Indicateur* and rejoiced that '[his] Romantic doctrine appealed even to common people' in Bordeaux. The catalogue of Foisset's library, with numerous volumes by Byron, Goethe and Schiller as well as French Romantics, also leaves little doubt of the magistrate's literary tastes.[15] Tellingly, major adversaries of free trade such as Saint-Chamans or Ferrier were hostile to the flouting of classical rules in literature.[16] Only a few months after expressing his support for protection against foreign competition, Adolphe Thiers, a rising star of the July Monarchy's politics, also defended the principles of classicism when he was admitted as a member of the Académie Française in 1834.[17]

In the wake of the 1830 Revolution, liberal exasperation with customs controls also made inroads in less elevated genres of literature. For example, it was prominent in the *Opinions de Monsieur Christophe* (1830–4), a series of pamphlets by Jacques Boucher de Perthes, a customs director at Abbeville better known for his contributions to the beginnings of palaeontology, which took aim at the encroachments of personal freedom by the state bureaucracy. The protagonist, Monsieur Christophe, was

[13] Gustave Flaubert to Louise Colet, 9 December 1852, in Gustave Flaubert, *Correspondance*, ed. Jean Bruneau, 4 vols. (Paris, 1991–7), vol. II, p. 202; Friedrich List, *Das nationale System der politischen Ökonomie* (Baden-Baden, 2008), p. 57.

[14] Honoré de Balzac, *Le Médecin de campagne*, first published in 1833, in *La Comédie humaine*, ed. Pierre-Georges Castex, 11 vols. (Paris, 1978), vol. IX, p. 429, and *Les Employés*, first published in 1844, in *La Comédie humaine*, vol. VII, p. 916; Stendhal, *Mémoires d'un touriste*, ed. Victor Del Litto, 3 vols. (Paris, 1981), vol. I, pp. 31–2, 59; Jules Michelet, *Voyage en Angleterre*, ed. Jean-François Durand (Arles, 2005), pp. 36–7 and Michelet, *Le Peuple*, pp. 68, 121.

[15] Fonfrède to Campan, 31 July 1827, BMB, MS 1089, fol. 49; see also the manuscript of an unpublished novel by Fonfrède, entitled 'Louise; ou, De l'amour au dix-neuvième siècle', BMB, MS 1085. On Foisset's books, see catalogue, ADCO, 34J 101.

[16] Auguste de Saint-Chamans, *L'Anti-romantique* (Paris, 1816); Ferrier, *Du système maritime*, p. 9.

[17] Adolphe Thiers, *Discours prononcé par M. Thiers, le jour de sa réception à l'Académie française* (Paris, 1834), pp. 1–2.

a winegrower, no doubt an allusion to the protests of the wine industry at the end of the Restoration, and the first pamphlet exposed Christophe's views on 'prohibitions and the liberty of commerce'. Responding to a cynical 'minister' who defended the prohibitive system, Christophe invoked the wisdom imparted upon him by his cousin, who was 'well versed in political economy', and concluded: 'Liberty essentially consists in the freedom of work and industry; all the others, including the freedom of expression or the press, are nothing without that one.' The pamphlet sought to render the principles of political economy through simple maxims, for instance, 'Frenchmen work, because Englishmen work', in order to stress the reciprocal nature of international trade. Above all, it denounced customs vexations as an aberration in modern liberal societies, comparing the harsh treatment of travellers in customs houses to that of Christian captives by 'Algerian privateers'. In the same way as the recent capture of Algiers by French forces in July 1830, the parallel implied, commercial reform would contribute to the progress of civilization.[18]

Not only winegrowers, but also smugglers, who were vilified as enemies of the state under the Restoration, were now celebrated as heroes of liberty. For instance, Pierre-Jean de Béranger, the immensely popular composer of liberal folk songs, wrote 'Les Contrebandiers' in 1833. 'Woe, woe to the [customs] clerks', Béranger had smugglers say, for 'the people support us / the people are our friend'. Béranger's smugglers claimed that they held the 'balance of trade' in their hands and shared out 'abundance' in accordance with the will of Providence. Their rifles defended 'liberty', and smuggling thwarted the arbitrary borders traced by kings, whose treaties often attempted to transform 'one people' into 'two enemy peoples': 'No; thanks to our efforts / This people will not in vain / Spin the same wool / Smile at the same wine.'[19] The free circulation of commodities, Béranger suggested, undermined the reactionary order of Vienna, an object of universal detestation among French liberals in the early 1830s.

In contrast to winegrowers or smugglers, customs officers became an object of mockery in the liberal literature. In a work attacking 'administrative *mœurs*', Boucher de Perthes contended that 'the mob' saw every customs officer as 'a rat, a stone marten, a fox or a wolf' and thought it 'always a good deed to throw a stone at him'. Those interested in politics

[18] Jacques Boucher de Perthes, *Opinion de M. Christophe sur les prohibitions et la liberté du commerce*, 2nd edn (Paris, 1831), pp. 12–13, 26, 63, 74–6; in total, 1,500 copies were printed of the work's two editions, see impressions 4619 (12 October 1830), AN, F18*II 20 and 1632 (7 June 1831), AN, F18*II 21.

[19] Pierre-Jean de Béranger, *Chansons nouvelles et dernières* (Paris, 1833), pp. 93–9.

considered the customs officer as 'the satellite of a tyrant or his minister', traders as 'the enemy of shopkeeping and liberty', elegant female travellers as 'a vampire, a monster who creases dresses and bonnets' and sea captains as 'a reef making the approach [to the shore] difficult'.[20] Liberal newspapers frequently gave vent to such anti-customs feelings. The Lyon workers' daily, *L'Écho de la Fabrique*, argued that 'if you wish to introduce, for your personal use, a needle, a corkscrew, twenty cigars, you are searched, molested, insulted and robbed, especially if you have the misfortune of wearing poor or modest clothes'.[21] An attack on 'mœurs douanières' in a Parisian daily castigated the 'fiscal executions' carried out by the 'border tyrants'. After bodies have been searched in a humiliating fashion, it was the turn of the luggage: 'Bundles, boxes, suitcases, all sorts of packages, everything is carelessly hurled off the top of coaches, often in the rain or in the open air; the covers are lifted off with a hammer … It is the very image of destruction.'[22] Few things were more at odds with the Romantic sensibility than customs controls, or, as Boucher de Perthes wrote of the customs declaration, 'Nothing resembles less a declaration of love.'[23]

This liberal and Romantic sensibility contributed to high expectations of commercial reform in the aftermath of the 1830 Revolution. In Bordeaux, as early as August 1830, *L'Indicateur* predicted that 'our entire political economy will be elevated to the same status as our institutions, and commercial liberty will not remain behind civil and religious liberties'.[24] When the new king, Louis-Philippe, visited eastern France in the summer of 1831, he was presented with several petitions in favour of the relaxation of customs controls. Even the Mulhouse cotton manufacturers in Alsace, who later became staunch supporters of protection against British competition, stated, 'Commerce only lives by liberty and sees every hindrance as a deadly threat'.[25] In response to the nationwide anti-customs clamour, the new regime carried out a substantial reform of commercial administration and legislation between 1830 and 1832. These changes to France's commercial system have often been overlooked because they did not affect much the level of protection against foreign competition, which is today considered as the essence of protectionism. But, as seen in the

[20] Jacques Boucher de Perthes, *Petit Glossaire; traduction de quelques mots financiers; esquisses de mœurs administratives*, 2 vols. (Paris, 1835), vol. 1, pp. 228–9.

[21] *L'Écho de la Fabrique*, 6 May 1832.

[22] 'Mœurs douanières fort exactes', *Le Temps*, 12 September 1834.

[23] Boucher de Perthes, *Petit Glossaire*, vol. 1, p. 206. [24] *L'Indicateur*, 19 August 1830.

[25] Memorandum by the Mulhouse Chamber of Commerce, 22 June 1831, Mulhouse, Centre Rhénan d'Archives et de Recherches Economiques (hereafter CERARE), Archives de la Chambre de Commerce de Mulhouse (hereafter ACCM), p. 561.

previous chapters, commercial liberty under the Restoration had a broader meaning than the reduction of tariffs.

First, the new regime sought to professionalize and depoliticize the administrative apparatus of commercial policy. Some changes were symbolic, such as the 'Douanes royales' becoming the 'Douanes nationales', or the *fleur-de-lys* on the uniforms and helmets of customs officers being replaced by the Gallic cock. Others were more substantial, with a sharp reduction in the powers of patronage and command of the customs director, a position rendered infamous by the extraordinary influence of Saint-Cricq and his *ultra* successors in the 1820s. The director appointed in January 1831, Théodore Gréterin, was a professional customs officer, who, despite two regime changes, retained his position until 1860. In customs houses, controls also became less overtly political. Imported books, for instance, continued to be inspected, but to detect the infringement of copyrights rather than to prevent the introduction of subversive ideas.[26] The institutions in charge of customs legislation were also overhauled in 1831. In Paris, a ministry of commerce, assisted by a conseil supérieur de commerce predominantly made up of experts and civil servants, was established.[27] In the provinces, members of the chambers of commerce were no longer appointed by prefects but elected by local manufacturers and merchants.[28]

Second, the *Résistance* government led by Casimir Perier from March 1831 until October 1832 pushed through substantial changes in the customs legislation. Import duties on several raw materials, including silks and mahogany, and export duties on a wide range of products, including wines and machinery, were reduced.[29] The Perier government also relaxed restrictions on the re-exportation of foreign goods and the importation of grain. A first law on re-exports, which extended the range of goods that could be re-exported and simplified customs procedures, was adopted by deputies almost unanimously (276 to 5), amid a concert of praise for the virtues of commercial liberty.[30] A second law, preceded by an official inquiry of the Conseil Supérieur de Commerce on warehouses, abolished the privileges of seaports for the storage of foreign goods.[31] The Minister of Commerce, the Comte d'Argout, hailed the measure as

[26] Clinquart, *L'Administration des douanes sous la restauration*, pp. 111–21, 256–7; Bordas, *Les Directeurs généraux des douanes*, pp. 503–61.

[27] 'Note sur l'histoire et les attributions du ministère de l'agriculture et du commerce', AN, F12 2491/A.

[28] Lemercier, *Un si discret pouvoir*, p. 32.

[29] AP, vol. LXXII, pp. 582–9 (17 December 1831).

[30] AP, vol. LXXII, p. 327 (8 December 1831).

[31] Ministère du Commerce, *Enquête relative à l'établissement demandé d'entrepôts de douanes* (Paris, 1831).

'an act of distributive justice', while the *rapporteur* of the law proposal at the Chamber of Deputies, the Parisian merchant Auguste Ganneron, described it as the implementation of 'the principles of liberty and equality that triumphed in July [1830]'. Representatives of the seaports rejected this isonomic interpretation of liberalism. Antoine Jay, a deputy for the Gironde, echoed Fonfrède's earlier protests against proposals to create a warehouse in Paris. Stressing the dangers of 'universal centralization' and of the proliferation of 'luxury' in the capital, Jay attributed the project to the influence of the 'economists', who treated liberty as a 'fact' when it should be considered as a 'sentiment'. Jay concluded with a rhetorical question: 'Is this really liberalism?' A robust majority of deputies (190 to 76) apparently thought so and adopted the law.[32]

In the spring of 1832, the replacement of the prohibition on grain imports by a sliding scale of duties – inspired by the sliding scale introduced in Britain in 1828 – marked the apex, but also the limits, of commercial reforms in the aftermath of the 1830 Revolution. The *rapporteur* of the law proposal, Charles Dupin, described the new legislation as worthy of Adam Smith and Turgot, because it dispelled 'the selfish delusion that a people's gain [drew] on another people's loss'. Yet Dupin and several other deputies introduced several technical modifications to the law proposal that increased the effective level of protection against grain imports. The July Monarchy, Dupin argued, ought to protect the many farmers, most of them grain producers, who owed their property to the 1789 Revolution, or else the July Revolution 'would be for small proprietors and for peasants not the revolution, but the counter-revolution of 1830'. To justify the increase in the level of protection, deputies also pointed to the different distribution of land property in England and France. In England, one deputy argued, 'two to three thousand families' owned the land between them, making the aristocracy the main beneficiary of agricultural protection. In France, by contrast, property of the land was divided between 'millions' of *paysans*, and protection served to defend the country's democratic social constitution.[33] These progressive, egalitarian justifications of protection foreshadowed a key theme of later protectionist propaganda against free trade.

The commercial reforms of 1830–2 closely resembled and matched the significance of the measures of liberalization adopted by Britain in the mid 1820s. Their economic impact was far from negligible. In a context

[32] AP, vol. LXXI, p. 500 (11 November 1831); vol. LXXII, p. 226 (3 December 1831) and pp. 546–8 (13 December 1831); vol. LXXIII, p. 247 (28 December 1831).

[33] AP, vol. LXXVI, pp. 31–66 (5 March 1832) and pp. 695–9 (23 March 1832).

of improved global economic conditions, they facilitated a 40 per cent increase in French exports and, testifying to the significance of the new legislation on transit and warehouses, a trebling of French re-exports between 1830 and 1836.[34] Their political impact was also appreciable. Together with the quelling of radical agitation, they consolidated the remarkable popularity of the Perier ministry among the well-to-do electorate. Rarely had France seemed closer to emulate the common liberal perception of the British model as a combination of representative institutions, political stability and economic efficiency.

II

The opening of commercial negotiations with Britain in November 1831 further illustrated the aspiration to convergence with the British model. The negotiations were a French initiative, emanating from two old Anglophiles, the Baron Louis, Minister of Finances, and Talleyrand, France's ambassador in London since the July Revolution. Instead of preparing a commercial treaty, an instrument condemned by economists as a tool of mercantile diplomacy, the joint commission set up in Paris was to propose tariff reductions in both countries. The leading French negotiators were the Baron Fréville, an administrator under Napoleon recently elevated to the peerage, and Tanneguy Duchâtel, the author of the winegrowers' *Mémoire* of 1829 against the prohibitive system. Their British counterparts were the diplomat George Villiers (later Lord Clarendon) and the merchant and publicist John Bowring.[35] These negotiations not only spurred French legislators into considering further relaxation of trade regulations but also furnished Bowring with an excuse for proselytizing a radical brand of free trade in the French provinces. Bowring's endeavours show that the influence of the British liberal model in 1830s France was direct as well as indirect, resulting from very practical efforts at disseminating liberal ideas as much as intellectual admiration for Britain's political and economic achievements.

Bowring was a notable figure in the global dissemination of Benthamite utilitarianism.[36] His energy, his command of a dozen European languages

[34] Ministère du Commerce, *Statistique de la France*, vol. VII, pp. 8–12.

[35] Guyot, *La Première Entente cordiale*, pp. 105–15; Lucy Brown, *The Board of Trade and the Free-Trade Movement, 1830–1842* (London, 1958), pp. 118–27; Barrie M. Ratcliffe, 'Great Britain and Tariff Reform in France, 1831–1836', in William H. Chaloner and Barrie M. Ratcliffe (eds.), *Trade and Transport: Essays in Economic History in Honour of T. S. William* (Manchester, 1977), pp. 98–135.

[36] David Armitage, 'Globalizing Jeremy Bentham', *History of Political Thought*, 32 (1) (2011): 63–82; Todd, 'John Bowring'.

and the web of contacts he had woven as a merchant in post-Napoleonic Europe – especially in Spain and France – led Bentham to appoint him as his personal secretary in 1820 and as the editor of the *Westminster Review* in 1824. Bowring enjoyed particularly strong ties with French liberals under the Restoration, as a result of which he was expelled and banned from re-entering French territory in 1822. In a pamphlet on the circumstances of his expulsion, Bowring declared himself to be in 'complete communion of thought and feeling … with the *Liberals* of France'.[37] In August 1830, he led a delegation of British radicals who had come to congratulate the Parisian people on the overthrow of Bourbon despotism. Bowring was also an early and fervent advocate of free trade, who edited, and provided a great deal of material for, Bentham's most strident text on the damages caused by restrictions on international trade.[38] Bowring was therefore well suited to the task of persuading France's new regime of embracing trade liberalization. Having been ruined by speculations in Latin American stocks and bonds in the late 1820s, he was also keen to obtain public employment and he owed his 1831 appointment as Trade Commissioner in Paris to Charles Poulett Thomson, Vice-President of the Board of Trade and an admirer of Bentham.

It is difficult to ascertain the chief motives of Bowring's spirited efforts to disseminate liberal ideas about trade across French society. The tone of his correspondence leaves little doubt as to the sincerity of his belief in the virtues of free trade. 'I scarcely ever get to bed till 3 in the morning', he wrote to Thomson, 'and never go to any place of amusement – or to any place but to advance over objects to which I am bound by flesh-blood-brains and every thought and feeling.' Villiers and he, Bowring recalled to his fellow commissioner, had 'sworn to each other upon the altar that the Baal of monopoly [in France] should be overthrown by these blessed hands of ours – and overthrown he *shall* be'.[39] Yet Bowring was also a mercenary. He repeatedly complained about the low level of his remuneration, threatening 'to throw up the matter in disgust' if his salary was not raised.[40] He eventually consented to stay in France on lavish terms (a £500 annual salary, a living allowance of £3, 3s. per day,

[37] John Bowring, *Details of the Arrest, Imprisonment and Liberation of an Englishman by the Bourbon Government of France* (London, 1823), pp. 2–3.

[38] Jeremy Bentham, *Observations on the Restrictive and Prohibitory Commercial System*, ed. John Bowring (London, 1821).

[39] Bowring to Thomson, 10 January 1833, Oxford, Bodleian Library (hereafter BODL), Clarendon Papers (hereafter MS Clar.) dep. c. 546/1/2, fols. 14–15; Bowring to Villiers, 7 April 1833, BODL, MS Clar., dep. c. 544, fols. 116–17.

[40] Bowring to Thomson, 27 February 1832, BODL, MS Clar., dep. c. 546/1/1, fols. 61–2.

a travel allowance of 2s. per mile and the payment of all his expenses), and he received another £750 for two reports on Franco-British commercial relations.[41] Benjamin Disraeli later denounced the 'ludicrously preposterous' level of Bowring's remuneration for his work of propaganda.[42] Moreover, Bowring was keenly aware that he was paid for 'opening the continental markets to English industry'.[43]

Such a combination of cosmopolitan ideals and zeal to promote British interests made Bowring a living example of what later historians have described as 'free trade imperialism'.[44] A quarter of a century later, still looking to open new markets for British exports as Plenipotentiary in the Far East, Bowring was responsible for the outbreak of the Second Opium War (1856–60) with China. In July Monarchy France, Bowring resorted to more peaceful means to propagate free trade. His tactics closely mirrored the strategy for trade liberalization described in the text of Bentham that Bowring had edited earlier. This pamphlet stressed the need to constitute 'counter-efficient influences' or new lobbies representing export-oriented industries and consumers in order to cancel the 'secret or corrupt influence' of the 'sinister interests' of import-competing industries.[45] Bowring therefore focused his efforts on regions involved in the production of silk textiles and wines, France's two main export industries.

Bowring and Villiers initially expressed great confidence in the negotiations' outcome. They found the 'faith' in free trade of their main French counterpart, Duchâtel, 'sound and strong'. They rejoiced at the 'triumphant' passage of the law on warehouses, which they viewed as 'a step towards the right road'. Villiers thought French officials were on the whole favourable to the reduction of protection: they 'fully admit the inefficiency of prohibitions – their cost to the public and their damage to the Treasury – they are forced to act cautiously with interests w[hi]ch have been created by the laws but they will steadily move towards a better system'.[46] Yet Bowring and Villiers soon became frustrated with the slow

[41] Bundles '1832', '1833' and '1834', Kew, The National Archives (hereafter TNA), T 1/4001; the reports were John Bowring and George Villiers, *First Report on the Commercial Relations between France and Great Britain* (London, 1834) and John Bowring, *Second Report on the Commercial Relations between France and Great Britain* (London, 1835).

[42] Parliament, *Hansard's Parliamentary Debates*, 3rd series, 156 vols. (London, 1830–91), vol. LV, cols. 700–14 (1840).

[43] Bowring to Thomson, 5 July 1833, BODL, MS Clar., dep. c. 546/1/2, fol. 118.

[44] John Gallagher and Ronald Robinson, 'The Imperialism of Free Trade', *Economic History Review*, new series, 6 (1) (1953): 1–15.

[45] Bentham, *Observations*, pp. 28–35.

[46] Bowring to Thomson, 18 December 1831, and Villiers to Thomson, 30 December 1831 and 20 January 1832, BODL, MS Clar., dep. c. 546/1/1, fols. 7, 17, 33.

pace of negotiations and what they perceived as the pusillanimity of the French government. In March 1832, the Conseil Supérieur de Commerce rejected the repeal, proposed by the joint commission, of the prohibition on imports of fine cotton twists. According to Bowring, opposition to trade liberalization was engineered by Saint-Cricq, a member of the Conseil Supérieur, where he 'took the part of the blasphemer'. The prospect of a 'change of system' made the architect of the prohibitive system 'furious', and he 'menaced the government with the turning out of I do not know how many provinces'.[47] Perier assured the British negotiators that he would see the joint commission's recommendations through, promising 'every time [that the Premier saw them] *qu'il s'en est occupé, qu'il s'en occupe, qu'il s'en occupera*'. Yet he seemed more adept at 'declining the verb' than at 'doing the thing'.[48]

As officials cited the hostility of the public to freer commercial intercourse with Britain as the main obstacle to reform, Bowring offered to tour the French provinces and enlighten opinion. The French government consented and offered him letters of recommendation to the prefects of the departments he was planning to visit. Bowring's tours might be construed as an attempt to transpose across the Channel the methods of 'irradiation, suscitation and permeation' employed by Benthamites to propagate their ideas in Britain.[49] Bowring recapitulated his strategy in later reports to Lord Auckland, the President of the Board of Trade. In each town he visited, Bowring sought 'to gather up the elements and form a nucleus [of convinced free-traders] there'; he then kept up a 'tremendous correspondence … to direct (as it were) all the elements over France to a common end': 'the overthrow of the monopolists'. These nuclei in turn propagated liberal ideas about trade, until public opinion was transformed: 'opinion – enlightened opinion – is the great instrument for carrying *our* object – without this we should have made no progress here – with it we shall carry everything'.[50]

In April and May 1832, Bowring galvanized support for commercial liberalization in Lyon, the capital of France's silk industry, and the south-east. At the Lyon prefecture, Bowring 'harangued' with success 'all

[47] Bowring to Thomson, 19 March and 29–30 March 1832, BODL, MS Clar., dep. c. 546/1/1, fols. 77, 89.
[48] Villiers to Thomson, 2 April 1832, BODL, MS Clar., dep. c. 546/1/1, fol. 100.
[49] Samuel E. Finer, 'The Transmission of Benthamite Ideas, 1820–50', in Gillian Sutherland (ed.), *Studies in the Growth of Nineteenth-Century Government* (London, 1972), pp. 11–32.
[50] Bowring to Auckland, 27 February, 10 March and 13 March 1834, London, British Library (hereafter BL), Auckland Papers (hereafter AUP), Add MS 34460, fols. 17–18, 42, 48.

the notables du commerce' to persuade them 'that the whole commercial system respecting England *must* be changed'. He met with 'all classes of persons – workmen – masters – chefs d'atelier – fabricants – bankers – and all the authorities … – the men of the movement and the men of the resistance'. 'Of success I do not doubt', Bowring commented on his own efforts, 'and engaged in this great work I often feel that I speak with the tongue of an angel.' He often encountered 'jealousy and distrust at first' but combated such feelings with assurances that the British government no longer wished to weaken French commerce or sought 'to infuse into [his interlocutors] a *wholesome uneasiness*' by suggesting that Britain may revert to higher barriers on imports of silk textiles unless France liberalized its own tariff. He also ensured, 'by a small expenditure', that local newspapers such as the workers' daily, *L'Écho de la Fabrique*, would support free trade. Bowring met with equal success in Grenoble, Saint-Etienne and Avignon. He stayed only briefly in Marseille before returning to London to see the ailing Bentham, who died on 6 June 1832. Bowring nonetheless judged his tour a success. He had ascertained that 'St Cricq [was] an object of great detestation in the south' and asserted to Thomson: 'Be assured this monstrous system of prohibition is tottering – and we have given it a push in happy hour.'[51]

Petitions from the Lyon Chamber of Commerce elicited by Bowring helped the government abolish the prohibition on the exportation of raw silks and several other minor restrictions in June 1832. A law proposal tabled in December 1832 confirmed the measures and recommended the repeal of several other prohibitions, including the ban on imports of cotton twists. In defence of the proposed legislation, Argout expressed the government's desire to rid France's commercial system of all its 'useless, vexatious, exorbitant' elements, with a view to establish a 'gradual liberty' of commerce. While rejecting the 'absolutism' of all the 'schools' of political economy, Argout noted that even François Ferrier recognized in principle 'the general advantages of the liberty of commerce' and paid homage to Say, who had died a few weeks earlier.[52] Yet Bowring and Villiers judged the proposed changes timid. They were also dismayed, in January 1833, by the appointments of Saint-Cricq as *rapporteur* of the proposed law and Adolphe Thiers, 'a prohibitionist as far as he has understanding of the matter', as Minister of Commerce in replacement of

[51] Bowring to Thomson, 16 April, 24 April and 5 May 1832, BODL, MS Clar., dep. c. 546/1/1, fols. 105, 112–13, 122–3.

[52] AP, vol. LXXXVIII, pp. 58–61 (3 December 1832).

Argout. To counterbalance Saint-Cricq's influence, the British negotiators redoubled their lobbying efforts. Bowring secured articles in favour of free trade in most radical and liberal newspapers. Apart from the royalist and pro-government news-sheets, Bowring reported, 'there is not one influential newspaper here which will not support us'.[53]

Despite the support of a great deal of the Parisian press and several notable political figures, including King Louis-Philippe and Victor de Broglie, the Anglophile son-in-law of Madame de Staël and Minister of Foreign Affairs, Bowring and Villiers remained worried by the influence of Saint-Cricq, who spoke as if 'a whole host of base grovelling creatures would obey his word of command'. Moreover, they did not trust French politicians. Except Broglie, Bowring contended, French ministers were 'Toads', and he found 'the bigotry and blind ignorance and wretched selfishness of the [parliamentary] Chambers' equally frustrating. He and Villiers felt as if they were 'keeping watch over the *condamnés des bagnes*' (convicts), an image that recalls Bentham's project of Panopticon to observe and encourage the moral improvement of convicts.[54] What began as a commercial negotiation was becoming an original transnational utilitarian experiment in the dissemination of economic ideas and redressing of debased political *mœurs*.

III

In order to overcome the reformist reluctance of July Monarchy politicians, the British negotiators set out to stir up agitation in favour of free trade in Bordeaux and other winegrowing regions. Soon after their arrival in France, Villiers already saw 'the wine question' as 'the leaven for the overthrow of the obnoxious interests', for 'such a community as the wine growers stunning the government with their miseries distinctly deduced from the law, will in the end make the devil himself strike his flag'.[55] In 1833, Bowring requested Thomson's permission to go on a new tour in the south-west, so that 'by and by we shall have Lyon and Bordeaux echoing each others' voices loudly enough to produce some vibration in Paris'. The nullification crisis, which saw cotton-exporting South Carolina use the threat of secession to obtain substantial reductions in the American

[53] Bowring to Thomson, 4 January, 14 January and 18 February 1833, BODL, MS Clar., dep. c. 546/1/2, fols. 1, 16, 79.

[54] Bowring to Thomson, 8, 11 and 22 February 1833, BODL, MS Clar., dep. c. 546/1/2, fols. 56, 64–5, 87–8.

[55] Villiers to Thomson, 23 December 1831, BODL, MS Clar., dep. c. 546/1/1, fols. 10–11.

Union's tariff between 1828 and 1833, served as a model of what the new propaganda tour should achieve. Bowring wanted to 'make a Carolina on the other side of the Loire', while Thomson counted on Bowring's 'talents for agitation' to 'set Guienne [the name of Bordeaux's province under the Old Regime] into a South Carolina fire'.[56]

Bowring's second tour was well timed because by the spring of 1833 the Bordelais merchants and winegrowers were thoroughly disillusioned by the results of commercial reform. Moreover, local politics were in flux and therefore malleable. The *Mouvement* narrowly lost the city to the *Résistance* at the municipal elections in November 1831. In subsequent years, Bordelais liberalism took on an increasingly conservative hue, and only with regard to international trade would the Gironde liberals maintain radical views.[57] The personal evolution of Fonfrède, the leader of the Bordelais liberal party under the Restoration, closely mirrored and perhaps helped to shape this nascent disjunction between political and commercial liberalism. In the autumn of 1830, he left the pro-*Mouvement* newspaper *L'Indicateur* for the moderate *Mémorial Bordelais*. In 1831, Fonfrède still compared himself to 'the remains of Patroclus, tugged by the two parties, the *Résistance* and the *Mouvement*'. It was the latter's democratic tendencies that made him tilt increasingly rightwards: 'Men gathered into masses are so *stupid*! Fie, no republic!'[58] In reality, Fonfrède did not renounce his republican longing for a government by a virtuous citizenry, but he feared that further lowering the franchise would encourage demagogic politics. His suspicion of egalitarianism cannot be reduced to a reflection of his personal interest, since it was his low tax returns, inferior to the eligibility threshold, that prevented him from becoming deputy for the suburbs of Bordeaux in the summer of 1831.[59]

The conservative drift of Bordelais liberalism is intriguing because the commercial reforms carried out by the Résistance government were a source of considerable frustration among the local *notables*. As in Nantes and Le Havre, merchants in Bordeaux protested against the creation of new warehouses in Paris and other inland cities. But while the Breton and Normand merchants clung to their commercial privileges stridently, their Gironde counterparts adopted a more sophisticated strategy, suggesting

[56] Bowring to Thomson, 5 January, 10 January and 11 February 1833, BODL, MS Clar., dep. c. 546/1/2, fols. 3, 14, 67; Thomson to Villiers, 5 March 1833, BODL, MS Clar., dep. c. 545, fol. 60.

[57] André-Jean Tudesq, 'Les Débuts de la monarchie de juillet', in Louis Desgraves and Georges Dupeux (eds.), *Bordeaux au XIXe siècle* (Bordeaux, 1969), pp. 61–82.

[58] Fonfrède to Campan, 3 July 1831, BMB, MS 1087, fol. 65.

[59] Hémardinquer, 'Henri Fonfrède', p. 452.

that they might consent to the new legislation on warehouses in return for a reduction of protection on imports. Drawing on memories of the Vendée royalist insurrection, the Nantes Chamber of Commerce implausibly contended that new warehouses might reignite 'civil war' in the royalist West.[60] By contrast, the Bordeaux chamber turned down a request from the Nantais merchants that they issue their own pamphlet in defence of the seaports.[61] Instead, in a petition to the Chamber of Deputies, the Bordelais merchants declared themselves willing to accept the 'injustice' of the new warehouses if 'the horizon of maritime trade was widened' thanks to 'a reduction of tariffs'.[62]

Fonfrède probably wrote or at least inspired the petition. In January 1832, he sought to further channel Bordelais commercial discontent into demands for tariff reduction in a new series of articles in *Le Mémorial*. The articles still denounced the abolition of the seaports' privileges on behalf of 'liberty' and 'equality' as hypocritical, since Paris and the north benefited from the more substantial advantage of high tariffs. Fonfrède also launched a new attack on industrialism, which he now unambiguously identified with the growth of manufacturing. While his earlier articles were concerned with the amoral materialism of the industrialists, this series was more specifically preoccupied with the social consequences of industrialization. Echoing Jean-Charles Simonde de Sismondi, he held the multiplication of large manufactures as responsible for crises of overproduction. Above all, he lamented the emergence of a new 'industrial feudality' that was 'not worth much more than landed feudality'. In his opinion, the rise of modern manufactures was eliminating small-scale independent producers, dividing society between 'a small number of large capitalists' who possessed most riches on the one hand and 'vast masses … of workers, without property and without any hope ever to acquire property, reduced … to resort to one of the following three means: *begging*, *revolting*, or *starving*' on the other.[63]

Fonfrède's critique of industrialization resembled the contemporary analysis of the first socialist thinkers. But, unlike the latter, Fonfrède did

[60] Petition of the Nantes Chamber of Commerce to King Louis-Philippe, 18 November 1831, AN, F12 2594. See also Chambre de Commerce de Nantes, *Un dernier mot sur les entrepôts intérieurs* (Nantes, 1831); [Anon.], *Pétition du commerce de Nantes à MM. les membres de la chambre des députés* (Nantes, 1831); and [Anon.], *Pétition du commerce du Havre à la chambre des députés contre l'établissement projeté des entrepôts intérieurs* (Le Havre, 1831).

[61] Bordeaux Chamber of Commerce to Nantes Chamber of Commerce, 27 August 1831, ADG, 02/081/278, register 1828–32, fol. 238.

[62] Petition from the Bordeaux Chamber of Commerce to the Minister of Commerce, 21 November 1831, AN, F12 2594.

[63] 'De l'entrepôt de Paris', 1st, 2nd, 3rd and 4th articles, *Le Mémorial Bordelais*, 7, 8, 10 and 12 January 1832.

not wish to overthrow the existing political and social order. Rather, he believed that the solution to the industrialist perversion of liberty lay in an absolute form of commercial liberty. A relaxation of restrictions on imports, especially manufactured imports, would halt or reverse the progress of industrialization and revive small-scale production: 'the only prop and stay that might prevent a general collapse and catastrophic events ... is the gradual adoption of commercial liberty and equality'.[64] Such a conception of free trade remained republican in the sense that it sought to preserve a body of economically independent citizens as a bulwark against both the nascent capitalist oligarchy and unruly proletariat. It differed sharply from the Benthamite utilitarian conception of free trade or the later messianic discourse upheld by Richard Cobden and other manufacturers who led the Anti-Corn Law League in the 1840s. Fonfrède's republicanism also stood at odds with the democratic preoccupations of most French republicans, who viewed the new urban proletariat as potential allies and favoured an extension of the franchise.

In the winter of 1833, a failed attempt to reform the commercial regime of sugar imports and re-exports further intensified Bordelais frustration. The legislation inherited from the Restoration, consisting in high duties on French colonial sugar, a prohibitive *surtaxe* on foreign sugar and bounties for the re-exportation of colonial sugar, was an unpopular symbol of the Bourbon regime's connivance with colonial planters. In 1832, a petition drafted by Fonfrède demanded the suppression of the *surtaxe* and the adoption of low and uniform duties on all sugar imports. 'We must increase our relations with the general production of the universe' the petition stated, 'and seek to obtain, thanks to this salutary exchange, vast outlets for our industrial and agricultural products, which our colonies are utterly unable to provide'.[65] The government was willing to reduce protection for colonial planters but favoured an increase in duties on colonial sugar in order to increase fiscal revenue. Rejecting the proposal, deputies instead reduced the *surtaxe*, but only by one-fifth, and abolished the bounty on re-exports of French colonial sugar.[66] The slight reduction in the tariff fell short of Bordelais hopes of a change of system, while the repeal of the bounty harmed the interests of Bordelais sugar refiners as well as colonial planters.

64 'De l'entrepôt de Paris', 5th article, *Le Mémorial*, 15 January 1832.

65 [Henri Fonfrède], *Observations à l'appui des réclamations du commerce de Bordeaux sur le privilège colonial et sur la surtaxe des sucres étrangers* (Bordeaux, 1832); Fonfrède described himself as the author of the pamphlet in *Le Mémorial*, 25 January 1833.

66 AP, vol. LXXVIII, pp. 349–60 (21 December 1832); vol. LXXX, pp. 555–65 (4 March 1833); vol. LXXXIII, p. 58 (23 April 1833).

Once again, Bordeaux lost a commercial advantage without obtaining a substantial compensation. Fonfrède vented the Bordelais fury in a new series of articles. The suppression of the *surtaxe*, he contended, offered 'an opportunity to abandon the prohibitive system, thanks to a simple and fecund experiment', for 'the radical, the fundamental, the unique vice of our present situation [was] the high level of tariffs'.[67] Fonfrède entreated his readers not to let themselves be deceived by the prohibitive system's new name: 'Prohibition is in itself so shameful and harmful that its very own partisans blush and seek to disguise it under the name of protective system.' In his opinion, whether imports were banned or rendered impossible by high tariffs amounted to the same policy: 'When the commerce of exchange is dead, what is the point of still attacking it? It would be like stabbing a dead man.'[68]

Bowring arrived in Bordeaux a few weeks later and stayed there for a month. Local discontent with the stalling of commercial reform ensured that he was well received. Soon after his arrival, he reported to Villiers that 'every thing [was going] on here exceedingly well' and he had no doubt that he would engineer 'a capital explosion' of free-trade opinions in Bordeaux. As in Lyon, he took care to promote liberal ideas about trade among all parties and all classes. His room was 'crowded from morning to night' with local leaders of the *Résistance* and the *Mouvement*, republicans and Saint-Simonians (disciples of Henri de Saint-Simon, the advocate of a new order governed by economic imperatives) and the editors of all the city's news-sheets. He dined with prominent merchants but also arranged a meeting with the *tonneliers*, or Bordelais dockworkers ('the counterparts to my Lyonnais *canuts*' or silk-workers, Bowring wrote), who agreed 'to petition for Free Trade'. Bowring's most significant success was the creation of two committees that would endeavour to propagate liberal ideas about trade in French opinion: the Commission Libre du Commerce, dominated by wealthy merchants, and a resurrected Comité des Propriétaires de Vignes. Bowring persuaded the Prefect of the Gironde to authorize the new organizations on the grounds that their object would be 'economic' and not 'political'. Instead of petitioning the government, the two committees aimed at 'taking hold of the subject – and (in a word)

[67] *Le Mémorial*, 19, 23, 25, 30 and 31 December 1832; quotations from 'Observations à l'appui des réclamations du commerce de Bordeaux', 19 December 1832, and 'Question des sucres', 30 December 1832.

[68] 'Admirables effets du système prohibitif ou protecteur' and 'Le Système protecteur étant essentiellement prohibitif, est essentiellement faux et mauvais', *Le Mémorial*, 5 and 6 January 1833; see also articles on the sugar tariff in *Le Mémorial*, 25, 26 and 28 January 1833.

popularizing it by their appeal to *public opinion*', with solemn calls to the nation for the abolition of customs protection.[69]

The only significant difficulty reported by Bowring was the survival of some Anglophobic feelings, although they tended to be confined to 'old people' who still feared 'les *astucieux anglais*' (the astute English). At a meeting of the Comité des Propriétaires de Vignes, 'a Jew called Perreira' harangued his colleagues on the dangers of agreements with Britain, citing how the latter had 'crushed' Portuguese commerce after the conclusion of the Methuen treaty in 1703. The Committee appointed a deputation of eight winegrowers headed by Perreira, who subjected Bowring to a thorough interrogation. The British agent felt that he successfully passed the test and 'made Mon. Perreira look rather sheepish in the flock'.[70] Bowring's accounts of how he surmounted this and other obstacles sound complacent. But the British Consul in Bordeaux confirmed that Bowring's mission had created 'the greatest interest' among 'the inhabitants of this part of France', who would henceforth support 'most energetically' the lowering of French tariffs.[71] 'Well done thou Prince of Agitation', Villiers congratulated his colleague.[72]

Before he left Bordeaux, Bowring was infuriated by the conclusions of the Customs Legislative Commission, delivered by Saint-Cricq on 3 April 1833. The report proposed to increase several tariffs and postpone for another two years the repeal of the prohibition on cotton twists. Against the doctrine of the 'economic school', it defended 'a system of reasoned protection' for French industries. Saint-Cricq wished, 'on the one hand, to protect effectively the country's labour, and, on the other, to study carefully, for each industry, the minimum rate of necessary protection, to prevent the damages that excessive protection might cause'.[73] Bowring's reaction to the report was incandescent: 'What a series of lies and frauds ... The press must speak out upon St-Cricq as the *English enemy*, the liar par excellence, the man whom *we hate* – Louis Philippe will listen – and others will listen too.' Bowring remained confident that the government's desire to consolidate good relations with Britain, combined with the pressure from public opinion he was helping to organize, would prevail over Saint-Cricq's

[69] Bowring to Villiers, 19, 25, 28 March and 7 April 1833, BODL, MS Clar., dep. c. 544, fols. 103–4, 107–8, 111, 115–17.

[70] Bowring to Villiers, 7 April 1833, BODL, MS Clar., dep. c. 544, fols. 115–17.

[71] Scott to Palmerston, 30 March 1833, TNA, FO/27/469, fol. 104.

[72] Villiers to Bowring, 2 April 1833, Cambridge (Mass.), Houghton Library, English manuscripts, MS 1247, fol. 35.

[73] AP, vol. LXXXII, pp. 111–31 (3 April 1833).

manoeuvres: 'you have no idea', he wrote to Villiers, 'what a mighty influence is awakened and how the holy spirit is spreading'.[74]

Leaving Bordeaux in mid-April, Bowring pursued his propaganda tour in Angoulême, Rochefort, La Rochelle, Nantes, Angers, Lorient, Brest, Morlaix, Saint-Brieuc, Saint-Malo, Caen, Le Havre and Rouen. In each town he recruited new forces 'for us to direct when we march again against the St Cricquian legions'. He focused his efforts on journalists, asserting towards the end of his tour: 'There are sixteen newspapers on the ground over which I have gone – There is not one of them that has not published several hearty articles in condemnation of the protecting system.' In Le Havre, for example, the editors of the main newspaper offered 'their columns on all occasions to advance the great work, and declar[ed] that they [felt] it to be their *apostolat*'.[75] Back in Paris, he renewed his efforts to entice the press to clamour for tariff reform. In addition to the newspapers enlisted in 1832, Bowring secured the support of the conservative *Messager* and of the republican *Bon Sens*. In his view, 'except the notoriously paid and prostitute newspapers, there is not one which is not our ally'. Parisian editors felt that they ought to 'respond' to the protests from the provincial newspapers 'and their responses will vibrate again thro' France'.[76]

Bowring certainly exaggerated the success of his propaganda in his reports, if only to justify his remuneration. But a great deal of evidence suggests that the impact of his second tour, along the Atlantic coast, seriously irked the French government. Upon his return to Paris in June, Bowring was summoned by Thiers to his office, where the Minister of Commerce gave the British agent a severe reprimand, saying that he had 'insurrectionized the south – *crushed* ... his ministère with representations – inflamed the popular passions' and 'that England had better mind her own commercial affairs and let France attend to hers'.[77] In the autumn, the joint Anglo-French commission charged with investigating tariff reductions was indefinitely suspended. Unfortunately, there is little information about what exactly Bowring said that succeeded in 'inflaming' the passions of his interlocutors. His reports suggest that he spent more time reassuring them about Britain's alleged aspirations to commercial supremacy than didactically expounding the economics of free trade. The very experience of an encounter with a francophone and Francophile emissary of the British government was an unusual experience in provincial towns

[74] Bowring to Villiers, 7 April 1833, BODL, MS Clar., dep. c. 544, fols. 113–15.
[75] Bowring to Villiers, 2 and 23 May 1833, BODL, MS Clar., dep. c. 544, fols. 123, 129.
[76] Bowring to Villiers, 9 and 11 June 1833, BODL, MS Clar., dep. c. 544, fols. 157, 159.
[77] Copy of a letter from Bowring to Villiers, 5 June 1833, BODL, MS Clar., dep. c. 546/1/2, fols. 113–15.

and is likely to have made a potent impression. However, his audience proved receptive because liberal ideas about trade were already gaining in popularity, especially in Bordeaux. Bowring may therefore be described as having played the role of catalyst, whose encouragements unleashed a new wave of protests in favour of free trade.

IV

The main fruit of Bowring's efforts in Bordeaux was the publication, in January 1834, of a strident *Adresse*, signed by 438 Bordelais merchants and demanding the advent of commercial liberty. '[No] document ever produced a greater sensation in the commercial and commercio-political world', Bowring claimed. Even the pro-government *Journal des Débats* reproduced large extracts, while the other Paris newspapers were 'balking out in its praise'.[78] *Le Constitutionnel*, the leading liberal sheet, described the *Adresse* as 'the manifesto of a revolution that [was] peaceful in its operation', but 'immense in its results'. In London, *The Times* hailed the Bordelais protests as so 'very able … that it would seem hardly possible for any member of the legislature who [read] the memorial not to yield to the wishes expressed by the memorialists'.[79] The chambers of commerce of Bordeaux, Le Havre, Nantes, Toulouse, Boulogne, La Rochelle and another Commission Commerciale in Le Havre expressed their solemn adhesion to the principles expounded in the *Adresse*. The following year, a pamphlet hostile to free trade by a customs official lamented that the *Adresse* had thrown the entire kingdom 'into a state of turmoil'.[80]

The very word *adresse* had revolutionary undertones: it was the *adresse* signed by 221 deputies in March 1830 that led to the demise of the Bourbon dynasty three months later. The signatories of the 1834 *Adresse* demanded that 'the liberal principle of the 1830 constitution' be extended to economic legislation: 'So that the word liberty has its value fully recognized in a society, it should not only be sanctioned by its political laws: it should, in addition, be applied to its economy, so that the individual will, in the exercise of industry, meets as few obstacles as possible.' The petitioners underlined the links between 'the so-called protective regime' and the 'despotisms' that governed France in the past, from the 'old monarchy' to the 'revolutionary government' of 1793 and 'the conquering genius of

[78] Bowring to Thomson, 7 February 1834, BODL, MS Clar., dep. c. 546/1/3, fol. 17.

[79] 'De l'adresse des négociants de Bordeaux aux chambres législatives', *Le Constitutionnel*, 8 February 1834; *The Times*, 6 February 1834.

[80] Saint-Ferréol, *Exposition du système des douanes en France* (Marseille, 1835), pp. 27–8.

the [Napoleonic] Empire'. Yet these regimes conformed to 'the law of their nature' in maintaining the principle of 'commercial privilege'. Harmony between the new 'fundamental law' of 1830 and 'France's political economy' therefore required the abolition of tariff protection. Trade liberalization would also enable France to pursue and encourage the regeneration of 'old Europe', but by more peaceful means than under the Revolution and Napoleon: 'France is the intellectual summit of the civilized world; every innovation has to start from her soil before it propagates gloriously.'[81]

The *Adresse* abided by the principles of liberal political economy more closely than the 1828 and 1829 petitions of the Gironde winegrowers. But it remained inspired by Fonfrède's hostility to industrialization and centralization. The Bordeaux merchants warned the government that the 'shocking discrepancy' in wealth between northern and southern France 'might damage patriotic feelings'. Although they recognized the need for a managed transition and did not demand the complete abolition of customs duties, they insisted that the 'liberty' of international exchanges ought to be recognized as 'the goal … of the new France'. The petitioners also portrayed themselves as the conservative defenders of 'order' against the 'anarchy' caused by the protective system, which they accused of breeding 'a civil war among workers'.[82] They even supported an extensive role for the state in the management of the economy, akin to the description of the government as 'delegated' by society in Guizot's writings during the Restoration. In their view, the government should 'direct human activity in every sphere' but 'with impartiality', and it should never remain 'idle or stationary; but, delegated by society, it must only seek to serve social interests'.[83]

The *Adresse* can therefore not be reduced to an expression of pure liberalism in the sense of an aspiration to a minimalist state. Rather, it combined an adhesion to a radical version of economic *laissez-faire* with a politically conservative concern about social stability. Such a combination recalls the conservative reinterpretation of Adam Smith's ideas by Edmund Burke and others at the turn of the nineteenth century, although there is no trace of direct influence. Fonfrède, a member of the Commission Commerciale, no doubt played a leading part in drafting the document. In a letter written fourteen months later, Théodore Ducos, a cousin of Fonfrède who later served as Minister of the Navy under Napoleon III, mentioned with

[81] Commission Commerciale de Bordeaux, *Adresse des négociants de Bordeaux aux chambres législatives* (Bordeaux, 1834), pp. 1–3, 5, 10–11, 22.

[82] *Adresse*, pp. 3, 8, 14–20.

[83] *Adresse*, p. 14; on Guizot's conception of government's power as delegated by society, see Rosanvallon, *Le Moment Guizot*, pp. 44–54.

nostalgia the times when they wrote together 'the work of the Commission libre'.[84] But the emphasis on the role of the state in managing society bore the mark of Henri Galos, Secretary of the Commission Commerciale who later became a staunch supporter of Guizot and Director of Colonies at the Ministry of the Marine between 1842 and 1848. Galos accepted that the Revolutions of 1789 and 1830 had been necessary to overthrow the old order. Yet he held deep sympathies for the ultramontane Catholicism of Lamennais, or even the utopian schemes of Saint-Simon and Charles Fourier, because these doctrines sought 'to reconcile authority and liberty, to reunite individual rights and social law'. The most urgent 'necessity' was, in his view, 'organization':

> The phases we have gone through have led us to a crossroads on the social terrain: if we persist on the path of individual liberalism, we shall fall in a bottomless abyss, if we embark on the path of unitary liberalism, we shall meet with a fine future of real improvement and true progress.[85]

The socially conservative undertones of the *Adresse* also certainly reflected the influence of Pierre-François Guestier, the President of the Commission Commerciale. A defeated candidate of the *Résistance* at the 1831 general election, Guestier upheld ideas that befitted his social station as a *grand notable* (he was the Gironde's largest tax-payer) and his fervent Anglophilia (he was a reformed Protestant who spoke English at home with his wife, Anna Johnston, of Scottish descent, and their three children). In an exchange of letters with Fonfrède, Guestier declared himself to be in agreement with the publicist on all issues except one, the distribution of property. While Fonfrède, like Benjamin Constant, still saw in numerous small estates the best means to defend property against the 'proletarian masses', Guestier praised large estates as a bulwark against revolutionary agitation. The wealthy merchant approved of the 1789 Revolution but regretted the 'constant fever' that had disturbed French society since its outbreak and, as a remedy, recommended the adoption of the 'English' rule of primogeniture.[86] It is likely that several other members of the Commission, who were almost all Protestant and often of northern European descent, shared Guestier's admiration for the British political and social model.[87]

[84] Ducos to Fonfrède, 11 March 1835, BMB, MS 1095, vol. 1, fol. 589.

[85] Galos to Fonfrède, 23 February 1835, BMB, MS 1095, vol. 1, fols. 545–7.

[86] Exchange of letters between Guestier and Fonfrède, August 1831, repr. in Guy Schyler, *Guestier: souvenirs et documents* (Bordeaux, 1993), pp. 142–6.

[87] Members of the Commission Commerciale included four merchants of Anglo-Irish or Scottish descent (John Exshaw, David Brown, David Johnston, Nathaniel Johnston), two merchants of

Finally, the *Adresse* owed a great deal to Bowring. The British agent did not only help to set up, in collaboration with Guestier ('the most enlightened merchant in France', in Bowring's description) and Fonfrède ('a mighty man [who] exercises a very extraordinary influence'), the Commission Commerciale.[88] He also provided his Bordelais allies with statistical data, which highlighted the harm done by French protective tariffs to Anglo-French commercial exchanges since the eighteenth century.[89] The statistics were appended, under the form of twenty pages of tables, to the twenty-five pages of text of the *Adresse*. Bowring also did his utmost to ensure extensive publicity for the manifesto. Despite the rupture of the Anglo-French commercial negotiations, Bowring returned to Paris in January 1834, officially to collect data on the French wine industry but with the supervision of the campaign for free trade as his real purpose. The French government was now ill disposed towards the British agitator. Bowring believed that he was placed under the surveillance of the police, while Thiers enjoined him to stop visiting 'the journalists' offices'. Bowring nevertheless remained 'in constant communication with the [Bordelais] commission' and had numerous praises for the *Adresse* inserted in newspapers.[90] 'I must say', Lord Granville, the British Ambassador in Paris, reported to Auckland, 'that the unremitting exertions of Bowring have had most extraordinary success – The Press both Parisian and Provincial has answered to his will.'[91]

The Bordelais campaign reached its apex a few weeks later, when the Gironde Comité des Propriétaires de Vignes, also presided by Guestier, issued its own manifesto, under the form of a petition against tariff protection, on 20 February 1834. The petition was adopted 'unanimously and by acclamation' by a 'very numerous' gathering of winegrowers at the Bordeaux Bourse du Commerce.[92] A Bordelais merchant who attended the meeting wrote (in English) to Bowring that if the government wanted 'to check the excess of [this] injured and enraged body of men', they would

Huguenot descent (Pierre-Antoine Bouscasse and Stanislas Ferrière), one reformed Protestant of Genevan descent (Guillaume Mestrezat) and one Lutheran of Prussian descent (Jacques-Henri Wustemberg). I could not identify the Commission's last three members (Louis Lafitte, Christoph Klipsch and John Violett), but Klipsch and Violett were probably Protestant and of foreign descent. See Cavignac, *Les Vingt-Cinq Familles*, pp. 89–106.

88 Bowring to Villiers, 25 March and 7 April 1833, BODL, MS Clar., dep. c. 544, fols. 107, 117.

89 Minutes of the Chamber of Commerce, 20 August 1833, ADG, 02/081/307, register 1830–4, fol. 127, which records that the statistics sent by Bowring were forwarded to Guestier.

90 Bowring to Thomson, 31 January and 14 February 1834, BODL, MS Clar., dep. c. 546/1/3, fols. 106, 130.

91 Granville to Auckland, [February 1834], BL, AUP, Add MS 34460, fols. 9–10.

92 *Le Mémorial*, 21 February 1834.

have to concede very substantial reductions in the tariff. '[The] Girondin spirit is awakened', Bowring's correspondent rejoiced:

> The whole population of the south could be raised in one day! Lyon awaits the [signal] of Bordeaux, and unless some wise concession be offered, unless the protected [sic] system be abandoned, the whole Midi will rise en masse and obtain commercial liberty ([the] sister of political) by force.[93]

Armand Dupérier de Larsan, a member of the winegrowers' committee in the 1820s, was now its secretary and drafted the petition. He reported to Bowring that 'opinion here [was] very heated indeed': 'we are tired of being legally plundered [by northern manufacturers] and we wish to bring matters to a head. Be confident that the day for true Reform is not far off. Mark my words'.[94]

The petition took the inflammatory rhetoric of the *Adresse* to new extremes. Drawing the same analogy as the merchants' protest, the winegrowers' petition regretted that 'the triumph of political and religious liberty' in 1830 was not followed by 'the triumph of a wise commercial liberty'. It also recalled, with nostalgia, Bordeaux's prosperity in the decades preceding the 1789 Revolution, before the 'restrictive economics' of the 'prohibitive or protective regime' annihilated France's wine exports to northern Europe. Foreign retaliation against high tariffs, the petition argued, encouraged the plantation of new vines from Crimea to South Africa, endangering French predominance on the global wine market. If barriers on imports were not soon removed, it concluded, the south of France should erect 'an internal customs line', separating it from the north and enabling it to pursue its own trade policy.[95] The project of customs secession, Dupérier insisted in a letter to Bowring, was 'not a utopia' but a pragmatic return to the diversity of customs regimes that prevailed in France before 1789. Dupérier entreated the British agent to ensure the maximum of publicity for the petition and 'to highlight the idea of an internal customs line'.[96]

The project of customs secession received a great deal of attention, but not all of the kind that Dupérier wished for. Etienne Hervé, who drafted the 1828 petition and was now a deputy for the Gironde, reported that in

[93] Violett to Bowring, 20 February 1834, BODL, MS Clar., dep. c. 546/1/3, fols. 40–1; the letter is damaged, making some interpolations necessary.

[94] Dupérier de Larsan to Bowring, 24 February 1834 (copy), BODL, MS Clar., dep. c. 546/1/3, fol. 45.

[95] Copy of the petition dated 17 May 1834, AN, F12 2506.

[96] Dupérier de Larsan to Bowring, 24 February 1834 (copy), BODL, MS Clar., dep. c. 546/1/3, fols. 44–5.

Paris, 'the petition from the winegrowers' committee seem[ed] close, very close to sedition'.[97] Although they sympathized with the winegrowers' grievances, left-wing newspapers such as *La Tribune* condemned 'this call for abrupt dislocation' as 'insane'. The legitimist press described the petition as further evidence that 'this government [could not] maintain social ties' (*La Gazette de France*) or that Louis-Philippe's regime would eventually result in 'the dissolution of France' (*La Quotidienne*).[98] In March, Aristide Dufour, a member of the winegrowers' committee visiting Paris, informed Bowring that the forces of 'Monopoly' were spreading rumours that the winegrowers wished to 'break up national unity' and turn Gironde into 'an English province'.[99] Dufour also reported to Fonfrède that only one topic succeeded in lifting the Chamber of Deputies out of its usual state of apathy, namely the Gironde department: 'then [deputies] become agitated; almost all members tremble at the mention of Bordeaux', 'a demanding and insatiable city', whose inhabitants considered 'Bordeaux as their sole homeland' and were not afraid of proclaiming 'the necessity for separation'.[100]

Bowring's prophecy of a Bordelais 'explosion' in favour of free trade was fulfilled. The tone of the *Adresse*, the winegrowers' petition and the personal correspondence between the campaigners testified to a remarkable degree of ideological fervour. But the socially conservative undercurrent of the protests, their strong regionalist connotation and the open involvement of a British agent risked undermining the appeal of such a radical conception of commercial liberalism outside the Gironde.

V

Following the publication of the *Adresse* and the winegrowers' petition, Bowring and his Bordelais allies experimented with new means of propagating free-trade ideas. In order to bolster the coherence of radical commercial liberalism, Fonfrède sought to define and retrace the genealogy of their ideological enemy, support for protective tariffs. At the general election of June 1834, the Bordelais merchants and winegrowers also offered their support to candidates committed to the advent of commercial liberty. Bowring sought to recruit new supporters in other winegrowing

[97] Hervé to Fonfrède, Paris, 27 February 1834, BMB, MS 1095, vol. 1, letter 144.

[98] *La Tribune*, 4 March 1834; *La Gazette de France*, 3 March 1834; *La Quotidienne*, 3 March 1834.

[99] Dufour to Bowring, [March 1834], BL, AUP, Add MS 34460, fols. 60–2.

[100] Dufour to Fonfrède, 1 May 1834, BMB, MS 1095, vol. 1, fols. 269–70.

regions such as Champagne, Burgundy and Languedoc. Yet the impact of the Bordelais campaign beyond the Gironde remained limited.

In response to the criticisms of Parisian newspapers, Fonfrède set out to write another series of articles to demonstrate, in plain French, the shortcomings of tariff protection. The publicist planned 'to put a leading article in the *Mémorial* every Sunday and Thursday with a view to instruct the middle classes and those who do not understand the advantages of commercial liberty until the subject is exhausted'.[101] The overarching theme of the articles was the need to complete the liberal Revolution of 1830. Fonfrède maintained that the Restoration was an 'economic despotism' as well as a 'political despotism'. The latter was overthrown, but 'despotic' conceptions of economics still prevailed. To sap their hold over minds, Fonfrède proposed a systematic investigation of the history and effects of prohibitive policies: 'we will gather together the system that has been scattered [in pamphlets, newspaper articles and parliamentary speeches] and we will assemble it in one block to demonstrate the incoherence of its parts, the error of its doctrines and the nonsense of its practice'.[102] A powerful case for free trade required to sketch out the contours of its ideological other, later to be described as protectionism.

To prove that the protective system was merely the prohibitive system under another name, Fonfrède insisted that high tariffs had the same nefarious consequences, for consumers and export industries, as prohibitions. Since they still aimed at preventing imports and indirectly exports, 'the doctrines of our tariffs [were] positively absolute and remain[ed] tarnished by the odious nature of prohibition'. Fonfrède scoffed at the argument that protection would be abolished as soon as national producers could sustain foreign competition. Even if one day they caught up with their rivals, which was unlikely without the pressure of foreign competition, their success would render imports unnecessary and prevent in another manner the regeneration of foreign trade. Protection therefore always resulted in the permanent abolition of commercial exchanges: 'Thus peoples isolate themselves, shun each other, hate each other. Such a project is profoundly immoral and retrograde, heartless and soulless.'[103]

Fonfrède proceeded to refute 'the main argument, the mighty argument' employed by 'les prohibitifs', namely that it was better to produce dearly

[101] Violett to Bowring, 20 February 1834, BODL, MS Clar., dep. c. 546/1/3, fols. 40–1.

[102] 'De l'exposé des motifs du projet de loi des douanes, par M. Thiers', *Le Mémorial*, 22 February 1834.

[103] 'Les Doctrines prohibitives sont absolues, fausses et ruineuses', *Le Mémorial*, 27 February 1834.

than not to produce at all. The publicist established the genealogy of this flawed line of reasoning, which underlined its illiberal origins: 'from Mr Ferrier it passed to Mr de Saint-Cricq, from Mr de Saint-Cricq it passed to Mr de Villèle and from Mr de Villèle it passed on to Mr Thiers', the new Minister of Commerce. In response, Fonfrède contended that 'productive forces' never remained idle. Even if producers worked less in a regime of free trade, they would produce more wealth 'because production channelled into its most natural and economical employments would necessarily be more fecund and better distributed'.[104] The journalist was confident that the increase in 'free labour' would more than compensate the reduction in 'prohibitive labour'. Fonfrède also sought to discredit one of the defenders of tariff protection's favourite examples, the alleged ruin of Portugal as a result of its commercial agreements with Britain. Despite severe prohibitions on imports, Spain had undergone the same economic decline as its Iberian neighbour. This suggested that 'theocracy' and Catholicism's contempt for productive labour rather than trade policy were responsible for the economic stagnation of both countries: 'it was not industrial products which should have been prohibited, but monks!' By contrast, Gallicanism and Anglicanism shielded France and, even more so, England from the negative economic consequences of 'papal despotism'.[105]

In response to Parisian attacks on the Bordelais lack of patriotism, Fonfrède drew a parallel with the accusations of 'federalism' levelled by the Montagne against the Girondins. The current debate on commercial liberty was the continuation of 'the great struggle that began in 1793' between proponents and opponents of centralization. The 'new Girondins', he maintained, did not want to disorganize society or destroy national unity any more than their predecessors.[106] Fonfrède's case for trade liberalization remained intertwined with the defence of his region's interests. Yet, perhaps as a result of Bowring's influence, it was no longer hostile to liberal political economy. On the contrary, Fonfrède now described himself as a supporter of 'the theories of economists' and wished to 'propagate [them] in people's minds'. His formerly vivid distrust of British policies also receded. He hailed Britain's efforts 'to relinquish the system of prohibitions' and asserted: 'I am not an *Anglomane* – but

[104] 'Les Doctrines prohibitives sont ruineuses', *Le Mémorial*, 3 March 1834.

[105] 'La Liberté commerciale est plus productive que le système prohibitif: l'exemple du Portugal n'est pas applicable à la question actuelle', two articles, *Le Mémorial*, 6 and 9 March 1834.

[106] '*Le Journal des Débats* et les pétitionnaires de la Gironde', three articles, *Le Mémorial*, 11, 12 and 13 March 1834.

neither am I an Anglophobe.'[107] In conclusion, Fonfrède reiterated his conviction that 'political absolutism' and 'prohibitive absolutism' were intimately linked to each other. The downfall of the former made the establishment of free trade inevitable and, if Louis-Philippe's regime continued to resist commercial liberalization, 'a commercial 29 July' would follow the 'political 29 July', when insurgents overthrew the Bourbons.[108]

The series of articles had echoes beyond Bordeaux. In 1832, Fonfrède asserted that the influence of *Le Mémorial* spread 'from Marseille to Nantes'.[109] In 1834, Bowring congratulated the publicist on 'the virile, irresistible and generous eloquence' of his articles and encouraged him to represent his department at the Chamber of Deputies: 'Say to 30 million Frenchmen from the parliamentary rostrum what you say to 3,000 in *Le Mémorial Bordelais* and you will have at your disposal the future of France, England and the entire world.'[110] The figure of 3,000 suggests that *Le Mémorial* was one of the most widely circulated provincial newspapers, while Fronfrède's polemical exchanges with *Le Journal des Débats* and other Parisian dailies about Bordelais patriotism confirms that his readership was not purely local. Bowring described Fonfrède as 'the most influential man in southern France' and reported an attempt by Thiers to 'silence' him: acting on the Minister's instructions, the local *procureur du roi* (magistrate in charge of prosecutions) and the Prefect of the Gironde visited Fonfrède, trying 'both promise and menace' and 'working on his Anti-English feelings' to persuade him to interrupt his series of articles. But their pleas left the 'incorruptible' publicist unmoved.[111]

Instead, it was Thiers who, on 6 April 1834, resigned the portfolio of commerce, although he stayed in the government as Minister of the Interior. The new Minister of Commerce was Duchâtel, an avowed advocate of trade liberalization. According to Bowring, Thiers's dismissal from the commerce department corresponded to a 'universal wish' and the reshuffle portended major legislative changes: 'the power of English influence … only requires to be watched and encouraged – and you will see it break down all the Customs House barriers'.[112] Yet the revolt of the Lyon silk-workers against the reduction of their wages and the repression of

[107] 'Les Doctrines prohibitives', *Le Mémorial*, 3 March 1834; 'La Liberté commerciale', *Le Mémorial*, 6 and 9 March 1834; 'Politique commerciale et coloniale de l'Angleterre et de la France', *Le Mémorial*, 3 April 1834.

[108] 'Le Fer, les machines à vapeur, les chaînes cables', *Le Mémorial*, 6 April 1834.

[109] Fonfrède to Campan, 17 February 1832, BMB, MS 1087, fol. 67.

[110] Bowring to Fonfrède, 16 February 1834, BMB, MS 1095, vol. 1, letter 140.

[111] Bowring to Auckland, 10 March and 7 April 1834, BL, AUP, Add MS 34460, fols. 44, 93.

[112] Bowring to Auckland, 7 April 1834, BL, AUP, Add MS 34460, fol. 95.

their insurrection and a smaller revolt in Paris between 9 and 15 April temporarily overshadowed all other concerns. Even the ever-buoyant Bowring recognized that the debate at the Chamber of Deputies on the Bordeaux petitions, on 12 April, was 'tame and unprofitable'.[113] The Chamber's customs commission issued a dilatory report on possible new legislative changes.[114] But on 2 June, in an attempt to appease the press and public opinion on the eve of a general election, Duchâtel issued an ordinance that authorized imports of cotton twists and reduced duties on coal and wool. The ordinance's preamble insisted on the need 'to multiply the exchanges [of France] with other peoples', and the liberal press hailed the measure as a significant step towards the abolition of 'commercial feudality'.[115]

Meanwhile, Bowring and his Bordelais allies prepared for the general election, seeking to transform the two Gironde committees into an electoral machine. In April, Bowring pointed out to his London employers that 'the organization [was] spreading to 40 departments who return 120 deputies, of which more than half [were] under the influence and [would] be nominated by the Commission des Vignobles'.[116] On 3 June 1834, the Comité des Propriétaires de Vignes and the Commission Commerciale merged into a 'Comité Électoral'.[117] A manifesto drafted by Fonfrède proclaimed, on a messianic tone, that the new committee pursued 'the progress of the human race' and 'the rapid and fraternal rapprochement of peoples'. In their opinion, 'political liberty would only be an illusion and a delusion, at once derisory and dangerous' as long as it was not completed by economic liberty. In order to ensure the triumph of 'veritable liberty', the committee pledged to spread correct ideas about trade: 'economic doctrines will be placed within the reach of all minds, of all beliefs, from the great Parisian city to the most humble of our villages'.[118] Yet the June election proved a relative disappointment. Candidates sponsored by the Comité Électoral won nearly all the seats in the Gironde, enabling Bowring to describe the department's deputies as 'a compact nucleus of commercial reformers'.[119] But it had little impact elsewhere.

Bowring's propaganda and the Gironde protests sustained a vigorous interest in political economy throughout the country. The first periodical

[113] Bowring to Thomson, 14 April 1834, BODL, MS Clar., dep. c. 546/1/3, fol. 49.
[114] AP, vol. LXXXIX, pp. 478, 519–55 (29 April 1834).
[115] *Le Constitutionnel*, 4 and 6 June 1834.
[116] Bowring to Auckland, 17 April 1834, BL, AUP, Add MS 34460, fol.111.
[117] Galos to Guestier, [13 May 1834], and Nathaniel Johnston to Guestier, [June 1834], reprinted in Schyler, *Guestier*, pp. 164–6, 168–9.
[118] 'Déclaration' by the Comité Électoral, in *Le Mémorial*, 21 June 1834.
[119] Bowring to Thomson, 4 August 1834, BODL, MS Clar., dep. c. 546/1/3, fol. 80.

dedicated to economics, the *Revue Mensuelle d'Économie Politique* was launched at the end of 1833. Its first issue paid homage to Bowring's efforts to spread free-trade ideas and rejoiced at the intensity of the debate on international trade: 'The customs question has become popular, everyone is concerned with it. What formerly interested only statesmen, the foremost merchants and the main speculators is now a pivotal issue around which the nation's most essential interests seem to revolve.'[120] Yet the monthly's circulation was under 500 copies, and it ceased publication in 1835.[121] The demand for works popularizing political economy remained high, with the publication, in 1834 alone, of a fourth edition of Say's *Catéchisme* (2,000 copies printed), a second edition of Jane Marcet's *Conversations* (500 copies) and a translation of Marcet's *John Hopkins' Notions on Political Economy* (500 copies), first published in Britain in 1833.[122] Nor was the interest in political economy and international trade confined to the capital, with the publication of works supporting the advent of commercial liberty, between 1833 and 1835, by merchants or journalists from Bordeaux, Le Havre, Marseille, Lyon, Dijon and smaller towns such as Saumur, Arras and Mont-de-Marsan.[123] The text published in Mont-de-Marsan was the first publication of Frédéric Bastiat, the future advocate of *libre-échange* and theoretician of radical economic liberalism. Bastiat's *Réflexions sur les pétitions de Bordeaux* hailed 'the unanimous concert of praise that welcomed, within and outside our country, the complaints of French commerce' but reproached Fonfrède and the petitioners the inconsistencies of their economic reasoning and the moderation of their practical demands.[124]

In 1834, the Chamber of Deputies also received no fewer than 108 petitions on customs legislation, almost all in favour of liberalization and often emanating from winegrowing regions. The petitions frequently adopted a revolutionary rhetoric, as with thirty-five inhabitants of Mâcon in Burgundy, who asked the Chamber of Deputies to emulate

[120] 'Mission du docteur Bowring en France' and 'Opinions diverses sur le système des douanes françaises', *Revue Mensuelle d'Économie Politique*, 1 (1833): 81–5 and 2 (1834): 302–21.

[121] Impressions 3480 and 3760 (21 August and 9 September 1833), AN, F18*II 23.

[122] Impressions 3037, 3199 and 3288 (21 July, 4 August, 8 August 1834), AN, F18*II 24.

[123] François Coudert, *Recueil d'économie politique* (Bordeaux, 1833); Jean-Baptiste Delaunay, *Lettre à M. Tanneguy Duchâtel* (Le Havre, 1834); François-Barthélémy Arlès-Dufour and André Dervieu, *Un mot sur les fabriques étrangères de soieries* (Lyon, 1834); Charles Louvet, *Dialogue sur la liberté du commerce* (Saumur, 1834); M. Bénard, *De la liberté du commerce* (Arras, 1834); Frédéric Bastiat, *Réflexions sur les pétitions de Bordeaux, Le Havre et Lyon concernant les douanes* (Mont-de-Marsan, 1834); [Anon.], *Paroles d'un négociant* (Paris, 1834), by a Marseille merchant; and Jules Pautet, *Manuel d'économie politique* (Paris, 1835), by a Dijon journalist.

[124] Bastiat, *Réflexions*, p. 1.

the 'Constituent Assembly' of 1789 and abolish commercial 'serfdom' and 'privileges'.[125] Another petition, signed by 2,405 winegrowers of the Côte d'Or, also in Burgundy, demanded the immediate reform of 'the customs system … in the concurrent interest of consumers, trade and exports'. The author of the petition was Théophile Foisset, the Secretary of the Beaune Comité des Propriétaires de Vignes in 1829. While the Gironde winegrowers feared the expansion of vine cultivation in South Africa, their Burgundian counterparts were more worried about the creation of the German customs union or Zollverein on 1 January 1834, which risked further reducing French wine exports to central Europe.[126] Paying homage to Fonfrède and replicating his efforts to popularize commercial liberty, Foisset also published a letter in *Le Spectateur de Dijon*, the local *Résistance* daily, which aimed 'to reduce the [customs] question to such simple ideas that its solution may be accessible to the most rudimentary intellects'.[127]

Bowring strove to coordinate the efforts of the Bordelais with other local advocates of commercial liberty, such as the Lyon merchant François-Barthélémy Arlès-Dufour or Le Havre merchant Jean-Baptiste Delaunay.[128] Yet his endeavours met with only limited success. The public outcry against the Gironde winegrowers' project of customs secession did not help. In Lyon, for instance, the Chamber of Commerce declined to express its support for the Bordelais *Adresse*, lest public opinion mistake its endorsement 'for an adhesion to the winegrowers' manifesto'.[129] The hostility of Thiers, even after he had to resign the portfolio of commerce, was another hindrance. In Marseille, the statesman's hometown, his local supporters also prevented the Chamber of Commerce from adhering to the Bordelais *Adresse*.[130] But it is hard to escape a sense that the radical commercial liberalism of the Bordelais, inspired by Fonfrède's regionalism and fanned by Bowring's encouragements, simply failed to elicit the same enthusiasm in other French regions.

The setbacks did not prevent Bowring, in August 1834, from setting out on a third tour in the wine districts of Champagne, Burgundy and Languedoc. In particular, he wished to 'bring Burgundy and Bordeaux

[125] 'Pétition des habitants de Mâcon', 16 November 1834, AN, C 2141.

[126] 'Pétition de cinquante communes de l'arrondissement de Beaune dans la Côte d'Or', February 1834, AN, F12 2506.

[127] *Le Spectateur de Dijon*, 13 February 1834.

[128] Bowring to Arlès-Dufour, 19 May 1833; quoted in Canton-Debat, 'Arlès-Dufour', p. 274; Guestier to Fonfrède, 21 May 1834, BMB, MS 1095, vol. 1, fol. 287; Bowring to Thomson, 15 August 1834, BODL, MS Clar., dep. c. 546/1/3, fol. 88.

[129] Arlès-Dufour to Galos, 26–7 March 1834, BMB, MS 1095, vol. 1, fols. 240–3.

[130] Bowring to Thomson, 4 April 1834, BODL, MS Clar., dep. c. 546/1/3, fols. 49–51.

into close alliance, which is what the Bordeaux people want'. Although the French government refused to give him letters of recommendations, his reputation, he explained in his reports, still earned him a warm welcome by winegrowers and merchants in Reims, Epernay, Cry, Châlons, Troyes, Beaune, Mâcon, Lyon, Marseille, Montpellier, Carcassonne, Toulouse and Bayonne. Bowring ended his tour with a second stay in Bordeaux, where he found his allies worried by the government's decision to hold an official inquiry on prohibitions of foreign manufactured products. Bowring and his Bordelais acolytes disapproved of the initiative, engineered in their view 'by the hostile party in order to stave off the question a little longer'.[131] Bowring helped the Commission Commerciale draft a *déclaration* that described the decision to hold an inquiry as a 'symptom of disorganization and weakening of the restrictive system' but condemned the undertaking as inevitably 'sterile'.[132] In Paris, only the radical press also censured the initiative, while mainstream liberal newspapers welcomed it as a sign of the continuation of commercial reforms.[133] The divergent reactions underlined the growing disjuncture between the radical conception of commercial liberty defended by the Bordelais liberals and the more emollient version espoused by a majority of French liberals.

The stalling of commercial reform in 1834 did not yet mark the end of the Anglo-French liberal rapprochement. It is even possible to argue that at this point it was the French free-traders, at least in Bordeaux, who were adopting a radical conception of commercial liberty and experimenting with new means of disseminating it. The endorsement of candidates by the Bordelais free-trade lobby at the 1834 general election prefigured the use of a similar electoral tactic by the Anti-Corn Law League after 1840.[134] Perhaps not coincidentally, the League was founded at a banquet given in honour of Bowring's efforts to spread free trade on the Continent at Manchester in 1838, and Bowring later described himself as the League's 'baptizer'.[135] Anglo-French exchanges of liberal ideas in the 1830s were

[131] Bowring to Thomson, 15 August, 9 September and 20–1 October 1834, BODL, MS Clar., dep. c. 546/1/3, fols. 100–1, 106–8.

[132] *Le Mémorial*, 22 October 1834.

[133] 'L'enquête n'est qu'un moyen de préserver le ministère des exigences impérieuses de la délibération', *Le Réformateur*, 27 October 1834; 'L'Enquête sur les douanes', *La Tribune*, 13 October 1834; 'Enquête commerciale', *Le National*, 21 September 1834; *Le Temps*, 21 September 1834; 'Réforme des tarifs', *Le Constitutionnel*, 23 September 1834; *Le Journal des Débats*, 21 September 1834; 'De la circulaire de M. Duchâtel', *Le Journal du Commerce*, 23 September 1834; *Le Courrier Français*, 27 September 1834. The royalist press (*La Gazette de France*, *La Quotidienne*) did not discuss the decision to hold an inquiry.

[134] Norman McCord, *The Anti-Corn Law League, 1838–1846* (London, 1958), pp. 83–90.

[135] Todd, 'John Bowring', p. 385.

reciprocal. British influence undeniably helped to catalyse the emergence of a radical form of commercial liberalism in some parts of France. But France might also be said to have served as a laboratory, before British free-traders repeated the experience at home, on a larger scale and with greater success, after 1838.[136]

Only with the benefit of hindsight is it possible to discern the seeds of the French protectionist divergence in the early 1830s. The limited national impact of the Bordelais campaign suggests that the conservative and regionalist version of free trade elaborated by Fonfrède and others was not well suited to economic, social and political circumstances outside the Gironde. Furthermore, although Bowring initially toured the French provinces with the blessing of the French government, his attempt at influencing French opinion offered formidable ammunition to the adversaries of commercial liberalization, who would be able to use it as evidence that free trade was a jealous ploy to consolidate British economic hegemony. In subsequent years, a growing anxiety with the spread of urban pauperism, embodied by the miserable condition of factory workers in British cities, would dent the enthusiasm of French liberals for the British economic model and enhance the credibility of such suspicions.

[136] On the reciprocity of transnational exchanges, see Michael Werner and Bénédicte Zimmerman, 'Beyond Comparison: *Histoire Croisée* and the Challenge of Reflexivity', *History and Theory*, 45 (1) (2006): 30–50.

CHAPTER 4

Inventing economic nationalism

In the liberal context created by the 1830 Revolution, the language of mercantile jealousy did not constitute an effective response to calls for free trade. The jealous conception of international trade as a zero-sum game stood profoundly at odds with liberal economic thinking. Jealousy was also tainted by its successive associations with illiberal politics, from the Republican Terror to the Napoleonic Empire to *ultra-royalisme* under the Restoration. Moreover, the growing contemporary enthusiasm for free trade in Britain was eroding the persuasive power of the British example, which until then had served in a French context to illustrate the compatibility of jealous policies with representative institutions. Resisting the radical conception of commercial liberty therefore required ideological innovation, or at least a reinvention of jealousy that would render it compatible with the discourse of political liberty and commercial society.

Such a reconciliation of jealousy with liberal precepts marked an important stage in the emergence of modern economic nationalism. The origins of nationalism as a political phenomenon remain disputed, but the prevailing view still locates its source in the era of Atlantic revolutions, before its intensification and expansion in the nineteenth century.[1] This chapter contends that the elaboration of new nationalist economic ideas formed a significant part of this process of intensification and can be construed as a response to the acceleration of globalization since the early 1820s.[2] The decisive innovation made by defenders of high tariffs in the 1830s lay in their harnessing of the fear of urban pauperism, euphemistically referred

[1] Classical statements of the modernist view on the origins of nationalism include Benedict Anderson, *Imagined Communities: Reflections on the Origins and Spread of Nationalism*, 2nd edn (London, 1991); Eric Hobsbawm, *Nations and Nationalism since 1780: Programme, Myth, Reality*, 2nd edn (Cambridge, 1992); and Ernest Gellner, *Nations and Nationalism*, 2nd edn (Oxford, 2006). On the early emergence of modern nationalism in France, see David Bell, *The Cult of the Nation in France: Inventing Nationalism, 1680–1800* (Cambridge, Mass., 2001).

[2] For an alternative view, which stresses continuity between early modern jealousy and modern economic nationalism, see Hont, *The Jealousy of Trade*, pp. 111–56, 447–528.

to as the *question sociale*, to present protection as an at least partial solution to this new danger of social and political unrest. Britain, the model to be emulated for traditional advocates of jealousy, now served as a foil. The misery and unruliness of its workers were reinterpreted as a consequence of its excessive reliance on foreign exchanges and predilection for free trade.[3] Through the British prism, the *question sociale* appeared as a consequence of the growing industrial specialization of Western Europe in global trade, making it possible to view the economic nationalism of the 1830s as the prefiguration of the late-nineteenth-century protectionist backlash against globalization.[4]

The new Anglophobic justification of protection recalls Johan Gottlieb Fichte's earlier defence, in the context of archaic globalization, of economic self-sufficiency as indispensable to the edification of a liberal order in *The Closed Commercial State*.[5] I found no trace of direct influence of Fichte's work in French debates, but it is noteworthy that as defenders of protection shunned the British example, they often cited the rapid progress of Germany, which did not seem to rely on overseas trade, as a possible alternative model. The formation of a German customs union or Zollverein in 1834 also fostered a sense that national economic solidarity, even in the absence of political unity, was necessary to sustain global competition. In any case, the French economic nationalists did not put forward theories that matched the intellectual sophistication and coherence of Fichte's work. As with the development of nationalism as a political doctrine, the invention and diffusion of economic nationalism was primarily the work of 'second-rank thinkers'.[6]

This chapter successively examines the liberal nationalist justifications of protection put forward by four such middle-brow, but extremely influential figures: the statesman Adolphe Thiers; the Lorraine agronomist Christophe-Joseph-Alexandre Mathieu de Dombasle; the Roubaix manufacturer Auguste Mimerel; and the navy engineer Charles Dupin. All four supported the liberal order established in 1830 and had defended

[3] On the emergence of the *question sociale* in France, see Giovanna Procacci, *Gouverner la misère: la question sociale en France, 1789–1848* (Paris, 1993) and Elizabeth M. Sage, *A Dubious Science: Political Economy and the Social Question in Nineteenth-Century France* (New York, 2009).

[4] O'Rourke and Williamson, *Globalization and History*, pp. 93–117; Conrad, *Globalisation and the Nation*, esp. pp. 27–76.

[5] Nakhimovsky, *Closed Commercial State*; on Fichte and the origins of modern nationalism, see Elie Kedourie, *Nationalism*, 4th edn (Oxford, 1993), esp. pp. 26–40.

[6] John Breuilly, 'On the Principle of Nationality', in Gareth Stedman Jones and Gregory Claeys (eds.), *The Cambridge History of Nineteenth-Century Political Thought* (Cambridge, 2011), pp. 77–109, at p. 78.

commercial liberty in the past, making them apposite examples of the protectionist turn of French liberalism after 1830. This chapter also considers the impact of this effervescence of nationalist ideas on Friedrich List, the German-American publicist who wrote his protectionist manifesto, the *National System of Political Economy*, while living in Paris in the late 1830s. List's interest and involvement in French debates certainly helped to inspire his opposition to global free trade as incompatible with the persistence of national politics. Yet the emphasis he placed on the limits of protection may also be construed as an implicit rejection of the self-sufficiency favoured by several French defenders of protection.

I

Adolphe Thiers was one of the first politicians of July Monarchy France to reject free trade openly, as Minister of Commerce, in the *exposé des motifs* of a customs law presented to the Chamber of Deputies in February 1834. From his promotion of Louis-Philippe's candidacy to the throne in July 1830 as a journalist in the columns of *Le National* until his tacit support for a conservative republic as President in the early 1870s, Thiers advocated liberal representative institutions with a rare constancy in nineteenth-century French politics. However, his fervent political liberalism was combined with a strident patriotism. As the instigator of the return of Napoleon's ashes in 1840 and the author of an epic *Histoire du Consulat et de l'Empire* (1845–62), he even made significant contributions to the elaboration of the Napoleonic legend, often seen as the root of a Caesarist streak in modern French political culture.[7]

Thiers's economics reflected the ambivalence of his politics. He initially opposed the system of the balance of trade and expressed support for commercial liberty. Under the Restoration, he condemned the prohibitive system as deriving from 'the prejudice … of an exclusively national commerce' and the delusion that 'a nation must constantly try to render itself independent of foreigners'. Such opinions were incontrovertible errors, he asserted, as demonstrated by 'the luminous discussions of our latest writers on political economy', at that date a probable reference to Jean-Baptiste Say.[8] A few years later, in an account of John Law's financial experiments

[7] John Bury and Robert Tombs, *Adolphe Thiers, 1797–1877: A Political Life* (London, 1986); Pierre Guiral, *Adolphe Thiers; ou, De la nécessité en politique* (Paris, 1986); on the combination of liberal and nationalist rhetoric at *Le National*, see Jeremy Jennings, 'Nationalist Ideas in the Early Years of the July Monarchy: Armand Carrel and *Le National*', *History of Political Thought*, 12 (3) (1991): 497–514.

[8] Adolphe Thiers, *Les Pyrénées et le midi de la France* (Paris, 1823), p. 58.

in the eighteenth century, Thiers also ridiculed the archaic doctrines that equated wealth with bullion.[9] In January 1832, Bowring, the agent of the British Board of Trade, still hoped to enrol Thiers, then Under-Secretary of State for the Treasury, as an ally in his campaign against tariff protection: 'We want to win over Thiers', he reported, 'and I was with him yesterday for four hours giving him information about the [British] Budget, in return for which I hope he will give our cause a lift.'[10]

Only after becoming Minister of Commerce in December 1832 did Thiers adhere to the necessity of commercial protection against foreign competition. The Customs Bill he introduced in the Chamber of Deputies on 3 February 1834 actually proposed several tariff reductions, significant for duties on wool and cattle and more modest for duties on coal and iron. But the law's *exposé des motifs* firmly rebutted the demands for 'unlimited freedom of exchange' made by some 'maritime cities', an allusion to the Bordelais *Adresse* in favour of commercial liberty, and sketched out a new rationale for tariff protection. Thiers likened his stance on commercial policy to 'the general spirit of government' of the July Monarchy, which shunned in equal measure the 'rash' spirit of 1789 and the 'reactionary' spirit of 1814. In commercial legislation as in politics, he asserted, the spirit of 1830 ought to be 'measured, practical, positive'. He condemned the 'harsh' and 'absurd' legislation of the 'Continental System' but also recalled the 'unfortunate results' of the commercial treaty of 1786 with Britain, 'conceived under the influence of systematic minds'. Commercial isolation would breed 'ignorance and the impoverishment of the mind', but absolute liberty would leave France with only 'one or two industries', hence the need to steer a middle course between 'absolute systems'.[11]

Commercial legislation, Thiers argued, should be based neither on the outdated doctrine of the balance of trade nor on the 'dogmatic science' of political economy but on the 'veritable science' of economics, 'this science, more modest and more useful, which limits itself to the observation of facts'. According to Thiers, this pragmatic science showed that early nineteenth-century nations were engaged in a competition for the possession of modern industries and that tariffs constituted a legitimate instrument in this economic struggle:

> Nations have an irresistible tendency to make industrial conquests at each other's expense. In order to succeed, they prohibit or increase the price,

[9] Adolphe Thiers, *Law: encyclopédie progressive* (Paris, 1826), pp. 3–4.

[10] Bowring to Thomson, 18 January 1832, BODL, MS Clar., dep. c. 546/1/1, fol. 30.

[11] AP, vol. LXXXVI, p. 118 (3 February 1834).

> thanks to tariffs, of certain foreign products, so as to give their own citizens an incentive to produce them. … It is the universal instinct of peoples; [following the example of the English and the French], the Americans, the Russians, the Germans do the same today.

Only thanks to tariffs did the English acquire 'cotton spinning and weaving from the Indians' and 'iron forging from the Swedes'. Conversely, absolute specialization under conditions of free trade was an absurd project, for Nièvre and French Flanders could not make Bordeaux wine or silk textiles. France therefore needed to continue, for the foreseeable future, the protection of its cotton, iron and coal-mining industries.[12]

Thiers conceded that modern nations' 'irresistible tendency' for tariffs could have harmful effects and needed to be restrained. Tariffs that expressed political hostility towards other nations, that favoured aristocratic landowners or that sought to foster industries ill-suited to the local climate should be avoided. He also accepted that protection should be limited in time: 'it ought to be temporary; it must end when the industry's education is over, once it has become adult'. Yet temporary does not mean brief, Thiers added, as illustrated by the example of Britain, which waited several decades before reducing its import duties on iron or cotton textiles, until its producers could sustain foreign competition.[13] Thiers's 'veritable science' of tariffs was an industrialist reinvention of jealousy: a liberal, attenuated version of jealousy, primarily concerned with the promotion of modern industries. Thiers's marriage to Elise Dosne, the daughter of a family of rich Lille textile manufacturers, in November 1833 certainly contributed to his reappraisal of the merits of protection. But whatever role his personal interest played, it is noteworthy that his liberal culture prevented him from employing the traditional language of jealousy, which set great store by the balance of trade and placed few limits on the desirable extent or level of tariffs. Tellingly, Thiers's personal library contained the treatises of Adam Smith, Jean-Baptiste Say and David Ricardo, but not those of Ferrier, Saint-Chamans or Vaublanc.[14]

However, the *exposé des motifs*' praises for the past work of the 'Administration' in matters of commerce betrayed the personal influence of Saint-Cricq, the architect of the Restoration's prohibitive system. When

[12] AP, vol. LXXXVI, pp. 119–21 (3 February 1834). [13] AP, vol. LXXXVI, pp. 120–4 (3 February 1834).

[14] 'Catalogue de la bibliothèque de M. Thiers', Paris, Fondation Dosne-Thiers, Fonds Thiers, I-2, items 368, 369, 374, 457, 742, 3750. Thiers owned copies of Adam Smith's *De la richesse des nations* (1822 edn), David Ricardo's *Principes d'économie politique* (1819 edn), Thomas Malthus's *Essai sur le principe de population* (1823 edn) as well as Say's *Traité d'économie politique* (1826 edn), Sismondi's *Nouveaux principes d'économie politique* (1819 edn) and Antoine Destutt de Tracy's *Traité d'économie politique* (1822 edn).

George Villiers, Bowring's colleague, called on Thiers at his private residence in 1833, he was shocked to find the young minister of commerce in the company of the old Director General of Customs and by the 'emulation' between them at whom would display 'the greater ignorance' in commercial affairs:

> I never heard such a duo before. One said we [Britain and France] must ever be rivals because we produce the same things so let each protect his own – then the other replied we want no theories we'll have no principles we know what to do with the country – then, morceau d'ensemble – we are not schoolboys we don't want to learn ... etc.[15]

Bowring later confirmed that Thiers was now 'wholly in St-Cricq's hands'.[16] The exalted account of British industrial progress in the *exposé* also certainly drew on Thiers's impressions while he travelled in Britain for several weeks in the autumn of 1833. His tour included visits to factories in the Midlands, Lancashire and Wales and seems to have persuaded him that only the safety offered by several decades of tariff protection enabled British manufacturers to make the large-scale investments required for the installation of machinery in branches such as coal-mining, cotton-spinning and metallurgy.

Thiers's reformulation of jealousy in liberal terms met with limited success. Bowring was dismayed: 'The *exposé* is wretched indeed – and must be *flétri*' (discredited).[17] The Bordelais press was incensed, disparaging the *exposé* as 'delirious babblings' (*La Guienne*), a 'heresy' (*L'Indicateur*) and a 'declaration of war' (*Le Mémorial*).[18] Apart from the pro-government *Journal des Débats*, the Parisian press was also hostile. The left-wing *Tribune* decried the exposé as a 'political, economic and administrative jumble' that reflected the principles of an 'oligarchy devoid of conscience or convictions'. The centre-left *Constitutionnel* derided the 'charlatanism' of this strange 'politico-economic manifesto'. The royalist *Quotidienne* scoffed at the language of 'technologue' adopted by Thiers and attributed his exaggerated enthusiasm for manufacturing to his recent '*industrial* journey' across England.[19] Faced with such criticisms, Thiers affected not to have written the *exposé* himself. But an official at the Ministry told Bowring that the Minister was indeed the author of the text. The agent of

[15] Villiers to Thomson, 22 February 1833, BODL, MS Clar., dep. c. 544, fols. 83–5.
[16] Bowring to Villiers, 25 May 1833, BODL, MS Clar., dep. c. 544, fol. 109.
[17] Bowring to Auckland, 10 February 1834, BL, AUP, Add MS 34459, fols. 514–15.
[18] *L'Indicateur*, 19 February 1834; *Le Mémorial*, 22 February 1834; *La Guienne*, 25 February 1834.
[19] *La Tribune*, 13 February 1834; *Le Constitutionnel*, 16 and 20 February 1834; *La Quotidienne*, 18 February 1834.

the British Board of Trade now described the *exposé* as a '*trouvaille*': 'our cause is gained – and gained by Thiers's folly rather than by our own wisdom'.[20]

The extent of discontent led Thiers to resign the portfolio of commerce on 6 April 1834. His 'veritable science' of tariffs, with its bellicose imagery of rivalry and conquests, perhaps resembled traditional jealousy too closely to appeal to liberal opinion. But the main cause of Thiers's fiasco probably lay in his loud enthusiasm for modern industries at a time of mounting anxiety about the parallel growth of manufacturing and urban pauperism – an anxiety nurtured by several workers' revolts in Paris since 1830 and the larger insurrections of the Lyon silk-workers in November 1831 and April 1834. Thiers's hostility to free trade would not abate in later years, but he would use different arguments, laying greater stress on tariffs as instruments of social stability.

II

In the summer of 1834, the Lorraine agronomist Mathieu de Dombasle better captured the country's mood with another response to the clamour for free trade, *De l'avenir industriel de la France*, first published under the less compelling title of *Des interêts respectifs du midi et du nord dans les questions de douanes*. The pamphlet met with a success rare for this type of publication, reaching its fourth edition by the end of 1835 and a total circulation of around 10,000 copies.[21] While Thiers supported tariffs in order to foster industrial growth, Dombasle instead defended protection as a means of preserving France's fragile social equilibrium from the instability induced by dependency on foreign markets.

By the early 1830s, Dombasle was France's most celebrated agronomist. He owed his fame to the development of a simple and effective plough after 1815 ('la Dombasle'), his efforts to disseminate agricultural best practices with publications such as the *Calendrier du bon cultivateur* (1821) and the foundation of an agricultural school at Roville (Meurthe) in 1822. The scholarship on Dombasle has questioned the significance of his innovations, highlighting his debt to the French tradition of agricultural improvement since the 1750s and the works of foreign agronomists such as John Sinclair and Albrecht Thaër, whose treatises Dombasle translated in the

[20] Bowring to Auckland, 15 February 1834, BL, AUP, Add MS 34459, fol. 517; Bowring to Auckland, 24 February 1834, BL, AUP, Add MS 34460, fol. 12.

[21] Louis Villermé, *L'Agriculture française: Mathieu de Dombasle, sa vie, ses œuvres, son influence* (Paris, 1864), p. 19.

1820s. But it has confirmed his importance as a 'popularisateur-diffuseur' of novel ideas and practices.[22] Dombasle expressed little interest in party politics in his writings, but he had served as a conscript in the Revolutionary armies in the 1790s and supported the liberal opposition under the Restoration. Despite his political leaning, Dombasle received the financial support of several royalist benefactors, who approved of his schemes of agricultural improvement. In particular, he earned the friendship of Alban de Villeneuve-Bargemont, an advocate of charity works and future major figure of social Catholicism, while the latter served as the royalist prefect of the Meurthe between 1820 and 1824.[23]

De l'avenir industriel did not reject free-market economics, praising instead the results of 'industrial liberty' within France's borders since its advent in 1789. Dombasle even confessed a youthful enthusiasm for the unlimited liberty of commerce: 'Which one of us', he asked, 'before the age of thirty, did not pay an admiring and fervent tribute to the doctrines of Adam Smith and Jean-Baptiste Say?'[24] Dombasle turned thirty in 1807, and it was perhaps his experience as a beet-sugar manufacturer during the Continental System, and the ruin of his factory when cane-sugar imports resumed in 1814, that made him realize the merits of protection.[25] The main argument put forward by Dombasle to justify his rallying to the regulation of imports lay in the vastly greater importance, for almost all national producers, of the domestic market over foreign exports. Even for France's south and most winegrowers, he retorted to the Bordelais petitions, 'the most important outlet [was] the market of the country itself'. In an attempt to reverse the usage established by Adam Smith's attacks on the 'mercantile system' of trade restrictions, Dombasle contended that it was the free-traders who should be labelled the 'Mercantile School', because they believed that 'external trade was the main source of wealth for nations'.[26]

Shunning complex economic theory, Dombasle appealed to *bon sens* (common sense), which 'made nations feel, early on, that it was better

[22] Fabien Knittel, 'Mathieu de Dombasle: agronomie et innovation' (unpublished doctoral thesis, University of Nancy II, 2007), p. 126; see also Fabien Knittel, 'L'Europe agronomique de C. J. A. Mathieu de Dombasle', *Revue d'Histoire Moderne et Contemporaine*, 57 (1) (2010): 119–38.

[23] André Tiano, *Alban de Villeneuve-Bargemont (1784–1850): le précurseur de l'État social ou un grand notable bien ordinaire?* (Nîmes, 1993), pp. 175–7.

[24] Christophe-Joseph-Alexandre Mathieu de Dombasle, *Des intérêts respectifs du midi et du nord dans les questions de douanes* (Paris, 1834), p. 57.

[25] See a petition by Dombasle against imports of cane sugar, 'Observations relatives au tarif des douanes', October 1814, AN, C2399.

[26] Mathieu de Dombasle, *Des intérêts*, pp. 8, 24–6.

for them to produce a good that they consumed, rather than buying it from abroad'. England, in the seventeenth century, was the first country to turn such feelings 'into a comprehensive and regular system', thanks to which 'all the industries of the United Kingdom experienced a development unprecedented in the history of the world'. Other nations had since imitated Britain, so that 'the system of protection [was now] the foundation of commercial public law between nations'. Dombasle drew from this observation a consequence that flew in the face of a widely held belief in the concurrent progress of industry and international trade: 'the progress of industry will always tend ... to reduce the total of importations by all nations', eventually extinguishing international exchanges, at least of manufactured commodities. According to Dombasle, such an autarkical 'industrial future' should be welcomed rather than feared. Scientific knowledge, art and literature would continue to circulate freely across borders, while the waning of commercial rivalries would facilitate 'the preservation of peace'. Moreover, freer trade increased the specialization in manufacturing, encouraging a precarious dependency on faraway markets and a dangerous concentration of workers in large cities, as illustrated by the destitution of English workers in Manchester and Birmingham, or the recent insurrections of silk-workers in Lyon. Industrial autarky, by contrast, would enhance social stability: 'Whenever a country consumes its own products, its industry adopts a remarkably stable character because it develops gradually all its branches and preserves a constant balance between them.'[27]

Dombasle conceded that his views gainsaid dominant ideas about international trade, which remained inspired by the 'liberal spirit' of the primacy of individuals and 'cosmopolitan philanthropy'. But he expressed his confidence that another principle inherited from the Revolutionary struggles, the 'patriotic spirit', consisting in the willingness of individuals to sacrifice themselves for the greater good and power of the nation, would eventually prevail. The present popularity of liberal ideas about trade, Dombasle contended, relied on a misguided alliance between 'men of progress' and 'modern political economy', an alliance 'contracted under the rousing charm of the word *liberty*'. The mistaken use of 'political ideas' in 'discussions about social economics' misled many into believing that 'a commercial reform' should be the natural consequence of the 'great political reform' of 1830: 'This is why today all the liberal political newspapers still defend, fervently, the doctrines of unlimited liberty in commerce: for them,

[27] Mathieu de Dombasle, *Des intérêts*, pp. 23, 30–2, 43–7.

all these are only questions of liberalism.' But the false analogy between political and commercial liberty would soon unravel: 'whether one lives in a Republic, an absolute Empire or a constitutional Monarchy, [interests] are entirely identical in all that concerns commercial relations with foreign nations'. Moreover, the dominance of the liberal spirit was confined to 'the surface of society', among 'a very small class ... but which speaks and writes a great deal'. Once the rest of the country was consulted, 'the immense majority of the population' would side with patriotic protection.[28]

De l'avenir industriel combined a liberal language with concerns drawn from early social Catholic doctrines. Dombasle was probably well acquainted with the work of his friend, Villeneuve-Bargemont, whose *Économie politique chrétienne* had only just been published, with 1,000 copies printed in June 1834.[29] Using the local data on poverty that Villeneuve-Bargemont collected while he served as prefect of the industrial department of Nord between 1828 and 1830, this treatise investigated the 'nature and causes of pauperism in France and abroad'. Villeneuve-Bargemont attributed the growth of this new sort of destitution to the relentless growth of manufacturing and the nefarious materialism of 'the theories of [Adam] Smith and his disciples'. In England, industrial exuberance and Smithian political economy had resulted in the parallel growth of fabulous riches for some and 'hideous pauperism' for masses of workers. Such disparity could not fail 'sooner or later to break out into a great political and social revolution', of which the recent multiplication of urban riots and industrial actions formed 'the preludes'. Against this 'English system', Villeneuve-Bargemont recommended the adoption of a 'French system', which would rely on a more equitable distribution of industrial riches and a greater emphasis on 'the development of agriculture' thanks to the creation of 'colonies' of cultivators in metropolitan France and the recently conquered regency of Algiers.[30]

Économie politique chrétienne was representative of a broader trend in conservative Catholic thought after 1830.[31] Other significant examples included the works of Louis-François Huerne de Pommeuse, an *ultra-royaliste* promoter of agricultural colonies within France, and Pierre

[28] Mathieu de Dombasle, *Des intérêts*, pp. 53–9, and third edition, under the title *De l'avenir industriel de la France* (Paris, 1834), pp. 71–2.

[29] Impression 2260 (2 June 1834), AN, F*18 II 24.

[30] Alban de Villeneuve-Bargemont, *Économie politique chrétienne, ou recherches sur la nature et les causes du paupérisme en France et en Europe*, 3 vols. (Paris, 1834), vol. I, pp. 23–4; vol. II, pp. 153–5.

[31] Georges Cahen, 'L'Économie sociale chrétienne et la colonisation agricole sous la Restauration et la Monarchie de Juillet', *Revue d'Économie Politique*, 17 (6) (1903): 511–46; Jean-Baptiste Duroselle, *Les Débuts du catholicisme social en France (1822–1870)* (Paris, 1951), pp. 59–79; André

Bigot de Morogues, a conservative supporter of the July Monarchy, on the dangers of urban pauperism.[32] This trend can be construed as a partial revival of the anti-luxury discourse of agricultural improvement, widespread among rural *notables* in the eighteenth century. Several chapters of the *Économie politique chrétienne* opened with an epigraph from Jacques Delille, the popular poet of agricultural improvement and rural life before the Revolution.[33] But while this agriculturalist discourse was often combined with the republican exaltation of virtue until 1789 and Delille wrote odes to the Supreme Being during the Terror, its revived form had distinct conservative undertones. The opening epigraph of *Économie politique chrétienne* was a passage from Burke's *Reflections on the Revolution in France*, and the book paid homage to several luminaries of counter-revolutionary political and economic thought, including Louis de Bonald, François Ferrier, Maurice Rubichon and Auguste de Saint-Chamans. Moreover, Villeneuve-Bargemont and most other advocates of an agricultural revival paid only incidental attention to the influence of trade policy. In *De l'avenir industriel*, Dombasle simultaneously harnessed these ideas to justify protection against foreign competition and offered a political reformulation acceptable to the 'patriotic' fraction of liberal opinion.

In Paris, the reception of *De l'avenir industriel* oscillated between critical and scornful. Élie Decazes, a Gironde politician and former Premier, reassured Fonfrède, who was worried by the pamphlet's success, that Dombasle was 'a dreamer whose work [was] rarely read'. Théodore Ducos, Fonfrède's cousin, concurred that deputies were unimpressed by the agronomist's ideas and considered the pamphlet 'no longer worth refuting'.[34] The Parisian press was equally disdainful. A review in *Le Temps* ironically lauded Dombasle for his 'courage in rejecting the current trends and honestly declaring himself the champion of the opposite principles'. The reviewer also pointed to what he perceived as a contradiction between

Gueslin, *L'Invention de l'économie sociale en France: le XIXe siècle français* (Paris, 1987); Geneviève Gavignaud-Fontaine, *Les Catholiques et l'économie sociale en France: XIXe–XXe siècles* (Paris, 2011), pp. 24–9; António Almodovar and Pedro Teixeira, '"Catholic in Its Faith, Catholic in Its Manner of Conceiving Science": French Catholic Political Economy in the 1830s', *European Journal of the History of Economic Thought*, 19 (2) (2012): 197–225.

32 Louis-François Huerne de Pommeuse, *Des colonies agricoles et de leurs avantages* (Paris, 1832); Pierre Bigot de Morogues, *Du paupérisme, de la mendicité, et des moyens d'en prévenir les funestes effets* (Paris, 1834).

33 Shovlin, *The Political Economy of Virtue*, pp. 76, 214; Jeremy Jennings, 'The Debate about Luxury in Eighteenth- and Nineteenth-Century French Thought', *Journal of the History of Ideas*, 68 (1) (2007): 79–105, esp. at pp. 99–100.

34 Decazes to Fonfrède, 11 September 1834, and Ducos to Fonfrède, 21 January 1835, BMB, MS 1095, vol. 1, fols. 310, 512.

Dombasle's support for industrial liberty within France and his hostility to the free circulation of commodities across borders. In a response to the review, the agronomist refuted the accusation, explaining that both opinions derived from a single principle, 'the individuality of nations'. National self-sufficiency, he argued, was not only compatible with, but also necessary for, the achievement of economic liberty: 'for all the parts [of a society] to be able to sustain a full liberty in their relations with each other', they needed the common bond of 'natural nationality', which provided 'sufficient homogeneity and sufficient common material interests'.[35]

Reactions to Dombasle's defence of protection were more positive outside Paris. At least three pamphlets published in 1834, authored respectively by a Nantes merchant, a Clermont-Ferrand manufacturer and a Normand landowner, expressed their admiration for *De l'avenir industriel*.[36] In their statements to the commercial inquiry organized by Duchatel in the autumn of 1834, the Le Puy Chamber of Commerce referred to Dombasle's pamphlet as 'the only system that truly suits France's material interests', while the Nevers chamber expressed its 'true sympathy' for 'the clear and rational ideas profusely spread by the work of M. Mathieu de Dombasle'.[37] Dombasle's reinvention of jealousy as a condition of domestic liberty appeared to have struck a chord among the provincial notables of early July Monarchy France.

III

The proceedings of the commercial inquiry held in October and November 1834 further highlighted the limits of public enthusiasm for commercial liberty. Northern and eastern industrialists who testified before the Conseil Supérieur de Commerce opposed the repeal of prohibitions with unexpected energy. Auguste Mimerel, a cotton and wool manufacturer from Roubaix (Nord), was the most defiant, stressing the need for solidarity between national producers and the danger of workers' revolts if British manufactured goods were allowed to enter the French market. Mimerel and other manufacturers frequently resorted to a language of raw and virulent

[35] *Le Temps*, 4 and 29 September 1834.

[36] Henry Ducoudray-Bourgault, *Réflexions d'un ancien commerçant sur l'industrie agricole, commerciale et manufacturière et particulièrement sur l'ouvrage récemment publié par M. de Dombasle* (Nantes, 1834); Auguste de Lamothe, *De l'abolition des droits de douane sur les houilles étrangères et des effets de cette mesure sur l'avenir industriel de la France* (Clermont-Ferrand, 1834); Jean-Jacques Lebaillif, *Essai sur la question de la liberté du commerce entre tous les peuples* (Falaise, [1834]).

[37] Ministère du Commerce, *Enquête relative à diverses prohibitions*, 3 vols. (Paris, 1835), vol. 1, pp. 149, 184.

nationalism. But in so far as they sought to justify protection on theoretical grounds, their arguments resembled Dombasle's defence of self-sufficiency rather than Thiers's call for the making of industrial conquests.

Upon learning, in September 1834, that the government would hold an inquiry on the repeal of prohibitions, fear swept France's industrial north-east. In Normandy, specialized in the production of cotton textiles, the Prefect of the Seine-Inférieure reported that 'there reign[ed] … an extreme anxiety, caused by the commercial inquiry'. 'The enemies of the government', he added, peddled rumours that ministers wished 'to sell France to England by opening our ports to foreign goods, that the ruin of national industry [would] inevitably follow, etc.'[38] In early October, an assembly of 500 manufacturers gathered in Rouen's town hall in order to appoint the region's delegates for the inquiry and mandated them that the 'system of prohibition' be maintained '*at all costs*'.[39] In Lille, another centre of textile production, the Prefect of the Nord received a delegation of foremen and workers who came to express 'their anxiety' over the inquiry.[40] Even liberal Alsace felt apprehensive. Mulhouse, sometimes described as the French Manchester for the number of its cotton manufactures, was 'as restless as if there was a [general] election'. The circular announcing the inquiry was 'commented upon in a thousand different ways'. Even those who had 'spent forty years … without worrying about political economy' now expressed misgivings: 'For many of our manufacturers, who were liberals under the Restoration, prohibition is the holy ark: touching it is like shaking the throne and encouraging the masses to revolt; indeed, it is worse than the Republic.'[41]

Dozens of chambers of commerce or ad-hoc commissions sent solemn petitions, often reproduced by national newspapers, for or against the repeal of prohibitions, to the Conseil Supérieur de Commerce. A majority – Alençon, Arras, Bar-le-Duc, Bordeaux, Boulogne, Calais, Grenoble, Le Havre, Limoges, Lyon, Marseille, Nantes, Niort, Orléans, Rennes, Rethel, Saumur, Tours, Valenciennes, Vire – still demanded their replacement by high or moderate import duties.[42] Yet the fiery rhetoric of industrial towns hostile to repeal made up for their smaller numbers. Pointing at Bowring's efforts to agitate public opinion, many denounced the decision to hold an inquiry as a bow to British pressures. A petition from Rouen complained that 'England … sustains and fosters these ideas [of commercial liberty], spreads them through emissaries'. Another petition

[38] Letter reproduced in Ministère du Commerce, *Enquête relative à diverses prohibitions*, vol. 1, p. 84.
[39] *Le Journal de Rouen*, quoted in *Le National*, 12 and 13 October 1834.
[40] *Le Courrier Français*, 18 October 1834. [41] Quoted in *Le Temps*, 22 October 1834.
[42] Ministère du Commerce, *Enquête relative à diverses prohibitions*, vol. 1, pp. 63–193.

from the same town insinuated that not only 'official' but also 'secret' agents of the British government had been travelling 'throughout all our southern departments' and 'taking advantage, skilfully, of the inclination for change that seems characteristic of the French mind' to 'sow, forcefully, ideas of commercial fraternity'.[43] Petitions by Amiens, Bolbec, Carcassonne, Dunkirk, Lille, Louviers Saint-Quentin, Sedan and Yvetot also denounced Britain's hypocritical support for trade liberalization now that its manufacturers no longer needed protection to sustain foreign competition, and no fewer than seven petitions recalled the 'disastrous' effects of the 1786 treaty of commerce with England.[44]

Two vehement petitions from Roubaix also introduced a novel theme to the defence of protection, insisting that the removal of restrictions on imports of manufactured goods would harm workers as well as factory owners and endanger social stability. A petition from the Roubaix 'manufacturers and spinners' exclaimed: 'Do the well-to-do mind paying five or ten more centimes for an alder of fabric, if at this small cost they ensure a living for the people, without making them blush and beg for it?' Another petition by the Roubaix 'cotton spinners' contended that 'if Napoleon was loved by the country' despite the decimation of the French population by his wars, 'it was because he provided his countrymen with work'. More menacingly, it also recalled that the ordinances of Charles X, which triggered the July Revolution, 'met with such prompt resistance' from the Parisian people because the suspension of freedom of the press 'left print workers jobless'. 'Above all', the petition concluded, 'remember that [the workers of] Lyon rose up twice [in November 1831 and April 1834] after the lowering of wages.'[45]

Unprecedented publicity amplified the impact of the industrialists' protests. National dailies commented at length on the chambers' manifestos and, from mid-October, reproduced in full the testimonies of manufacturers before the Conseil Supérieur du Commerce. Between 19 October and 1 November, *Le Journal des Débats* dedicated on average 25 per cent of its printed space to the Inquiry's proceedings. The figure remained 16 per cent from 2 to 15 November, before falling to 4.5 per cent from 16 to 29 November.[46] The controversy on international trade now enjoyed a broad and growing audience. However, most of this press coverage, especially on

[43] Ministère du Commerce, *Enquête relative à diverses prohibitions*, vol. 1, pp. 85–6, 101.

[44] Ministère du Commerce, *Enquête relative à diverses prohibitions*, vol. 1, pp. 92, 94–7, 128, 250, 272, 324–6, 329, 338, 375.

[45] Ministère du Commerce, *Enquête relative à diverses prohibitions*, vol. 1, pp. 136–40.

[46] My calculations, based on *Le Journal des Débats*, 19 October–29 November 1834.

the left of the political spectrum, remained favourable to commercial liberty and castigated the defence of protection by manufacturers as archaic and self-interested.[47]

During debates about a possible commercial treaty between France and Belgium in 1842, memories of the 1834 inquiry were vivid enough for *Le National* to publish the parody of a cotton and wool manufacturer's testimony. The part of the manufacturer was played by Jérôme Paturot, the anti-hero invented by the liberal writer, Louis Reybaud. A credulous character, Paturot fell victim to all sorts of practical and ideological swindles, from the Saint-Simonian religion to the colonization of Algeria. His incarnation as a manufacturer hostile to free trade implicitly categorized protectionism as another malady of the times. In the 1842 parody, Paturot's limited intelligence prevented him from answering the questions put to him by the members of the Conseil Supérieur de Commerce on production costs. Instead, he merely rejected the repeal of prohibitions on the grounds that the raw materials he bought and the products he sold were 'Frrench': 'I only honour Frrench sheep. … and Frrench shepherds, Mister president! And Frrench meadows! And Frrench dogs! On this point, you see, my convictions are firm. Long live Frrench sheep!'[48] Paturot's pronunciation was almost certainly an allusion to another fictional character, Nicolas Chauvin, a grotesque but irresistible patriotic conscript, who made his first appearance in Parisian vaudevilles in 1840 and also emphasized the *r* in the words *France* or *français*. The origins of *protectionnisme* were intertwined with those of *chauvinisme*, another contemporary neologism.[49]

There was also an echo, in Paturot's imaginary testimony, of Auguste Mimerel, the real manufacturer of cotton and wool textiles who represented the Lille, Roubaix and Tourcoing chambers of commerce at the commercial inquiry.[50] Mimerel probably contributed to the drafting of the threatening Roubaix petitions cited above, and his testimony before the Conseil Supérieur de Commerce stood out for its vehemence and insolence. Mimerel's politics were liberal. On the eve of the July Revolution, the royalist Prefect of the Nord identified him and his brother, a justice of the peace, as the 'leaders of the hostile party' in Roubaix, who

[47] See, for instance, 'Enquête commerciale', *Le National*, 15 October 1834, and 'L'Enquête n'est qu'un moyen de préserver le ministère des exigences impérieuses de la délibération', *Le Réformateur*, 27 October 1834.

[48] Louis Reybaud, *Jérôme Paturot à la recherche d'une position sociale*, 4th edn (Paris, 1846), pp. 232–40.

[49] Gérard de Puymège, *Chauvin, le soldat-laboureur* (Paris, 1993), pp. 51–7.

[50] Frédéric Delattre, 'Pierre-Auguste Mimerel', *Mémoires de la Société d'Émulation de Roubaix*, 35 (1961), 81–5; Jean Piat, *Quand Mimerel gouvernait la France* (Roubaix, 1992).

exercised 'a regrettable influence over the main manufacturers and their workers'.[51] Even on the issue of international trade, until the early 1830s, Mimerel employed a liberal rhetoric. In an 1832 letter to the Prefect of the Nord, for instance, he protested against the seizure of foreign wool illegally introduced into France on the grounds that 'the spirit and the imperative of our century … require[d] new commercial liberties rather than new harsh measures [of repression against smuggling]'.[52] It was the threat of the repeal of prohibitions in 1834 that turned him into a staunch defender of protection, who went on to become the leading figure of a new anti-free-trade lobby in the 1840s, the Association pour la Défense du Travail National.

In his testimony, instead of merely defending protection for manufacturers, Mimerel insisted that all French producers, including those of raw materials and semi-finished products, were entitled to restrictions on imports: 'all industries are in contact with each other', he told the Conseil Supérieur de Commerce, 'and if we ask for protection for ourselves, we must also want it for the others'. Such a stance contradicted the short-term interests of manufacturers, but it broadened the potential appeal of nationalist economics. Mimerel's emphasis on solidarity between national producers led him to embrace a conception of protection closer to self-sufficiency than the pursuit of industrial conquests. To explain his views, he contrasted France's situation with Britain's:

> The English … are in intercourse with all the peoples of the world. If a commercial crisis occurs in a country, they are affected by it, whereas it does not concern us; for if we do not enjoy the same advantages as our neighbours, we are not exposed to such frequent perturbations.

Mimerel's boisterous attitude during his testimony, as when he accused the Minister and President of the Conseil Supérieur, Duchâtel, of having broken an unofficial promise not to call into question the protection of French industries, ensured that his defence of protection received a great deal of publicity.[53]

The strident hostility of Mimerel and other manufacturers to the repeal of prohibitions stalled projects of reform. Bowring attributed the manufacturers' firmness to the encouragement of 'the knave', Thiers, who had organized a meeting with several leading manufacturers 'and told them

[51] The Prefect of the North to the Minister of the Interior, 20 January 1830, AN, F7 6776, folder 24.

[52] Mimerel to the Prefect of the North, November 1832, Archives Départementales du Nord (hereafter ADN), P 52/20.

[53] Ministère du Commerce, *Enquête relative à diverses prohibitions*, vol. III, pp. 191–2, 206–7.

that he desired to thwart Duchâtel and would do all he could to make the enquête a means of keeping out English goods'.[54] In an attempt to counteract the unfavourable impression made by the inquiry, Bowring called for the assistance of his friend, Thomas Perronet Thompson, the author of a pamphlet widely disseminated in Britain, the *Catechism on the Corn Laws*.[55] Thompson spent six weeks in France. He rejoiced that '[t]he Free Trade question' was 'fiercely agitated in France just now' yet regretted that 'the balance of vigour' seemed to be tilting 'rather on the wrong side'. In his opinion, the difficulty lay in the relative lack of interest of 'the republican or popular party' in the free-trade cause. He even noticed 'a curious *cross* in the question': 'the more liberal and republican departments are interested in the monopolies, and the juste milieu [conservative *orléaniste*] and possibly even royaliste departments against it'.[56]

In order to redress the balance, Thompson sought to galvanize support for free trade on the left of the French political spectrum. He was particularly keen to reverse the impression, given by Mimerel and others, that workers were hostile to free trade. 'Respecting the ouvriers', he wrote to Bowring, 'I think between us we can indite a petition for them.'[57] The project of a petition on behalf of French workers did not materialize. But with the help of a French journalist, Thompson wrote a refutation of the manufacturer's patriotic tirades before the Conseil Supérieur de Commerce, the *Contre-enquête*. Perhaps to conceal the British inspiration of the pamphlet, this counter-inquiry was allegedly conducted by 'l'homme aux quarante écus', the character invented by Voltaire to ridicule Physiocratic doctrines. In the didactic vein of earlier works seeking to popularize Smithian political economy, the pamphlet used the concrete examples of the glove-making and wig-making industries to illustrate the advantages of freer international trade. On a more polemical note, the *Contre-enquête* attacked the Roubaix workers' threat of an 'uprising' if prohibitions were repealed: the lowering of wages in industries that diminished 'the wealth and power of France', it contended, would be compensated by an increase in 'the wages of workers whose industry is useful' for France.[58] The pamphlet was printed, with a print run of 1,000,

[54] Bowring to Thomson, 31 October 1834, BODL, MS Clar., dep. c. 546/1/3, fol. 115.

[55] Michael J. Turner, 'The "Bonaparte of Free Trade" and the Anti-Corn Law League', *Historical Journal*, 41 (4) (1998): 1011–34.

[56] Thompson to Bowring, 22 and 28 October 1834, BJL, Thompson MSS, 4/5.

[57] Thompson to Bowring, 3 November 1834, BJL, Thompson MSS, 4/5.

[58] [Benjamin Laroche and Thomas Perronet Thompson], *Contre-enquête, par l'homme aux quarante écus* (Paris, 1834), p. 10; the text was published, alongside an English translation, as 'Contre-enquête/Counter-inquiry', *Westminster Review*, 43 (1835): 227–58.

but not circulated, probably at the request of the French government.[59] The attitude of French authorities and the ebbing of support for free trade led Bowring and Thompson to abandon their campaign and return to Britain at the end of 1834.

In Bordeaux, Bowring's French allies were also stunned by the stridency of the opposition to free trade. Disillusioned, Fonfrède drew the conclusion from the inquiry that in northern industrial regions 'the population believed in the prohibitive regime as much as in God'. The prevalence of 'the blind prejudice of industrial nationalism' in the northern 'masses' derived in his view from the 'immense irritation' of national feelings during the Napoleonic wars, which manufacturers kept up and channelled in a way favourable to their interests.[60] It was an early use of the term 'nationalism' and probably one of the very first in an economic context.[61] The apparent adhesion of the masses to economic nationalism hardened Fonfrède's hostility to the 'democratic school' and its project of extending the electoral franchise. Such an extension could only delay the abolition of economic protection and the advent of 'true liberty'.[62] As noticed by Thompson in his observation about the 'cross' of commercial and partisan opinions, the rise of nationalist economic ideas was severing the ties between economic and political radicalism.

IV

The backlash against trade liberalization at the commercial inquiry left French advocates of free trade in disarray. '[D]efeat has dispersed the combatants', Adolphe Blanqui commented.[63] In 1836, a major parliamentary debate on customs legislation sanctioned the division of Restoration liberals between opponents and supporters of protection. The divide only imperfectly mirrored the split between *Mouvement* and *Résistance* since 1830. Furthermore, it proved that Thompson's alleged cross between political and economic remained incomplete, since right-of-centre, conservative liberals, who remembered the Napoleonic era as one of national glory

[59] Impression 5185, 20 November 1834, AN, F18*II 24.

[60] 'De la liberté sociale', *Le Mémorial*, 17 January 1835.

[61] Sauvigny, 'Liberalism, Nationalism and Socialism', p. 160; Jacques Godechot, 'Nation, patrie, nationalisme et patriotisme', *Annales de l'Histoire de la Révolution Française*, 206 (1971): 481–501.

[62] 'De la liberté sociale', 'Liaison de la liberté politique et de la liberté commerciale' and 'La Liberté protège mieux que la prohibition' (two articles), *Le Mémorial*, 17, 21, 24 and 26 January 1835; these four articles were also published as a pamphlet, *La Liberté protège mieux que la prohibition* (Paris, 1835).

[63] Blanqui to Fonfrède, 17 May 1835, BMB, MS 1095, vol. 1, fols. 617–19.

and social stability, were the most likely to espouse the nascent discourse of national economics. The case of Charles Dupin, a former officer in the Napoleonic navy who recanted his former liberal opinions about trade, illustrates this confluence of economic nationalism with social conservatism and its justification by the danger of pauperism.

The two customs law proposals debated by deputies in the spring of 1836 merely confirmed the changes in the tariff enacted since the July Revolution and reduced import duties on a dozen of supplementary minor articles such as hats, copper and saltpetre. Thiers, Premier since February 1836, probably introduced the proposals as a means of bringing the controversy over commercial reform to a formal end. His minister of commerce, Hippolyte Passy, was reputed to be an admirer of Adam Smith. But Henri Galos, sent by the Bordelais merchants to lobby ministers and deputies in Paris, reported that since he became minister, Passy was content to 'paraphrase' Thiers, who himself had 'resurrected the entire system of M. de Saint-Cricq'. 'With regard to the implementation of commercial liberty', a melancholy Galos concluded, 'we are in a reactionary movement'.[64]

Despite its modest economic significance, the 1836 law proposals, the first on tariffs to be considered by the chambers since 1826, proved one of the lengthiest parliamentary debates under the July Monarchy, suggesting that contemporaries felt a need for ideological clarification.[65] The 1836 debate was extremely polarized. An opening three-day 'general discussion' saw fourteen deputies taking the floor to defend, alternately, commercial liberty and the protective system. As one of the seven advocates of liberty – Jacques-Henri Wustemberg, a conservative deputy for the Gironde – put it, the point of the discussion was not to settle 'a question of tariffs' but to decide between two 'systems of public economics': the 'regime of prohibitions' on the one hand and a 'more generous and liberal commercial legislation' on the other.[66] Comte Jaubert, one of the seven defenders of protection and an ally of Thiers, drew a parallel between this polarization of economic opinions and the political division of the liberal party after 1830: 'the economic school', he contended, was to 'the system of protection' what 'the *Mouvement* was to the *Résistance*'. In his view,

[64] Galos to Fonfrède, 27 April 1836, BMB, MS 1095, vol. II, fols. 186–92.

[65] The reproduction of the proceedings takes up 413 pages of the *Archives Parlementaires*, more than twice, for instance, the length of the debate on the controversial *loi infâme* that limited press freedom the previous year; compare AP, vol. XCVIII (21–9 August 1835) and AP, vols. CI, CII and CIII (13 April–5 May 1836).

[66] AP, vol. CII, p. 27 (14 April 1836).

commercial liberty and the *Mouvement* enjoyed the support of 'the same individuals', stemmed from 'the same hazardous theories, the same despotism of alleged principles, the same cosmopolitan spirit' and shared 'the same will to pit the different classes of society against each other'.[67]

Alphonse de Lamartine, one of the seven orators hostile to protection, implicitly agreed with Jaubert's political analogy, describing the advocates of commercial liberty as 'revolutionaries', who wished to complete the work that 'our fathers from 1789 have gloriously pursued and achieved in the moral order, namely political reform', by achieving it in 'the material order'. 'The Revolution is not done', the poet-politician declared, 'or rather it is only half-done': 'having introduced liberty into institutions and overthrown personal feudalism, it must now overthrow industrial feudalism … and introduce liberty into things'.[68] However, neither Jaubert's analysis nor Lamartine's lyrical flight accurately reflected political reality. Jaubert's equation of the 'economic school' with the *Mouvement* even elicited indignant protests on the left side of the assembly.[69] Out of the seven orators who advocated commercial liberty, three supported the *Résistance*, one sat with the centrist *Tiers-parti*, Lamartine – a former *ultra* in the process of rallying the republican opposition – formed a political category of his own, and only two voted with the *Mouvement*.[70] Had Jaubert drawn the converse parallel between political and economic opinions, he would have been nearer the truth. Of the seven orators who paid allegiance to protection during the general discussion, all but one – a republican – belonged to the pro-*Résistance* majority.[71]

Support for protection had Napoleonic as well as conservative undertones. One of the seven orators who defended protection, Hector-Napoléon Soult, was the son of a Napoleonic field marshal. During the debates that followed the opening discussion, three Napoleonic generals and several other dignitaries of the imperial regime declared themselves against commercial liberty.[72] Charles Dupin, another of the seven orators who opposed free trade during the opening discussion, offers a compelling example of the role played by memories of Napoleon's reign

[67] AP, vol. CI, pp. 720–1 (13 April 1836). [68] AP, vol. CII, p. 48 (14 April 1836).

[69] AP, vol. CI, p. 720 (13 April 1836).

[70] The three conservatives were Jacques-Henri Wustemberg, Alexandre Anisson-Dupéron and François Bignon; the centrist was Prosper Duvergier de Hauranne; and the supporters of the *Mouvement* were Alexandre de Laborde and Armand Lherbette.

[71] The republican was Etienne Garnier-Pagès, and the six conservative defenders of protection were Henri-Emmanuel Poulle, Hippolyte Jaubert, Laurent Cunin-Gridaine, Jean-Jacques Meynard, Charles Dupin and Hector-Napoléon Soult.

[72] General Demarçay, General Bugeaud and General Tirlet.

as an era of domestic stability rather than territorial expansion, in galvanizing support for tariff protection.[73] Dupin served with distinction as an engineer in the Napoleonic navy in Boulogne, Antwerp, Genoa, Toulon and the Ionian islands. Since Dupin fervently disseminated liberal ideas about trade under the Restoration, his case is also a spectacular instance of the protectionist turn taken by many French liberals after the 1830 Revolution.

As seen in the previous chapter, Dupin already played an ambivalent part in the reform of the legislation on the grain trade in 1832. By 1833, Bowring lamented that 'Saint-Cricq [was] an angel compared to *Charles Dupin*'. A member of the Chamber of Deputies' customs commission, Dupin 'resisted every change even the slightest with all the acharnement (tenacity) which such a vain, shallow and spiteful creature [was] capable of'. Dupin's reputation as an expert on British economic affairs, Bowring added, made him an influential enemy of commercial reform.[74] Yet his publicly expressed views remained ambiguous. His personal manifesto for the 1834 general election rejected free trade in a contorted liberal language: he vowed to fight 'monopolies' but not 'at the expense of French workers' and to promote 'commercial liberty', although he refused to 'prostitute the sacred name of liberty' to the abolition of all taxes on 'the exchanges of goods with other countries'.[75]

Dupin's speech of April 1836 on customs legislation condemned free trade more forcefully. It made a strong impression on its audience, producing a 'general sensation' in the chamber and receiving the 'marked adhesion' of numerous deputies. It was also published under the title *Défense du système protecteur*.[76] Dupin focused his attack on the political and social implications, rather than the economics, of free trade. It began with a proposal that 'the alleged science of *economics*' be renamed as 'anti-political economy' because it threatened to disorganize 'the state of our society'. Dupin first sought to refute the contention that protection violated the principles of political liberty enshrined in the constitutional Charter of 1830. Even under a liberal political order, he recalled, 'criminal and civil laws' proscribed and punished actions that contravened the 'public' or

[73] On the political and social impact of Napoleonic memories, see Sudhir Hazareesingh, *The Legend of Napoleon* (London, 2004) and Nathalie Petiteau, *Lendemains d'empire: les soldats de Napoléon dans la France du XIXe siècle* (Paris, 2003).

[74] Bowring to Thomson, 4 and 6 January 1833, BODL, MS Clar., dep. c. 546/1/2, fols. 1, 7.

[75] 'A MM. les électeurs du 10ème arrondissement de Paris', Nevers, Archives Départementales de la Nièvre, Dupin MSS, 4J 2, fols. 23–4.

[76] Charles Dupin, *Défense du système protecteur de la production française et de l'industrie nationale* (Paris, 1836).

'national interest'. In the same way as the Code Civil promulgated by Napoleon protected weaker individuals such as wives, children or orphans, a liberal government should protect weaker industries from foreign competition. Retorting to suggestions that the origins of trade restrictions lay in feudal or aristocratic power, Dupin cited the examples of several major advocates of protection, from Colbert in the seventeenth century to Necker, François de Neufchâteau and Chaptal during the Revolution, who were averred enemies of the aristocracy.[77]

Dupin then rejected the claim that protection harmed most the interests of the poorest, 'the people par excellence', or those sometimes referred to as 'proletarian' – the use of the latter word revolted him, when all Frenchmen, 'under the glorious equality of the tricolour flag', had a chance of rising to the upper echelons of society. In reality, Dupin contended, 'not just international, but cosmopolitan competition' constituted 'the gravest danger that threaten[ed] the working class'. Against this danger, national protection played the role of a collective insurance, 'a vast association of mutual assistance', against the hazards of economic life. Without protection, 'the terrifying struggles between industries from different nations' led industrialists to treat their workers with unspeakable cruelty. The miserable conditions of British workers exemplified the results of 'the immoderate desire to crush foreign industries by the means of unlimited competition'. Dupin mentioned the British legislation that limited child labour (the 1833 Factory Act) but only to describe the need of it as evidence of the 'barbary of liberty' in a country where 'even life [was] put at an unlimited discount'.[78]

Instead of adopting free trade, Dupin concluded, the July Monarchy should emulate Napoleon's commercial policy. Admittedly, Napoleon had been 'the greatest prohibitor of modern times' and the Continental System harmed the interests of workers *qua* consumers. And yet, 'far from being an object of detestation for workers, Napoleon was their idol', because they saw him as 'the true founder of modern factories of textiles and of a multitude of other products'. It was why, upon his return from Elba in 1815, 'the *paysan*, the cultivator, the mere worker, the proletarian, surrounded him and hailed him as their emperor and father'. If the July Monarchy wished to enjoy the same popularity among the people, Dupin pleaded, it needed to inscribe 'on the tricolour flag, like the Emperor: National industry! National protection! National defence!' Dupin also used arguments borrowed from the traditional language of mercantile jealousy, recalling that

[77] AP, vol. CII, pp. 32–4 (14 April 1836). [78] AP, vol. CII, pp. 34–5 (14 April 1836).

Britain only achieved its present prosperity thanks to more than a century of protection. Notwithstanding his critique of working conditions in British factories, he marvelled at how British cotton manufacturers had finally 'triumphed over India'. But what made Dupin's defence of protection distinctive and earned him prolonged plaudits at the end of his speech was his insistence that commercial restrictions may help solve the social question and reduce risks of popular rebellion.[79]

Dupin's concern with the treatment of workers in modern factories led him to become a promoter of France's first piece of social legislation, a law that limited child labour in 1841, despite his earlier mocking of British legislation. He also became an indefatigable advocate of savings banks for workers as a protection against the vagaries of factory employment. His defence of protection as a means of attenuating the consequences of competition for workers therefore formed part of a broader, paternalist response to the social question. Yet he remained a fervent advocate of the development of industry, or what he called 'productive forces', and was not averse to using the language of jealousy to stress the need for France to rise to the British industrial challenge. He also retained a concern for the preservation of France's naval and colonial power that would later set him at odds with advocates of self-sufficiency in the mould of Dombasle or Mimerel, and lead him to reject the label of *protectionniste*.[80] In the mid 1830s, however, Dupin's very reputation as an advocate of modern industry helped render the repudiation of free trade and the use of arguments drawn from the language of self-sufficiency more acceptable among conservative liberals.

V

A comparison with contemporary German debates about international trade highlights both the originality and the transnational dimension of the effervescence of nationalist economic ideas in France in the 1830s. The economic unification of Germany, under the aegis of Prussia with the creation of the Zollverein in 1834, made a powerful impression in France. The teleological appreciation of the Zollverein as a preliminary stage of German political unification has lost its standing in the recent

[79] AP, vol. CII, pp. 35–7 (14 April 1836).

[80] David Todd, 'La Nation, la liberté et les colonies dans la pensée économique de Charles Dupin' and Part 4, 'Charles Dupin et la question sociale', in Carole Christen and François Vatin (eds.), *Charles Dupin (1784–1873): ingénieur, savant, économiste, pédagogue et parlementaire du Premier au Second Empire* (Rennes, 2009), pp. 177–89, 207–69.

historiography. Yet the contemporary economic significance of the advent of a market of 25 million consumers, the largest in Europe after France's, should not be neglected.[81] Influence, however, was reciprocal. The model of the French protective system and its defence by Thiers, Dombasle or Dupin, at a time when the progress of free trade in Britain rendered the British example less pertinent, offered useful lessons for German advocates of protection. Friedrich List's influential *National System of Political Economy*, in particular, needs to be relocated in the French context of the liberal reinvention of jealousy. List spent half of the 1830s in France and initially conceived his treatise as a contribution to French debates, which refuted calls for self-sufficiency as much as it condemned free trade as a British ploy.

In Britain, anxiety that the Zollverein might erect high tariffs against British imports provided free-traders with a new compelling argument for the repeal of the Corn Laws and other obstacles to German agricultural exports.[82] In France, the creation of the Zollverein became perceived as a potential model to emulate as well as a threat. Combined with the rapid agricultural and industrial progress of several German states, it altered the traditional perception of Germany as economically backward.[83] Dombasle, who did not live far from the German border and admired the innovative use of fertilizers recommended by German agronomists, used the example of prosperous and self-sufficient Germany as a foil against the extrovert and perilous model of British economic growth. He attributed Germany's rapid economic growth 'to the good fortune it has had of not possessing colonies and of being exempt, thanks to its position, from these temptation of foreign trade' that slowed down economic progress in France. German foreign trade was, he contended, declining. Yet this country had taken 'giant steps in the development of agricultural and manufacturing industries', and 'nowhere else had the well-being of the working classes improved as rapidly'. While

[81] Most members of the German confederacy joined the Zollverein upon its creation, and, by 1836, only Austria, Hanover and the Hanseatic cities remained outside the customs union; see William O. Henderson, *The Zollverein*, 3rd edn (London, 1984), pp. 70–102, and Hans-Werner Hahn, *Geschichte des deutschen Zollverein* (Göttingen, 1984), pp. 43–87. On the economic significance of the Zollverein and its disputed impact on identity and nationalism in Germany, see Rolf H. Dumke, *German Unification in the Nineteenth Century: The Political Economy of the Zollverein* (Munich, 1994); Abigail Green, 'Representing Germany? The Zollverein at the World Exhibitions, 1851–1862', *Journal of Modern History*, 75 (4) (2003): 836–63; and Hans-Werner Hahn and Marko Kreutzmann (eds.), *Der deutsche Zollverein: Ökonomie und Nation im 19. Jahrhundert* (Cologne, 2012).

[82] Brown, *The Board of Trade*, pp. 107–10; John R. Davis, *Britain and the German Zollverein, 1848–1866* (Basingstoke, 1997), pp. 11–47.

[83] Schui, *Early Debates about Industry*, pp. 40–6.

Britain would 'fulfil its inevitable destiny of slow decline or abrupt catastrophe', Dombasle predicted, Germany would soon become 'one of the richest and most prosperous nations in the world'.[84]

An anxious preoccupation with German commercial unification frequently surfaced during the 1836 parliamentary debate about customs legislation. Most deputies concurred with Saint-Marc de Girardin, a conservative deputy and author of a recent report that praised the quality of German secondary education, that the Zollverein should not be construed as 'a work of commercial liberalism', even though it abolished internal customs barriers, but as a 'miniature' version of 'the Continental System'. Thiers, then Premier, answered reproaches that he did not try to prevent the formation of the German customs union while he was Minister of Commerce in 1832–4 with an assertion that the creation of the Zollverein was 'a spontaneous movement of all German peoples, which no one could oppose'. As a regular contributor to the *Augsburg Allgemeine Zeitung* in the 1820s, Thiers had forged strong ties with German liberals, and he cited his personal observation of the 'unanimous cry … against this infinite division of customs' within Germany, when he visited the country in the late 1820s, to justify his inaction.[85] It is likely that his witnessing of protests for German commercial unification also helped to forge the conviction he expressed in 1834 that national economic solidarity constituted an irrepressible 'instinct'.

Thiers's conviction was certainly reinforced by his close frequentation, in the 1830s, of another collaborator of the *Allgemeine Zeitung*, who had played a prominent part in the agitation for German commercial unification, Friedrich List.[86] An adversary of reaction in post-Napoleonic Germany, List held not only the French political model but also the French economic model in high esteem.[87] In an 1819 petition to the German Confederacy's Diet on the hindrances to domestic trade caused by internal customs, he claimed that all the Germans who wished to 'work and trade' looked 'with envy across the Rhine, where a great people (*Volk*) can carry out commercial operations along free rivers and open roads, from the Channel to the Mediterranean, from the Rhine to the

84 Mathieu de Dombasle, *Des intérêts respectifs*, pp. 44–5, 62–6.

85 AP, vol. CIII, pp. 99, 102 (2 May 1836); on Thiers's links with German liberals, see Robert Marquant, *Thiers et le baron Cotta: étude sur la collaboration de Thiers à la Gazette d'Augsbourg* (Paris, 1959).

86 On the friendship between List and Thiers, see Eugen Wendler, *Friedrich List: politische Wirkungsgeschichte des Vordenkers der europäischen Integration* (Munich, 1989), pp. 74–9.

87 Biographical elements are drawn from Paul Gehring, *Friedrich List: Jugend und Reifejahre, 1789–1825* (Tübingen, 1964) and William O. Henderson, *Friedrich List: Economist and Visionary* (London, 1983).

Pyrenees, and from the Dutch border to Italy'. At that date, like most French Restoration liberals, List still opposed what remained perceived as the commercial dimension of reaction and used a liberal phraseology. The 1819 petition looked forward to the advent of 'the universal liberty of commerce', while a memorandum he addressed the following year to the Austrian Chancellor, Klemens von Metternich, proposed to convene a European 'commercial congress' that would discuss the lowering of customs barriers across the Continent.[88]

Forced to flee Wurttemberg to avoid imprisonment in 1822, List found refuge in Strasbourg. Associating with French liberals as well as other German exiles, he appreciated the greater freedom of thought and the combination of French and German cultures that prevailed in the Alsatian capital: 'I would rather be a cheese seller here [in Strasbourg]', he wrote to his wife, 'than a Councillor of State in Stuttgart', the capital of Wurttemberg.[89] It was during this stay that List became interested in French debates about international trade, reading several French works on political economy and reporting on French political and economic affairs for the *Neckar Zeitung*, Wurttemberg's radical news-sheet. In particular, he castigated the prohibitive commercial legislation propounded by the Villèle government as 'charitable increases' of import restrictions in favour of 'the aristocracy' and at the expense of exporters in Alsace, Lyon and other French regions.[90] When French authorities discovered that List was the author of these and other 'virulent' articles against the government in the *Neckar Zeitung*, they had him expelled to Switzerland.[91]

Under the pressure of the Wurttemberg government, List eventually agreed to emigrate to North America. Several entries in his diary as he travelled across France before embarking for the USA in 1825 suggest that his views on international trade were already beginning to change. He remained convinced that barriers on internal exchanges ought to be removed. 'The advantages of the reunion with a large nation can be felt in every class [*Stand*] in Alsace', an entry dated from Strasbourg read.[92] But

[88] 'Bittschrift an die Bundesversammlung', 14 April 1819, and 'Denkschrift, die Handels- und Gewerbsverhältnisse Deutschlands betreffend', 15 February 1820, in Friedrich List, *Schriften, Reden, Briefe*, ed. Erwin von Beckerath, Karl Goeser, Friedrich Lenz et al., 10 vols. (Berlin, 1927–35), vol. I.2, pp. 491–5, 527–47.

[89] List to Caroline List, May 1822, in List, *Schriften*, vol. VIII, p. 221.

[90] 'Französiche Gränze', *Neckar Zeitung*, 23, 27 April and 16 May 1822.

[91] Prefect of the Bas-Rhin to the Minister of the Interior, 18 September 1822, reprint in List, *Schriften*, vol. VIII, p. 239.

[92] Quoted in Hans Gehrig, *Friedrich List und Deutschlands politisch-ökonomosiche Einheit* (Leipzig, 1956), p. 92.

the industrial prosperity of the Seine valley, which he witnessed on his way from Paris to Le Havre, led him to record strong doubts about the liberal prescriptions of Smithian political economy with regard to international exchanges of commodities:

> When will the sight of such industrious regions finally bring the obstinate followers of Adam Smith back to their senses? This master of political economy may have rendered, in other respects, a vast number of services to nations; but all these services do not compensate, in our view, the harm done by this tiny whim, the whim of the so-called free circulation [of merchandise], in the mind of our theoreticians.[93]

List's rejection of free trade therefore pre-dated his five-year stay in the USA, even though his encounter with arguments in favour of the 'American System' of high tariffs no doubt reinforced his convictions.[94] The main theoretical reference approvingly cited by List in his own contribution to the defence of protection in the USA, *Outlines of American Political Economy* (1827), was Jean-Antoine Chaptal's 'celebrated work *De l'industrie française* (1819)', because it contained 'a most practical and material refutation' of Smith and Say's liberal doctrine about foreign trade.[95] The concept of 'productive powers', introduced by List in the *Outlines* as an alternative to 'value' in order to measure economic development, probably owed something to the popularity of *industrialisme* in France in the mid 1820s. Its phrasing recalls Dupin's emphasis on 'forces productives', the eponymous concept of the latter's 1827 work on French economic development, although List and Dupin almost certainly forged these cognate phrases independently from each other.

The July Revolution incited List to return to Europe, and he settled in Paris for most of 1831. Now a diplomatic agent of the American republic, he sought in vain to negotiate a commercial agreement between France and the USA and to promote a plan for the construction of a national network of railways in France. At this stage, List still employed an ambivalent language about international trade, not unlike the contorted pronouncements of Thiers, Dupin and other French industrialist liberals in the aftermath of the July Revolution: List described himself as 'partisan

93 'Tagesbuch', April 1825, in List, *Schriften*, vol. VIII, pp. 58, 77.

94 Tribe, *Strategies of Economic Order*, pp. 32–65; see also Klaus Schafmeister, *Entstehung und Entwicklung des Systems der politischen Ökonomie bei Friedrich List: eine Rekonstrucktionsanalyse seiner Beiträge zur wirtschaftlichen Entwicklung in Württemberg 1806–1823 und Pennsylvania 1806–1835* (St Katharinen, 1995).

95 Friedrich List, *Outlines of American Political Economy/Grundriß der amerikanischen politischen Ökonomie* (Wiesbaden, 1996), p. 47.

of the theory of the liberty of commerce' and 'cosmopolitan by principle', although he also believed 'in the necessity of a wise protection for national industry'.[96] List's projects elicited only limited interest in France, and he returned to Germany, where he successfully campaigned for the construction of the Confederacy's first major railway line, between Dresden and Leipzig. But he failed to obtain the position of manager of the new Saxon railways and decided to try his luck in France again, arriving in Paris as the correspondent of the *Allgemeine Zeitung* in the summer of 1837.

List's second, three-year-long stay in Paris proved decisive for the formulation of his critique of free trade. In December 1837, he submitted an essay for a *concours* of political economy organized by the Académie des Sciences Morales et Politiques, the old bastion of liberal *idéologie* resuscitated by Guizot in 1832, on the conditions required for the adoption of 'the liberty of commerce' by a nation. The question had been proposed by Charles Comte, goaded by Bowring, in 1833.[97] None of the seven essays submitted by December 1835 was deemed worthy of the prize, and the competition was reopened in 1836. But new guidelines by Charles Dupin, a member of the Académie, urged the competitors to reject the interpretation of *liberté*, upheld by 'a few speculative theoreticians', as the 'absolute abolition' of restrictions. Such a definition, Dupin asserted, amounted to 'a misuse of language', for repealing trade barriers would not free but 'enslave', 'stifle' and 'kill several kinds of national commerce'.[98]

Published in the early twentieth century under the title *Le Système naturel d'économie politique*, List's essay sketched out the most important aspects of his future 'national system' of political economy. The text based its opposition to free trade in industrial countries less developed than Britain on a severe critique of the abstract and deductive methodology of the 'school' of political economy. It refined the contrast drawn in the *Outlines* between the economists' 'theory of values' and List's own 'theory of productive powers'; it rejected 'cosmopolitan' or 'individual' economics in favour of 'national or political economics' on the grounds that it was 'from the nation' that individuals drew 'all the benefits of civilization'; and the last section illustrated the argument with a survey of the commercial history of modern European nations and the USA. Rather than

96 Frédéric List [sic], 'Idées sur des réformes économiques, commerciales et politiques applicables à la France', *Revue Encyclopédique*, 49 (1831): 473–90 and 50 (1831): 37–52.

97 Minutes, 20 and 26 July 1833, Paris, Institut de France, Archives de l'Académie des Sciences Morales et Politiques (hereafter AASMP), 2D1, fols. 90–1; Bowring to Villiers, 6 June 1833, BODL, MS Clar., dep. c. 546/1/2, fols. 114–15.

98 Minutes, 28 December 1836, AASMP, 2D2, fols. 15–19.

condemning free trade as always harmful, *Le Système naturel* stressed that it suited the interests of the dominant manufacturing nation, Britain, and of stagnant agrarian societies. The essay only recommended protection for Britain's less advanced industrial rivals, including Belgium, France, Germany and the USA.[99]

Le Système naturel was written for a French audience. It attacked Say rather than Smith as the leading 'cosmopolitan' economist. It paid homage to the works of Chaptal and Dupin and praised the commercial policies of Colbert and Napoleon. List's text also cautiously distinguished his conception of protection as a means of encouraging the growth of manufacturing industries from both the mercantilist balance of trade and protection as a means of achieving self-sufficiency. Discussing the views of Ferrier, List considered his practical recommendations sound in France's present circumstances but underlined that they were 'based upon principles which have long been shown to be erroneous'. It is also possible that List borrowed his description of Smith and Say's political economy as the 'veritable mercantile system', because it corresponded with the interests of merchants, from Dombasle's *De l'avenir industriel.* But at the same time the essay took a swipe at advocates of self-sufficiency, condemning tariffs on raw materials or agricultural products as harmful to industry.[100] List expressed little interest in the social question, in either *Le Système naturel* or his later writings.[101] List's nascent system of political economy amounted to an industrialist reinvention of jealousy, which combined *industrialisme* with an optimism on the social consequences of industrialization that may have originated from his American experience.

Again, none of six new essays submitted to the Académie was deemed worthy of the prize, although List's and two others were awarded citations as 'remarkable works'. The diverse origins of the competitors to the 1835 and 1837 sessions of the *concours* further testified to the transnational impact of French debates about international trade, at least on the European continent. Out of twelve competitors, seven were not French, including a Dutch professor of classics, two Belgian publicists

99 'Le Système naturel d'économie politique/Das natürliche System der politischen Ökonomie', in List, *Schriften*, vol. IV, pp. 155–545, esp. p. 180; List wrote the essay with the help of his daughter Émilie, who had a perfect command of French.

100 'Le Système naturel', pp. 158, 313–24, 354, 376–84.

101 William O. Henderson, 'Friedrich List and the Social Question', *Journal of European Economic History*, 10 (2) (1981): 697–708. On French influences on the essay, see Edgar Salin and Artur Sommer, 'Die positiven Quellen der Preisschrift', in List, *Schriften*, vol. IV, pp. 50–145; Henderson, 'Friedrich List and the French Protectionists'; and William O. Henderson, 'Introduction', in Friedrich List, *The Natural System of Political Economy*, trans. William O. Henderson (London, 1983), pp. 17–25.

and three German competitors (a Hamburg lawyer, a Stuttgart merchant and a Wittemberg bailiff) in addition to List.[102] The topic selected by the Academy to replace the question on free trade, on the present and future consequences of the 'German commercial association', also confirmed a growing French interest in the economic unification of Germany.[103]

List attributed his failure to obtain the prize to the dominance of the 'cosmopolitan school' in the Académie's section of political economy. But he was determined to revise and expand the essay into a book, which he planned to publish simultaneously in French and German and which would lay the foundations of 'a new system of political economy'.[104] Between 1838 and 1840, List worked on the book while reporting on French affairs for the *Allgemeine Zeitung*. He also translated several French publications into German, including *Des idées napoléoniennes* (1839), a manifesto by the future Napoleon III, which described domestic economic improvement as the chief objective of Napoleonic politics. In the spring of 1840, List hailed the return of his friend Thiers as Premier, arguing that he 'alone has proved … that he could analyze the trade relations of England and France with greater depth than theoreticians'.[105] Thiers offered List a well-paid position in the French administration to oversee the construction of a national rail network. However, List turned down the offer and returned to Germany, perhaps as a result of the European crisis over Eastern affairs that threatened to erupt into a Franco-German war in the summer of 1840.

List failed to complete the French version of his treatise, but the German version came out in Stuttgart in May 1841. *Das nationale System der politische Ökonomie* was longer and more polished than the hastily written *Système naturel*. Yet the German treatise only differed in substance from the French essay by the greater emphasis placed on history as the necessary linchpin of a new, empirical science of political economy. In particular, List expanded his survey of national commercial histories and moved it from the end to the beginning of the work.[106] This emphasis played an important role in List's legacy, enabling the mostly German proponents of the 'historical school' of economics in the late nineteenth century to hail List as a precursor.[107] However, even List's insistence on

[102] AAMSP, 386 and 389; the other five French competitors were two Paris 'writers', a Lyon 'man of letters', a municipal official at Valence (Drôme) and a Paris 'worker'.
[103] Académie des Sciences Morales et Politiques, *Concours de l'Académie* (Paris, 1901), p. 3.
[104] List to Johann Georg Cotta, 6 September 1838, in List, *Schriften*, vol. IV, pp. 48–9.
[105] 'Die handelsverhältnisse von England und Frankreich', *Allgemeine Zeitung*, 5 March 1840.
[106] List, *Das nationale System*, pp. 97–182.
[107] Yuichi Shionoya (ed.), *The German Historical School: The Historical and Ethical Approach to Economics* (London, 2001); Erik Grimmer-Solem, *The Rise of Historical Economics and Social Reform in Germany, 1864–1894* (Oxford and New York, 2003).

the significance of history for economics probably owed a great deal to his involvement in French debates about international trade. It was perhaps inspired by his almost daily frequentation of Thiers, a historian as well as a politician, between 1838 and 1840. List published his 'L'Économie politique devant le tribunal de l'histoire' in *Le Constitutionnel*, the mouthpiece of Thiers's centre-left faction, in 1838. The article drew on several staples of French debates, including the nefarious consequences of past commercial agreements with Britain, and warned readers against the danger of turning France, after Portugal, into a second 'English vineyard'.[108] The eighteen chapters of the incomplete manuscript of the French version of the treatise, probably written in 1838, also prefigured List's stress on history in *Das nationale System*. The introduction described 'the history of civilization and the commerce of modern nations' as the 'touchstone' of his theory and was followed by a dozen historical chapters that closely resembled the first part of the final German version, except for a more strident emphasis on the success of Colbert and Napoleon's economic policies.[109]

List's industrialist defence of protection has exercised a global and enduring influence, with translations of *Das nationale System* in numerous languages, including Hungarian (1844), French (1851), English (1856 in the USA, 1860 in Australia, 1885 in Britain), Romanian (1887), Swedish (1888), Japanese (1889), Russian (1891), Bulgarian (1926), Mandarin (1927), Finnish (1935), Spanish (1942) and Korean (1983).[110] List's book also had a significant intellectual impact in several countries where it was not translated into indigenous languages, from colonial India, to Ireland after its independence, to post-Ottoman Turkey.[111] The transnational – German, French and American – origins of List's ideas certainly contributed to their global appeal, by detaching his reflections from a single national context. Yet it is telling that his attempt to found a new political economy came to fruition in 1830s France, where the question of the relationship between political liberty and free trade was posed with such acuity, his views echoing and responding to the ideas of French nationalists. List's French translator found it necessary to forewarn his readers that they would 'recognize [in this book], admittedly under a more scientific form, ideas that have been common among us for a long time'. But recognizing the reciprocity

[108] *Le Constitutionnel*, 25 September 1839; reprinted in List, *Schriften*, vol. v, pp. 99–111.

[109] Unfinished manuscript of French treatise, [1838], SR, List MSS, Fasc. 23.3.

[110] Eugen Wendler, 'Einführung', in List, *Das nationale System*, pp. 13–49, at p. 26.

[111] Eugen Wendler (ed.), *'Die Vereinigung des europäischen Kontinents': Friedrich List, gesamteuropäischen Wirkungsgeschichte seines ökonomischen Denkens* (Stuttgart, 1996); Manu Goswami, 'From Swadeshi to Swaraj: Nation, Economy, Territory in Colonial South Asia', *Comparative Studies in Society and History*, 40 (4) (1998): 609–36, esp. at pp. 617–18.

and multiplicity of cross-border interactions in the debate about international trade, he also described his translation as evidence that France could 'import useful truths from across the Rhine as well as from across the Channel'.[112]

A common feature of the attempts to reinvent jealousy under a liberal guise in the 1830s lay in the exaltation of the nation as a political limit to the expansion of the global market. The language of *patrie* and nation, with its egalitarian undertones, still formed part of the liberal revolutionary legacy and therefore helped to dissociate tariff protection from its real or alleged reactionary origins. Unlike the language of the balance of trade, which tended to be used alongside nostalgia for guilds and other forms of economic regulation under the Old Regime, this novel emphasis on the nation as a community of economic solidarity between citizens was compatible with economic liberty within national borders. However, defenders of protection assigned different purposes to national solidarity, ranging from the industrialist jealousy favoured by Thiers and List to the self-sufficient form of economic development defended by Dombasle and Mimerel, with Dupin steering an awkward but rhetorically effective middle course that combined the two objectives. A common dislike of free trade and British commercial dominance helped to conceal such differences. But, as nationalist economic ideas gained ground in subsequent years, the contradictions between these different conceptions became more apparent, requiring further elaboration of the goals and limits of protection.

[112] List, *Le Système national*, p. xxx. List's translator, Henri Richelot was an analyst of foreign customs legislation at the Ministry of Commerce; see folder 'Richelot', AN, F12 5069.

CHAPTER 5

The contours of the national economy

By the mid 1830s, at least three strands of ideas hostile to free trade could be discerned: a mercantile jealousy revived by François Ferrier, Auguste de Saint-Chamans and Vincent Viénot de Vaublanc in the 1820s, acutely concerned with the preservation of France's colonial trade; the industrialist reformulation of jealousy promoted by Adolphe Thiers and Friedrich List after the 1830 Revolution; and an aspiration to self-sufficiency, with an emphasis on an adequate balance between agricultural and industrial growth, of which Mathieu de Dombasle and Auguste Mimerel emerged as the main spokesmen in the same years. The middle period of the July Monarchy, until the mid 1840s, saw these three strands vying to make their mark on the nascent French protectionist ideology in a succession of practical commercial controversies about the linen tariff, a project of customs union with Belgium and the sugar tariff. These debates posed two crucial questions about the extent and purpose of protection: should it solely encourage modern manufactures, or should it also preserve traditional modes of industrial production? And should it be reserved to contemporary metropolitan France, or could it be extended to nearby territories that were French before 1815, and to colonies, old – in the Antilles – and new – in North Africa?

These discussions took place in the context of a global industrial depression between 1837 and 1843, triggered by a sudden withdrawal of British capital from the USA.[1] In response to the collapse of demand for industrial products, Western European manufacturers formed new lobbies that sought to influence commercial policy. In Britain, the Anti-Corn Law League, founded by Manchester manufacturers in 1839, orchestrated an unprecedented public campaign for the adoption of free

[1] Jessica M. Lepler, *The Many Panics of 1837: People, Politics, and the Creation of a Transatlantic Financial Crisis* (Cambridge, 2013); and Alasdair Robert, *America's First Great Depression: Economic Crisis and Political Disorder after the Panic of 1837* (Ithaca, NY, 2012), esp. pp. 28–30; on the repercussions of the crisis in Europe, see Lévy-Leboyer, *Les Banques européennes*, pp. 551–94.

trade.[2] In France, by contrast, manufacturers created lobbies dedicated to the defence of protection and loosely coordinated by a Comité pour la Défense du Travail National after 1842.[3] Under the influence of Mimerel, these lobbies adopted the language of self-sufficiency rather than industrialist jealousy and promoted protectionist ideas discreetly but effectively through subsidies to the mainstream press. Another influence on French debates about international trade was the abolition of slavery in British colonies (1833–8) and the acceleration of the plantation colonies' economic decline in the Caribbean.[4] Rejecting the alternative between an increase in protection for French planters and the liberalization of colonial trade, Dombasle and others propounded instead the development of beet-sugar production in metropolitan France. Their campaign gained new supporters for self-sufficiency, ranging from liberal adversaries of colonial slavery to the future Napoleon III.

Although the government's policy remained hesitant between these various commercial options, self-sufficiency made the most significant inroads in public opinion, often as a result of anxieties about the social question: the decline of the rural linen industry evoked fears of mass migration to the cities, while the cultivation of the sugar beet and new beet-sugar factories in the countryside seemed likely to slow down urbanization. In the meantime, liberal ideas about trade became increasingly relegated to the margins of intellectual and political life. The emerging contours of the protected national economy were territorially exclusive but socially inclusive, forming a coherent liberal yet paternalist response to the transformations of the global economy.

I

The first lobby to emerge in response to the manufacturing slump of the late 1830s was the Comité de l'Industrie Linière, founded in 1837 and which became the Union des Cultivateurs, Filateurs et Tisserands de Lin et de Chanvre in 1842.[5] Despite a steady decline since the 1780s,

[2] McCord, *The Anti-Corn Law League*, pp. 34–54; Paul A. Pickering and Alex Tyrrell, *The People's Bread: A History of the Anti-Corn Law League* (London, 2000), Chapter 10; Cheryl Schonhardt-Bailey, *From the Corn Laws to Free Trade: Interests, Ideas, and Institutions in Historical Perspective* (Cambridge, Mass., 2006), Chapter 3.

[3] Bertand Gille, *Recherches sur la formation de la grande entreprise capitaliste, 1815–1848* (Paris, 1959), pp. 129–62.

[4] On British abolition and its impact in France and the world, see Robin Blackburn, *The Overthrow of Colonial Slavery* (London, 1988), Chapter 12, and Seymour Drescher, *Abolition: A History of Slavery and Anti-Slavery* (Cambridge, 2009), Chapter 10.

[5] Comité des Lins, *Compte-rendu* (Paris, 1845) offers a brief survey of the Committee's history.

the traditional domestic linen industry remained France's largest for the volume of its output and the number of workers.[6] Flax and hemp were secondary but widespread crops in northern and western France as well as in Belgium and Germany. Local farmers or agricultural workers spun and wove the fibres into cheap linen (or hemp) cloth, which was sold at the town market or to merchant entrepreneurs who marketed their products in other regions and foreign markets. This domestic industry, requiring only rudimentary tools and relying on a gendered division of labour of female spinners and male weavers, constituted a crucial complementary source of income in the densely populated countryside of Flanders, Picardy, Normandy and Brittany. Exports to French and Spanish colonies ensured its prosperity until the second half of the eighteenth century. Yet the rise of the cotton industry, combined with the collapse of France's and Spain's Atlantic empires between 1790 and 1820, ushered in an era of stagnation and recurring crises for linen production.[7]

In the late 1830s, the creation of new factories employing mechanized flax-spinning in Leeds, Dundee and Belfast resulted in a dramatic increase in British exports of linen yarns and textiles to the Continent and turned the industry's slow decline into an acute crisis. In Silesia and Belgian Flanders, armed forces had to quell several revolts engendered by extreme rural destitution.[8] Poignantly capturing this social disruption, Heinrich Heine's poem, 'Die schlesischen Weber' (1844), had Silesian weavers put a curse on their 'false fatherland' (Germany, not Silesia) because it abandoned them to the influx of cheap British imports.[9] In France, too, protection against cheap British products was soon construed as a matter of national solidarity. The commercial malaise began in 1837, with imports of British linen yarns increasing more than 170 per cent on the previous year (3,200 versus 1,175 tons) and imports of British cloth more than 400 per cent (475 versus 85 tons). The surge continued until 1842, when imports of British yarns reached 10,695 tons and British cloth 1,820 tons.[10] Fear

[6] François Crouzet, 'Essai de construction d'un indice annuel de la production industrielle française au dix-neuvième siècle', *Annales: Économies, Sociétés, Civilisations*, 25 (1) (1970): 56–99.

[7] Hugh D. Clout, *Agriculture in France on the Eve of the Railway Age* (London, 1980), pp. 147–8; Tessie P. Liu, *The Weaver's Knot: The Contradictions of Class Struggle and Family Solidarity in Western France, 1750–1914* (Ithaca, NY, 1994), pp. 22–44.

[8] On the British linen industry, see Negley B. Harte, 'The Rise of Protection and the English Linen Trade, 1690–1790', in Negley B. Harte and Kenneth G. Ponting (eds.), *Textile History and Economic History* (Manchester, 1973), pp. 74–112, and William G. Rimmer, *Marshalls of Leeds: Flax Spinners, 1788–1886* (Cambridge, 1960); on the rise of British exports to the Continent and its consequences, see Sidney Pollard, *Peaceful Conquest: The Industrialisation of Europe* (Oxford, 1981), pp. 110–11.

[9] First published as 'Die armen Weber'; *The Complete Poems of Heinrich Heine*, trans. Hal Draper (Boston, Mass., 1982), pp. 544–5.

[10] Lévy-Leboyer, *Les Banques européennes*, p. 108.

that the trouncing of French producers by their British competitors would accelerate rural migration to industrial cities and aggravate the social question compounded more traditional feelings of mercantile jealousy.

What contemporaries described as the *question des lins* (linen question) pitted against each other divergent conceptions of protection rather than advocates and opponents of free trade. Even the handful of industries that employed linen products as raw materials such as producers of twisted yarns or household linen in the Lille region couched their opposition to any increase in the tariff in the jealous language of the 'protection' due to their work and expressed regrets that they could not advocate, in the present circumstances, 'so desirable a preference' for French products.[11] The main debate opposed advocates of a large tariff increase, sufficient to slow down the de-industrialization of the French northern countryside, and those of a moderate rise, which would enable French manufacturers to compete with Britain without reducing the pace of industrial progress.

An extraordinary wave of petitions – at least 215 between January 1837 and June 1839 – by rural weavers and spinners, sometimes signed by entire villages, clamoured for a ban or a prohibitive tariff on industrial British linen products. The potential benefits of cheap imports of foreign yarns held little attraction for weavers because the spinners whose piecework remuneration had collapsed were often their mothers, wives or daughters. Probably drawn up by local *notables*, the petitions drew heart-rending pictures of rural destitution. 'As a result of the calamitous importation of British mechanical yarns', the inhabitants of Tassigny (Calvados) lamented, 'our land has sunk in the most woeful state of wretchedness'. The remuneration of 'the women of [their] country, who spin yarns every day', had fallen from 'between fifteen and twenty *sous*' (0.75 to 1 francs) to 'barely … four or five *sous*' (0.20 to 0.25 francs) a day for 'the most hard-working'. It was 'distressing', the petitioners concluded, 'to see most of these women either killing themselves at work, or forced to beg for some bread'.[12]

In addition to such appeals to patriarchal compassion, the petitions systematically invoked the preference due to their 'French', 'national' or 'indigenous' industry. According to the inhabitants of Pont-Audemer (Eure), 'on national markets a preference should be given to national

[11] 'Les Fabricants de linge de table, coutils, voile et autres étoffes de lin et étoupe, des villes de Lille, Roubaix, Tourcoing, Armentières, etc. à M. le Ministre du Commerce', July 1837, AN, F12 2536; 'Mémoire adressé à messieurs les membres de la Chambre des Députés par les fabricants de fil retors des villes de Lille, Bailleul, Wervicq et Comines', 1 March 1838, AN, F12 2537.

[12] Petition by the inhabitants of Tassilly to the Minister of Commerce, [1838], AN, F12 2537.

labour', while those of Abscon (Nord) wondered why the government seemed to consent 'to the annihilation of a most national industry, which has enabled entire populations to earn a living for centuries, to the benefit of foreigners'. Showing that the debate about international trade had not left even small towns and villages indifferent, several petitions attacked the 'theories of economists', holding them responsible for the government's apparent lack of concern for the condition of French linen producers: 'In vain', the petitioners of Runan (Côtes-du-Nord) asserted, 'will one invoke the liberty of commerce or the interests of consumers [against our demands]. The salvation of the people is the supreme law. Liberty only comes next.'[13]

An early advocate of a moderate increase in the linen tariff was Adolphe Thiers, who had witnessed the progress of British flax-spinning manufactures during his industrial tour of England in 1833. Yet his proposal for a small rise of duties on linen yarns was defeated by the objections of Bowring and the British Board of Trade in 1834. Paying homage to Thiers's prescience, List later cited the episode as an example of how Britain used free trade to promote its commercial interests and of 'what the English call a *trick*': the Board of Trade dismissed linen as 'one of the least important' products for Anglo-French trade, while British officials already knew that it was about to become 'one of England's most important exports'.[14] In 1837, a group of capitalists who had invested in modern flax-spinning factories founded a Comité de l'Industrie Linière to promote an increase in the tariff. Its leading figures were Xavier Defitte and Ernest Feray, two political allies of Thiers. Deputies affiliated with the Comité repeatedly raised the linen question in the chamber, while Defitte and Feray wrote several pamphlets underscoring the need for a tariff increase. The Comité Linier also lamented the plight of rural workers, but mostly in order to channel public sympathy in favour of protection for their modern factories: 'It is not a fictitious industry that we ask you to create; it is the country's oldest industry, the poor's industry that we wish to preserve under a new form … French workers, it is the national market that we are asking the government to preserve for us.'[15]

[13] Petition by the inhabitants of the Pont-Audemer arrondissement to the Minister of Commerce, [1837], and petition by the inhabitants of Abscon to the Minister of Commerce, 20 December 1838, AN, F12 2536; petition by the inhabitants of Runan to the Minister of Commerce, 27 January 1839, AN, F12 2537.

[14] Articles published in the *Allgemeine Zeitung* in July–August 1839, reprinted in List, *Schriften*, vol. v, pp. 122–57.

[15] Xavier Defitte and Ernest Feray, *Nécessité d'une prompte et efficace modification à notre tarif de douanes, relativement aux fils et aux toiles de lin et de chanvre* (Corbeil, 1838), p. 4; see also Comité

The pressure from the petitions and the Comité Linier led the government to hold an official inquiry on the linen tariff. The Conseil Supérieur de Commerce interviewed fifteen witnesses, most of them manufacturers affiliated with the Comité. Its conclusions reflected the industrialists' view, stating that 'one must look away from the sufferings [of rural spinners] inseparable from a transition that nothing can stop' and proposing a moderate increase in the tariff, 'so that the labour lost by one class of Frenchmen be transferred to another class and does not inevitably fall into the hands of foreigners'.[16] Yet the suggested increase, to average duties of 8 per cent *ad valorem* on foreign yarns and 15 per cent on foreign cloth, remained below the manufacturers' expectations. Furthermore, the government delayed the implementation of the Conseil's recommendations so as not to jeopardize ongoing commercial negotiations with Britain and Belgium.[17]

Irritated by the government's prevarication and desire to improve Anglo-French relations, the Comité and the petitioners used an increasingly Anglophobic language that also helped to conceal their divergent goals. Alluding to the alleged weakness of the July Monarchy vis-à-vis Britain, petitioners from Vimoutiers (Orne) warned that the postponement of the tariff increase might 'give credence to what some people repeat every day, namely that we are not free to make our own decisions, and that since the [Napoleonic] Empire we have to endure a foreign yoke'. A petition from Plouëc (Côtes-du-Nord) insisted that Britain had only one goal, 'universal monopoly' and that, not content to have deprived France of its foreign markets, 'it is on our soil that it tries to establish itself, no longer seeking to enslave us with her armies as before, but bringing ruin and misery to our countryside and among our workers'.[18] The pamphlets of the Comité Linier also continued to combine regrets for the production of linen textiles by 'free and independent' rural workers, rendered unsustainable by the competition of British 'machine-beings' and calls for the creation of modern factories, lest the linen industry in France meet the fate of the cotton industry in 'Hindoostan'.[19]

des Lins, *Résumé de la question des fils et des toiles de lin et de chanvre* (Paris, [1838]) and *Des modifications de tarif réclamés par la filature du lin et la fabrication des toiles en France* (Paris, [1838]).

16 Ministère du Commerce, *Enquête sur les fils et tissus de lin et de chanvre* (Paris, 1838), pp. 274–7.

17 Guyot, *La Première Entente cordiale*, pp. 145–51, 247–50.

18 Petition by the cloth-weavers and merchants of Vimoutiers to the Minister of Commerce, 26 April 1838, AN, F12 2536; petition by the inhabitants of Plouëc to the Minister of Commerce, 18 March 1839, AN, F12 2537.

19 Estancelin, *De l'importation en France*, pp. 39–41.

In what was becoming a trope of anti-free-trade propaganda, the Comité Linier also drew on economic memories of the Napoleonic era to bolster the legitimacy of its demands. A first flax-spinning machine had been devised by the engineer Philippe de Girard in the early 1810s, as part of a competition organized by the Napoleonic administration with a view of remedying poor supplies of raw cotton during the Continental Blockade. Publications by the Comité Linier interpreted this early attempt at mechanization as evidence of Napoleon's special concern for the linen industry. To those who consented to its disappearance, a pamphlet responded: 'Napoleon, whose genius saw through the future and who fully understood the influence that the linen industry must have on the country's destiny, shouts at you from his grave: No!'[20] Other pamphlets on the linen question by provincial notables, such as a Breton mayor, a Breton commercial judge or a justice of the peace in Picardy, focused on the social disruption caused to the countryside by British imports.[21]

After commercial negotiations with Britain broke down in the wake of the 1840 Eastern crisis, a customs law increased duties on imports of linen yarns from 4 per cent to 12 per cent *ad valorem* in February 1841.[22] From Germany, Friedrich List hailed this first significant increase in the French tariff since the July Revolution as evidence of the declining influence of 'the supporters of Smith and Say'.[23] Yet flax-spinning manufacturers still found the increase insufficient. Moreover, weavers were unhappy about the lack of a corresponding rise of duties on linen cloth. The decision not to increase the tariff on cloth was intended to facilitate the conclusion of a commercial agreement with Belgium, with linen cloth still making up more than half of Belgian exports to France in the early 1840s.[24] The linen question was becoming increasingly intertwined with the project of a commercial rapprochement, and possibly a customs union, with Belgium.

This project was partly inspired by the idea of a 'Latin Zollverein' or 'Union du Midi' advocated by the publicist Léon Faucher. A progressive

[20] Victor Chapelle, *Pétition adressée à MM: les membres de la chambre des députés relativement à la filature du lin* (Paris, [1841]), p. 1; see also Ernest Feray, *Réponse sur les négociations commerciales ouvertes entre la France et l'Angleterre* (Paris, 1839), and Comité des Lins, *Réclamations de l'industrie française des toiles de lin et de chanvre* (Paris, 1842).

[21] Pierre-Marie Le Mesl, *Mémoire sur la nécessité de prohiber l'importation des fils de lin de provenances étrangères* (Saint-Brieuc, 1838); Moret de Moy, *Misère des classes laborieuses et ses causes, démontrées par les faits, par l'abandon de l'intérêt agricole, et notamment de l'industrie des lins* (Saint-Quentin, 1840); Charles Homon, *Question des lins et des chanvres* (Morlaix, 1842).

[22] *Le Moniteur Universel*, 13 February 1841.

[23] 'Das neue Gesetz über den französischen Handelstarif', *Allgemeine Zeitung*, supplement, 11 February 1841.

[24] Lévy-Leboyer, *Les Banques européennes*, pp. 104–5.

liberal, Faucher viewed a customs union with Belgium as a preliminary step towards the abolition of customs barriers first from Andalusia to Flanders and then across Europe.[25] The project of a customs union with Belgium also benefited from the support of Guizot, leader of the government since 1840, and King Louis-Philippe, both sensitive to the geopolitical advantages of a reinforcement of French influence in a country that many still wished to annex on behalf of the natural frontiers doctrine. Fearing for the recent independence (1831) of their country, Belgian negotiators eventually rejected a customs union but agreed to a limited convention that would facilitate Belgian exports of manufactured goods in return for the lowering of Belgian duties on French silks and wines. The proposed agreement constituted a dilemma for French nationalists, caught between memories of expansion during the Revolution and the fear of competition with more advanced Belgian industries. The latter feeling prevailed, accelerating the drift of French manufacturers towards a conception of protection as self-sufficiency, which privileged the well-being of existing French citizens over territorial aggrandizement.[26]

Supporters of the commercial agreement or *unionistes* and their adversaries or *anti-unionistes* waged a fierce battle through the press. The main *unioniste* newspapers were *Le Journal des Débats* (pro-government, conservative), *Le Courrier Français* (liberal, edited by Faucher) and *Le Siècle* (liberal), whereas *Le Constitutionnel* (centre-left, under Thiers's influence), *La Presse* (conservative, under Comte Molé's influence) and *Le Commerce* (controlled by manufacturing interests) led the *anti-unioniste* campaign. *Unionisme* usually combined an exaltation of France's leadership in Europe with a preference for free trade, while *anti-unionisme* stood for a narrow interpretation of protection as reserved to French nationals and hostility to Guizot, the adversary of Thiers and Molé. Subsidies handed out by both sides played a key role in determining newspapers' stances. During their stay in Paris, Belgian delegates spent over 1,000 francs a month in gifts and subscriptions to promote the agreement in the press.[27] Yet the *anti-unionistes*, thanks to the support of manufacturers, probably outspent the defenders of the treaty, leading Faucher to complain of 'an avalanche of prohibitive interests' over the press.[28]

[25] Léon Faucher, 'L'Union du midi', *Revue des Deux Mondes*, 4th series, 9 (1837): 517–59, and *L'Union du Midi* (Paris, 1842).

[26] Henry-Thierry Deschamps, *La Belgique devant la France de Juillet* (Paris, 1956), pp. 110–19.

[27] Deschamps, *La Belgique*, pp. 119–38.

[28] Faucher to Henry Reeve, 8 April 1842, in *Léon Faucher*, 2 vols. (Paris, 1867), vol. 1: *Correspondance*, pp. 117–18.

The pressure orchestrated by manufacturing interests kept growing in the run-up to the July 1842 general election. Even royalist and radical sheets such as *La Quotidienne* or *Le National* supported the demand put forward by *anti-unioniste* newspapers for an immediate increase in the linen tariff. *Le Constitutionnel* described such an increase as 'a measure of justice and fairness, … fundamentally corresponding with the national interest … because this industry, thanks to its close connections to agriculture as well as by itself, affects our production as a whole'. The government eventually bowed to the pressure. Probably prompted by ministers, *Le Journal des Débats* and *Le Siècle* conceded the need for an increase in the linen tariff. Only Faucher's *Courrier Français* continued to shun the extension of the protective system to the last 'free branch of French industry'.[29] Excusing Guizot, a Belgian negotiator admitted that his conservative majority was at risk of losing between twenty and thirty seats if it did not give in to public opinion.[30] Guizot himself was a deputy for Lisieux, in linen-producing Normandy. On 26 June, two weeks before the election, the government raised import duties on linen yarns and cloth to, respectively, 26 per cent and 30 per cent *ad valorem*.

Immediately after Guizot's comfortable victory at the election and in return for reductions in Belgian duties on French silks and wines, the 16 July 1842 Franco-Belgian commercial convention annulled, for linen imports from Belgium, the increase of 26 June and restored the 1841 tariff. Thanks to the new preferential tariff, Belgian imports recovered, while British imports of yarns and cloth declined by 40 per cent and 70 per cent respectively between 1842 and 1843. There was an echo of the Continental System in this encouragement of intra-continental trade at the expense of British commerce. But the arrangement proved a Pyrrhic victory for the *unioniste* camp, as the Guizot government would soon abstain from further defying manufacturing interests and the press over the Belgian question. The success of the campaign for an increase in the linen tariff, at least on British imports, therefore demonstrated the progress of ideas of protection as self-sufficiency. It also highlighted the growing influence of industrial lobbies on the controversy about international trade.

[29] *Le Constitutionnel*, 27 May 1842, and *Le Courrier Français*, 28 June 1842. See also *La Quotidienne*, 12 February 1842; *Le Commerce*, 25 May 1842; *La Presse*, 25 May 1842; *Le National*, 25 May 1842; *Le Journal des Débats*, 28 June 1842; *Le Siècle*, 2 June 1842.

[30] Deschamps, *La Belgique*, p. 161.

II

Given the lack of records other than published sources on the activities of the Comité de l'Industrie Linière, one can only imagine the behind-the-scenes pressures that it exercised on politicians or the payments it made to newspapers. The surviving minutes of another lobby spawned by the industrial depression of the late 1830s, the Comité de l'Industrie Cotonière de l'Est, held at the Centre Rhénan d'Archives et de Recherches Économiques in Mulhouse, offer more concrete evidence of how manufacturers sought to influence public opinion. The same source also sheds light on how and why French manufacturers gradually abandoned the industrialist discourse in favour of self-sufficiency.

The Mulhouse manufacturers offer a particularly interesting example of this shift because until 1830 these dynamic entrepreneurs were reputed for their liberal opinions on economic as well as political issues. A Restoration prefect of the Haut-Rhin described Mulhouse as 'a seat of seditious machinations' hatched by the manufacturers who were 'all Protestants, all with the liberal party'.[31] Thanks to the growth of cotton-spinning, weaving and dyeing, the population of 'le Manchester français' grew 120 per cent between 1815 and 1844.[32] In 1831, the Chamber of Commerce still presented King Louis-Philippe with a petition demanding the repeal of all prohibitions, including the prohibition on cotton textiles: 'We are confident that in conditions of universal competition of industry, France would occupy a leading rank.'[33] The following year, Ferdinand Koechlin, one of the town's leading manufacturers, considered the reduction of protection inevitable because 'the cry "no more prohibitions" and "liberty of commerce" [was] becoming more common every day' and, despite some apprehension, deemed that such a measure corresponded with 'France's general interest'. The same year, the Société Industrielle de Mulhouse, an organization dominated by local manufacturers, chose for its prize competition of political economy a question on the best means to ensure a smooth transition towards 'a system of liberty of commerce'.[34]

31 Prefect of the Haut-Rhin to the Minister of the Interior, 17 April 1827 and 2 December 1829, AN, F 7 6771, folder 10.

32 Georges Livet and Raymond Oberlé (eds.), *Histoire de Mulhouse des origines à nos jours* (Strasbourg, 1977), pp. 173–245; see also Michel Hau and Nicolas Stoskopf, *Les Dynasties alsaciennes: du XVIIe siècle à nos jours* (Paris, 2005), pp. 115–229.

33 Memorandum by the Mulhouse Chamber of Commerce, 22 June 1831, CERARE, ACCM, 561.

34 Ferdinand Koechlin to Emile Dollfus, 1832, CERARE, Archives de la Société Industrielle de Mulhouse (hereafter ASIM), 96 A 1901; minutes of the Comité de Commerce of the Société Industrielle de Mulhouse, CERARE, ASIM, 96 B 1533, fols. 27–8. On the Société, see Florence Ott, *La Société Industrielle de Mulhouse, 1826–1876: ses membres, son action, ses réseaux* (Strasbourg, 1999).

Only when confronted with the concrete prospect of free trade, with the 1834 inquiry on prohibitions, did the Mulhouse manufacturers begin to modify their liberal industrialist language. The Chamber of Commerce acknowledged that, on several occasions, it had expressed the view that 'it would be desirable to render our system of customs less hostile to neighbouring states'. But, in the present circumstances, it asserted, 'the continuation of the current system is indispensable to the preservation of industry', or else 'France would be turned into a drain for all sorts of cheap English goods'. The Chamber of Commerce even raised a subscription and set up a 'commission du Haut-Rhin', which collected statistics in order to demonstrate the impossibility for French manufacturers of competing with their British and Swiss rivals at the 1834 inquiry.[35] The Chamber's opposition to the repeal of prohibitions was not unanimous: the President of the Chamber, Nicolas Koechlin (Ferdinand's brother) resigned in protest. Despite his support for free trade, Nicolas Koechlin, a *Mouvement* deputy for Mulhouse since 1830, was re-elected in 1837 and 1839.[36]

The ambivalence of the Mulhouse manufacturers on the regulation of international trade persisted when they founded, on 23 January 1839, the Comité de l'Industrie Cotonnière de l'Est. The seven founding members were major industrialists from the Haut-Rhin. In July, they were joined by seven representatives from neighbouring departments (Bas-Rhin, Vosges, Meurthe, Doubs and Haute-Saône) and by a Mulhouse publisher, whose newspaper *L'Industriel Alsacien* served as the Comité's mouthpiece.[37] The founding members of the committee would not all become convinced protectionists. One of them, Jean Dollfus, a manufacturer of dyed cotton fabrics in Mulhouse, later distinguished himself as a fervent advocate of free trade, both in France under Napoleon III and in Bismarck's Germany after the annexation of Alsace in 1871. The committee's objectives corresponded with neither the promotion of free trade nor the defence of the protective system but with the pursuit of local industrial interests. It still used an industrialist rather than a liberal or a nationalist phraseology. For instance, it called not only for bounties on French exports of cotton yarns and textiles but also for the repeal of the preferential tariff in favour of raw cotton imported via French ports. The Committee even declared itself willing to support 'the repeal of the prohibition [on cotton textiles], if

35 Minutes of the Mulhouse Chamber of Commerce, 15 October 1834, Archives Municipales de Mulhouse (hereafter AMM), 66TT/63, folder 3.

36 Nicolas Koechlin, *Réplique aux délégués de la chambre de commerce de Mulhouse* (Paris, 1835).

37 Minutes of the Comité de l'Industrie Cotonnière de l'Est (hereafter CICE), 23 January 1839 and 11 July 1839, CERARE, ACCM, 679, fols. 1, 33–4.

it [was] replaced by sufficient protective duties and above all if French manufactures [were] placed in conditions as advantageous as their competitors' by the reduction of duties on raw materials.[38]

The Committee had at its disposal a remainder of 5,000 francs from the defunct Commission du Haut-Rhin and collected 11,000 francs in yearly fees from its adherents. The funds were intended to ensure 'publicity' for its demands through three main channels: a salaried agent in Paris, the publication of pamphlets and the insertion of articles in the press.[39] In March 1839, the Committee paid for the publication and dissemination of a first pamphlet, against the 'monopoly' enjoyed by French seaports on the importation of American raw cotton. Funds also served to finance the sending of three delegates to Paris, where they met with several deputies and officials from the Ministry of Commerce. In May, the committee recruited Henri Bresson, a conservative deputy for the Vosges, as a permanent representative in Paris. Bresson agreed to serve *gratis* save for his expenses. In July, he had articles on the raw cotton duties printed in *Le Constitutionnel* and had them reproduced as a pamphlet that was distributed to deputies, peers and other officials.[40]

Bresson also suggested that in order to increase their influence, the Alsatians should emulate the 'manufacturers of linen textiles' and establish a 'national committee' in alliance 'with Rouen, Saint-Quentin, Lille, etc.'. An informal proposal from the Mulhouse committee elicited little enthusiasm from the manufacturers from other regions, perhaps because the Alsatians seemed insufficiently committed to national protection. In its response to the committee, the Société Industrielle et Commerciale de Saint-Quentin declined to undertake any collective action, lest it revived the debate on the prohibition of foreign textiles.[41] In October 1840, the Committee replaced Bresson, who had obtained few results, with a salaried agent named Mr Hadol, a solicitor from the small town of Remiremont (Vosges). Hadol received 1,000 francs per quarter, to be complemented by bonuses if he could obtain favourable changes in the legislation. In addition to promoting the objectives defined in 1839, Hadol was instructed to defend 'the prohibitive customs duties against English products, in all the branches of industry where we still cannot compete with England'.[42] This

[38] Minutes of the CICE, 13 February 1839 and 6 March 1839, CERARE, ACCM, 679, fols. 5–6, 8.

[39] Minutes of the CICE, 9 September 1840, CERARE, ACCM, 679, fols. 66–8.

[40] Minutes of the CICE, 6 March, 1 May and 11 July 1839, CERARE, ACCM, 679, fols. 9, 23–4, 32–3.

[41] Minutes of the CICE, 31 July and 23 October 1839, CERARE, ACCM, 679, fols. 36–40.

[42] Minutes of the CICE, 22 July 1840, 21 October 1840 and 27 January 1841, CERARE, ACCM, 679, fols. 56–7, 69, 78.

inflexion in favour of protection reflected the fears aroused by commercial negotiations with Britain and Belgium.

Hadol's reports on his activities confirmed the prevalence of corruption in the Parisian press described by Balzac in *Illusions perdues*. According to the Committee's agent, *Le Constitutionnel* would publish articles supporting their demands in return for '50 yearly subscriptions, or 4000 francs', while *Le Courrier Français* required 'thirty subscriptions, or 2400 francs'; '*Le Siècle, L'Estafette, Les Débats, La France*', he added, only needed 'to be paid' in order to endorse their views. The least expensive was *Le Commerce*, which only required a few 'honnêtetés' or petty bribes of approximately 500 francs, because its reputation as a mouthpiece of business interests made it less effective. The minutes of the Comité des Industries Cotonnières de l'Est do not indicate the amount or recipients of its subsidies. But the casual tone of Hadol suggests that such payments were common practice, explaining how the press became increasingly hostile to free trade after 1840. In March 1841, the Alsatian manufacturers considered and rejected a suggestion made by Hadol of creating their own Parisian newspaper. They preferred 'to employ different newspapers in turns' because a special sheet would not have as much influence as one that seemed to defend their interests 'of its own accord'.[43] In the spring of 1841, the Committee obtained the partial abolition of the preferential tariff on raw cottons imported via French ports. Yet, after learning that Hadol now worked as the 'commercial and industrial editor' of an unnamed Parisian newspaper, it decided to dispense with his services.[44] Hadol's professional trajectory shows how porous the boundaries between lobbying and journalism were at the time.

In 1840, three more manufacturing lobbies were founded: the Comité des Intérêts Métallurgiques (for metal-working, soon known as the 'Comité des Forges'), the Union des Houillères Françaises (for coal extraction) and the Comité Central des Fabricants de Sucre (for beet sugar). These organizations exercised a discreet but significant influence on economic policy until at least the First World War.[45] In 1842, the fear of a customs union with Belgium even induced manufacturers, led by Auguste Mimerel, to establish a national organization. In March, Mimerel submitted to the Mulhouse committee a proposal 'to unite French industry into a single *faisceau* (beam)'. The national organization would comprise four

[43] Minutes of the CICE, 27 January, 17 March and 14 April 1841, CERARE, ACCM, 679, fols. 78–9, 81–3.

[44] Minutes of the CICE, 17 November 1841 and 16 February 1842, CERARE, ACCM, 680, fols. 1, 4–5.

[45] Gille, *Recherches*, pp. 129–47; Smith, *Tariff Reform in France*, pp. 90–114.

main branches: ironworks, wool, cotton and remaining industries. The projected yearly contributions were relatively modest, at 5,000 francs per branch, to be divided on a regional basis – in the case of cotton between Normandy (1,500 francs), Alsace (1,500 francs), the Nord (1,200 francs) and Picardy (800 francs). In the future, a new branch would be created as soon as the output of an industry reached approximately 150 million francs.[46]

The organization's immediate goal was to derail negotiations with Belgium. But Mimerel hoped that this new 'common centre' of French industries would become a permanent means of fending off attempts to call protection into question. He also insisted that it ought to defend protection for all producers: 'it would provide help and support not only to well organized industries; the country's labour, whether it derives from agriculture, industry or commerce, this is what we want to shelter from every attack'.[47] The Mulhouse committee initially declined Mimerel's invitation to become part of the organization. But after the Guizot government made new commercial overtures to Belgium in the early autumn, the Alsatian manufacturers reversed their decision.[48] The Comité pour la Défense du Travail National held its founding meeting in Paris on 5–7 November 1842. More than 100 delegates attended, most of them from the Paris region, Normandy, Alsace and the Nord. They elected Mimerel as President and Henri Barbet, the Mayor of Rouen, as Vice-President. A solemn resolution asserted that 'all the French industries form[ed] a single family, founded and developed under the same system of protection for national labour'. Opposing any further lowering of the French tariff on Belgian imports, the manufacturers' manifesto promised 'to present, without delay, a common defence and to act upon the minds, thanks to publicity and the demonstration of facts'.[49]

Mimerel elaborated upon his conception of protection in a pamphlet published at the end of 1842 and entitled *Du paupérisme dans ses rapports avec l'industrie en France et en Angleterre*. Anxiety about the *question sociale* had reached new heights since the publication of the statistician Louis-René Villermé's *Tableau de l'état physique et moral des ouvriers* (1840), a heart-rending description of the destitution of textile workers

[46] Copy of a letter from Mimerel to Nicolas Schlumberger père dated 22 March 1842, in minutes of the CICE, 15 April 1842, CERARE, ACCM, 680, fols. 6–7.

[47] Copy of 'Projet d'association en un seul faisceau de l'industrie française', in minutes of the CICE, 15 April 1842, CERARE, ACCM, 680, fols. 8–9.

[48] Minutes of the CICE, 2 November 1842, CERARE, ACCM, 680, fols. 10–11.

[49] *Le Commerce*, 6 and 8 November 1842; see also the petition by the Comité de la Défense du Travail National, 'Aux membres du Conseil du Roi', 7 November 1842, AN, F12 6240.

in northern factories, and of an equally alarming *La Misère des classes laborieuses en France et en Angeleterre* (1840) by Eugène Buret, a disciple of Sismondi. Simultaneously responding to Villermé and suggestions by free-traders that tariffs were a manifestion of manufacturers' greed, Mimerel wished 'to demonstrate that protection was not established in favour of a privileged few, but mostly in favour of workers, and ultimately of the entire nation'. Pointing out that 'the hideous wound of pauperism' primarily affected British cities, he attributed its extent across the Channel to Britain's liberal trade policy and increasing reliance on exports. Mimerel also attacked the materialistic doctrines of the economists and the socialists as having contributed to the spread of pauperism, which consisted in 'moral poverty' as much as 'real destitution': 'multiplying desires for multiple pleasures eventually results in rendering unbearable a condition, which, under the influence of different ideas, might have been envied, because it satisfied all the necessities of life'. Only when workers were subjected to foreign competition, Mimerel contended, could their wages fall below the subsistence level and poverty become material as well as moral: 'if foreign labour cannot access our market, workers, rare in relation to the number of machines, will receive constant and high salaries for a long time'.[50]

Protection, in Mimerel's opinion, constituted the foundation of France's 'economic system', which guaranteed limited but stable outlets for French products and a better balance between agricultural and industrial development. The phrase echoed the 'French system' propounded by Villeneuve-Bargemont (a royalist deputy for the Nord department since 1840), and the substance recalled Dombasle's analysis in *De l'avenir industriel.* Mimerel also contrasted France's system to the 'disorderly state' of the British economy. Britain's reliance on foreign markets left it vulnerable to 'the jolts that might affect Germany, America, China' and 'its thirst for external outlets [was] so devouring, that quenching it would require setting the whole world on fire'. It was in order to secure 'the privilege of supplying cheap textiles to all nations' that Britain reduced its workers to a state of 'abject destitution'. Unlike the royalist Villeneuve-Bargemont, however, Mimerel attributed the Anglo-French economic contrast to divergent political values, themselves rooted in differences of 'social organization and customs'. While France's system reflected its egalitarianism, symbolized by the inheritance rules of the

[50] Auguste Mimerel, *Du paupérisme dans ses rapports avec l'industrie en France et en Angleterre* (Lille, [1842]), pp. 4–5, 10.

Code Civil, Britain's proclivity for immense industrial concerns mirrored its preference for aristocratic primogeniture. The British privileged classes shared between them the benefits of the export trade, condemning their workers to 'debasement' and using the sophistry of political economy to justify such exploitation: 'in the eyes of this science that ignores mercy, the free man of England is nothing more than a tool of production, the least valuable of all'. Indeed, it was 'not even as valuable as a slave', he added in a disapproving allusion to the popularity of the anti-slavery movement in Britain.[51]

Du paupérisme drew on the old republican critique of Britain as a soulless oligarchy but turned the conclusion on its head, using it to defend protection instead of propounding the liberty of commerce, as, for instance, in Say's *De l'Angleterre* (1815). Mimerel's pamphlet contained several gross misrepresentations. In the early 1840s, workers' wages were higher and social legislation more advanced in Britain than in France – but Mimerel would have disputed the contradiction since he disapproved of social legislation such as the 1841 law on child labour as 'coercive', favouring instead the revival of 'patronage' as a means of improving workers' conditions.[52] The pamphlet also ignored that the growth of France's foreign trade was then experiencing a significant acceleration, from an annual rate of 1.5 per cent in 1825–34 to 4.5 per cent in 1835–44.[53] However, in some respects, the contrast drawn by Mimerel between the British and French economic systems foreshadowed the conclusions of several historians on the existence of a French path of industrialization, slower but more balanced and more humane than that of Britain.[54]

In spite of – or thanks to – the liberties taken by Mimerel with economic and social reality, his campaign for the defence of national labour met with swift success. At the end of November 1842, the Guizot government formally renounced any further commercial negotiation with Belgium. In December, the ironworks branch of the Comité pour la Défense du Travail National took financial control of the *Courrier Français*, the last vocal support of free trade in the press.[55] Dismissed from his position as editor of the *Courrier*, Faucher travelled in England and published a well-documented analysis of British politics and economics. Although critical of the extent of inequalities in Britain, this work sought to correct several exaggerations of Mimerel's Anglophobic propaganda.

[51] Mimerel, *Du paupérisme*, pp. 16–17, 19–24. [52] Mimerel, *Du paupérisme*, pp. 27–8.
[53] Toutain, 'Les Structures du commerce extérieur', p. 61.
[54] O'Brien and Keyder, *Economic Growth in Britain and France*; Horn, *The Path Not Taken*.
[55] Deschamps, *La Belgique*, p. 263.

Faucher conceded that Britain's reliance on exports exposed its immense manufacturing sector to frequent 'commercial hurricanes' and gave vivid descriptions of workers' destitution in London and northern industrial cities. But, in an attempt to revive Say's republican critique of Britain's political economy, he attributed the prevalence of poverty in British cities to the enduring dominance of the 'aristocratic principle' in British politics and was confident that the imminent abolition of the Corn Laws and the rise of the middle classes would at least alleviate the sufferings of workers.[56] France's controversy on international trade was increasingly entangled with the debate about the merits and dangers of industrialization across the Channel.

III

After their relative victory over the promoters of industrialist jealousy in the linen and Belgian question, the partisans of self-sufficiency also prevailed over both the free-traders and the defenders of mercantilist protection in the fiercely debated *question des sucres* at the turn of the 1840s. Again, the fear of pauperism contributed to the outcome of the controversy, with the new beet-sugar industry appearing as a means of slowing down migration towards cities. But the sugar question was primarily a dispute about the economic advantages and drawbacks of colonial expansion and might even be construed, in the absence of a major abolitionist movement, as a surrogate debate about the future of slavery in French overseas possessions.[57]

The sugar question was ignited by the rapid growth of the beet-sugar industry in the 1830s. The first beet-sugar factories were established during the Continental Blockade, with the encouragement of the Napoleonic administration, as a remedy to the collapse in imports of cane sugar. The resumption of cane-sugar imports at the end of the Blockade ruined most of these ventures. But improvements of the fabrication processes devised in the 1820s permitted a rapid rise in the output of metropolitan beet sugar, from 5,000 tons in 1829 to 20,000 in 1834 and 40,000 in 1836. This surge

[56] Léon Faucher, *Etudes sur l'Angleterre*, 2 vols. (Paris, 1845), vol. I, pp. xiv–xv, 443–70 and vol. II, pp. 337–87; see also Philip Morey, 'Through French Eyes: Victorian Cities in the Eighteen-Forties Viewed by Léon Faucher', forthcoming in *Historical Research*.

[57] Seymour Drescher, 'British Way, French Way: Opinion Building and Revolution in the Second French Slave Emancipation', *American Historical Review*, 96 (3) (1991): 709–34; and Jennings, *French Anti-Slavery*; on the equally complex articulation, for different reasons, between the sugar tariff and the abolition of slavery in Britain, see Richard Huzzey, 'Free Trade, Free Labour, and Slave Sugar in Victorian Britain', *Historical Journal*, 53 (2) (2010): 359–79.

in the production of beet sugar also relied on the inadvertent protection offered by the fiscal duties of 45 francs per 100 kilograms on all imports of cane sugar, including French colonial sugar. Although the latter remained sheltered from foreign cane-sugar competition by a *surtaxe* or additional tax of 60 francs per 100 kilograms, the boom in the beet-sugar industry resulted in the steady decline in the price of sugar on the French market and the stagnation of cane-sugar imports from the colonies at about 80,000 tons per year after 1830. In addition to an economic crisis in the colonies, the rise of the untaxed metropolitan beet-sugar industry caused a significant shortfall in fiscal revenue, since duties on cane-sugar imports represented 5 per cent of all Treasury receipts.[58]

Combined with the abolition of slavery in British colonies in the 1830s, the stagnation of the colonial sugar trade reinforced a sense that the days of slavery and the plantation economy were numbered. But the economic difficulties of planters also strengthened the opposition of the colonial lobby to abolition and probably helped to delay the emancipation of French slaves until after the fall of the July Monarchy, in April 1848.[59] Bordeaux remained the main port for exchanges with Caribbean islands, and Henri Fonfrède was one of the first to stress the connection between the sugar question and France's imperial future. Despite his conservative drift on most political issues after 1830, the city's leading publicist retained radical opinions on the colonial question as well as free trade. As early as 1834, Fonfrède condemned French endeavours to colonize North Africa, which he described as 'the protective system jumping across the Mediterranean'. He supported the spread of European civilization overseas but favoured 'the moral propagation of ideas' over a 'colonial propagation' by 'pilfering, ineffective and barbaric' means. So, while most of the press stood behind France's Algerian war effort in the 1830s, Fonfrède reviled the immorality of the massacres perpetrated by French troops as 'a crime of lese-nation and lese-mankind', which illustrated 'the barbaric results of Europe's civilizing efforts'. In his view, the economic decline of France's old colonies and the difficulties of the Algerian conquest proved that the 'colonial system [was] as dead and buried as the Polish nation'. Unable to comprehend attempts at resuscitating it in Africa while it was withering away in

58 E. Boizard and H. Tardieu, *Histoire de la législation des sucres (1664–1891)* (Paris, 1891), pp. 24–86; figures drawn from 'Sucres de toutes origines soumis aux droits et consommés en France', 15 February 1850, AN, F12 2550/A and Ministère du Commerce, *Statistique de la France*, vol. VII, pp. 244–5.

59 Butel, *Histoire des Antilles françaises*, pp. 246–59; Frédéric Régent, *La France et ses esclaves: de la colonisation aux abolitions* (Paris, 2007), pp. 263–89.

America, he described his own programme for Algeria with a neologism that would be little used until the next century: 'décolonisation'.[60]

In 1836, Fonfrède used the sugar question as further evidence that the colonial system was doomed. But, rather than welcoming the rise of the beet-sugar industry, he demanded uniform taxation on all three types of sugar – foreign cane sugar, colonial cane sugar and metropolitan beet sugar – in the hope of developing France's trade with the rest of the world rather than protecting French colonial or metropolitan producers. He even reserved his most acerbic comments for beet sugar, in which he viewed an extreme example of the unnatural economic change brought about by protection: just as 'evil yields evil' and 'despotism yields despotism', he argued, 'the prohibitive system yields indigenous sugar'. But he also condemned 'old colonial fashions'. Instead, he viewed the sugar question as an opportunity to adopt a new economic course, 'in which the old and contradictory routines of prohibitive madness would no longer keep our thoughts in a languishing state of oppression, restriction and torture'. He recommended the adoption of a uniform tax of 25 francs per 100 kilograms on all types of sugar, which would wipe out the beet sugar industry and enable France to become again, as before 1789, 'an entrepôt of foreign sugar for the other states of Europe'. Such a 'fragment of commercial liberty', he hoped, would also help persuade the masses that 'if all mankind's production were treated according to the same principles, ... all the goods, all the raw materials, all the incentives to work, all the fuels, irons and metals, all the skills [would become] simultaneously cheaper'.[61]

The Bordelais merchants, often the creditors of French planters in the Antilles, only supported Fonfrède's crusade for a single tax on sugar with reluctance, as a means of garnering broad support against the threat posed by beet sugar. From Paris, Tanneguy Duchâtel, the former Minister of Commerce, reported that Fonfrède's articles on the sugar tariff made a 'powerful impression' on state officials and deputies, who worried about the shortfall of revenue induced by the growth of the beet-sugar industry.[62] Yet, in 1837, the government opted for the defence of the colonial system, with a proposal to reduce duties on colonial cane sugar from 45 to 25

60 'Affaire d'Alger – Commission d'Afrique', *Le Mémorial*, four articles, 30 September 1834 and 1, 2 and 3 October 1834; 'Un mot sur la colonisation d'Alger', 'Comment la civilisation commence – Comment la colonisation finit', 'La Presse parisienne – Alger – Le mémorial bordelais', *Le Mémorial*, 12, 22, 24, 28, 29 and 31 December 1835; 'De la lettre de M. Mauguin, président du conseil des colonies' and 'De la décolonisation d'Alger', *Le Mémorial*, 26 and 31 January 1836.

61 'Question des sucres', six articles, *Le Mémorial*, 9, 11, 12, 13, 14 and 15 April 1836.

62 Guestier to Fonfrède, 30 March 1836, and Duchâtel to Fonfrède, 27 April 1836, BMB, MS 1095, vol. 11, fols. 165–70, 185–6.

francs per 100 kilograms. In the Chamber of Deputies, one of the measure's chief defenders was Alphonse de Lamartine, a supporter of both free trade and French overseas expansion, on the grounds that 'colonies are part of France' and that planters deserved the same fiscal treatment as metropolitan producers. Yet, led by representatives of beet-sugar-producing departments (Nord, Pas-de-Calais, Aisne, Somme), deputies rejected the proposal, preferring instead to create a modest tax of 15 francs per 100 kilograms on beet sugar.[63] Defenders of beet sugar favoured a new domestic tax over a reduction in import duties because they knew it would be easy to evade. Official figures based on tax receipts, which indicate a decline of the output of beet sugar from 48,000 tons in 1837 to 28,000 in 1840, can therefore not be trusted, and the price of sugar on the French market continued to decline.[64]

Fonfrède's disappointment accelerated his drift to the right of the political spectrum and led him to call for the limitation of the legislative chambers' powers. The hardening of his distrust in the representative element of the constitution was connected with the contemporary struggle between the government of Comte Molé, backed by King Louis-Philippe, and the parliamentary 'Coalition' of Guizot, Thiers and the leader of the dynastic left, Odilon Barrot, between 1837 and 1839. In 1838, Fonfrède left the pro-Coalition *Mémorial* and, with the financial support of several Bordelais merchants, founded his own pro-Molé newspaper, *Le Courrier de Bordeaux*. In a vehement series of articles, Fonfrède described the refusal of deputies to alter the 'Satanic' legislation on sugar as evidence that the powers of the parliamentary chambers had become excessive, especially in matters of economic legislation. 'The Crown', he argued, 'should have the power to determine the industrial and economic course of the country', because the chambers, and 'especially the elected chamber', lacked 'the knowledge and ability to use such a power for the benefit of social progress'. Despite his own role in the 1830 insurrection in defence of the representative chamber, Fonfrède considered it 'a great deal and … often too much to let [deputies] dominate *the civil and political order*; but *the industrial and economic order* should be placed out of their immediate reach'. The publicist now described himself as an adversary of 'parliamentary democracy'.[65]

Free-traders such as Fonfrède, equally enraged by the mercantile preference for colonial sugar and the protection of metropolitan beet sugar,

[63] AP, vol. CXI, pp. 732–5 (26 May 1837) and CXII, p. 121 (1 June 1837).

[64] 'Sucres de toutes origines soumis aux droits et consommés en France', 15 February 1850, AN, F12 2550/A.

[65] 'Du dégrèvement des sucres', six articles, *Le Courrier de Bordeaux*, 1, 4, 18, 19, 23 and 30 October 1838; on Fonfrède's intervention in this constitutional debate, see Rosanvallon, *La Monarchie impossible*, pp. 158–60.

raised the issue of the sugar tariff in the hope that a liberal legislation would appear as the only reasonable solution of the complex sugar question. Fonfrède's frustration with the economically illiberal tendencies of elected chambers foreshadowed the exasperation of several other free-traders who, under the Second Empire of Napoleon III, would further reappraise the merits of a strong executive branch of government. By contrast, the defence of metropolitan or 'indigenous' beet sugar enabled the promoters of self-sufficiency to stress the compatibility of their ideas with representative government and to gain new supporters on the left of the political spectrum.

A case in point was the propaganda in favour of indigenous sugar by Mathieu de Dombasle, himself a former beet-sugar manufacturer during the Continental Blockade and whose defence of economic autarky, *De l'avenir industriel de la France* (1834), had already met with a warm reception in provincial opinion. Dombasle was no less opposed than Fonfrède to colonial expansion. In *De l'avenir de l'Algérie*, published in 1838, he conceded that 'a very imposing majority of the French population' supported the conquest of North Africa, but he declared himself resolutely hostile, both on humanitarian and economic grounds. Stressing the incompatibility of liberalism with colonialism, he argued that nothing was 'less liberal than the domination of a people over another' and pointed out that French rule had placed Arabs under 'a far harsher yoke than that [of the Turks], from which we claimed to liberate them'. He also condemned the exportation of capital to the colony, where it would obtain low returns and create new competitors for Mediterranean French producers. 'And then blood', he concluded, 'always more blood, and all this not even in the real interest of the country'.[66]

Between 1835 and 1843, Dombasle published six pamphlets and numerous articles on the sugar question. His writings underlined the global economic and geopolitical consequences of what he described as a 'révolution sucrière' (sugar revolution). As a result of political revolutions in the New World since the 1770s, there remained only a few 'fragments' of the 'colonial colossus' erected by Europeans in the Americas, and even these were bound to succumb to 'the atmosphere of liberty and independence that surrounds them' in the near future. Furthermore, the inevitable abolition of slavery in the Americas, propounded by Britain's cynical efforts to increase the profitability of its Indian possessions, would further reduce

[66] Christophe-Joseph-Alexandre Mathieu de Dombasle, *De l'avenir de l'Algérie* (Paris, 1838), pp. 3, 15–17, 20.

the supply of American sugar and make France dependent upon British and Dutch importations from their Asian colonies. Only the domestic production of beet sugar could guarantee France's future independence: 'The discovery of indigenous sugar has substituted an industrial revolution advantageous to Europe to a commercial revolution advantageous to English India.'[67]

Dombasle's second major argument in favour of beet sugar lay in the supplementary economic activity it generated in the countryside. As with the introduction of the turnip in eighteenth-century England, the sugar beet made possible the adoption of more productive crop rotations. The cultivation of the sugar beet also encouraged farmers to hoe the soil, further increasing returns. Beet-sugar factories could therefore become a formidable source of progress and prosperity in rural France: 'Each sugar refinery established in regions where techniques are not very advanced forms a centre around which radiate agricultural improvements of all kinds.' The beet-sugar industry exemplified the complementary relations between agriculture and manufacturing that Dombasle called for in *De l'avenir industriel* and would reduce the influx of impoverished rural workers in urban centres. Dombasle conceded that the rise of beet sugar would hasten the ruin of France's colonies and risked reducing its naval power but insisted that the country's 'true strength' lay in a capacity to raise 'numerous land armies' anyway. He also accepted that beet sugar would reduce external outlets for French products. But the loss of foreign markets would be more than compensated by new outlets 'in the interior' that would not 'be exposed to the hazards of a maritime war'.[68]

Dombasle's case for indigenous sugar inspired many other defenders of the new industry. Citing the agronomist, a pamphlet by Thémistocle Lestiboudois, a deputy for the Nord, denied that colonies formed 'an integral part of France' and considered them doomed by the forthcoming abolition of slavery.[69] A pamphlet by a committee of beet-sugar industrialists in Valenciennes and Avesnes (Nord) also cited Dombasle's pamphlets before calling into question the very nationality of planters in French colonies: 'And who are these colonists, Gentlemen? French citizens, they claim to be; enjoying the same rights as us; bearing the same

[67] Christophe-Joseph-Alexandre Mathieu de Dombasle, *De l'impôt sur le sucre indigène: nouvelles considérations* (Nancy, 1837), pp. 15–19; see also Christophe-Joseph-Alexandre Mathieu de Dombasle, *Du sucre indigène* (Nancy, 1835), *Questions des sucres: nouvelles considérations* (Nancy, 1838), *Question des sucres: conséquences du système adopté* (Nancy, 1839), *Question des sucres* (Nancy, 1840) and *La Question des sucres en 1843* (Nancy, 1843).

[68] Mathieu de Dombasle, *De l'impôt sur le sucre indigène*, pp. 12, 22–5.

[69] Thémistocle Lestiboudois, *Des colonies sucrières et des sucreries indigènes* (Lille, 1839), p. 6.

charges as us!' 'These are all lies', the pamphlet asserted, because colonists were subjected neither to the land tax nor to the military service. 'There is between them and us', it concluded, 'neither equality of rights nor equality of charges. To us the laws of free nations; to them the laws of barbaric nations: caste and colour distinction, slavery.'[70] Dombasle's conception of protection as self-sufficiency channelled anti-colonial and anti-slavery feelings more effectively than Fonfrède's more traditional liberal hostility to the colonial system.

IV

In the early 1840s, defenders of beet sugar gained further ground in public opinion and defeated two attempts by the government to suppress the new industry. In 1840, they saw off a ministerial project to raise the tax on indigenous sugar to the same level as customs duties on colonial sugar, or 45 francs per 100 kilograms. General Bugeaud spearheaded opposition to the project. Although Bugeaud is still identified with the most brutal phase of French colonization in North Africa, before becoming Governor-General of Algeria in 1841 he was better known as a promoter of agricultural improvement in his native Périgord and frequently expressed sceptical views on overseas expansion.[71] Hence his determined support, in 1840, for the beet-sugar industry, as a source of prosperity for metropolitan agriculture and greater stability for French society. 'Keep [workers] in the countryside', he urged deputies, 'and you will not need to make such extraordinary expenses [on outdoor relief] and these populations will retain a better morality ... If there is one means of extinguishing pauperism, or at least of diminishing it significantly, it is certainly by encouraging the cultivation of the sugar beet' and, more generally, 'domestic production.'[72]

On the sugar question, advocates of industrialist jealousy tended to side with the promoters of self-sufficiency. Adolphe Thiers attacked the project of tax equalization on the grounds that discouraging any 'national industry' would be 'a serious fault'. He also feared that the repeal of protection for one industry might serve to justify similar measures for 'all [France's] other protected industries'. The need to protect the beet-sugar industry, he added, further illustrated what he had earlier described as the 'veritable

[70] [Anon.], *Observations sur la question des sucres* (Valenciennes, 1839), pp. 14–15.
[71] Anthony T. Sullivan, *Thomas-Robert Bugeaud: France and Algeria, 1784–1849 – Politics, Power, and the Good Society* (Hamden, Conn., 1983), pp. 37–44, 66–8.
[72] Debates at the Chamber of Deputies (7 May 1840), *Le Moniteur Universel*, 8 May 1840.

science' of economics: 'It may not be a very imposing sort of political economy', he concluded, 'but it is the most accurate, the one that corresponds with historical facts.'[73] Friedrich List, Thiers's friend, was enthusiastic about the prospects of beet sugar and considered investing in a sugar factory himself in 1836.[74] In the German press, List condemned the 1840 equalization project in harsh terms, describing the author of the proposal, the conservative minister Laurent Cunin-Gridaine, as a 'new Herod' for his project of 'industrial assassination'.[75] A large majority of deputies (230 to 67) rejected the project, voting instead to increase the tax on indigenous sugar to 25 francs per 100 kilograms, a level still insufficient to halt the new industry's growth.[76]

Following a succession of good cane harvests in the Antilles and a further decline in the price of sugar on the French market, the controversy over the sugar tariff reached its maximum intensity between 1841 and 1843. New lobbies orchestrated an unusual agitation in defence of colonial or beet sugar, drowning the voice of free-traders. Colonial planters had informal delegates lobbying ministers and deputies since the early years of the Restoration. In 1840 or 1841, a formal Conseil des Colonies elected Charles Dupin, a delegate for Martinique since the mid 1830s, as their president. Perhaps influenced by the planters' subsidies, Dupin upheld a conception of protection that would extend to French overseas producers. His service in the Napoleonic navy and knowledge of British affairs made him an adequate spokesman of colonial interests. In the late 1830s, he became a leading defender of the *pacte colonial*, a new phrase that underlined the allegedly reciprocal nature of mercantilist legislation on colonial trade, whereas in reality the Old Regime's *exclusif* was only intended to benefit metropolitan France.[77] Dupin also propounded a reduction of duties on colonial sugar as a means of bolstering French naval power, since the colonial trade played a crucial role in the training of sailors for the French navy. Conversely, abandoning colonial sugar in favour of beet sugar would reduce France to a 'third-rank' naval power and jeopardize its influence outside Europe.[78]

After becoming President of the Conseil des Colonies, Dupin published four more pamphlets that demanded an outright ban on the

[73] Debates at the Chamber of Deputies (8 May 1840), *Le Moniteur Universel*, 9 May 1840.
[74] Henderson, *Friedrich List*, pp. 80–1.
[75] *Allgemeine Zeitung*, 1 February 1840.
[76] Debates at the Chamber of Deputies (12 May 1840), *Le Moniteur Universel*, 13 May 1840.
[77] On the *pacte colonial* as a nineteenth-century misconstruction of pre-1789 legislation on the colonial trade, see Tarrade, *Le Commerce colonial*, vol. 1, pp. 85–6.
[78] Charles Dupin, *Tableau des intérêts de la France* (Paris, 1836) and *Faits et calculs* (Paris, 1837).

production of beet sugar, in return for an indemnity for beet-sugar manufacturers (the scheme mirrored proposals for the abolition of slavery in return for an indemnity to planters). His fundamental argument was the Frenchness of colonial producers, making them entitled to the same protection against foreign competition as metropolitan manufacturers and workers. As evidence of their French economic nationality, Dupin offered calculations showing that the inhabitants of Martinique, Guadeloupe and Bourbon, including slaves, consumed on average 198 times more French wine and 660 times more French textiles than the inhabitants of the rest of the world. Although Dupin insisted that even slaves, as 'human beings', deserved economic protection, his attack on the beet-sugar industry was also an implicit defence of slavery. The 'greatest benefit' of sugar plantations, he argued, lay in 'compelling the black race to retain the industrious habits it has received under European direction, as a precious element of civilizing activity'. Dupin also described himself as the true defender of 'Napoleonic ideas', on the grounds that in times of peace, Napoleon would have done everything in his power to promote French naval power.[79] Dupin's conviction that the protective system should be extended to 'overseas Frenchmen' also applied to Algeria, and he later became the main sponsor of the commercial incorporation of North African departments to France under the Second Republic.[80]

The Conseil des Colonies' campaign for the ban of beet-sugar production received the support of most maritime cities. After Fonfrède died in 1841, the Bordeaux merchants set the publicist's anti-colonial scruples aside and coordinated a campaign of petitions in favour of the proposal. The chambers of commerce of Bordeaux, Nantes, Saint-Malo, Granville, Cherbourg, Le Havre and Dieppe petitioned for a ban, while those of Marseille, Rouen and Lorient demanded at least the equalization of taxes on colonial and beet sugar.[81] In December 1842, the Bordeaux Chamber of Commerce sent two delegates to organize a new committee in Paris, which would insert 'in the capital's newspapers as many articles as they [would] deem necessary on the matter of the important sugar question'. A Commission Permanente des Délégués des Ports was founded in Paris the following month. In its first three months, the new lobby spent 3,000

79 Charles Dupin, *La Vérité des faits sur les cultures comparées des colonies et de la métropole* (Paris, 1842), pp. 33–4, 37, and *Appel au bon sens* (Paris, 1843), pp. 10–13, 28; see also his *Observations exposées au conseil général d'agriculture* (Paris, 1842) and *Mémoire adressé par le conseil des délégués des colonies aux ministres du roi sur la question des sucres* (Paris, 1842).

80 Todd, 'La Nation, la liberté et les colonies', p. 188.

81 Petitions on the sugar tariff, 1841, AN, F12 2541.

francs 'on the drafting, printing and publishing' of pamphlets and articles in the press. The creation of new colonial and maritime lobbies responded to the foundation of a very active Comité des Fabricants de Sucre Indigène in 1840. According to the Bordeaux delegates, the beet-sugar lobby wielded an extraordinary influence. Its members were 'constantly in Paris', promoting 'their interests with unyielding perseverance': 'influential in the ministerial offices and with the Parisian press, they wage a relentless war against maritime trade'.[82]

A good illustration of the propaganda skills of the beet-sugar committee was the circulation, under its auspices, of two editions and, in total, 4,000 copies of a pamphlet in favour of indigenous sugar by Louis-Napoléon Bonaparte, the pretender to the imperial throne.[83] The future Napoleon III wrote the *Analyse de la question des sucres* in the fortress of Ham, where he was held prisoner since his failed coup of Boulogne in August 1840. Citing Dombasle, Napoleon's nephew underlined the benefits of sugar-beet cultivation for agriculture and asserted that indigenous sugar would solve, 'at least to a large extent, one of today's most important problems, the condition of the working classes', by keeping workers in the countryside and 'disseminating sources of labour instead of gathering them in the same location'. Promoting the new industry therefore conformed to the conception of a Napoleonic policy he already expounded in *Des idées napoléoniennes* (1839), which consisted in 'promoting affluence' in order to 'preserve order'. Louis-Napoléon's pamphlet reinforced the Napoleonic legitimacy of the beet-sugar industry, putting it on a par with the Code Civil and other legacies from the imperial era.[84] The following year, the pretender reiterated his support for economic self-sufficiency in a more detailed analysis of the social question, *Extinction du paupérisme* (1844).

A desire to placate the planters and fiscal considerations nonetheless led the Guizot government to table a law proposal for a ban combined with an indemnity for beet-sugar manufacturers in January 1843.[85] The proposal brought the sugar controversy to a paroxysm. According to the catalogue of the Bibliothèque Nationale de France, no fewer than 140 works on the

[82] Minutes of the Bordeaux Chamber of Commerce, 13 April 1842, 21 December 1842, 8 February 1843 and 29 March 1843, ADG, 02/081/307, register 1841–3, fols. 63–5, 101–2, 108, 118.

[83] 'Avis de l'éditeur', in Louis[-Napoléon] Bonaparte, *Analyse de la question des sucres*, 2nd edn (Paris, 1843); impression 8087 (14 December 1842), AN, F18*II 29.

[84] Louis[-Napoléon] Bonaparte, *Analyse de la question des sucres* (Paris, 1842), pp. 5, 43, 47.

[85] 'Note portée au Conseil des Ministres', 15 March 1842, AN, F12 2550/A; *Le Moniteur Universel*, 11 January 1843.

sugar question were published between 1837 and 1843, including 53 in 1843 alone.[86] The conservative daily *La Presse* spoke, in April 1843, of 'a torrent of pamphlets'.[87] Of a sample of 32 pamphlets published in Paris in 1842 and 1843, the average number of copies printed stood at 1,040: the total number of copies printed therefore probably neared 50,000 in 1843 and certainly exceeded 100,000 for the years 1837–43.[88] Such figures were extraordinary for the time. Places of publication confirm that the controversy was not confined to Paris, with 43 pamphlets out of 140 published in the provinces, including 14 in the Nord department.

Supporters and opponents of indigenous sugar were equally well represented in this pamphlet war. But pamphlets in defence of beet sugar were perhaps more fervent, stressing that protection should be restricted to metropolitan producers. 'It is in vain', a typical pamphlet by the member of an agricultural society in Valenciennes (Nord) asserted, 'that some claim that the two types of sugar are equally French; that the manufacturer of indigenous sugar and the colonial producer should enjoy equal rights; that a French colony stands in the same relation to a French department as a French department to another French department.'[89] An anonymous pamphlet published in Douai (also in Nord) insisted, in poor verses, that beet sugar primarily benefited the less well off: 'The good citizens of the fields, our kind country folk / Sensible people, as worthy as those eloquent babblers / They know, indeed, how reckless it is / To try and divest France from such a treasure!' Beet sugar, the poem continued, was the industry of 'the poor', 'the destitute' and 'masses of workers'.[90]

The propaganda in favour of beet sugar, with the probable assistance of subsidies from the Comité des Fabricants de Sucre, had a noticeable impact on the press. In 1837, all the ten leading Parisian newspapers except *Le Siècle* supported the producers of colonial sugar.[91] Six years later, four of the five

[86] Titles including the word *sucre* or *sucres*, excluding 32 technical works on the manufacturing of sugar also published between 1837 and 1843; Bibliothèque Nationale de France, catalogue BN-Opale plus (www.bnfol.fr, accessed 3 April 2005). The figure 140 is a low estimate: it does not include works on the sugar tariff that did not contain the word *sucre* or *sucres*, while the *dépôt légal* or obligation to provide the Bibliothèque Nationale with a copy of every printed work was not always abided by in the nineteenth century, especially by publishers outside Paris.

[87] *La Presse*, 29 April 1843.

[88] Impressions 1103, 1660, 2110, 8087, AN, F18*II 29; impressions 93, 198, 259, 302, 398, 423, 699, 701, 804, 824, 840, 1091, 1126, 1135, 1348, 1377, 1682, 1778, 1899, 2318, 2493, 2631, 2648, 2649, 2784, 2824, 3067, 3245, AN, F18*II 30.

[89] Edouard Grar, *Question des sucres* (Valenciennes, 1843), pp. 5–6.

[90] [Anon.] ('A. B.'), *Question des sucres examiné d'un point de vue moral* (Douai, 1843), pp. 2–3.

[91] 'Question des sucres', *Le Siècle*, 10 May 1837; *Le Journal des Débats*, 23 May 1837; *La Quotidienne*, 24 May 1837; 'Question des sucres – Résumé', *La Gazette de France*, 31 May 1837; *Le Commerce*, 22 May 1837; *La Presse*, 23 May 1837; 'De la loi sur les sucres', *Le Constitutionnel*, 23 May 1837; 'Projet

newspapers with a circulation above 10,000 (*Le Siècle*, *Le Constitutionnel*, *Le Journal des Débats* and *Le National*) defended beet sugar, while only *La Presse* and five less important sheets (*L'Univers*, *Le Commerce*, *Le Courrier Français*, *La Gazette de France*, *La Quotidienne*) continued to demand new measures in favour of colonial sugar producers.[92] The distribution of newspapers between advocates and opponents of beet sugar suggested the emergence of a divide between a left hostile to colonial planters and a right more sensitive to their plight. *Le Constitutionnel* and *Le Siècle* were affiliated with the centre-left, and *Le National* with the radical left. By contrast, *La Presse* was a stalwart support of the conservative Guizot government, while the royalist dailies, *La Gazette* and *La Quotidenne*, were the most vigorous advocates of colonial sugar.

By eight votes – including Alexis de Tocqueville's – to one, a special commission of the Chamber of Deputies recommended to reject the proposed ban as an 'anti-French act'. In full session, Lamartine still defended the interdiction of an industry that stemmed from Napoleonic 'despotism'. Acknowledging the growing popularity of beet sugar, he accused 'words' of having 'deceived [public] opinion' especially the labelling of the new industry as 'national', when 'its real name' was 'false, violent, artificial'. 'You cannot call it national', he entreated his colleagues, 'unless what it has cost to the country in subsidies, in broken contracts, be in your eyes the tariff of nationality.' Lamartine's attack elicited an indignant response from Augustin Corne, a left-wing deputy for the Pas-de-Calais, who recalled that beet sugar was national 'by its very origin, since it was created by a decree passed by the Emperor … whose name … is sufficiently national'. It was also 'national', he continued, because it would 'set Europe free from the supremacy of tropical countries' and 'from the commercial vassalage to England' and because it employed 'free men … ready to defend their country', unlike the planters and their slaves.[93] Corne's tirade encapsulated the main themes of the propaganda for economic self-sufficiency, from the reverence for Napoleon to the fear of British dominance and hostility to the colonial system.

de loi sur les sucres', *Le Courrier Français*, 22 May 1837; *L'Univers*, 24 May 1837; *Le National*, 22 May 1837.

92 'Question des sucres', *Le Siècle*, 15 January 1843; 'Question des sucres', *Le Constitutionnel*, 19 January 1843; *Le Journal des Débats*, 6 January 1843; 'Question des sucres', *Le National*, 14 January 1843; *La Presse*, 2 January 1843; 'Question des sucres', *L'Univers*, 14 January 1843; 'Question des sucres', *La Quotidienne*, 9 May 1843; *Le Courrier Français*, 10 January 1843; 'Question des sucres', *La Gazette de France*, 6 January 1843; *Le Commerce*, 1 January 1843.

93 Debates at the Chamber of Deputies (12 and 13 May 1843), *Le Moniteur Universel*, 13 and 14 May 1843.

Deputies rejected the ban by 286 votes to 97. Instead, they adopted a gradual increase of 5 francs per year in the domestic tax on beet sugar until it reached the level of duties on colonial sugar in 1848.[94] This fourth and last law on the taxation of sugar under the July Monarchy constituted a relative victory for the defenders of self-sufficiency: tax evasion, further improvements of the fabrication process and the abolition of slavery in 1848 facilitated the continued expansion of the beet-sugar industry. Between 1845 and 1862, its output rose by 360 per cent, to 162,000 tons, while imports of colonial sugar rose by only 24 per cent, to 112,500 tons.[95]

V

Just as free trade elicited a mounting fervour in Britain at the turn of the 1840s, the radical conception of protection as a means of achieving self-sufficiency was making rapid progress in French opinion. It was an article underlining this Anglo-French divergence in the *Journal des Économistes* that made Frédéric Bastiat's reputation among economists in 1844.[96] Bastiat's account, published the following year, of the popular success met by the Anti-Corn Law League, *Cobden et la ligue*, was also a lament over the decline of liberal ideas about trade in France. At the end of the Restoration, Bastiat recalled, 'the authority of the Smiths and the Says' over matters of international trade was 'no longer in dispute'. But fifteen years later, 'far from having gained any ground', political economy had 'not only lost some', it had 'almost none left, except for the narrow stretch upon which [stood] the Académie des Sciences Morales [et Politiques]'.[97]

Bastiat's pessimistic judgement was only a slight exaggeration. In Paris, a new generation of lecturers on political economy – the Italo-Genevan Pelegrino Rossi at the Collège de France, Joseph Garnier at the École de Commerce de Paris and the Polish refugee Louis Wolowski at the Conservatoire des Arts et Métiers – lacked the messianic enthusiasm of their predecessors.[98] Moreover, at the instigation of Thiers in 1840, Rossi was replaced at the Collège de France by Michel Chevalier, an

94 Debates at the Chamber of Deputies (19 May 1843), *Le Moniteur Universel*, 20 May 1843.

95 'Rapport', 22 April 1863, AN, F12 2550/A.

96 Frédéric Bastiat, 'De l'influence des tarifs français et anglais sur l'avenir des deux peuples', *Journal des Économistes*, 9 (1844): 244–71.

97 Frédéric Bastiat, *Cobden et la ligue* (Paris, 1845), in *Œuvres complètes de Frédéric Bastiat*, ed. Prosper Paillotet and Robert de Fontenay, 2nd edn, 6 vols. (Paris, 1862–4), vol. III, pp. 78–9.

98 Pelegrino Rossi, *Cours d'économie politique*, 2 vols. (Paris, 1840–1); Joseph Garnier, *Eléments de l'économie politique* (Paris, 1846); Louis Wolowski, *Cours de législation industrielle*, 3 vols. (Paris, 1840–4).

ex-Saint-Simonian.[99] Upon learning that Chevalier would succeed him, Rossi allegedly quipped, 'It will give him … an opportunity to learn political economy'.[100] Instead, Chevalier's early lectures contested the 'ban' on government intervention in the economy decreed by 'economic science'. Attributing the earlier enthusiasm for *laissez-faire* to a legitimate distrust of inept authorities under the Old Regime, he considered that modern European governments, being committed to material and moral progress, not only had a 'right' but a 'duty' to stimulate economic activity. As for external trade, Chevalier admitted that it constituted a formidable source of prosperity for Britain. But he thought it impossible for France to replicate the British model, because 'we are not a trading or a manufacturing nation' but 'first and foremost an agricultural nation'. Even for French manufactures, he contended, the best chance of new outlets lay in the expansion of domestic agriculture.[101]

With the help of the republican publisher Gilbert-Urbain Guillaumin, liberal disciples of Say reorganized themselves outside official institutions, launching a monthly periodical, the *Journal des Économistes*, in 1841 and founding a Société d'Économie Politique, which organized informal dinners, in 1842.[102] But their audience remained limited. By 1845, the *Journal des Économistes* still had fewer than 600 subscribers.[103] From just five in 1842, membership of the Société d'Économie Politique only rose to eighty in 1849. Moreover, unlike the debates of the Restoration, when free trade seemed a natural response to the plight of the winegrowing industry and dissatisfaction with the reactionary tendencies of the regime, the main controversies of the middle period of the July Monarchy – on the linen tariff, commercial negotiations with Belgium or the sugar tariff – left less obvious room for the advocacy of radical commercial freedom. The contributions of the economists to these debates were confused and contradictory. Charles Coquelin, the future editor of the *Dictionnaire d'économie politique* (1854), espoused the language of industrialist jealousy

99 Le Van-Lemesle, *Le Juste ou le riche*, p. 94; on Chevalier's politics and economics, see Jean Walch, *Michel Chevalier, économiste saint-simonien* (Paris, 1975) and Michael Drolet, 'Industry, Class and Society: A Historiographic Reinterpretation of Michel Chevalier', *English Historical Review*, 123 (504) (2008): 1229–71.

100 Alphonse Courtois, *Notice sur la vie et les travaux de Michel Chevalier* (Paris, 1889), p. 14.

101 Michel Chevalier, *Cours d'économie politique*, 3 vols. (Paris, 1842–50), vol. II, pp. 19–22, 74–86; vol. II corresponds with the lectures given by Chevalier in the academic year 1842–3.

102 Lucette Le Van-Lemesle, 'Guillaumin, éditeur d'économie politique, 1801–1864', *Revue d'Économie Politique*, 95 (2) (1985): 134–49; Michel Lutfalla, 'Aux origines du libéralisme économique en France: le *Journal des Économistes*, analyse de la première série, 1841–1853', *Revue d'Histoire Économique et Sociale*, 50 (4) (1972): 494–517.

103 Bastiat to Félix Coudroy, May 1845, in *Œuvres complètes*, vol. I, p. 51.

to promote the creation of flax-spinning factories in France.[104] The *Journal des Économistes* condemned the project of commercial treaty with Belgium as a preferential agreement that violated the principles of political economy.[105] Blanqui, Say's leading disciple, defended the beet-sugar industry as a means of encouraging agricultural progress and supported the 'eviction' of the indigenous population in order to accelerate the introduction of new cultures by European settlers in Algeria.[106]

Despite Fonfrède's death in 1841, the Gironde merchants and winegrowers remained more fervent defenders of free trade than the Parisian economists. But they were increasingly isolated. An attempt to found a permanent Union Nationale des Viticulteurs, with representatives from other departments, as a response to the influence of manufacturing lobbies, floundered in 1842–3.[107] Edited by Fonfrède's friend Charles-Alcée Campan, the *Courrier de la Gironde* upheld the same combination of radical commercial liberalism and trenchant conservatism as the publicist at the end of his life, but without his inflammatory eloquence. In 1843, Campan also resolved to publish an edition of Fonfrède's journalistic writings. With the consent of the deceased publicist's sisters, he gathered his articles in *L'Indicateur*, *Le Mémorial* and *Le Courrier*, 'set them in order' and separated 'what was doctrine' from circumstantial comments.[108] Campan's editorial work in the two volumes concerned with 'public economics' attenuated the radical and heterodox origins of his views. Positive references to Jean-Jacques Rousseau or Gabriel de Mably, two authors reputed as democratic, disappeared, while those to Charles Secondat de Montesquieu and Germaine de Staël, more acceptable to conservative opinion, were preserved. Campan's editorial work also selected the targets of Fonfrède's diatribes according to the new divide between partisans and adversaries of free trade. In the section on *industrialisme*,

[104] Charles Coquelin, 'De l'industrie linière en France', *Revue des Deux Mondes*, 4th series, 19 (1839): 61–96, 194–234, and *Essai sur la filature mécanique de lin et de chanvre* (Paris, 1840).

[105] Hippolyte Dussard, 'Quelques réflexions à propos du traité belge', *Journal des Économistes*, 3 (1842): 72–82.

[106] Adolphe Blanqui, *Cours d'économie industrielle*, 3 vols. (Paris, 1837–9), vol. 1, pp. 463–88; and *Algérie: rapport sur la situation économique de nos possessions dans le nord de l'Afrique* (Paris, 1840), pp. 52–4.

[107] [Anon.], *Compte-rendu des séances de l'assemblée générale des départements vinicoles* (Bordeaux, 1843), and Union Vinicole, *Assemblée générale des délégués des départements* (Bordeaux, 1843); on lobbying by the Gironde winegrowers in the mid 1840s, see Fernand Paillère, *La Lutte en Gironde pour l'amélioration des échanges entre les nations, 1842–1937* (Bordeaux, 1937), pp. 18–29, and Albert Charles, *La Révolution de 1848 et la Seconde République à Bordeaux* (Bordeaux, 1945), pp. 31–3.

[108] 'Convention entre Charles-Alcée Campan et les demoiselles Zoé et Clémentine Fonfrède, sœurs et uniques héritières de leur frère M. Henri Fonfrède', BMB, MS 1089.

Campan removed attacks on the free-trader Charles Dunoyer and kept those on Dupin, an advocate of protection. He also replaced the name of Saint-Cricq, the architect of prohibitive policies under the Restoration, with the new phrase 'les protectionnistes'.[109]

Campan hoped to obtain 300 subscriptions to Fonfrède's works and print 1,000 copies in total. We do not know whether he reached such an ambitious goal. But a list of 193 subscribers dating from 1845 confirms the regional or even local nature of Fonfrède's readership: nearly three-quarters (144) of the subscribers lived in Bordeaux, six in other Gironde towns, eight in Toulouse and only eighteen in Paris. Given the high price of the subscription (75 francs for the ten volumes), 150 subscribers for a single department is an extremely high figure. The subscription slips sometimes indicate the profession of the subscribers: a majority were merchants, but there were also several deputies, a former prefect, an architect, a dentist and a chemist.[110] Fonfrède's free-trade ideas remained popular among the Gironde conservative *notables*, but their impact outside the department was slight.

Only at the other extreme of French intellectual and political life, among the first utopian socialists, did free-trade ideas seem to gain some new supporters around 1840. In the early 1830s, several socialist thinkers or radicals who would later become socialists already supported commercial reform. These included Charles Fourier, who expressed sympathy for the complaints of the Bordelais merchants, and also Ange Guépin, a future Fourierist, and Philippe Buchez, a future Christian socialist.[111] In 1834, *Le Réformateur*, the most sympathetic national daily to early socialist doctrines, asserted that prohibitions only benefited 'a privileged few' and were 'detrimental to the masses'.[112] In relation to international trade as with many other issues, the early socialists did not yet distinguish themselves very clearly from traditional radical protests against the corrupt and oligarchical tendencies of monarchical power.[113]

[109] Henri Fonfrède, *Œuvres de Henri Fonfrède*, ed. Charles-Alcée Campan, 10 vols. (Bordeaux, 1844–7), vol. VII, p. 386, vol. VIII, pp. 93–157.

[110] 'Liste des souscripteurs', BMB, MS 1089.

[111] Charles Fourier, 'Déclin de Bordeaux, ridicule distribution de l'industrie française', *La Réforme Industrielle*, 16 December 1833; Ange Guépin, *Traité d'économie sociale* (Paris, 1833), p. 86; Philippe Buchez, 'Économie politique: considérations sur le mode de répartition des charges publiques', *L'Européen*, 24 March 1832.

[112] 'L'Enquête n'est qu'un moyen de préserver le ministère des exigences impérieuses de la délibération', *Le Réformateur*, 27 October 1834.

[113] On continuity, in an English context, between radicalism and early socialist protests, see Gareth Stedman Jones, *Languages of Class: Studies in English Working Class History 1832–1982* (Cambridge 1983), pp. 90–178.

This radical legacy continued to influence socialist perceptions of the controversy on international trade in subsequent years. In 1840, Victor Considérant, Fourier's main disciple after the master's death in 1837, called on France to 'multiply its communications, connections, and relations with neighbouring Nations'. 'No more prohibitions!', he added, 'No more tariffs! No more customs on your borders, civilized nations!' Considérant even praised the merits of 'foreign competition', which would 'continuously stimulate' French industries. Considérant also refused to side with either colonial planters or metropolitan producers in the sugar question, preferring to use the controversy as evidence of the incoherence of capitalism and of the need for 'Direction' by the government in 'the industrial and social life of Nations'.[114]

The perpetuation of radical hostility to restrictions on international trade also loomed large in Etienne Cabet's influential utopia, the *Voyage en Icarie*, published in 1840. En route from London to Icarie, the narrator was 'annoyed and outraged by the customs officers' and 'arrested and imprisoned for several days for having reacted to the insolence of a customs officer'. Upon arriving by sea in Icarie, he asked the captain of his ship if the boats he could make out at the entrance of the harbour were 'customs boats': 'Customs!', the captain exclaimed, 'We haven't had any Customs for fifty years. The good ICAR [founder of the utopian government] destroyed that den of thieves, more ruthless than pirates or storms.' After he landed in the port, the narrator walked through a gate with the inscription, 'in enormous letters: *The Icarian nation is brother of all other nations*', and spent his first night at the Hôtel des Étrangers, located on the site of the old customs house. There were no merchants in Icarie, but the nation's representatives conducted foreign trade relations. They shunned self-sufficiency and welcomed the international division of labour: 'The Republic does not cultivate or manufacture products that it may easily obtain from another country if its agriculture and industry may be utilized more effectively for other products.'[115]

Louis Blanc's influential diatribe against capitalist anarchy, *Organisation du travail* (1840), offered only more qualified support for free trade. Blanc admitted that the defenders of the prohibitive system were right 'relatively speaking', because the abolition of protection would plunge French workers in a state of destitution. However, 'from an absolute point of view, they [were] wrong', because the international division

[114] Victor Considérant, *De la politique générale et du rôle de la France en Europe* (Paris, 1840), pp. 77–84, and *Projet de loi sur les sucres: un enseignement donné au pays* (Paris, 1840), pp. 1–2.

[115] Etienne Cabet, *Voyage en Icarie* (Paris and Geneva, 1979), pp. 9–10, 164.

of labour would improve the standard of living of all consumers. He therefore supported the abolition of 'customs, prohibitions, tariffs' but in combination with a socialist overhaul of the domestic market: 'the best, the only means of achieving the liberty of commerce, without causing dreadful upheavals and deadly unrest', was 'the substitution of a system of association and solidarity to what has been falsely given a beautiful name: the liberty of industry'.[116]

Liberal economists, Bordelais merchants and the first socialists formed too small and disparate a constituency to challenge the progress of nationalist economic ideas. In the case of the socialists, support for free trade was rarely a major preoccupation and often remained conditional upon a more drastic reorganization of society. The triumph of free trade in capitalist Britain in 1846 would lead even most socialists to reconsider and endorse protection.

As global exchanges of commodities continued to intensify at the turn of the 1840s, the social and colonial questions modified the terms of the debate on international trade, but with contrary results in Britain and France. In Britain, free trade increasingly appeared as a remedy to both the miserable conditions of factory workers – by reducing the price of necessities – and the decay of the old colonial system – by curtailing colonial dependence on the metropolitan market. In France, an aspiration to self-sufficiency rather than free trade tended to supersede support for mercantile or industrialist jealousy. According to its French promoters, self-sufficiency would shelter factory workers from the downward pressure on wages implied by international competition and render colonial undertakings, or at least plantation colonies, unnecessary. The manufacturers' lobbies that emerged out of the late 1830s depression helped to steer ideological change in both countries, but not as conspicuously in France as in Britain and in an opposite direction.

While the growing popularity of free trade helped to fashion Victorian liberalism and ensure its dominance of British politics until the late nineteenth century, the more discreet rise of self-sufficiency severed the connection that existed in the mind of most French liberals ten or fifteen years earlier between commercial and political liberty. On the one hand, the apparent decline of liberal ideas about trade led some radical free-traders to call into question the merits of representative government, paving the way for the emergence of an economic liberalism indifferent or hostile to liberal institutions. On the other hand, disdain for foreign trade was

[116] Louis Blanc, *Organisation du travail*, 2nd edn (Paris, 1841), pp. 138–43.

no longer confined to reactionary royalist writers. The main advocates of self-sufficiency were conservative liberals devoid of nostalgia for the Old Regime, and their ideas were making some converts among more progressive liberals. The triumph of free trade in Britain at the end of the 1840s would further reveal the extent of Anglo-French ideological divergence and intensify support for the defence of national labour on the left of the political spectrum.

CHAPTER 6

The Englishness of free trade and the consolidation of protectionist dominance

The triumph of the Anti-Corn Law League in 1846 revived the energies of French free-traders. Inspired by the success of Richard Cobden's organization, Frédéric Bastiat founded an Association pour la Liberté des Échanges that made a new attempt to persuade French opinion of the merits of the free exchange of commodities across borders. The Association's propaganda combined a messianic aspiration to global peace and prosperity borrowed from the British Anti-Corn Law League with a liberal constitutional interpretation of French political history. It also sought to transpose to France the techniques employed by British free-traders to propagate their views, including meetings, cheap pamphlets and a newspaper dedicated to their cause, *Le Libre-échange*. Bastiat's campaign may be construed as an effort to halt and reverse the growing chasm between French and British liberalism by condemning in equal measure the glorification of revolutionary violence and economic nationalism.

This attempt to reconcile French liberalism with British reformism and cosmopolitanism ended in dismal failure.[1] Bastiat's campaign benefited from the sympathy of the Guizot government, the support of Parisian economists and the financial assistance of the Bordelais bourgeoisie. But, once more, enthusiasm for free trade remained confined to the Gironde and a narrow section of the middle class in large cities. Instead, Bastiat's efforts mainly resulted in the reinforcement of protectionist ascendancy. Led by Auguste Mimerel, an Association pour la Défense du Travail National founded dozens of local committees, organized vocal protests against the temptation to emulate British policy and circulated its own vituperative newspaper, *Le Moniteur Industriel*. Denouncing *libre-échange* – a phrase introduced by Bastiat in order to regenerate support for commercial

[1] For more optimistic assessments of the results of Bastiat's campaign for free trade in France, see Tyrrell, '"La Ligue Française"' and Anthony Howe, 'Re-forging Britons: Cobden and France', in Sylvie Aprile and Fabrice Bensimon, *La France et l'Angleterre au XIXe siècle* (Paris, 2006), pp. 89–104.

liberalism – as an ideological ploy engineered by England and its French supporters as traitors, Mimerel's counter-campaign gained the backing of not only most manufacturers but also grain producers and even some maritime merchants. By describing protection as a means of preserving the egalitarian legacy of the 1789 Revolution from social and economic anglicization, it even extended support for protectionism to the radical and socialist left.[2]

Following the 1848 Revolution, the reaction against 'English free trade' continued under the fragile Second Republic. Adolphe Thiers, a leading defender of capitalist competition within national borders against socialist doctrines, simultaneously asserted himself as the main advocate of protectionism. Despite their reactionary origins and conservative undertones, protectionist ideas continued to appeal to a significant fraction of the left. On the other hand, following the crushing defeat of Bastiat's crusade, the ex-Saint-Simonian Michel Chevalier became the champion of a conception of free trade detached from political liberalism. The ideological contrast with Britain was now stark and appeared well entrenched.

I

The resurgence of protests in favour of trade liberalization in France was an indirect consequence of the repeal of the Corn Laws by Robert Peel, under the pressure of Cobden's League, in 1846. But it resulted more immediately from the efforts of an energetic and talented polemicist, Frédéric Bastiat. 'I am not only of the association', Bastiat wearily explained about his role in the Association pour la Liberté des Échanges, modelled on the British Anti-Corn-Law League, 'I am the entire association.'[3]

Bastiat's passionate free-trade convictions originated from an original combination of resentment against prohibitions in the south-west, liberal political economy and admiration for Richard Cobden's campaign in Britain.[4] Born and raised in the Landes near Bordeaux, Bastiat

[2] On the French left, nationalism and the revolutionary legacy in the mid nineteenth century, see François Furet, *La Gauche et la Révolution au XIXᵉ siècle: Edgar Quinet et la question du jacobinisme* (Paris, 1986), esp. pp. 11–27; Sophie Wahnich, *L'Impossible citoyen: l'étranger dans le discours de la Révolution française* (Paris, 1997), pp. 243–327; and Philippe Darriulat, *Les Patriotes: la gauche républicaine et la nation, 1830–1870* (Paris, 2001), pp. 55–106.

[3] Bastiat to Félix Coudroy, 1 October 1846, in *Œuvres complètes*, vol. 1, p. 75.

[4] Robert de Fontenay, 'Notice sur la vie et les écrits de Frédéric Bastiat', in Bastiat, *Œuvres complètes*, vol. 1, pp. ix–xli; Maurice Baslé and Alain Gélédan, 'Frédéric Bastiat, 1801–1850: théoricien et militant du libre-échange', in Yves Breton and Michel Lutfalla (eds.), *L'Économie politique en France au XIXᵉ siècle* (Paris, 1991), pp. 83–110; Gérard Minart, *Frédéric Bastiat (1801–1850): le croisé du libre-échange* (Paris and Dunkirk, 2004).

devoured the works of Adam Smith, Jean-Baptiste Say, Charles Comte and Charles Dunoyer in the early 1820s. A devout Catholic, he wished to become a priest. But after a brief career as a merchant specialized in the importation of Spanish goods, Bastiat instead put his fervour at the service of free trade. His interest in the issue was aroused by the Bordelais agitation at the turn of the 1830s. In 1829, he wrote an unpublished memorandum in support of winegrowers' protests and, in 1834, some *Réflexions* that paid homage to Fonfrède's eloquence but condemned the relative moderation of his demands.[5]

A visit to London in October 1840, during which he attended meetings of the Anti-Corn Law League, rekindled his interest in economic agitation. In 1841, Bastiat made a first proposal for the creation of a national 'association' representing the interests of winegrowers, modelled on the 'committees' of beet sugar and textile producers. In 1843, he compared the destitution of southern French winegrowers to the poverty of British factory workers, attributing both to the 'economic error' of the 'prohibitive regime', and called again on an association of winegrowers that would mobilize 'financial and intellectual resources' for 'the cause of liberty'.[6] But it was the contrast he drew between the decline of free trade in France and its imminent triumph in Britain, in the *Journal des Économistes* in 1844 and *Cobden et la ligue* in 1845, that established his reputation as an eloquent advocate of commercial liberty. Bastiat planned at first to take over the editorship of the *Journal des Économistes*. But a second stay in Britain in the summer of 1845, where he met and began a friendship with Cobden, persuaded him instead to try and found an association modelled on the British League.

In accordance with the parallel he had drawn between French winegrowers and British factory workers, Bastiat sought to turn Bordeaux into the Manchester of his French League. He first expounded his project of a 'ligue anti-protectionniste' in *Le Mémorial Bordelais* in February 1846. His explicit model was the foundation of the Anti-Corn Law Committee by seven Lancashire manufacturers in 1838 and the religious animus that inspired them:

> What made the success of the League in England is one thing, one thing only: *faith in an idea*. They were only seven but they believed; and because they believed, they had the will; and because they had the will, they moved

[5] Bastiat, *Réflexions sur les pétitions*, pp. 1–2.

[6] Frédéric Bastiat, *Le Fisc et la vigne* (Paris, 1841) and *Mémoire sur la question vinicole* (Mont-de-Marsan, 1843), repr. in *Œuvres complètes*, vol. 1, pp. 243–60, at pp. 256–8, and pp. 261–83, at pp. 274–6, 280.

> mountains. The question from my point of view is not whether there are [talented] men in Bordeaux, but whether there is faith in Israel.[7]

Another lesson Bastiat drew from the British example was the need for large financial resources in order to 'spread economic truth ... with sufficient profusion to alter the course of national will'. Calling for large donations, he reminded his readers that 'intellectual communications' always required 'material vehicles'.[8]

At its founding meeting on 23 February 1846, members of the Bordelais Association pour la Liberté des Échanges elected Pierre-Lodi Duffour-Dubergier, the city's conservative mayor, who had himself attended meetings of the Anti-Corn Law League in Britain, as President.[9] Duffour-Dubergier's acceptance speech combined the messianic phraseology of Bastiat, calling for 'the day of light and of the righting of wrongs', with a critique of France's proclivity for political upheavals, even though its 'ten revolutions' had failed to establish true 'liberty'. In order to complete the great proclamations of 1789 on the rights of man, he concluded, it was time to follow Britain's example and recognize 'the most just and natural right of a free citizen: the right to use his money and his labour as he sees fit, the right to buy whatever he likes from wherever he likes'.[10] *Libre-échange* as the completion of the 1789 Revolution became a leitmotiv of the French free-traders' campaign. But the disavowal of revolutionary violence and admiration for the British tradition of reform indicated a preference for a liberal rather than democratic interpretation of the revolutionary legacy.

Bastiat's hope for generous donations was not disappointed. Within six weeks, the Bordeaux Association raised over 85,000 francs from 559 subscribers.[11] The figure exceeded the 20,000 francs that Mimerel hoped to collect from the members of the Comité de la Défense du Travail National and bore comparison with the £5,000 (approximately 125,000 francs) raised by the Anti-Corn Law League in its first year.[12] The average

[7] Frédéric Bastiat, 'Projet de ligue anti-protectionniste', 2nd article, *Le Mémorial*, 9 February 1846.

[8] Frédéric Bastiat, 'Projet de ligue anti-protectionniste', 3rd article, *Le Mémorial*, 10 February 1846.

[9] Henri Courteault, 'La Formation commerciale d'un jeune bordelais il y a cent ans', *Revue Philomatique de Bordeaux*, 26 (1923): 62–70.

[10] Association pour la Liberté des Échanges de Bordeaux, *Fondation de la société, 23 février 1846: Manifeste* (Bordeaux, 1846), pp. 5–10. Other members of the Association's executive committee were also *notables*: Bruno Devez, a banker and proprietor of vineyard; Adrien Duchon-Doris, a merchant; Armand Lalande, a wine merchant; François Samazeuilh, a banker and Deputy Mayor; Jules Hovyn de Tranchère, a landowner; Gustave Brunet, a local erudite. I could not identify the remaining four others of the committee: Paul Vignes, Jules Fauche, A. Duvergier and Durin.

[11] Lists of 'souscripteurs', published in *Le Courrier de la Gironde*, 2, 6, 12, 19, 25, 30 March and 8 April 1846.

[12] McCord, *The Anti-Corn Law League*, pp. 64–6.

donation of 153 francs suggests that the majority of subscribers were prosperous merchants and landowners. The Bordelais Association used the funds to issue affordable pamphlets,[13] to organize a prize competition on the benefits of free trade for the working classes,[14] and, almost certainly, to subsidize the local press: from the spring of 1846, the liberal *Indicateur*, the conservative *Mémorial*, the *Courrier* edited by Fonfrède's disciples and even the royalist *Guienne* clamoured for the advent of *libre-échange*.[15]

Le Mémorial and *Le Courrier* best represented the messianic fervour that seized Bordeaux at the end of the July Monarchy. In *Le Mémorial*, a member of the Association's committee described his colleagues and himself as 'fervent apostles of economic faith', who would bring about the 'regeneration' of France: 'A day will come when, aided by our efforts, economic liberty will shove reprobate restrictive tariffs in the darkness of oblivion. French and foreign products, fast and abundant, will travel along all existing routes.'[16] Another contributor to *Le Mémorial*, the lawyer Félix Coudroy, a friend of Bastiat and admirer of the counter-revolutionary thinkers Joseph de Maistre and Louis de Bonald, explained that it was 'the *faculty to exchange* that placed man at the forefront of creation' and described the defenders of protection as 'lunatics' for daring 'to hold their wisdom in higher regard than God's wisdom'.[17]

The editors of the *Courrier* supported the campaign of the Association with equal enthusiasm, although they tended to invoke Fonfrède rather than the Creator: 'This is what Fonfrède wanted and therefore we want it too', an anonymous article declared about the repeal of barriers on foreign trade. In the vein of Fonfrède's earlier emphasis on the linguistic dishonesty of the advocates of prohibitions, a long series of articles dissected the 'cabalistic language' of the protectionists, in which one said 'Protection for Spoliation, Tribute for Exchange, National labour for Monopoly, Invasion for Abundance'; this 'holy dialect ... also comprised several idioms,

[13] These included *Fondation de la société de Bordeaux* (50 centimes), *Progrès de la navigation commerciale d'Angleterre* (40 centimes), Henri Fonfrède, *Du système prohibitif* (1 franc), *De la consommation des vins de France en Angleterre* (20 centimes), *Lettre adressée à M. Charles Dupin* (20 centimes), *Rapport de la commission de navigation sur la réforme douanière* (20 centimes), *Banquet offert à Richard Cobden* [à Bordeaux] (30 centimes); publications cited on the back cover of a pamphlet by the national Association pour la Liberté des Échanges, *Deuxième séance publique* (Paris, 1846).

[14] *Le Libre-échange*, 14 March 1847.

[15] André-Jean Tudesq, *Les Grands Notables en France, 1840–1849*, 2 vols. (Paris, 1964), vol. II, pp. 609–10.

[16] Jules Fauche, 'Association en faveur de la liberté des échanges', *Le Mémorial*, 23 February 1846.

[17] Félix Coudroy, 'De l'Association en faveur de la liberté des échanges', *Le Mémorial*, 1 March 1846.

such as France must produce its *own* iron, its *own* cattle etc.'.[18] Despite Fonfrède's own anti-clerical opinions, even the *Courrier* sometimes used religious images, asserting that 'God had given commercial liberty to man' and accusing the protectionists of 'blaspheming' against 'Providence'.[19]

Only a few weeks after the creation of the Association, Bastiat rejoiced that 'Bordeaux was in a true state of *agitation*', as Britain had been since the beginning of the 1840s. Spurred by this success, he sought to establish a national association based in Paris. Even in the French capital Bastiat thought that he could perceive 'a great change in opinion', due to the impression made by Peel's decision to repeal the Corn Laws, and that the 'triumph' of free trade in France was 'perhaps not as far off as we supposed at first'. Newspapers praising Peel's courage and welcoming the foundation of the Bordelais Association included the government's main mouthpieces, *Le Journal des Débats* and *L'Époque*, which nurtured hopes among free-traders that François Guizot wished to emulate the British Premier and defy his own conservative majority. Lest propaganda in favour of free trade frightened voters, Tanneguy Duchâtel, Minister of the Interior, delayed the official authorization of the national association until after the July 1846 general election. The resounding electoral success of Guizot and his supporters cleared the last hurdle for Bastiat's attempt to transpose agitation for free trade on the French national stage.

II

In the vein of the propaganda used by Bastiat in Bordeaux, the national Association pour la Liberté des Échanges (hereafter ALE) sought to fuse the language of liberal constitutionalism with a religious fervour resembling the crusade of the British League. At its founding meeting, held in front of an audience of 1,500 in the salle Montesquieu on 28 August 1846, members of the executive committee confirmed Eugène d'Harcourt, scion of a prestigious aristocratic family and a leading advocate of liberal Catholicism in the Chamber of Peers, as their president. Harcourt's inaugural speech placed the struggle for *libre-échange* in the continuity of France's great Revolution: 'Having fought hard to conquer all our liberties for fifty years, including the liberty of man and the freedom of the press,

[18] 'Liberté commerciale' and 'Réponse aux prohibitionnistes, XVII – Résumé', *Le Courrier de la Gironde*, 25 March and 17 October 1846.

[19] 'Du libre-échange considéré comme droit national', and 'Liberté commerciale', *Le Courrier de la Gironde*, 22 and 26 September 1846.

we demand one last liberty, which is their natural complement and not the least important, because it affects all interests: the liberté des échanges.' Harcourt's speech also had religious undertones, as when he attributed the uneven distribution of productions across the globe to a design of 'Providence', which wanted 'to force men to obtain [these productions] and communicate between them by means of the liberté des échanges'.[20]

Other members of the ALE's executive committee also described the campaign for *libre-échange* as the continuation of the French Enlightenment and Revolutionary struggles. Adolphe Blanqui insisted that *libre-échange* was a French invention: it was 'the axiom of Turgot and of the economists of the eighteenth century, these contemporaries of Voltaire, Rousseau and Montesquieu, of all our great philosophers and founders of all our civil, political and even commercial liberties'. Another member of the committee, a Parisian bronze producer, called on the French of 1846 to follow 'the example set by our fathers, who conquered the foundations of all our liberties' in 1789. Just as Britain adopted the 1832 Reform Act under the inspiration of the 1830 Revolution, Léon Faucher argued, France ought to emulate the British example of 'commercial revolution'.[21] Pious commercial liberalism did not resonate in Paris as well as in the Gironde, since in ten months the ALE collected only 25,000 francs from 569 subscribers, less than a third of the sum collected by the Bordeaux association in six weeks. However, the lower average sum subscribed (44 versus 153 francs) suggests that the appeal of *libre-échange* extended to slightly lower social strata than in Bordeaux. The 522 Parisian subscribers who indicated their occupation on subscription lists included 65 shopkeepers and 82 artisans or skilled workers, who together gave 1,666 francs to the ALE. Yet the most significant contributions still originated from the Parisian elite, with 23 politicians and state officials giving between them 6,250 francs, and 14 bankers and manufacturers giving 3,425 francs.[22]

Rather than petitioning the government, the ALE addressed itself directly to public opinion. Between September 1846 and January 1848, it organized six more meetings in the salle Montesquieu. References to the Enlightenment and the early constitutional phase of the 1789 Revolution continued to abound. At the third meeting, a law professor compared customs duties to the tithe and called for a '4 August [1789] of industrial

[20] Association pour la Liberté des Échanges, *Première séance publique* (Paris, 1846), pp. 5–6.
[21] Association pour la Liberté des Échanges, *Première séance*, pp. 7, 17, 20.
[22] 'Liste des souscripteurs', *Le Libre-échange*, 13 June 1847.

privileges'. At the fifth meeting, Louis Wolowski, the Polish refugee and economist, lambasted 'industrial chauvinism' and asserted that France had, during the Revolution, 'raised the flag of human fraternity too high' to abandon its mission to liberate European peoples.[23] Attendance at these meetings fluctuated between 1,000 and 2,000. Although not insignificant, such numbers fell far short of the enormous audiences of the British League's meetings in London or Manchester. Gilbert-Urbain Guillaumin, the economists' publisher, circulated accounts of the meetings, with 3,000 copies printed of the first meeting's proceedings.[24] Guillaumin also published or reissued scores of books and pamphlets on international trade.[25]

However, the ALE's main effort to promote free trade was the publication, from November 1846, of a new weekly, *Le Libre-échange*. The enterprise absorbed three-quarters of the association's financial resources.[26] Bastiat, editor and main contributor, projected a circulation of 6,000 – a very high figure for a specialized newspaper.[27] Bastiat chose to publish the newspaper from Paris rather than Bordeaux because 'for the same expense' it would have 'ten times more influence' than if it was published in the provinces.[28] The newspaper's title was not the first occurrence of *libre-échange*. The phrase had been used, without a hyphen, and often as a translation of 'free trade' since the early 1830s. An early indigenous use can be found in the widely circulated *Livre du peuple* (1837) by Félicité de Lamennais, a heterodox Catholic thinker admired by Bastiat. Among other means of liberating the people from its moral and material servitude, Lamennais recommended to suppress 'the countless obstacles that interrupt or hinder communications from one country to another and the free exchange [*libre échange*] of their productions'.[29] But the expression only gained wide currency as a result of Bastiat's campaign, with no published title including 'libre-échange' or 'libre échange' until 1845, ten titles in 1846 and twenty-seven in 1847.[30]

[23] *Le Libre-échange*, 29 November 1846, and Association pour la Liberté des Échanges, *Cinquième séance publique* (Paris, 1847), p. 4.

[24] Impression 5722 (8 October 1846), AN, F18*II 33.

[25] Guillaumin's publications under the auspices of the ALE included: Frédéric Bastiat, *Sophismes économiques* (Paris, 1846); Eugène d'Harcourt, *Discours en faveur de la liberté du commerce* (Paris, 1846); *Banquet offert à Richard Cobden* (Paris, 1846); Gustave de Molinari, *Histoire du tarif*, 2 vols. (Paris, 1847); and Alexandre Anisson-Dupéron, *Essai sur les traités de commerce de Methuen et de 1786 dans leurs rapports avec la liberté commerciale* (Paris, 1847).

[26] *Le Libre-échange*, 13 June 1847.

[27] Impression 7401 (28 November 1846), AN, F18*II 33.

[28] Bastiat to Coudroy, 19 February 1846, in *Œuvres complètes*, vol. 1, p. 66.

[29] Félicité de Lamennais, *Le Livre du peuple*, 2nd edn (Paris, 1838), p. 9.

[30] Bibliothèque Nationale de France, catalogue BN-Opale plus (http://catalogue.bnfol.fr, accessed 16 May 2005).

The radical ring of *libre-échange* worried some supporters of commercial liberalization. At a preliminary meeting for the creation of a local branch of the ALE in Le Havre, several participants suggested the adoption of a more moderate slogan, 'which might not please the ear as much, but would satisfy reason better'.[31] The criticisms prompted Bastiat to defend the new slogan in a tirade that echoed the combination of religiosity and democratic aspirations of the British League's propaganda:

> *Libre-échange*! This word makes our strength. It is our sword and our shield. *Libre-échange*! It is one of those words that move mountains. … The liberty of commerce, free relations between peoples, the free circulation of things, men and ideas, the free disposal for every one of the free fruits of their labour, the equality of all before the law, the extinction of national animosities, the peace of nations ensured by their mutual solidarity, all financial reforms made possible and easy thanks to peace, human affairs dragged away from the dangerous hands of diplomacy, the merging of ideas and consequently the gradual ascendancy of the democratic idea, here is what will inflame our country, here is what is included in this word: *libre-échange*; and one must not be surprised if its appearance provokes so many protests. It was the fate of *libre-examen* and all the other liberties from which it derives its popular origin.[32]

The connection established by Bastiat with *libre-examen* (free enquiry), a word associated with the Protestant Reformation in French, underlines again the role played by religious inspiration in the campaign for *libre-échange*.

Le Libre-échange resumed earlier efforts for the dissemination of political economy. In a parody of Robinson Crusoe published by the newspaper, Friday sought to teach Robinson the benefits of bartering vegetables for game with a neighbouring island, while Robinson absurdly reproached Friday for not having read the newspapers of the defender of 'national labour': 'It would have taught you this: all the time that you save is a net loss. It is not eating that matters, but working.'[33] *Le Libre-échange* also reproduced Dupin's 1827 dialogue between Lefranc and Prohibant.[34] In accordance with Bastiat's cosmopolitanism, the newspaper issued optimistic reports on the progress of free trade not only in Britain but also in the USA, Germany and Italy.[35] Commenting on the calls for the prohibition of French industrial products by a new protectionist association

[31] *Le Libre-échange*, 6 December 1846. [32] *Le Libre-échange*, 20 December 1846.
[33] *Le Libre-échange*, 21 March 1847. [34] *Le Libre-échange*, 30 May–1 August 1847.
[35] 'Extrait du rapport annuel fait par M. Walker, ministre des finances des Etats-Unis', 'La Liberté commerciale devant les électeurs du Royaume Uni', 'La Presse allemande au point de vue du

in Spain, it contrasted the harmony between free-traders of all nationalities with the conflicting interests of protectionists from different countries.[36] The cosmopolitan aspirations of the French free-traders culminated with a 'Congrès du Libre-échange', hosted by the new Belgian Association pour la Liberté Commerciale in Brussels. The ALE's nineteen delegates at the congress outnumbered each of the other foreign delegations, which included nine Britons, nine Dutchmen, seven Germans, three Americans, two Italians, two Poles, one Spaniard, one Swede and one Moldovan.[37]

Yet, within France, Bastiat's campaign met with limited and diminishing success. In the autumn of 1846, local branches of the ALE were created in Lyon and Marseille, but neither of them was very active.[38] Local branches were also created in Le Havre and Nîmes, but they refused to endorse the national association's name, Le Havre opting for the name Association pour la Réforme Commerciale.[39] Pamphlets in favour of *libre-échange* published outside Paris and Bordeaux were few and far between.[40] At a meeting held in Marseille in September 1847, Lamartine, who enjoyed a growing political audience at the end of the July Monarchy, nonetheless threw his weight behind the campaign for *libre-échange*. Having compared protected industries with the former privileged orders and consumers with the Third Estate before 1789, the poet asserted that *libre-échange* was 'the word of God'. If a 'divine legislator' governed commerce and industry, he added, 'he would establish the fraternity of trade, labour and transport, … he would immediately establish *libre-échange*'. By contrast, if God entrusted the government of commerce to 'a spirit of iniquity, darkness, evil and death', this devil would establish 'the prohibitive system' and, 'adding hypocrisy to cruelty', he would 'taint it with national fallacies' and 'call it the protective system'.[41]

libre-échange' and 'Ligue douanière italienne', *Le Libre-échange*, 23 January, 8, 24 October and 14 November 1847.

[36] 'Association espagnole pour la défense du travail nationale', *Le Libre-échange*, 7 November 1847.

[37] Association belge pour la Liberté Commerciale, *Congrès des économistes de Bruxelles* (Brussels, 1847); see also *Le Libre-échange*, 19 and 26 September 1847.

[38] According to the catalogue of the Bibliothèque Nationale, the Lyon association published two pamphlets, *Liberté des échanges: association lyonnaise* (Lyon, 1846) and *Liberté des échanges: Le Libre-échange à Lyon* (Lyon, 1847) and the Marseille association none.

[39] *Le Libre-échange*, 6 December 1846 and 3 January 1847.

[40] Isolated efforts included Charles Morlot, *La Comédie du libre échange: dialogues sur la liberté commerciale* (Le Havre, 1847), and Ponce Nollet, *Libre-échange, apologie du Cobden de Rheims*, a pamphlet in praise of Léon Faucher's efforts to spread free trade (Épernay, 1847).

[41] Alphonse de Lamartine, *Discours de M. de Lamartine à la réunion publique de l'association pour la liberté des échanges à Marseille* (Paris, 1847), pp. 2–7; see also *Le Libre-échange*, 5 and 12 September 1847.

Lamartine's inflamed speech caused a momentary sensation but did not stem the decline of the campaign for *libre-échange*. After its sixth public meeting on 30 March 1847, the ALE held none until 7 January 1848, and only 500 copies were printed of this seventh meeting's proceedings.[42] From 6,000, the circulation of *Le Libre-échange* dropped to approximately 1,500 per week.[43] The newspaper's geographic reach remained limited, with 500 copies sold in a single department, the Gironde.[44] Donations did not cover the ALE's expenses, and the national association owed its financial survival to subsidies from the Bordeaux and other provincial associations.[45] Except in and around Bordeaux, *libre-échange* failed to become a dominant ideology in the same way as free trade in Britain. The causes of this relative failure remain open to question, but it tends to confirm that, unlike in Britain, explicit religiosity was never a useful ally of liberal and radical causes in nineteenth-century France.[46]

A major weakness of the ALE's campaign was the tension between the democratic sympathies of its most active leaders (Bastiat, Harcourt, Wolowski, Faucher) and the conservative tendencies of the bulk of its supporters. Already in 1845, Faucher lamented that he was 'the only politician in France who combined support for commercial liberty and political liberty'.[47] In 1846, Bastiat regretted that the merchants of the Bordeaux association 'branded him as a radical'. Most deputies and peers who belonged to the executive committee of the ALE were stalwart supporters of the conservative Guizot government. The ALE's platform, adopted in August 1846, described free trade, alongside private property, as one of 'the foundations of order'.[48] Anonymous pamphlets in Bordeaux and Lyon accused the ALE of being the enemy of 'political liberty' and of despising 'democracy' and 'workers'.[49] In 1847, the departure of Faucher and Wolowski further weakened the progressive wing of the Association.[50] Bastiat explained his own resignation as editor of *Le Libre-échange* in January 1848 by 'the

[42] Impression 407 (22 January 1848), AN, F18*II 35.
[43] AN, BB/17A/145, cited in Deschamp, *La Belgique*, p. 328.
[44] *Le Courrier de la Gironde*, 4 March 1847. [45] *Le Libre-échange*, 13 June 1847.
[46] Jean Baubérot and Séverine Mathieu, *Religion, modernité et culture au Royaume-Uni et en France, 1800–1914* (Paris, 2002).
[47] Faucher to Nathalis Briavoine, 17 August 1845, in *Léon Faucher*, vol. 1, p. 165.
[48] Association pour la Liberté des Échanges, *Déclaration* (Paris, 1846).
[49] Bordelais pamphlet quoted in 'Nos libre-échangistes', *Le Moniteur Industriel*, 5 November 1846; [Anon.], *De l'influence de la démocratie dans les questions du libre-échange et de l'octroi* (Lyon, 1847), p. 2.
[50] *Le Libre-échange*, 2 May 1847; see also 'Un schisme dans le Comité du libre-échange', two articles, *Le Moniteur Industriel*, 25 and 29 April 1847.

divergence of political ideas' with other members of the ALE, who did 'not permit [him] to give the newspaper a sufficiently democratic direction'.[51]

When Richard Cobden visited France in the summer of 1846, he accurately perceived the contradictions and limitations of the French campaign for free trade. He was delighted by the warm atmosphere of the banquet given in his honour in Bordeaux, an event attended by nearly 500 Bordelais: it was, in his opinion, 'a splendid affair'. By contrast, he found the dinner organized by the Société des Économistes in Paris hushed and stilted.[52] His overall verdict on the French free-traders was damning: next to the British League, they were 'mere children'.[53]

III

The failure of *libre-échange* to win over public opinion also resulted from the virulent counter-campaign of the Association pour la Défense du Travail National. Since the protectionist association did not have financial means vastly superior to those of the ALE, its success can be attributed, at least in part, to the greater resonance of its propaganda. The latter's core theme may be described as economic Anglophobia, consisting in some elements of industrialist jealousy combined with a defence of a more self-sufficient, democratic and humane French economic model. According to the protectionists, the adoption of free trade would not only consolidate British industrial hegemony but would also spread British materialism, selfishness and acceptance of widening inequalities in France. Protection, by contrast, stood for the defence of the prevalence of small independent producers inherited from the Revolution.

Guizot's policy of cooperation with Britain since 1840 reinforced suspicions that France might follow the example set by Britain's commercial revolution.[54] At the ALE's first meeting, Adolphe Blanqui stated that 'a minister', who everyone understood to be Guizot, had told him about the campaign for *libre-échange*: 'Be strong and we shall protect you.'[55] In response, Mimerel and several leading manufacturers revived the Comité pour la Défense du Travail National. In a letter circulated in September 1846, they denounced the ALE's attempt to 'naturalize ... this English import', *libre-échange*, and proposed to transform the committee in a

[51] Bastiat to Coudroy, 22 July 1846 and 13 February 1848, in *Œuvres complètes*, vol. 1, pp. 73, 79–80.
[52] Cobden, *The European Diaries of Richard Cobden*, pp. 46–52.
[53] Richard Cobden to Frederick Cobden, 4 September 1846; quoted in Howe, *Free Trade*, p. 76.
[54] Collingham, *The July Monarchy*, pp. 318–27; Bullen, *Palmerston, Guizot*, pp. 25–49.
[55] Association pour la Liberté des Échanges, *Première séance publique* (Paris, 1846), p. 34.

permanent association that would seek to 'stop the contagion'.[56] The President of the new Association pour la Défense du Travail National (hereafter ADTN) was the conservative peer and Alsatian manufacturer Antoine Odier. But Odier, a former agent of the Compagnie des Indes Orientales dissolved in 1793, was eighty years old. The most active leading members of the ADTN were its vice-president, Mimerel, its secretary, the Seine-et-Marne earthenware manufacturer Louis Lebeuf, and the Seine-inférieure woollen manufacturer and centre-left deputy Victor Grandin. Most other members of the ADTN's executive committee were also industrialists from the Paris, Lille and Rouen areas.[57]

In response to the circular letter, dozens of local committees sprang up in manufacturing regions. The Lille committee was founded on 12 October 1846, at a meeting attended by 600 'industrialists', a figure that suggests the presence of small manufacturers and artisans alongside large factory owners. The new committee's secretary, the beet-sugar manufacturer Charles Kolb-Bernard, lambasted Britain's hypocritical preaching of free trade after it followed a policy of 'absolute prohibition' for centuries. Mocking the humanitarian language of the free-traders, he conceded that free trade corresponded with the British conception of 'human fraternity', since it reserved 'a birthright [for England] based on the spoliation of other nations'.[58] Such allusions to primogeniture served to recall the aristocratic and unequal nature of British society. In the Nord, committees were also founded at Roubaix, Armentières, Tourcoing, Valenciennes and Avesnes. The Roubaix committee solemnly pledged 'not to hand over the bread and well-being of French workers to England'.[59] A resolution adopted by the Armentières committee asserted that *libre-échange* 'would necessarily imply … the annihilation of French industry to the benefit of our eternal and jealous rival', England.[60]

The reaction against *libre-échange* soon spread to the east, Picardy and Normandy. On 21 October, the Mulhouse Comité de l'Industrie Cotonnière de l'Est opened its membership to other producers than cotton manufacturers, transforming itself into a local committee of the

[56] Letter published in *Le Moniteur Industriel*, 29 October 1846.

[57] List of members in 'Association pour la Défense du Travail National – Premier compte-rendu des travaux du comité central et de la commission permanente', *Le Moniteur Industriel*, 1 November 1846.

[58] 'Manifestation contre le libre-échange à Lille', *Le Moniteur Industriel*, 15 October 1846.

[59] 'Manifestation du comité du protecteur du travail national à Roubaix', 16 October 1846, ADN, 79J 36.

[60] 'Manifestation de la ville d'Armentières pour la défense du travail national', 9 November 1846, ADN, 76J b13, folder 42.

ADTN.[61] In November, it issued a manifesto describing *libre-échange* as a 'utopia' and concluded, 'A single consideration, in our eyes, dominates the question: the access to our markets for *English* products!'[62] By the end of November 1846, local committees were also created in Saint-Quentin (Aisne), Rouen (Seine-Inférieure) and Elbeuf, Louviers and Caudelec-les-Elebeuf (Eure).[63] By February 1847, the ADTN could boast twenty-nine local branches, including new committees in Normandy and committees in Amiens and Abbeville (Somme), Charleville and Sedan (Ardennes), Troyes (Aube), Saint-Dizier (Haute-Marne), Bar-le-Duc (Meuse) and Metz (Moselle). The industrial north-east predominated, but committees were also established in Nantes (Loire-Inférieure), Limoges (Haute-Vienne), Saint-Etienne (Loire) and Carcassonne (Aude).[64]

The primary function of local committees was the raising of funds. In Lille, 144 members offered voluntary contributions amounting to 11,500 francs. In Roubaix, local producers were asked to make a contribution equal to 5 per cent of their *patente* (business tax): 214 out of 256 producers complied, and the Committee collected over 2,500 francs. In Armentières, the committee requested 10 per cent of the *patente* from industrial producers and tradesmen and 2 francs per horse that they owned from farmers.[65] In Mulhouse, the Committee set subscription fees at 1 centime per spindle for spinners, 1 centime per three pieces of cloth for weavers and printers and 50 centimes per worker employed for other manufacturers, thus raising 8,000 francs.[66] Local committees gave a large share of the collected funds to the central committee. By 29 November 1846, Lille and Rouen had sent 4,000 francs each; Mulhouse, 3,000 francs; Roubaix, Tourcoing and Elbeuf, 2,000 francs each. The twenty-eight members of the central committee each made a personal contribution of 300 francs, adding 8,500 francs to the Association's funds.[67] The total of these sums amounted to 25,500 francs. It did not include contributions by secondary committees, and it is possible that the ADTN did not publicly acknowledge all the

[61] Minutes of the CICE, 21 October 1846, CERARE, ACCM, 680, fols. 22–3.

[62] *L'Industriel Alsacien*, 22 November 1846.

[63] 'Deuxième compte-rendu des travaux de la commission permanente', *Le Moniteur Industriel*, 29 November 1846.

[64] 'Association pour la Défense du Travail National – Troisième compte-rendu', *Le Moniteur industriel*, 18 February 1847.

[65] 'Souscription [de Lille], résumé général', 'cotisations [du comité de Roubaix]', 'Manifestation de la ville d'Armentières', ADN, 76J b13, folder 42.

[66] Association pour la Défense du Travail National de Mulhouse, *Première publication* (Mulhouse, 1846), p. 7.

[67] 'Deuxième compte-rendu' and 'Manifestation de la ville d'Amiens pour la défense du travail national', *Le Moniteur Industriel*, 29 November 1846.

contributions it received. But it is unlikely that its financial means substantially exceeded those of their adversaries, since the Bordeaux association alone raised 85,000 francs in 1846.

Most expenses, the ADTN's secretary explained in January 1848, served to finance the 'publicity' of protectionist ideas. They helped publish six pamphlets, with a relatively modest circulation of 1,000 to 2,000 copies.[68] As with the ALE, 'the largest share of expenses' was dedicated to the Association's newspaper, *Le Moniteur Industriel*. Subsidies to the periodical included: payments to 'several writers', including a journalist who went to Britain to 'study on the spot the results of [the free trade] system'; the supply of free copies to the members of the parliamentary chambers; the dispatching of free copies to clubs and circles where public opinion remained 'uncertain'; and the dispatching of free copies to provincial newspapers, so that they could reproduce articles and 'find readers that our newspaper could not have reached'.[69]

Founded in 1835, the biweekly *Moniteur Industriel* was initially an industrialist rather than a protectionist publication. Concerned with the promotion of modern industries and railways, it favoured the replacement of prohibitions by protective duties and a customs union with Belgium.[70] Only after a group of Parisian manufacturers bought the sheet in 1845 did *Le Moniteur Industriel* become staunchly opposed to free trade, adding 'journal de la défense du travail national' to its title in the autumn of 1846. After its takeover by protectionist manufacturers, it saw its circulation double, from 2,000 to 4,000 copies.[71] Its virulence and frequent insinuations that French free-traders must be in the pay of the British government led *Le Libre-échange* to dubb it 'the *Père Duchesne* of the protectionist league', by analogy with the Hébertiste revolutionary sheet, which clamoured for the execution of British spies during the Terror. The reference associated protectionism with Revolutionary Jacobinism.[72]

Le Moniteur Industriel's initial attacks on *libre-échange* drew on industrialist jealousy. Invoking 'practice', 'experience' and 'history', a profession of faith in September 1846 asserted that 'there [were] more important interests for peoples than the liberty of commerce, namely the unshakeable

[68] Impression 6782 (30 October 1846), AN, F18*II 33; impressions 1108 (27 February 1847), 3569 (12 June 1847) and 7355 (22 October 1847), AN, F18*II 34; and impressions 127 (10 January 1848) and 1044 (30 January 1848), AN, F18*II 35.

[69] Association pour la Défense du Travail National, *Réunion annuelle du comité central: séance du 17 janvier 1848* (Paris, 1848), pp. 45–9.

[70] 'Du système de prohibition', 'Un mot sur la prohibition' and 'De l'association douanière entre la France et la Belgique', *Le Moniteur Industriel*, 5 June 1836, 10 February 1842 and 25 August 1842.

[71] Deschamps, *La Belgique*, p. 333.

[72] *Le Libre-échange*, 20 December 1846.

possession of large industries. Every economic measure that takes this into account is a good one; every measure that does not must be rejected'. Systematically comparing production costs in France and abroad, it concluded that only high tariffs or prohibitions would enable France to produce iron, coal or cotton, wool and linen textiles.[73] The adoption of free trade by Britain, *Le Moniteur Industriel* insisted, was a jealous ploy: it was not 'to implement Adam Smith's doctrines' that Robert Peel repealed the Corn Laws but 'to maintain and extend England's domination over all the markets of the globe'.[74] Yet, in the following months, the newspaper's industrialist arguments were increasingly combined with the promotion of self-sufficiency, with, for instance, a frequent emphasis on the need to defend grain and other agricultural productions against foreign competition.[75]

The strident Anglophobia that permeated the newspaper's pages helped to conceal potential contradictions. Comparing the 'libre-échangistes' to the Physiocrats who had applauded the 1786 commercial treaty and the naive supporters of Bowring in the early 1830s, *Le Moniteur Industriel* recalled that Britain's attempts to flood the French market had always benefited from more or less credulous French complicities.[76] *Le Moniteur Industriel* even drew a parallel between Bastiat's League, which worked 'for the benefit of England', and the Catholic *Ligue* during the sixteenth-century wars of religion, which 'worked for the benefit of Spain, Rome and the [German] princes': 'Beneath the mask, then of religion, today of liberty, it is still foreigners who pull the strings and manipulate French puppets in their own interest.'[77] The 'libre-échangistes', the newspaper insisted, took 'their instructions … from London', although British policy was 'the embodiment of national selfishness': it 'broke the chains of thousands of blacks' with the abolition of slavery, but only in order to increase the profits it derived from its Indian possessions, and it now strove to fasten 'those of millions of whites' with free trade.[78]

Le Moniteur Industriel lambasted the inhumanity of Britain's society as well as its ambition to crush other nations. In 1847, a series of ten letters by the journalist sent to observe the results of free trade across the

73 'Sur les arguments du libre-échange', 'Progrès de l'industrie minière en France' and 'Sur l'industrie du fer', *Le Moniteur Industriel*, 20 September, 18 and 22 October 1846.

74 'Sur les réformes de sir Robert Peel', *Le Moniteur Industriel*, 1 February 1846.

75 'Sur les subsistances et sur notre agriculture', *Le Moniteur Industriel*, 27 September 1846.

76 'Simples rapprochements', *Le Moniteur Industriel*, 18 October 1846.

77 'La Ligue', *Le Moniteur Industriel*, 4 October 1846.

78 'L'Angleterre et le libre-échange français', three articles, *Le Moniteur Industriel*, 25 October, 1 November and 8 November 1846.

Channel not only warned readers that French producers could never sustain British competition but also denounced the de-humanizing consequences of Britain's economic superiority, including an atmosphere of 'incessant mobility', the 'daily and unchanging organization of individual labour' that resembled 'the regularity and accuracy of mechanical power', and 'these countless factories, … volcanoes of smoke' that shrouded entire cities in 'eternal clouds'. The reporter for *Le Moniteur Industriel* also noted, with a hint of anxiety, the extraordinary national and racial diversity that one encountered in port cities such as London, not only the 'groups of emigrants' from all over Europe and bound for the New World but also 'these Hindu, Malay, Chinese, North and South American sailors or workers' who could be seen amid the 'perpetual loading and unloading of goods'. British commerce, he concluded, was 'monstrously powerful', in a way that could not and probably should not be emulated.[79]

Le Moniteur Industriel's fervent Anglophobia was often combined with attacks on a French elite often suspected of 'Anglomania' in the early nineteenth century.[80] The ALE was led by an aristocrat (Harcourt) and received the support of literary luminaries (Lamartine) and high-quality newspapers (*Le Journal des Débats*). In contrast, Mimerel, Lebeuf and Grandin bore undistinguished names and only represented the provincial bourgeoisie. When *Le Journal des Débats* declared its support for *libre-échange*, *Le Moniteur Industriel* denounced the newspaper's predilection for 'big financiers', 'men of letters', 'artists', 'philosophers' and 'economists', none of whom – unlike 'manufacturers', 'engineers' and 'workers' – made a significant contribution to 'the strength, wealth and well-being of France today'.[81] The free-traders did not conceal their sense of cultural superiority. According to Faucher, the protectionists did not travel, did not know foreign languages and read very little: 'As a result, they are frightened by everything that comes from outside; they would be more liberal if they were more educated.'[82] In response, the defenders of protection flaunted their parochialism as evidence of their patriotism. In the Chamber of Deputies, having sufficiently mispronounced the names of several British politicians as to provoke the hilarity of his colleagues, Grandin retorted that he did not pronounce English 'as well as Messieurs les libre-échangistes', to whom 'this language [was] very familiar'. 'I try

[79] 'Observations d'un Français en Angleterre', ten articles, *Le Moniteur Industriel*, 17 June–1 August 1847.
[80] Tombs and Tombs, *That Sweet Enemy*, pp. 332–3.
[81] 'Le Journal des débats et nos industries', *Le Moniteur Industriel*, 12 April 1846.
[82] 'Du manifeste publié par le comité central de la prohibition', *Le Libre-échange*, 11 April 1847.

to read and pronounce names', he asserted, 'as someone who only knows French'.[83]

This suspicion of the elite's cosmopolitan and especially Anglophile tendencies facilitated a rapprochement between the protectionists and the radical left. Deriding the frequent references of the free-traders to 1789, *Le Moniteur Industriel* reclaimed the legitimacy of the Revolutionary legacy for the ADTN, sneering at 'the Lilliputians of the Montesquieu bazaar' who dared to compare themselves to 'the giants of the French Revolution'. It was, the newspaper asserted, 'the Ancien Régime that gave us libre-échange with the treaty of 1786', while the Revolution, 'with its national and democratic spirit, gave us back the protective system'. Far from representing the privileged classes, the leaders of the ADTN were all 'commoners, who only owed their condition to industry'. In contrast, the ALE was 'in large majority composed of members of the superior classes' and chose as its president 'a duke and large landowner' (Harcourt). Likewise, the leaders of the Bordeaux association were all 'counts, marquesses and barons', whose commercial firms were 'half-denationalized by the nature of their business'. Yet *Le Moniteur Industriel* simultaneously sought to portray protectionism as a means to overcome such social divisions, claiming that the protective system was 'neither aristocratic nor democratic' but 'national'. *Libre-échange*, by contrast, was neither 'French' nor 'humanitarian', but 'English'.[84]

IV

The campaign of the ADTN was a resounding success. In private, Bastiat himself expressed admiration: 'The prohibitionists practice agitation wholeheartedly and in the English manner. Newspapers, subscriptions, appeals to workers, threats to the government: nothing is missing. When I say in the English manner, I mean that they display a lot of energy and demonstrate a good understanding of agitation.' Bastiat also conceded that the success of the protectionists had less to do with their financial resources – 'our adversaries are not only [material] *interests*' – than with the popularity of Anglophobic propaganda: 'If this hatred of perfidious Albion was only a fashion', he lamented to Cobden, 'I would patiently wait for it to pass. But it has deep roots in [French] hearts. It is

[83] 'Le Libre-échange à la chambre des deputés', *Le Moniteur Industriel*, 11 February 1847.
[84] 'L'Aristocratie du système protecteur et la démocratie du libre-échange', *Le Moniteur Industriel*, 7 November 1847.

universal.'[85] The reaction against the triumph of free trade in Britain saw the protectionists consolidate their dominance among manufacturers and gain new supporters among maritime merchants and agricultural producers.

Since the early 1830s, the Mulhouse industrialists had been wary of paying allegiance to the protective system because they wished to obtain a lowering of duties on raw materials. Their rallying to the campaign of the ADTN was therefore a significant sign of the progress of protectionist ideas. Disappointed by the manifesto of the Mulhouse committee, Bastiat distinguished between traditional protectionists and the new 'liberal protectionists', such as the Mulhouse manufacturers, who had only just decided to side with 'national hatreds'.[86] Mulhouse was even one of the most active of the ADTN's local committees. Between 1846 and 1850, it collected more than 20,000 francs in subscriptions.[87] By the end of 1848, it had published fifteen pamphlets: three accounts of its activities and twelve reports on the region's different branches of industry, each concluding that French industries could not sustain British, Swiss or German competition.[88] The report on the cotton industry drew on the observations of an agent sent to Manchester, who reported that the main goal of British free-traders was 'to seize hold of our immense market'. The agent also believed that free trade worsened the conditions of factory workers and that, thanks to the protective system, 'the French nation taken as whole is happier than the English nation'.[89] Free copies of the Mulhouse committee's pamphlets were addressed to 400 'correspondents' throughout France, including members of the parliamentary chambers, publicists and businessmen.[90]

L'Industriel Alsatien, the weekly mouthpiece of the Mulhouse committee, reproduced articles from *Le Moniteur Industriel* and denounced in its own words the Englishness of *libre-échange*. Cobden, the newspaper argued, was 'no doubt a very good Englishman', but 'doctrines' emanating from 'our most constant, perfidious, relentless and implacable enemies,

85 Bastiat to Cobden, 22 November 1846, 25 December 1846 and 9 November 1847, in *Œuvres complètes*, vol. 1, pp. 145, 151, 167.

86 'Le Comité de l'association de Mulhouse', *Le Libre-échange*, 27 December 1846.

87 Of these 20,000 francs, 6,500 were sent to the Central Committee and the rest was spent locally; see 'Compte-rendu de l'assemblée générale des membres de l'association formée à Mulhouse pour la défense du travail national', 3 July 1850, CERARE, ACCM, 799.

88 Pamphlets collected in *Association pour la défense du travail national, formée à Mulhouse le 4 novembre 1846* (Mulhouse, 1848).

89 Risler Heilmann to Emile Dollfus, 14 March 1847, CERARE, ASIM, 99/A/732.

90 'Correspondants', CERARE, ACCM, 799.

the ENGLISH!' ought to be considered with suspicion.[91] *L'Industriel Alsatien* also contested the attempt of the free-traders to describe themselves as the sole representatives of liberalism. Being 'liberal in political economy', it contended, did not imply 'wanting to change everything at a stroke'. The newspaper attacked the resemblance between the phrase 'liberté des échanges' and other popular principles such as 'liberté individuelle' or 'liberté de la presse'. The abolition of barriers on international trade, *L'Industriel Alsatien* suggested, should instead be described as 'unlimited competition': the new name 'would make a lot of people ... think again' about the desirability of free trade.[92] Apart from the Lyonnais silk-weavers, all French industries therefore rallied behind the ADTN. In eighteen cities where no committee of the ADTN was founded, chambers of commerce or consultative chambers of arts and manufactures issued manifestos of adhesion to the Association's principles. Toulouse, for instance, denounced the 'paid missionaries, sent in France by Britain in order to preach libre-échange', while Bar-le-Duc railed against 'the Englishman Cobden and his French apostles ... salaried by England'.[93]

The ADTN also succeeded in extending support for protection to a fraction of maritime shipping. This branch of activity had stagnated since the 1820s, while British and American shipping grew rapidly.[94] The Bordeaux Chamber of Commerce and the ALE attributed this relative decline to the protective system, which not only slowed down the growth of trade but also increased construction costs for shipbuilders.[95] The ADTN pointed instead to the nefarious consequences of the reciprocal treaties of navigation concluded with the USA in 1822 and Britain in 1826 and suggested restoring preferential duties in favour of French shipping.[96] Such a return to mercantilist practices held limited appeal for large port cities such as Bordeaux, Marseille or Le Havre, which stood to lose too

[91] 'De la liberté des échanges', 'Sur la liberté du commerce', 'Ce qu'il faut croire du libéralisme commercial de l'Angleterre', 'La Cause de la liberté du commerce est-elle désintéressée?', *L'Industriel Alsacien*, 27 September 1846, 4 October 1846, 2 May 1847 and 16 January 1848.

[92] *L'Industriel Alsacien*, 14 February 1847 and 'La Liberté des échanges devrait s'appeler la Concurrence illimitée', *L'Industriel Alsacien*, 9 January 1848.

[93] Chambre de Commerce de Toulouse, *Lettre sur la question du libre-échange* (Toulouse, 1847), p. 10; Chambre Consultative des Arts et Manufactures de Bar-le-Duc, *Délibérations* (Bar-le-Duc, [1846]), pp. 8–9.

[94] Lévy-Leboyer, *Les Banques européennes*, pp. 246–54.

[95] 'Rapport de la commission de navigation sur la réforme douanière', *Le Mémorial Bordelais*, 16 and 17 August 1846; Chambre de Commerce de Bordeaux, *Des intérêts maritimes et de la protection* (Bordeaux, 1847).

[96] 'Le Libre-échange et le système protecteur considérés du point de vue de la marine nationale' and 'Association pour la défense du travail national à la marine marchande', *Le Moniteur Industriel*, 1 November and 17 December 1846.

much from Anglo-American retaliation. But it helped the ADTN obtain the adhesion of smaller ports such as Dunkirk or ports in marked decline such as Nantes. The Dunkirk Chamber of Commerce admitted that if *libre-échange* were adopted, British trade 'would subjugate all the world's consumers to its monopoly', while the Nantes Comité pour la Défense du Travail National declared its adhesion to 'the principle of protection, because it is thanks to its application that France [was] the world's second industrial nation', after Britain.[97]

Protectionist ideas met with even greater success among agricultural producers, rendered apprehensive by the abolition of the British Corn Laws. *Le Moniteur Industriel* insisted that, unlike in Britain, industry and agriculture in France were 'not in conflict with each other; on the contrary, they esteem[ed] and support[ed] each other'. All French producers understood 'that sacrificing agricultural labour to the benefit of Russia and the United States and industrial labour to the benefit of England would simultaneously exhaust the two sources of national wealth'. Reviving an argument dating back to the early 1830s, the protectionist newspaper insisted that the protection of agriculture had different purposes in Britain, where land property was 'constituted aristocratically', and in France, where it belonged to a 'multitude of families from all classes of society'.[98] Grain producers, in particular, proved sensitive to these arguments. In November 1846, a 'congrès agricole' attended by representatives from seven northern departments (Nord, Pas-de-Calais, Aisne, Ardennes, Oise, Somme and Marne) condemned the deceptive appeal of 'liberty' on behalf of 'the principle of equality': since production costs were unequal in Britain and France, *libre-échange* was 'in England's interest' and protection necessary to preserve equality.[99]

The ADTN also proposed that agricultural societies in France's eighty-six departments join the association without having to contribute to its funds. Fifty-three such societies accepted the offer. To justify their adhesion, rural *notables* insisted that French producers could not compete with English landlords, American slaves, Russian serfs or Egyptian fellahs: the higher production costs of French agriculture, they argued, were the price of the French farmers' equality and liberty.[100] Reports by

97 Chambre de Commerce de Dunkerque, *Lettre sur la question du libre-échange* (Dunkerque, 1847), p. 4; Association de Nantes pour la défense du travail national, *Réforme commerciale* (Nantes, [1847]), p. 13.

98 'Solidarité de l'agriculture et des autres branches du travail national' and 'L'Agriculture et ses protecteurs', *Le Moniteur Industriel*, 4 and 18 March 1847.

99 Congrès Agricole, *Protection du travail national* (Amiens, 1846), p. 15.

100 See, among others, Société d'Agriculture de l'Ain, *Opinion et vote de la société d'agriculture de l'Ain sur la question du libre-échange* (Bourg-en-Bresse, 1847); Société d'Agriculture du Calvados,

agricultural societies were often printed and distributed in each department. The Commission d'Agriculture de Draguignan, for example, had 500 copies of its report in favour of the defence of national labour printed and distributed – 260 for each mayor of the Var and 240 to other local *notables*, making for a high rate of dissemination in a department with a population just a little over 300,000.[101] At a national Congrès Central de l'Agriculture held in Paris in March 1847, a crushing majority of attendees (500 to 4) rejected a statement in favour of *libre-échange*, and in January 1848, 42 delegates of agriculture attended a general assembly of the ADTN.[102]

As a result of the ADTN's successful campaign, support for *libre-échange* in the national press rapidly dwindled. In September 1846, three centre-left newspapers – *Le Siècle* (circulation: 33,000 copies), *Le Commerce* (3,000) and *Le Courrier Français* (2,000) – and the two main pro-government sheets – *Le Journal des Débats* (9,000) and *L'Époque* (11,000) – praised Peel's decision to abolish the Corn Laws and the creation of the ALE.[103] The other major liberal newspapers – the conservative *La Presse* (18,000), the centre-left *Le Constitutionnel* (25,000), the centre-left *L'Esprit Public* (4,000) and the Catholic *L'Univers* (4,000) – rallied to the defence of the protective system. The royalist newspapers, *La Quotidienne* (3,000) and *La Gazette de France* (3,000) also condemned the ALE's propaganda.[104] But, after November 1846, *Le Journal des Débats* stopped publishing articles in favour of *libre-échange*. In January 1847, *Le Siècle* opposed the repeal of

Le Libre-échange apprécié par l'agriculture à sa juste valeur (Caen, 1847); Société d'Agriculture de l'Aube, *Rapport sur la théorie du libre-échange* (Paris, 1847); Société d'Agriculture de la Haute-Garonne, *Question du libre-échange: rapport à la société d'agriculture de Haute-Garonne* (Toulouse, 1847); Société d'Agriculture de l'Ariège, *Du libre-échange en matière d'agriculture* (Foix, 1847); Société d'Agriculture de la Haute-Saône, *État de l'industrie agricole en France, ce qu'elle doit redouter de la concurrence étrangère* (Vesoul, 1847); Pierre-Paul Jaenger [of the Société d'Agriculture du Bas-Rhin], *Mémoire sur le libre-échange* (Colmar, 1847); Société d'Agriculture de l'Aisne, *Rapport de M. Bauchart sur la question du libre-échange, au point de vue agricole* (Saint-Quentin, 1848); E. Hecquet d'Orval [of the Société d'Agriculture de l'Arrondissement d'Abbeville], *Quelques mots contre le libre-échange* (Abbeville, 1848).

101 Commission d'Agriculture de Draguignan, *Libre-échange: défense du travail national* (Draguignan, 1847), pp. 29–30; results of the 1851 Census, Institut National de la Statistique et des Études Économiques, 'Recensements de 1851 à 1921' (www.insee.fr accessed, 11 August 2014).

102 'Congrès central de l'agriculture – Vote sur le libre-échange', *Le Moniteur Industriel*, 28 March 1847; Association pour la Défense du Travail National, *Réunion annuelle*, pp. 5–7.

103 *Le Journal des Débats*, 8 April 1846; *L'Époque*, 8 September 1846; 'Du mode d'application de la liberté commerciale', *Le Siècle*, 5 September 1846; *Le Commerce*, 11 September 1846; 'Effets réels de la concurrence étrangère', *Le Courrier Français*, 5 October 1846. On the circulation of national dailies in 1846, see Bellanger et al., *Histoire de la presse*, vol. II, p. 146.

104 'Défense du travail national', *L'Esprit Public*, 2 September 1846; *Le Constitutionnel*, 6 December 1846; *L'Univers*, 14 October 1846; *La Presse*, 13 September 1846; 'Le Libre-échange', *La Quotidienne*, 27 November 1846; 'Défense du travail national', *La Gazette de France*, 29 November 1846.

protection for French agriculture. And, in October 1847, *Le Conservateur*, a new pro-government newspaper, which replaced *L'Époque*, described itself as 'protectionist'.[105] In November 1847, Bastiat reported to Cobden that the allies of the ALE 'were becoming discouraged or indifferent' and lamented 'the void that [was] growing around us'.[106]

The progress of protectionist ideas thwarted a modest attempt of the Guizot government to reform customs legislation. It is difficult to determine the personal opinion of Guizot, who never expressed much interest in economic issues, on trade policy.[107] In April 1846, he asserted to the Chamber of Deputies that he wished 'to uphold the conservative system, the protective system', and the statement has been used to describe him as a protectionist. But the speech was made on the eve of a general election, in response to centre-left deputies who accused him of planning the sacrifice of French industry to preserve the Anglo-French entente. Moreover, Guizot admitted in the same speech that he wished to 'modify [the protective system], to loosen and relax it whenever new needs and new possibilities [became] apparent' and that France should 'gradually reform her tariffs, extend her trade abroad, gain for ourselves guarantees of good relations and peace, and improve the condition of consumers'.[108] Confidential testimonies by contemporaries tend to confirm that Guizot favoured a reduction of French tariffs.[109] In April 1847, the government proposed a reduction of the iron tariff and the suppression of duties on several minor items. But Cunin-Gridaine, Minister of Commerce, insisted that the government remained committed to 'protected labour', while *Le Libre-échange* described the moderation of suggested changes as a 'sad and bitter disappointment'.[110] In any event, the Chamber of Deputies' customs commission, of which Thiers was a member, condemned 'the English system' of commercial policy and rejected the proposal.[111]

[105] 'Du libre-échange au point de vue de l'intérêt agricole de la France', *Le Moniteur Industriel*, 28 January 1847; *Le Libre-échange*, 3 October 1847.

[106] Bastiat to Cobden, 15 November 1847, in *Œuvres complètes*, vol. 1, p. 168.

[107] Rosanvallon, *Le Moment Guizot*, pp. 268–9.

[108] Debates at the Chamber of Deputies (1 April 1846), *Le Moniteur Universel*, 2 April 1846; see also Guizot's speech on commercial negotiations with Belgium, in debates at the Chamber of Deputies (25 March 1845), *Le Moniteur Universel*, 26 March 1845.

[109] In 1835, for example, Galos wrote to Fonfrède that in a private meeting 'Monsieur Guizot insisted that his ideas [on commercial reforms] agreed with yours'; Galos to Fonfrède, 11 July 1835, BMB, MS 1095, vol. 1, fols. 656–63.

[110] *Le Libre-échange*, 12 April 1847; see also 'Du projet de loi sur les douanes', *Le Moniteur Industriel*, 15 April 1847.

[111] 'Projet de loi sur les douanes', *Le Moniteur Industriel*, 16 December 1847.

The difficulties encountered by commercial reform disappointed another liberal intellectual, Alexis de Tocqueville. The author of *Democracy in America* shared Guizot's relative lack of interest in economic issues, even though he took some notes on Say's *Cours complet d'économie politique* on his way to the USA in 1831.[112] Yet following his travels in England in 1835, he expressed some concerns about the spread of pauperism, which led him to endorse Villeneuve-Bargemont's views on France's commercial system as 'less brilliant' but 'more secure' than England's and to echo Dombasle's prediction that in the future all nations will 'make themselves most of the products necessary or useful to them'. This concern probably explains his support for beet sugar in 1843.[113] But the success of the Anti-Corn Law League revived his sympathy for free trade, and he had several conversations with Cobden when the latter visited Paris in 1846.[114] The notes Tocqueville wrote the following year to define the platform of a new group of centre-left deputies showed a strong hostility towards 'customs', because they tended to 'make dearer inside the kingdom everything that it taxes at the border'. But Tocqueville's adhesion to free trade went against the grain, and he himself acknowledged that the success of the protectionist campaign made commercial reform impossible in the near future: 'Customs laws are the most in need of modifications, but at present they are a holy ark.'[115]

When a general assembly of the ADTN met in Paris on 17 January 1848, Mimerel celebrated its success: 'everywhere our views, our intentions' had been 'understood'. He entreated the Association's delegates to remain vigilant, for the triumph of protection would only be assured after the 'problematic science' of political economy, from which derived the free trade 'hallucination', was vanquished. As a next stage of their campaign, he therefore called for the foundation of a new science of economics that would abide by 'the true idea of an enlightened and moderate protection'.[116] The need to create a new science of economics, inspired by practical experiences and respectful of social complexities, was also a frequent theme in the columns of *Le Moniteur Industriel*. This new science, the protectionist newspaper argued, should reach conclusions 'varying according to facts' and political and geographical circumstances: 'the

[112] Alexis de Tocqueville, *Œuvres complètes*, 18 vols. (Paris, 1951–83), vol. XVI, pp. 425–34.
[113] Tocqueville, *Œuvres complètes*, vol. III.2, pp. 708–9, and vol. XVI, pp. 140–7, esp. pp. 145–6.
[114] Cobden, *European Diaries of Richard Cobden*, pp. 48–50.
[115] Alexis de Tocqueville, *Textes économiques: anthologie critique*, ed. Jean-Louis Benoît and Eric Keslassy (Paris, 2005), p. 190.
[116] Association pour la Défense du Travail National, *Réunion annuelle*, pp. 28, 36–8.

true economist … has no preconceived idea, no fixed system, no proud and imperious theory; he is the servant of facts and not the creator of a dogma; he aspires not to invent, but to observe and develop'. Above all, it would demonstrate the untruths of *libre-échange*, 'the eldest son and spoilt child of political economy'.[117]

Several authors tried to fulfil the hopes of the ADTN and sketch out the contours of a new nationalist science of economics. A 'secretary' of the protectionist association, probably Lebeuf, did not only lambast the Englishness of free trade in *Examen des théories du libre-échange*, a work published under the auspices of the ADTN.[118] He also called into question the principle of non-intervention of the state in the economy, an 'error of the free-traders' that originated from 'their false conception of social power': 'the State', the author argued, could limit the right to exchange goods because it ought to 'watch over the development of wealth' and was 'the personification of the country'. In the last resort, however, the necessity of protection remained grounded in the preservation of national identity and power: 'Nationalities are not the products of whims or accidents: their raison d'être is indelible. Each has its own character, its own genius and its own original instincts.' As a source of inspiration, the *Examen* cited the 'national system of political economy' of 'doctor List'.[119]

List's *National System* was translated into French in 1851, but the success of his work in Germany already served to legitimize the campaign of the ADTN.[120] In another sign of the early impact of List on French debates, *Le Libre-échange* recalled that List disapproved of the protection of agricultural products and raw materials: 'next to the furious intolerance of the French protectionists, his moderation would almost pass as liberalism'.[121] List himself, in the *Zollvereinsblatt*, had indeed condemned the exaggerations of the French protective system. But 'the experience of France', he also wrote, proved that 'too much protection [was] still better than no protection'.[122] In the weeks preceding his death in November 1846, List's

117 'De l'économie politique' and 'De l'économie politique considérée comme science', *Le Moniteur Industriel*, 8 April 1847 and 10 February 1848.

118 Association pour la Défense du Travail National, *Réunion annuelle*, pp. 26–7.

119 Association pour la Défense du Travail National, *Examen des théories du libre-échange et des résultats du système protecteur* (Paris, 1847), pp. 3–5.

120 However, an extensive summary of List's ideas in French was already available in Henri Richelot, *L'Association douanière allemande* (Paris, 1845), pp. 186–242.

121 Charles Coquelin, 'Le Docteur Frédéric List et sa doctrine', three articles, *Le Libre-échange*, 11 April, 18 April and 23 May 1847.

122 'Frankreichs Handelssystem', *Das Zollvereinsblatt*, 27 March 1843; see also 'Die französische Praxis der politischen Ökonomie' and 'Die Theorie und die Praxis der politischen Ökonomie in Frankreich', *Das Zollvereinsblatt*, 15 April and 11 November 1844.

German newspaper hailed the ADTN's efforts to bring to a halt the 'free trade mania' on the Continent.[123] Another work published in 1847 relied on the ideas of 'doctor List' to assert that the origins of wealth lay in the 'national spirit'.[124] Several pamphlets hostile to free trade cited the national solidarity of the Zollverein as an example to emulate, while the report of the agricultural congress of northern departments praised the 'wisdom' of Germany, which 'reserved the Germanic market to products made by German hands'.[125]

Another noteworthy attempt to found a new political economy was the *Économie pratique des nations* by Thémistocle Lestiboudois, a defender of beet sugar and centre-left deputy for the Nord. Lestiboudois used a wide array of statistics and some mathematic formulae to demonstrate that free trade would disadvantage all nations except Britain. But beneath this positivist veneer, Lestiboudois's work was also an attempt to promote a more democratic and almost republican conception of economics. Instead of the 'liberty' of 'consumers', he contended, the 'initial principle' of this 'social science' ought to be 'the absolute equality' of 'citizens', animated by patriotic virtue: 'Citizens of the same country, we shall rely on each other, ... because we share a common material well-being, identical feelings, a common renown, the same thoughts, the same beliefs, the same opinions, the same needs, the same PATRIE!' In order to thwart Britain's ambition to establish world 'supremacy' and spread the selfish values of free trade, Lestiboudois also called for the extension of protection to a 'united central Europe' under the joint leadership of France and Germany.[126] This amounted to a reformulation of the anti-English Continental blockade or system, propounded by Alexandre Hauterive and François Ferrier more than forty years earlier, in the language of egalitarian republicanism.

The campaign of the ADTN failed to give birth to a new science of economics. But its relentless identification of Smithian political economy with British materialistic and aristocratic free trade contributed to the discipline's declining popularity in nineteenth-century France. The Anglophobic propaganda of the protectionists also nurtured the interest,

[123] 'Der Tarifkampf in Frankreich', four articles, *Das Zollvereinsblatt*, 5, 19, 26 October and 2 November 1846.

[124] Hantute, *Du libre-échange* (Paris, 1847), pp. 37, 68.

[125] Charles Maître, *Richard Cobden* (Paris, 1846), pp. 33, 77–80; Gustave Goldenberg, *Libre-échange et protection* (Paris, 1847), pp. 28–32, 58–9; Jules Lebastier, *Défense du travail national* (Paris, 1847), pp. 144–5; Congrès Agricole, *Protection du travail national*, p. 14.

[126] Thémistocle Lestiboudois, *Économie pratique des nations* (Paris, 1847), pp. 30–3, 45, 463–4; see also the glowing review of the book in *Le Moniteur Industriel*, 15 August 1847.

as an alternative to British values, in 'German' ideas of organic solidarity, which would continue to grow in subsequent decades.[127]

V

The rejection of British materialism and aristocratic values facilitated another significant success of the protectionist campaign: the rallying, on the eve of the democratic Revolution of 1848, of the majority of the radical left to the defence of national labour. As seen in the previous chapter, until the early 1840s, French radicals continued to favour the abolition of barriers on international trade as a means of reducing the price of essential commodities and encouraging fraternity between workers of all countries. Yet in the last years of the July Monarchy, most early socialists rejected *libre-échange*, sometimes entering into a surprising alliance with the protectionist capitalists.

At first, most representatives of the radical left refused to take sides between the ALE and the ADTN. Only *Le Populaire*, edited by the utopian Etienne Cabet, praised the repeal of the British Corn Laws and called for the abolition of customs barriers 'throughout the universe'. But the republican *La Réforme* announced that it would stay neutral in 'this civil war among the rich and powerful'. According to the Fourierist *La Démocratie Pacifique*, the debate on free trade pitted against each other 'the different factions of the bourgeoisie, without regard for the interests of the people'.[128] In November 1846, these two newspapers, together with the radical *Le National* and the socialist monthly *L'Atelier*, supported an attempt to create a 'Société pour la Défense des Intérêts Ouvriers dans la Question de la Liberté Commerciale'. But, fearing the effect of its propaganda on workers, the government did not authorize the creation of what would have been a third association in the controversy on free trade.[129]

Le Populaire and *La Réforme* did not intervene further in the debate. But the other newspapers of the radical left expressed increasingly vociferous hostility to *libre-échange*. Calling into question the patriotism of

[127] Yves Breton, 'Les Économistes français et les écoles historiques allemandes: rencontre entre l'économie politique et l'histoire?', *Histoire, Économie et Société*, 7 (3) (1988): 399–417; Alain Gélédan, 'Paul Cauwès, un nationaliste pour l'état régulateur', in Yves Breton and Michel Lutfalla (eds.), *L'Économie politique en France au XIXe siècle* (Paris, 1991), pp. 335–51. On the broader 'German' turn of French intellectual life in the second half of the nineteenth century, see Claude Digeon, *La Crise allemande de la pensée française, 1870–1914*, 2nd edn (Paris, 1992).

[128] *Le Populaire*, 28 August 1846; 'De la liberté commerciale', *La Réforme*, 14 September 1846; 'La Ligue anglaise et la ligue française', *La Démocratie Pacifique*, 11 September 1846.

[129] *L'Atelier*, November 1846; *La Réforme*, 1 December 1846.

Bastiat and his associates, *Le National* railed against 'les *free-traders*' of the 'Montesquiou's Hall' (the spelling was intended to suggest a British pronunciation), who wished to 'turn France into England'. Other radical newspapers became worried about the impact of British competition on French workers' salaries. *La Démocratie Pacifique* took the view that free trade would result in lower wages 'directly, by making entrepreneurs and bosses reduce, as much as they can, their workers' pay, and indirectly, by doing away with several industries and creating new ones where work will be relentless and more difficult, and by giving birth to new monopolies'. Free trade, the Fourierist daily concluded, was brought to France by 'English missionaries', and its adoption would accentuate 'all the bad aspects of industrialism' and 'Economism'. *La Fraternité*, a 'communist' newspaper, held similar views: 'For us *libre-échange* … is the unrestrained dominance of capital: it is the right, for the capitalist, in the name of liberty, to hold to ransom the working populations, and to oppress and enslave a nation.'[130]

The socialist newspaper that attacked free trade with the greatest virulence was *L'Atelier*, despite the earlier support of its editor, the Christian socialist Buchez, for commercial liberty in the early 1830s. 'Do not forget the countless machines at work across the Channel', the monthly, allegedly written by workers, instructed its readers in October 1846. 'To fight against them, manufacturers in France will only be able to do one thing: first to lower, then to lower, and always to lower our meagre wages.' 'The free-traders across the Channel', *L'Atelier* added the following month, 'are the friends of the people as much as the wolf is the friend of sheep.' The first issue of the *Revue Nationale*, another journal founded by Buchez in May 1847, extolled the beneficial effects of protection for workers and defined the publication's purpose as the defence of 'national activity' against 'foreign hostilities'.[131] The *Revue Indépendante*, edited by the humanist socialists Pierre Leroux and George Sand, also deemed 'the absolute individualism' of British free trade incompatible with France, 'the country of democracy and equality'.[132]

The ADTN stoked the Anglophobia of the radical left, especially among workers. In October 1846, the protectionist association sent to local

[130] *Le National*, 4 November 1846; 'La Vie à bon marché' and 'Le Libre-échange, dernière ressource de l'économisme', *La Démocratie Pacifique*, 3 December and 23 December 1846; 'De l'influence du libre-échange sur la condition des salariés', *La Fraternité*, 25 January 1847.

[131] *L'Atelier*, November 1846, December 1846 and January 1847; 'De la liberté et de la protection commerciale', *Revue nationale*, 1 (1847): 15–18.

[132] 'Le Libre-échange', *Revue indépendante*, 2nd series, 6 (1846): 33–64.

committees leaflets and posters of a short text addressed to factory workers and entitled 'On the Entry of English Goods'. In the text, an imaginary worker asked, 'Is it not true that we need to work to earn a living, and that giving work to the English to produce the clothes of the French is the same as giving the bread of the French to the English?' The text added, about free trade: 'This doctrine is brought in France by an Englishman [Cobden]. What is astonishing is that some Frenchmen repeat his lessons. They do not seem to realize that in this way they work to ruin their country and bring about the rule of the English in France.' The text concluded with an exhortation to set aside class conflicts, because 'when it comes to the English, masters and workers in France only have one interest, one idea, one heart'.[133] The ADTN sent 100 posters and 1,000 leaflets to the Lille committee, asking the city's manufacturers to 'hand out the fliers to their workers and post the placards in their workshops'.[134] The Mulhouse committee also received the posters and leaflets but only handed out the latter because several members deemed the text too inflammatory.[135]

When the government refused to authorize the formation of an association to defend the interests of workers in the controversy over *libre-échange*, the ADTN invited workers to join the protectionist association and considered giving workers several seats on its central committee.[136] *Le Moniteur Industriel* insisted that it did not profess 'republican doctrines' but rejoiced that throughout the country the democratic press – not only *Le National* and *L'Atelier* in Paris, but also *L'Impartial* in Lille, *Le Censeur* in Lyon and *Le Peuple Souverain* in Marseille – sided with the protectionists against free trade.[137] According to *Le Libre-échange*, Albert Gazel, a collaborator of Louis Blanc, became one of the main editors of the *Moniteur Industriel* in the autumn of 1847, sealing an objective alliance between protectionists and socialists.[138]

In addition to Anglophobia, protectionists and socialists found common ground in their detestation of liberal political economy. In September 1846, the conservative daily *La Presse* published a review of Bastiat's *Sophismes economiques* by François Vidal, a Fourierist. Vidal disparaged Bastiat's 'old economics', inspired by 'the worship of Jean-Baptiste Say,

[133] Text reprinted in *Le Moniteur Industriel*, 29 October 1846.

[134] Association pour la Défense du Travail National to the Lille Committee, ADN, 76J b13, folder 42, [October 1846].

[135] Association pour la Défense du Travail National de Mulhouse, *Réunion du 11 novembre 1848* (Mulhouse, 1848), pp. 3–4.

[136] 'Troisième compte-rendu', *Le Moniteur Industriel*, 18 February 1847.

[137] *Le Moniteur Industriel*, 5 July 1846, 1 November 1846 and 4 February 1847.

[138] *Le Libre-échange*, 7 November 1847.

winegrowing interests and the liberty of commerce': these 'liberals of the old Restoration' had become 'the laggards of economics'. Vidal confessed that he had read with enthusiasm, in his youth, Say's *Traité* and *Cours complet*, but Sismondi and other authors critical of the 'liberal school' had dispelled his illusions. The days of 'liberalism, a purely negative system', he concluded, were over, because public opinion realized that 'industrial and commercial anarchy' was 'as harmful as political anarchy'.[139] Pierre-Joseph Proudhon, the libertarian author of *What Is Property?* (1840), did not share such qualms about the danger of anarchy. But his critique of Smithian economics, the *Système des contradictions économiques* (1846), accused the 'Anglo-French agitation' in favour of free trade of seeking to transform the worker into 'the serf of the cosmopolitan idler', by depriving labour of a 'fatherland' and subjecting it to a global coalition of 'monopolists'. Paying homage to Dombasle's 'common sense, full of verve and originality', he provocatively described himself as a supporter of 'the balance of trade' as a means of keeping in check the alienation of domestic property to foreign capitalists.[140]

Wishing to remind the Fourierists of their former support for free trade, *Le Libre-échange* reproduced passages from Victor Considérant's earlier writings against customs protection. Despite the evidence, Considérant retorted: 'We [the Fourierists] are and have always been protectionist', although he would have preferred the substitution of the 'direct protection' of workers by the state to the 'indirect protection' offered by customs.[141] The rallying of the radical left to protectionism was a crushing blow for Bastiat: 'What most distresses me', he wrote to Cobden, 'whose heart is filled with the purest democratic feeling, is to see French democracy taking the lead in the opposition to the liberty of commerce.' Yet Bastiat, showing the extent of Anglophobia on the left, understood and almost excused the other radicals' distrust of England, which retained 'the capacity to crush all the navies of the world' and remained 'governed by a cynical oligarchy'. It was such legitimate suspicions that prevented France 'from understanding *libre-échange*'.[142] Conversely, Friedrich List's *Zollvereinsblatt* celebrated socialist support for protection as a major victory. It translated several articles of *L'Atelier* and rejoiced that in France even 'the lowest strata of society, the workers' understood that 'a vast and

[139] François Vidal, 'Les Sophismes économiques de M. Bastiat', *La Presse*, 3 September 1846.
[140] Proudhon, *Système*, vol. II, pp. 1–103, at pp. 3, 54, 57.
[141] *Le Libre-échange*, 12 December 1847 and 2 January 1848.
[142] Bastiat to Cobden, 9 November 1847, in *Œuvres complètes*, vol. I, pp. 166–7.

powerful national industry' was as indispensable to 'national independence' as 'a powerful national army'.[143]

The adhesion of French workers to national protection was perhaps not as wholehearted as the attitude of the socialist press suggests. *L'Atelier*, for example, although it claimed to be written exclusively by workers, mostly reflected Buchez's personal views.[144] However, recent painstaking research has argued that it was in the course of the 1840s that national consciousness superseded regional or professional identity in the French working classes.[145] In any case, the about-turn of the radical left's leaders on international trade was in itself significant because it deprived the free-traders of potentially useful allies. In a speech delivered at the Association Démocratique de Bruxelles in January 1848, one major socialist figure, Karl Marx, declared his support for *libre-échange*. But his speech was also a virulent attack on the 'abstract' rhetoric of 'liberty' and 'universal fraternity' of the British free-traders and French *libre-échangistes*. Indeed, Marx only favoured free trade because it would replicate, 'in gigantic proportions on the market of the universe', 'the destructive phenomena to which free competition gives rise within a country' and therefore hasten 'social revolution'.[146] Such an ambiguous adhesion, if Bastiat was aware of it, is unlikely to have given him much solace.

VI

The dominance of protectionism and the divorce between commercial and political liberalism were confirmed under the Second Republic established by the 1848 Revolution. For the vast majority of liberals, protection seemed a more natural bulwark for the preservation of the endangered social order. Adolphe Thiers, who emerged as the main leader of the 'parti de l'ordre', simultaneously defended liberal capitalism within France in his best-selling *De la propriété* (1848) and protection from foreign competition in his *Discours sur le régime commercial de la France* (1851). The latter drew on protection as a means of promoting self-sufficiency rather than industrialist jealousy and connected protective tariffs with the defence of liberal institutions. In contrast, Michel Chevalier, who superseded Bastiat

[143] 'Die nationalökonomische Bewegung in Frankreich', *Das Zollvereinsblatt*, 30 November 1846.

[144] Armand Cuvillier, *Un journal d'ouvriers: l'Atelier, 1840–1850* (Paris, 1954), pp. 46–52.

[145] Pierre-Jacques Derainne, 'Le Travail, les migrations et les conflits en France: représentations et attitudes sociales sous la Monarchie de Juillet et la Seconde République' (unpublished doctoral thesis, University of Bourgogne, 1999).

[146] Karl Marx, *Discours sur la question du libre-échange* (Brussels, 1848) reprinted in *Misère de la philosophie* (Paris, 1908), pp. 273–300, at pp. 296–7, 299–300.

as the champion of free trade, propounded a conception of commercial liberty indifferent to parliamentary liberalism, which would prove well suited to the authoritarian politics of the Louis-Napoléon Bonaparte's Second Empire.

The proclamation of the Second Republic in February 1848 did not bring the controversy on *libre-échange* to an immediate end. In March, the ALE posted placards in Paris that called for the abolition of import restrictions on foodstuffs: 'The French Republic', the text asserted in an allusion to the repeal of the Corn Laws, 'cannot refuse to French workers what the British aristocracy was forced to grant to the workers of Britain.'[147] *Le Libre-échange* also condemned the spontaneous expulsion of British, Belgian and Italian workers by their French counterparts that took place in the Nord and Normandy in the aftermath of the Revolution.[148] The organ of the French free-traders attributed the outburst of xenophobia to the protectionist propaganda of the previous two years against the 'mangeurs de rosbif'. Workers, the newspaper argued, applied the lessons of the ADTN on 'national labour' but preferred to ban the latter 'in the flesh' rather than 'under the form of commodities'.[149]

In April 1848, however, the ALE was disbanded, and *Le Libre-échange* ceased publication. Bastiat attempted to launch a new sheet to defend free-market ideas, but Parisian printers refused to condone a 'counter-revolutionary' enterprise and print the newspaper. Hostile to the Ateliers Nationaux, which commissioned state-funded public works to reduce unemployment, Bastiat attributed the effervescence of socialist projects to the doctrines spread by the protectionists: 'the dominant idea, which has conquered all the classes of society, is that the State ought to provide everyone with a living'.[150] 'Protectionism', he explained in a pamphlet on the causes of the 1848 Revolution, 'as it spreads, becomes Communism.'[151] Exhausted by his work on *Harmonies économiques* (1850), a more theoretical condemnation of state intervention in the economy, and demoralized by the decline of moderate republicanism in the Constituent and Legislative Assemblies, in which he served as a deputy for the Landes, Bastiat withdrew to Rome, where he died in December 1850.

147 Association pour la Liberté des Échanges, *Subsistances publiques: la vie à bon marché* (Paris, [1848]).

148 Derainne, 'Le Travail, les migrations et les conflits', pp. 239–42; Bensimon, 'British Workers', pp. 178–85.

149 'Dialogue entre un membre du comité Odier-Mimerel et un ouvrier sur le chemin de fer d'Orléans' and 'L'expulsion des ouvriers étrangers', *Le Libre-échange*, 19 March and 9 April 1848.

150 Bastiat to Coudroy, 9 June 1848, in *Œuvres complètes*, vol. 1, p. 82.

151 Frédéric Bastiat, *Protectionisme et communisme* (Paris, 1849), p. 4; sic for the spelling *protectionisme*.

For a time, most free-traders and protectionists focused their energies on fighting the socialist danger. In Bordeaux, the Association pour la Liberté des Échanges became an electoral committee, which organized the successful campaign of the 'party of order' (alliance of conservative factions) in the Gironde at the general election of May 1849.[152] In November 1848, the ADTN subsidized the diffusion of 10,000 copies of a popular edition of Thiers's anti-socialist pamphlet, *De la propriété*.[153] Even the more progressive Mulhouse committee of the ADTN contributed to anti-socialist propaganda, organizing an inquiry into the condition of Alsatian workers that highlighted the benevolence of their employers and a gradual improvement in their standard of living.[154] The ADTN also obtained, as a substitute for the Ateliers Nationaux, new bounties on exports of manufactured products in June 1848.[155] But, on the whole, the concern with international trade receded to the background in the early years of the Second Republic, with not a single parliamentary debate on customs legislation between 1848 and 1850.

Only in 1851, after the threat of social revolution had waned, did the controversy over commercial policy resurface. The resurgence was in part an echo of the first universal exhibition, conceived as a pageant to free trade and held in London between May and October.[156] In the midst of preparations for the exhibition, in February 1851, the cotton cloth printer Jean Dollfus submitted to his colleagues at the Société Industrielle de Mulhouse a radical proposal for the repeal of all prohibitions on manufactured products and the replacement of import duties on raw materials by an income tax.[157] Dollfus's plan, explicitly inspired by British fiscal and commercial policy in the 1840s, can be interpreted as yet another attempt to reverse Anglo-French divergence.[158] Most of the other Mulhouse manufacturers rejected it.[159] But the liberal *Journal des Débats* endorsed the

152 Charles, *La Révolution de 1848*, pp. 197–214.

153 Adolphe Thiers, *De la propriété*, ed. Comité Central de l'Association pour la Défense du Travail National (Paris, 1848), pp. i–iii; impression 6657 (21 November 1848), AN, F18* II 35.

154 Association pour la Défense du Travail National de Mulhouse, *Enquête industrielle dans les départements de l'Est* (Mulhouse, 1848).

155 *Le Moniteur Industriel*, 11 June 1848.

156 Jeffrey Auerbach, *The Great Exhibition of 1851: A Nation on Display* (New Haven, Conn., 1999), pp. 159–89; Kaiser, 'Cultural Transfers of Free Trade'; Whitney Walton, 'Political Economists and Specialized Industrialization during the French Second Republic, 1848–1852', *French History*, 3 (3) (1988): 293–311.

157 Jean Dollfus, *Communication sur l'opportunité d'une réforme dans le système protecteur des douanes* (Mulhouse, 1851).

158 Martin Daunton, *Trusting Leviathan: The Politics of Taxation in Britain, 1799–1914* (Cambridge, 2001), pp. 78–90; Nicolas Delalande, *Les Batailles de l'impôt: consentement et résistances de 1789 à nos jours* (Paris, 2011), pp. 63–8.

159 On reactions to Dollfus's proposals in Mulhouse, see AMM, 66TT 4, folders 8, 9 and 10.

proposal and gave it extensive publicity, contending that it was time to renounce the protective system, this legacy of 'the Convention and the [Napoleonic] Empire', 'two governments animated by the most furious bellicose passions', which symbolized the derailing of the 1789 Revolution from its initial liberal course.[160]

In June 1851, Pierre-Henri Sainte-Beuve, a moderate conservative deputy for the Oise, tabled an ambitious legislative proposal inspired by Dolfuss's project, consisting in the repeal of all duties on raw materials and foodstuffs and the replacement of prohibitions by *ad valorem* duties of 10 per cent on cotton and wool yarns and 20 per cent on all other manufactured products. In defence of his proposal, Sainte-Beuve eulogized the model of 'England, the motherland of free trade', solemnly read out passages of *The Wealth of Nations* and contended that commercial reform had helped to spare Britain from the revolutionary turmoil of 1848. Sainte-Beuve's proposal received the wholehearted support of a conservative representative for the Gironde, Jules Hovyn de Tranchère, who complained that 'for the past sixty years', the French had 'done too much politics' and 'not sufficiently concerned [themselves] with economic questions'.[161] Sainte-Beuve's proposal was an attack on the radical as well as protectionist tendencies of French liberalism.

Leading the opposition to the proposal, Thiers rejected this interpretation of French political and economic history as a failure to emulate Britain's more peaceful and prosperous course. Instead, he contended, it was Britain, with the adoption of free trade, which was overthrowing its aristocracy, fifty years after France: 'it is a part of the 1789 Revolution that has been accomplished in England'. The rise of democracy, Thiers continued, had different commercial implications, dependent on different social circumstances and national characters. In Britain, due to the concentration of land property in the hands of a few thousand families and a national preference for 'speciality' in production, it required the abolition of the Corn Laws and free trade. But in France, land belonged to 'the people' and millions of 'paysans': such a wide distribution of property was 'one of the most beautiful aspects of our situation, of our civilization'. Moreover, the French national character prized 'universality' above all else: 'this character of universality that can be found in our arts and literature also permeates our industries, we make everything'. The 'relative dearness' of French products resulting from protection was 'a condition

160 *Le Journal des Débats*, 22 March 1851.

161 Debates at the Legislative Assembly (26, 27 and 28 June 1851), *Le Moniteur Universel*, 27, 28 and 29 June 1851.

of universality' and social stability. As an alternative model to Britain better suited to France's new constitution, Thiers cited the American protectionist republic, which disproved 'the assimilation of political liberty and commercial liberty' made by some free-traders. He also condemned political economy as 'the most hollow, puerile and sometimes disastrous kind of literature'.[162]

The Legislative Assembly rejected Sainte-Beuve's proposal by 428 votes to 199.[163] At first sight, this division appeared to reflect the struggle between the party of order and the republican, democrat and socialist opposition. The bulk of the nays (388 out of 428) came from the ranks of the conservative majority. An unpublished caricature by Honoré Daumier, probably intended for the satirical *Charivari* and reproduced on the cover of this book, subscribed to this interpretation. In the cartoon, 'Commerce', in the shape of the god Mercury, walks on crutches into the Hôtel Dieu, Paris' main poorhouse, under the malevolent gaze of three individuals: Thiers, leader of the *orléaniste* royalists; Pierre-Antoine Berryer, leader of the *légitimiste* royalists; and 'Ratapoil', an imaginary character who embodied Bonapartist jingoism.[164] In contrast, out of the 199 deputies who voted for the proposal, 177 – including Alphonse de Lamartine, Félicité de Lamennais and Victor Hugo – sat on the left of the Assembly.

Yet such a reading oversimplified the connections between political and commercial opinions. The 1851 debate over the Sainte-Beuve proposal mainly took place within the conservative majority. Dollfus, Sainte-Beuve and Hovyn de Tranchère supported the party of order. The results of the division therefore rather highlighted the weakness of support for free trade among conservatives, with only twenty-two deputies – almost all elected in the Gironde and the Hérault, two wine-producing departments – who endorsed Sainte-Beuve's proposal. Moreover, the yes votes from the left did not necessarily mark an adhesion to the version of free trade defended by Sainte-Beuve. The republican *Charivari* regretted that during the parliamentary discussion, the left remained silent: 'What! On the generous

[162] Debates at the Legislative Assembly (27 and 28 June 1851), *Le Moniteur Universel*, 28 and 29 June 1851.

[163] Details of the Assembly's division in *Le Moniteur Universel*, 29 June 1851.

[164] Honoré Daumier, 'Le Commerce finissant, grâce à eux, par aller à l'hôpital', unpublished litograph, November 1851, Bibliothèque Nationale de France. The cartoon was part of a series by Daumier on 'Le Commerce', the publication of which was interrupted by the coup of 2 December 1851; see 'Le Commerce: Comment voulez-vous que je marche si vous me retenez toujours!' and 'Le Commerce: Quand donc, messieurs, finirez vous de jouer à ce jeu là … cela commence à m'ennuyer de payer tous les frais de la partie', *Le Charivari*, 25 November and 2 December 1851.

side [of the Assembly], thronged with representatives of new ideas, no one stood up to refute the retrograde theories of Mr Thiers; privileges and monopolies.'[165] The yes votes from the left were primarily a manifestation of personal hostility to Thiers, the leader of the majority. For instance, the socialist Vidal, who had ridiculed Bastiat's campaign in 1846, nonetheless voted for the Sainte-Beuve proposal. Despite the animus against Thiers, a significant minority of left-wing deputies (33 out of 195), including Edgar Quinet and Victor Schoelcher, rejected the Sainte-Beuve proposal. Alexandre Ledru-Rollin, the leader of the radical left in exile in London since 1849, had also recently pronounced himself against free trade in *De la décadence de l'Angleterre*: 'Starving one's own workers and ruining foreign nations, this is and will always be the fatal consequence of *libre-échange*', at least as long as 'a revolution of justice and equality' will not have overthrown aristocracies 'everywhere'.[166]

Thiers's speech in defence of protection represented the dominant view on the right. The ADTN sponsored its publication, both as a separate pamphlet entitled *Discours sur le régime commercial de la France*, of which 2,000 copies were printed, and as an addendum to a new edition of *De la propriété*.[167] Yet Thiers's advocacy of self-sufficiency was effective, at least in part, because of his insistence on the politically and socially progressive nature of protection in France. During the speech, his eulogy of the 1789 Revolution elicited strident protest from the *légitimiste* right. In a letter congratulating Thiers on 'this beautiful and frank exposition of the principles of Protection', Lord Derby, the leader of the protectionist Tories, also expressed some reservations on its 'democratic' undertones.[168] Thiers's contention that protection completed the 1789 Revolution may have irked some of his reactionary allies, but it confused and disarmed potential support for free trade on the left.

As a result, staunch support for free trade remained confined to a handful of conservatives who hoped that the material improvement brought about by the multiplication of commercial relations would tame revolutionary passions. The main response to Thiers's *Discours* did not emanate from the left but from Michel Chevalier, a supporter of Guizot before 1848 and a staunch adversary of socialism during the

165 *Le Charivari*, 29 June 1851.

166 Alexandre Ledru-Rollin, *De la décadence de l'Angleterre*, 2 vols. (Paris, 1850), vol. II, pp. 217–18.

167 Adolphe Thiers, *Discours sur le régime commercial de la France* (Paris, 1851) and *De la propriété* (Paris, [1851]); AN, F18*42, impression 5567 (8 July 1851).

168 Lord Derby to Thiers, 6 August 1851, BNF, NAF, MS 20618, fols. 92–5; on the reception of Thiers's defence of protection in Britain, see also Adolphe Thiers, *Speech of Mr Thiers on the Commercial Policy of France and in Opposition to the Introduction of Free Trade in France*, trans. M. de Saint-Felix (London, 1852).

Second Republic, who published an *Examen du système protecteur* at the beginning of 1852. Chevalier's conversion to free trade was recent.[169] In the 1830s, he expressed his dislike of 'the zealots of the absolute liberty of commerce' and in 1843 still insisted that French industries should not be left 'without any defences against the attacks of British factories'.[170] It was only in 1846 that Chevalier, as economics editor of *Le Journal des Débats*, declared the protective system to be an 'absurdity in the time we live in', considering it irremediably 'shaken' by Britain's adhesion to free trade. He joined the ALE but played a discreet role in its campaign, only contributing a short speech at its second meeting.[171] It is likely that Chevalier kept his distance from the campaign because he did not feel in agreement with the democratic language employed by Bastiat to promote free trade.

Tellingly, Chevalier's *Examen du système protecteur* never used the phrase *libre-échange*, employing instead the less radical sounding *liberté du commerce* or *liberté commerciale*. This systematic response to Thiers's *Discours* was published soon after Louis-Napoleon Bonaparte's coup of 2 December 1851, which suspended the constitution of 1848 and prepared the imperial restoration of December 1852. This context gave a special resonance to Chevalier's assertion in the *Examen* that 'political liberty' was only a secondary objective of human societies: it mattered only to a few educated individuals, while 'for the immense majority', it was 'a disturbance in their lives'. The principal 'goal' of society and 'distinctive sign' of civilization lay instead, he contended, in 'civil liberty', of which the freedoms to produce and exchange were essential components. In an echo of Say's attack on the daily nuisance of protection for ordinary Frenchmen in the *Cours complet*, Chevalier described the protective system as a constant violation of civil liberty:

> Let the French citizen consider all the articles that he wears, even his simplest clothes, or let him go on a tour of his bedroom: he is compelled, absolutely and physically compelled, despite his alleged liberty, to buy nine tenths of the common objects that he will find in France, even if his taste or preference for cheaper products would lead him to buy them from foreign countries.

[169] Jean-Baptiste Duroselle, 'Michel Chevalier et le libre-échange avant 1860', *Bulletin de la Société d'Histoire Moderne*, 2nd series, 5 (1956): 2–5.

[170] Michel Chevalier, *Lettres sur l'Amérique du Nord*, 2 vols. (Paris, 1836), vol. II, p. 207, and 'Comparaison des budgets de 1830 et de 1845', *Journal des Économistes*, 5 (1843): 345–89.

[171] *Le Journal des Débats*, 8 April 1846; Association pour la Liberté des Échanges, *Deuxième séance publique*, pp. 6–11.

In addition to improving the material 'well-being' of revolt-prone ordinary Frenchmen, the liberty of commerce would reduce the 'national hatreds' cultivated by the protectionists and risks of war in Europe.[172]

Chevalier's economic arguments in favour of free trade were not original. But his disregard for political liberty stood in sharp contrast with the involvement of Say and most of his followers in the struggles against illiberal regimes, from the Terror to the reactionary tendencies of Charles X. It may be construed as a radical interpretation of Say's insistence, in the famous preliminary discourse of his *Traité*, on the separation of political economy from politics. Chevalier's authoritarian conception of free trade was also combined with an unusual enthusiasm for overseas expansion. Bastiat opposed colonial ventures and castigated the colonization of Algeria as a formidable waste of taxpayers' money.[173] In contrast, since his exploration of North America in the mid 1830s, Chevalier frequently expressed his admiration for the colonial aptitude of the 'Anglo-Saxon race' and called on France and the 'Latin race' to step up its involvement in European efforts to bring civilization to the rest of the world. He reiterated his plea for overseas expansion in the conclusion of the *Examen*, in some considerations on the 1851 London exhibition. While in the eyes of many French observers the exhibition confirmed the dangerous superiority of British manufacturers over their Continental rivals, for Chevalier it manifested the superiority of the entire 'Western civilization' over its stagnant 'Muslim' and 'Eastern' worlds. France needed to emulate not British parliamentary institutions, the book argued, but British free trade in order to assuage the restless masses and participate in the global expansion of European industry.[174]

The triumph of democratic free trade in Britain precipitated its defeat in France after 1846. Whereas the *libre-échange* of Bastiat failed to enthuse public opinion, Anglophobic protectionism successfully laid claim to the social legacy of the 1789 Revolution. The rout of libre-échange also allowed Chevalier, after the 1848 Revolution, to promote another conception of free trade, inimical to political liberalism and concerned with the resurgence of French overseas expansion as well as the taming of domestic revolutionary tendencies. Although Chevalier's free trade enjoyed limited popular support, it exercised formidable influence on the

172 Michel Chevalier, *Examen du système commercial connu sous le nom de système protecteur* (Paris, 1852), pp. 9, 17–18, 61.

173 Bastiat, 'De l'influence des tarifs', p. 261; see also 'L'Algérie' in Frédéric Bastiat, *Ce qu'on voit et ce qu'on ne voit pas* (Paris, 1850), pp. 61–7.

174 Chevalier, *Examen*, pp. 271–319.

foreign, commercial and colonial policies of Napoleon III's authoritarian regime: the 1860 commercial treaty with Britain, instigated by Chevalier, constituted its triumph.[175] But the unpopularity of free trade and the Second Empire's adventurous foreign policy also helped Thiers become a leading figure of the liberal opposition in the 1860s and first President of the republican regime proclaimed in 1870.[176] The protectionist language elaborated by Thiers and others, combining conservative and democratic aspirations, would even dominate debates about international trade in subsequent decades, when nineteenth-century globalization reached its maximum intensity.

[175] Arthur Dunham, *The Anglo-French Treaty of Commerce and the Industrial Revolution in France* (Ann Arbor, Mich., 1930), pp. 29–63; Asaana Iliasu, 'The Cobden-Chevalier Commercial Treaty of 1860', *Historical Journal*, 14 (1) (1971): 67–98; on the conservative enthusiasm for economic reforms in the 1850s throughout Europe, see Christopher Clark, 'After 1848: The European Revolution in Government', *Transactions of the Royal Historical Society*, sixth series, 22 (2012): 171–97.

[176] Bury and Tombs, *Thiers*, pp. 166–74; Robert Schnerb, 'La Politique fiscale de Thiers', *Revue Historique*, 201 (1949): 186–211, esp. pp. 207–9, and 202 (1949): 184–220, esp. pp. 210–18.

Conclusion

The controversy on commerce after Napoleon appears to verify François Furet's contention that nineteenth-century French politics were primarily a contest over the legacy of the 1789 Revolution.[1] Under the Bourbon Restoration, royalist thinkers and politicians embraced restrictions on foreign trade as a means of reducing political restlessness, which the cross-border circulation of commodities was suspected of fostering. In response to these reactionary economics, Benjamin Constant and Jean-Baptiste Say, but also lesser known opponents of the regime such as Henri Fonfrède, endeavoured to rehabilitate *laissez-faire* in foreign trade as an indispensable complement of political liberty. The Revolution of 1830 did not only consecrate a liberal interpretation of the Constitutional Charter but also seemed to herald an era of commercial liberty. In 1831, the British radical Thomas Perronet Thompson thought it possible that 'the theory of Free Trade [might be] proclaimed in France first'; it 'would have', he added, 'a magical effect here [in Britain]'.[2]

Commercial liberalism in post-Napoleonic France cannot be reduced to an aspiration for economic growth and especially not modern industrial growth. In the eyes of its supporters, the repeal of restrictions on commercial exchanges was first and foremost designed to consolidate individual and political freedoms: for Constant, it formed a fundamental part of modern liberty; in the eyes of Say, it was a natural complement of the virtuous economic order he propounded; and, according to Fonfrède, it would reverse a regional concentration of wealth that endangered true liberty. Constant and Say expressed reservations about materialistic interpretations of liberty, while Fonfrède proved an eloquent adversary of the *industrialisme* of Henri de Saint-Simon and other advocates of economic growth at all costs. Despite some nuances between its proponents,

[1] Furet, *La Révolution*, vol. II.

[2] Thompson to Bowring, 6 December 1831, BJL, Thompson MSS, 4/4.

commercial liberalism after 1815 remained inspired by a republican concern for the equal treatment of responsible citizens by a regenerated state. It was often combined with an adhesion to a moderate interpretation of the Revolutionary legacy, oscillating between Feuillant constitutionalism and Girondin republicanism. Taking up the torch of commercial liberty and renaming it *libre-échange* in the 1840s, Frédéric Bastiat even offered a democratic and messianic reinterpretation inspired by the language of British free trade.

The defeat of free trade in France cannot be attributed to the aloofness of its advocates any more than to the cold materialism of their doctrines. On the contrary, the French free-traders proved as intent as their British counterparts upon popularizing liberal ideas about trade. Their polemical writings, from Say's *Catéchisme* and Charles Dupin's *Le Petit Commerçant* to Bastiat's weekly *Le Libre-échange*, were lucid and engaging. They experimented with new means of exercising pressure on the political process, from attempts to influence electoral results in the early 1830s to the raising of large funds to propagate *libre-échange* in the 1840s. The defeat of free trade resembles and needs to be explained in connection with the contemporary failure of the constitutional liberalism promoted by François Guizot and Alexis de Tocqueville. The triumph of free trade in Britain is acknowledged to have facilitated the intellectual hegemony and political dominance of liberalism in the Victorian era.[3] Conversely, its declining popularity in France after 1830 can be viewed as a contributing factor to the demise of the moderate, liberal and Anglophile interpretation of the 1789 Revolution.

The chief cause of the defeat of free trade lay in the emergence of an alternative interpretation of 1789 that stressed the necessity of protection in order to defend the economic and social legacy of the Revolution. This new protectionist discourse retained elements of mercantile jealousy, but it reformulated them in the language of industrialism. Adolphe Thiers sketched out this industrialist reformulation of jealousy after the 1830 Revolution, before his friend Friedrich List expounded it systematically in his *National System of Political Economy* a decade later. Yet the protectionist discourse also drew on an aspiration to self-sufficiency and social stability first formulated by royalist adversaries of the liberal order such as the royalist Alban de Villeneuve-Bargemont, an early propagator of the fear of pauperism. Polemicists such as the agronomist Mathieu de Dombasle and

[3] Eugenio Biagini, *Liberty, Retrenchment and Reform: Popular Liberalism in the Age of Gladstone, 1860–1880* (Cambridge, 1992); Jon Parry, *The Politics of Patriotism: English Liberalism, National Identity and Europe, 1830–1886* (Cambridge, 2006); Trentmann, *Free Trade Nation*.

the manufacturer Auguste Mimerel helped reconcile such anxieties with adhesion to the post-Revolutionary social and political order. Advocates of protection typically expressed nostalgia for the Napoleonic era, viewed as a successful ending and completion of the Revolution, rather than for the constitutional liberalism of 1789–92 or the experiment in moderate republicanism of the Directory in 1795–9. Protection also appealed, less consistently, to those who considered themselves the heirs of the Montagne of 1793–4, for example the radical republicans and socialists of the 1840s.

While the free-traders forged the concept of protectionism in such a way as to identify a common adversary, the advocates of protection employed Anglophobia to conceal the contradiction between industrialist jealousy and the aspiration to self-sufficiency. The notion of economic Anglophobia captures what might be considered as the essence of nineteenth-century French protectionism: a simultaneous fear of being surpassed by Britain, inspiring calls to emulate British industrialization, and of anglicization, that is to say of becoming more urbanized, more individualistic and more vulnerable to workers' revolts. In the wake of Revolutionary France's defeat against Britain, economic Anglophobia was more likely to be evoked by advocates of free trade such as Say or Constant. Yet, as the progress of political and commercial reform across the Channel improved the free-traders' perception of Britain, defenders of protection after 1830 exploited the antagonism towards Britain ruthlessly in their books, pamphlets, newspapers, posters and leaflets. Whether such Anglophobic rhetoric was affected or sincere, its repeated and intensive use suggests that it was not ineffective. Numerous testimonies, including by the protectionists' adversaries, confirm that it played a key role in galvanizing opposition to free trade.

Despite its reverence for Napoleon and xenophobic – almost exclusively anti-English – proclivities, protectionism after 1830 remained a liberal discourse. Thiers, Dombasle, Mimerel and Dupin were stalwart advocates of economic liberty within national borders. Unlike earlier defenders of the mercantile system, they also firmly supported the need for representative institutions. Their political liberalism even appeared at times more progressive than that of the free-traders, who feared that an extension of the franchise might further entrench protectionist dominance. Neither in theory nor in practice are nationalism and liberalism absolutely incompatible.[4] The wave of revolutions that started in Paris and swept across

[4] Will Kymlicka, *Politics in the Vernacular: Nationalism, Multiculturalism and Citizenship* (Oxford, 2001), pp. 203–20.

Europe in 1848 is often described as an eruption of nationalist liberalism. But in a longer term perspective, severing the ties between commercial and political liberty created new ideological possibilities and help set France on a political trajectory divergent from Britain's. Both Bonapartist authoritarian jingoism (before Napoleon III renounced his earlier support for protection at the end of the 1850s) and democratic conservative republicanism after 1870 proved congenial receptacles for the protectionist discourse elaborated under the July Monarchy.

The ephemeral victory of free trade under the Second Empire paradoxically confirmed the dissociation of commercial from political liberty. Michel Chevalier, the negotiator of the Anglo-French treaty of 1860, did not share the republican sympathies of earlier defenders of free trade. Instead, the ex-Saint-Simonian propounded an industrialist and imperialist conception of commercial liberty that was at best indifferent to political liberty. Chevalier's version of free trade may have enjoyed some support from Bonapartist officials and financial and export-oriented business interests, and it helped to justify the Second Empire's policy of global and often coercive interventionism, from Cochinchina to Mexico. But it remained unpopular among the *notables* and public opinion. The use of a treaty to circumvent the strident opposition of the usually servile Legislative Body (the regime's lower chamber) was castigated as a commercial *coup d'état* as scandalous as the political coup of 1851. When the British economist Nassau William Senior attended a party in the French capital thrown to celebrate the ratification of the treaty, he was dejected to find there, in addition to Richard Cobden and Michel Chevalier, only 'some fifty other free-traders, almost as many as Paris can furnish'.[5] The entry for *libre-échange* in Flaubert's *Dictionnaire des idées reçues*, a compendium of platitudes in the France of Napoleon III, read: 'Cause of all our difficulties.'[6]

Free trade is often cited as one of the factors that nurtured public disaffection with the Second Empire after 1860.[7] Conversely, it is probable that the return to protection after 1870 contributed to the enduring stability of the Third Republic, the regime which finally succeeded in ending the Revolution. Thiers, the regime's first president, increased tariffs

[5] Nassau William Senior, *Conversations with M. Thiers, M. Guizot, and Other Distinguished Persons, during the Second Empire*, 2 vols. (Edinburgh, 1878), vol. II, p. 314.

[6] Gustave Flaubert, *Dictionnaire des idées reçues: édition diplomatique des trois manuscrits de Rouen*, ed. Léa Laminiti (Naples and Paris, 1966), p. 97.

[7] Roger Price, *The French Second Empire: An Anatomy of Political Power* (Cambridge, 2001), pp. 230–40.

on agricultural goods and raw materials as early as 1872. Further tariff increases followed in 1881, 1885 and 1887. Protection from foreign competition was extended to Algeria in 1884 and France's new Indochinese colony in 1887. The return to protection culminated with the adoption of Jules Méline's 1892 tariff, which raised customs barriers on a wide range of primary and industrial products. Méline, a former ally of Jules Ferry, was a leading figure of conservative republicanism. His protectionist measures and policy of appeasement with the Catholic Church facilitated the acceptance of the republican regime by the right, symbolized by the *Ralliement* of Catholics in the 1890s.[8]

Méline's insistence on the need to promote agricultural as well as industrial growth recalled the support his fellow Lorrain, Mathieu de Dombasle, showed for self-sufficiency six decades earlier. However, two notable differences reflected global political and economic transformations since the 1830s: instead of a Germany now perceived as overly reliant on industrial exports, Méline upheld the republican USA as a model of balanced economic development, where high tariffs ensured the equal dynamism of agriculture and manufacturing; and, unlike Dombasle, who opposed overseas ventures, Méline supported the colonial expansion initiated by Ferry in the 1880s, but in order to provide new lands for French agriculturalists, in a perspective of imperial autarky, rather than to facilitate the intensification of global commercial exchanges. Méline noted the resemblance between his views and Joseph Chamberlain's contemporary scheme of imperial preference, but he preferred to compare France's colonial demesne to the prosperous agricultural West of America.[9] As in the 1840s, the progressive elements of the protectionist discourse in the 1890s disarmed the potential opposition of the radical left. Jean Jaurès, among others, rejected free trade on the grounds that it would mainly benefit large capitalists, even if he only offered qualified support for the regime's protectionist policies.[10]

Protectionism was part of the great compromise of the 1880s that brought French political instability to an end until the mid twentieth

[8] Smith, *Tariff Reform in France*, pp. 181–8, 200–1; Eugen O. Golob, *The Méline Tariff: French Agriculture and Nationalist Economic Policy* (New York, 1944), esp. pp. 206–15; Herman Lebovics, *The Alliance of Iron and Wheat in the Third French Republic, 1860–1914: Origins of the New Conservatism* (Baton Rouge, La., 1988); Rita Aldenhoff-Hübinger, *Agrarpolitik und Protektionismus: Deutschland und Frankreich im Vergleich, 1879–1914* (Göttingen, 2002), esp. pp. 132–46; Pierre Rosanvallon, *La Société des égaux* (Paris, 2011), pp. 183–93.

[9] Jules Méline, *Le Retour à la terre et la surproduction industrielle* (Paris, 1905), esp. pp. 259–66 and 274–6.

[10] See writings and speeches collected in Jean Jaurès, *À qui profite le protectionnisme?*, ed. Igor Martinache (Paris, 2012).

century. It is also possible to interpret France's strong support for European integration in its first decades, when it relied on a common external tariff and high barriers on agricultural imports, as an attempt to perpetuate this model of adaptation to globalization after the end of colonial empires. One may even consider the practical and, to a lesser extent, rhetorical abandonment of protectionism as one of the factors behind France's political and economic malaise since the 1980s.

However, the significance of French debates about commerce after 1815 extends beyond modern French political, economic or imperial history. From the perspective of global economic history, it may be considered as one of the main matrices of recurring backlashes against modern globalization, including the extensively studied rise of protectionist sentiments and policies in the years 1870–1914. At first, the fragile victory of free trade under the Second Empire facilitated the lowering of trade barriers throughout the Europe in the 1860s. Just as the 1860 commercial treaty was instigated by the regime of Napoleon III rather than Britain, it was France that took the lead in concluding further treaties with most Continental powers in subsequent years, ushering in a brief era of European and almost global free trade until the 1870s.[11] Conversely, the abandonment of free trade in France coincided with the adoption of protection by all major independent states, with the notable exception of Britain, and even autonomous British dominions in the late nineteenth century. The commercial policies of Germany and the USA, the two rising economic and geopolitical powers of the age, no doubt played a more important direct role than French policies in inspiring the global spread of protectionism after 1880. Yet *fin-de-siècle* German and American protectionism often reproduced, consciously or not, several features of the earlier French protectionist discourse, including the intensive use of Anglophobic rhetoric to conceal the divergent motives and objectives of protectionist interests.[12]

The impact of tariffs or their repeal on economic development, in France and elsewhere in the nineteenth century, remains disputed.[13] In any event, it

[11] Peter T. Marsh, *Bargaining on Europe: Britain and the First Common Market* (New Haven, Conn., 1999).

[12] Charles E. McClelland, *The German Historians and England: A Study in Nineteenth-Century Views* (Cambridge, 1971), Chapter 9; Grimmer-Solem, *The Rise of Historical Economics*, esp. pp. 118–26; Richard F. Bensel, *The Political Economy of American Industrialization* (Cambridge, 2000), Chapter 7.

[13] The classical defence of protection in the nineteenth century is Bairoch, *Commerce extérieur*; for a review of the available evidence and literature, which tends to contradict Bairoch's thesis, see Jean-Perre Dormois, *La Défense du travail national? L'Incidence du protectionnisme sur l'industrie en Europe (1870–1914)* (Paris, 2009).

appears to have been exaggerated by contemporaries. In the case of France, for instance, despite the prevalence of protectionism, the share of imports in gross domestic product rose from 3 per cent in 1820 to 17 per cent in 1910.[14] The decline in transport costs and the increase in the circulation of information were much more potent economic factors than low or high customs duties, explaining why globalization continued to accelerate in a context of rising tariffs after 1870.[15] The significance of free trade and protectionism lay in their political rather than their economic impact. They are best understood as democratic or populist reconfigurations of earlier patterns of thought about the links between commerce and politics, which served to express feelings of hope or anxiety about the pace of nineteenth-century globalization.

This analysis of the emergence of a protectionist discourse in post-Napoleonic France should also be viewed as a contribution to the intellectual history of globalization. Efforts to historicize the concept of globalization have played an important part in the development of various forms of world history. Similarly, the history of how contemporaries themselves apprehended the intensification of economic and cultural exchanges appears as a promising avenue of the international or transnational turn of intellectual history.[16] The awareness of the global emerged in the late eighteenth century.[17] But it became pervasive in the aftermath of the age of global revolutions, owing to an abrupt acceleration in the progress of transport and communications. Thus, in 1832, Michel Chevalier could imagine a world in which, thanks to railways, one could depart from Le Havre in the morning, have lunch in Paris and catch in Toulon a steamboat bound to Algiers or Alexandria in the evening. In such a world, he added, thanks to the telegraph, 'vast nations' would become 'moderately sized provinces' and existing nation-states would be able to govern entire 'continents'.[18]

Globalization is usually considered, in the first instance, as an economic phenomenon, with countless political, social and cultural

[14] Toutain, 'Les Structures du commerce extérieur', p. 56.

[15] Findlay and O'Rourke, *Power and Plenty*, pp. 396–407.

[16] On the utility and potential pitfalls of an intellectual history of globalization, see Samuel Moyn and Andrew Sartori, 'Approaches to Global Intellectual History', in Samuel Moyn and Andrew Sartori (eds.), *Global Intellectual History* (New York, 2013), pp. 3–30, esp. pp. 17–24; on the variety of possible approaches to global intellectual history, see also Shruti Kapila, 'Global Intellectual History and the Indian Political', in Darrin M. McMahon and Samuel Moyn (eds.), *Rethinking Modern European Intellectual History* (Oxford, 2014), pp. 253–74.

[17] Armitage, *Foundations*, p. 37; this early awareness was not confined to prominent thinkers, as shown by Emma Rothschild, *The Inner Life of Empires: An Eighteenth-Century History* (Princeton, NJ, 2011).

[18] Michel Chevalier, *Système de la Méditerranée* (Paris, 1832), pp. 37–8; on time, space and global political imagination, see Duncan Bell, *The Idea of Greater Britain: Empire and the Future of World Order* (Princeton, NJ, 2007), Chapter 3.

consequences. Debates about economics, and in particular about the circulation of commodities, capital, entrepreneurs and workers therefore constitute a privileged field of enquiry for the intellectual history of globalization. Analysing cross-border exchanges of ideas about these circulations may also help attenuate the frequent bias in intellectual history, especially among specialists of political economy, in favour of the production of ideas and at the expense of mediation and reception. Such a supply-side approach to the history of economic ideas prevails equally in works that express sympathy for neo-classical or Marxian economics, perhaps not coincidentally since these schools of economic thought pay limited attention to the role of demand in economic processes.[19] Yet contemporary go-betweens and propagators of ideas about the intensification of transnational exchanges in the nineteenth century were keenly aware of the necessity of adapting their message to diverse audiences and of eliciting and sustaining demand for their ideas. Friedrich List, for instance, reformulated his message ceaselessly, combining his defence of industrialist jealousy with Jacksonian populism in America, Thiers's historicism in France and support for national unification in Germany. His adversary Bowring described his own work of propaganda as consisting in making free-trade ideas 'vibrate' across entire regions or nations. Bastiat stressed that the dissemination of political and economic ideas required 'material vehicles' and therefore financial support.

The analogy with economic processes is not perfect, because the concept of demand for ideas is infinitely more elusive than the concept of demand for commodities or capital. Drawing on Bowring's contemporary image of vibrations, it may be more pertinent to try and interrogate what can be described as the resonance of ideas. The concept of resonance appears compatible and even complementary with contextualism, since the discursive and political context plays a determining role in explaining the resonance of certain ideas. It also allows for a more complex rendering of processes of dissemination than the discredited diffusionism often assumed by practitioners of supply-side intellectual history: instead of trickling down, concepts are echoed and refashioned, in a constant dialogue with local, regional and national preoccupations.[20] Resonance does

[19] As an example of a neo-classical approach, see Douglas Irwin, *Against the Tide: An Intellectual History of Free Trade* (Princeton, NJ, 1996); for a Marxian perspective, see Andrew Sartori, 'Global Intellectual History and the History of Political Economy', in Samuel Moyn and Andrew Sartori (eds.), *Global Intellectual History* (New York, 2013), pp. 110–33.

[20] On the resonance of liberalism outside Europe, see Christopher A. Bayly, *Recovering Liberties: Indian Thought in the Age of Liberalism and Empire* (Cambridge, 2011).

not imply quantification, but it requires paying greater attention to the material aspects of intellectual contests, from the income that contestants derived from their engagement to the economics of publishing books, pamphlets or newspapers. Digital tools will also offer new means of assessing the resonance of certain ideas, or at least certain words. For example, Google Ngram shows that the frequency of the phrase *travail national* in French-language printed works multiplied fifteenfold between 1840 and 1848, by which date it was nearly seven times more frequent than *libre-échange* (or *libre échange*) and two-thirds as frequent as the phrase 'free trade' in 1846 – its year of peak usage in the nineteenth century – in British English.[21]

Another advantage of resonance, well illustrated by the case of free trade, is that it makes room for a plurality of echoes, forestalling the temptation – particularly acute if one is concerned with the intellectual history of present-day concepts such as globalization – of linear teleology. The resonance of free trade, following its triumph in Britain, was global. Yet it was not a process of uniform diffusion, only halted or slowed by archaic or atavistic forms of resistance. The protectionist discourse that emerged in France after 1830 was not only a rejection of free trade but also a reinvention, mostly carried out by supporters of a liberal order, of the political and social significance of commerce. British free trade did not merely fail to spread to France. Instead, its very triumph in Britain contributed to the decline of liberal ideas about trade and the rise of protectionist sentiments across the Channel. The concept of resonance may also facilitate the adoption of transnational perspectives, because the format of actual echo chambers often differed from the conventional units of analysis such as the nation or Europe. Loud echoes endorsing British free trade can be detected in several regions or sections of existing nation-states, usually around a port city with a hinterland rich in primary products: Bordeaux and its wine (as seen in this book), but also Charleston and its cotton or Hamburg and its grain. Echoes subsequent to the eruption of protectionism in France can be identified not only in Germany and the USA in the second half of the nineteenth century, but also in Japan, Latin America, India and China in the twentieth century. Of course, the nineteenth-century controversy over free trade has resonated across time as well as space, and its echoes are still perceptible in current debates about globalization.

21 Google Ngram Viewer (https://books.google.com/ngrams, accessed 14 September 2014).

Bibliography

Archives

Archives Nationales (Pierrefitte-sur-Seine [Paris]):

C and CC (Assemblées parlementaires)
F7 (Police)
F12 (Commerce et Industrie)
F18 (Librairie, Imprimerie, Presse, Censure)

Archives des Affaires Etrangères (La Courneuve [Paris]):

Fonds divers, Ameriques
Mémoires et documents, Angleterre

Centre des Archives d'Outre-Mer (Aix-en-Provence):

11COL (Correspondance du ministère des Colonies)
CC9 (Saint-Domingue)

Archives des Douanes (Bordeaux):

2 B, 3 B (Registres d'ordres)

Institut de France (Paris):

Concours de l'Académie des Sciences Morales et Politiques
Procès-verbaux de l'Académie des Sciences Morales et Politiques

Bibliothèque Nationale de France (Paris):

Nouvelles Acquisitions Françaises, Jean-Baptiste Say MSS
Nouvelles Acquisitions Françaises, Adolphe Thiers MSS

Paris, Fondation Dosne-Thiers:

Fonds Adolphe Thiers

Archives Départementales de la Côte d'Or (Dijon):

34J (Fonds Théophile Foisset)

Archives Départementales de la Gironde (Bordeaux):

02/081 (Chambre de commerce de Bordeaux)
5P (Douanes)

Archives Départementales de l'Hérault (Montpellier):

5P (Douanes)

Archives Départementales de la Meurthe-et-Moselle (Nancy):

P1, P8 (Douanes)

Archives Départementales de la Moselle (Metz):

6P (Douanes)

Archives Départementales de la Nièvre (Nevers):

4J, 20J (Fonds Dupin)

Archives Départementales du Nord (Lille):

76J, 79J (Association pour la Défense du Travail National, Chambre consultative de Roubaix)
P52 (Douanes)

Archives Départementales du Bas-Rhin (Strasbourg):

79J (Chambre de commerce de Strasbourg)
P312-P319 (Douanes)

Archives Départementales du Haut-Rhin (Colmar):

5P (Douanes)

Archives Départementales du Var (Draguignan):

2U 180 (Justice, cour prévôtale)

Archives Municipales de Bordeaux (Bordeaux):

Fonds Famille Guestier
Fonds Jacques-Henri Wustemberg

Bibliothèque Municipale de Bordeaux (Bordeaux):

MS 1085–96, MS 1960–4 (Fonds Henri Fonfrède)

Archives Municipales de Mulhouse (Mulhouse):

66TT (Fonds Jean and Émile Dollfus)

Centre Rhénan d'Archives et de Recherches Economiques (Mulhouse):

Chambre de Commerce de Mulhouse
Société Industrielle de Mulhouse

The National Archives (Kew [London]):

FO (Foreign Office)
T (Treasury)

British Library (London):

Auckland MSS

Bodleian Library (Oxford):

Clarendon MSS

Brynmore Jones Library (Hull):

Thomas Perronet Thompson MSS

University College London (London):

Ogden MSS

Houghton Library (Cambridge, Mass.):

MS 1247 (letters to John Bowring)

Stadtarchiv Reutlingen (Reutlingen, Germany):

Friedrich List MSS

Periodicals, including newspapers

The place of publication is Paris unless otherwise stated.

Allgemeine Zeitung (Augsburg)
Das Zollvereinsblatt (Stuttgart)
Journal d'Agriculture et des Manufactures des Pays-Bas (Brussels)
Journal des Économistes
L'Atelier
La Démocratie Pacifique
L'Époque
L'Européen, Journal des Sciences Morales et Économiques

La Fraternité
La Gazette de France
La Guienne (Bordeaux)
La Presse
La Quotidienne
La Réforme Industrielle
La Tribune
Le Charivari
Le Commerce
Le Constitutionnel
Le Courrier de Bordeaux (Bordeaux)
Le Courrier de la Gironde (Bordeaux)
Le Courrier Français
Le Globe
L'Indicateur Bordelais
L'Industriel Alsacien
Le Journal de Paris
Le Journal des Débats
Le Journal du Commerce
Le Libre-échange
Le Mémorial Bordelais (Bordeaux)
Le Moniteur Industriel
Le Moniteur Universel
Le National
Le Populaire
Le Réformateur
Le Siècle
Le Spectateur de Dijon (Dijon)
Le Temps
L'Univers
Neckar Zeitung (Stuttgart)
Revue Britannique
Revue des Deux Mondes
Revue Encyclopédique
Revue Indépendante
Revue Mensuelle d'Économie Politique
Revue Nationale: Recueil d'Économie Politique
The Economist (London)
The Times (London)
Westminster Review (London)

Online resources

Bibliothèque Nationale de France, Catalogue BN-Opale plus (www.bnfol.fr).
Google Books, works in French (http://books.google.fr).
Google Ngram Viewer (https://books.google.com/ngrams).
Institut National de la Statistique et des Études Économiques, 'Recensements de 1851 à 1921' (www.insee.fr).
Oxford English Dictionary (www.oed.com).
The Times Digital Archive, 1785–2008 (http://gale.cengage.co.uk/times.aspx).
The Transatlantic Slave Trade Database (www.slavevoyages.org).

Official publications

Académie des Sciences Morales et Politiques, *Concours de l'Académie* (Paris, 1901).
Bowring, John, *Second Report on the Commercial Relations between France and Great Britain* (London, 1835).
Bowring, John and George Villiers, *First Report on the Commercial Relations between France and Great Britain* (London, 1834).
Mavidal, Jérôme and Émile Colombey (eds.), *Archives parlementaires*, 126 vols. (Paris, 1862–1912).
Ministère du Commerce, *Enquête relative à diverses prohibitions*, 3 vols. (Paris, 1835).
Enquête relative à l'établissement demandé d'entrepôts de douanes (Paris, 1831).
Enquête sur les fers (Paris, 1829).
Enquête sur les fils et tissus de lin et de chanvre (Paris, 1838).
Enquête sur les sucres (Paris, 1829).
Statistique de la France, 10 vols. (Paris, 1838).
Parliament, *Hansard's Parliamentary Debates*, 3rd Series, 156 vols. (London, 1830–91).

Primary printed sources

Anisson-Dupéron, Alexandre, *Essai sur les traités de commerce de Methuen et de 1786 dans leurs rapports avec la liberté commerciale* (Paris, 1847).
[Anon.] ('A. B.'), *Question des sucres examiné d'un point de vue moral* (Douai, 1843).
[Anon.] ('A. G.'), *Réfutation du mémoire intitulé: mémoire sur la prohibition des mousselines* (Paris, 1816).
[Anon.] ('A. G.* and A. P.*'), *De l'influence désastreuse de la fraude sur l'industrie française et sur les finances de l'État* (Paris, 1816).
[Anon.] ('G.'), *De l'influence du système maritime de l'Angleterre sur le repos de l'Europe, son commerce et son industrie* (Paris, 1815).
[Anon.] ('L.N.D.'), *Observations sur le traité de commerce projeté entre la France et l'Angleterre* (Paris, 1814).
[Anon.] *Compte-rendu des séances de l'assemblée générale des départements vinicoles* (Bordeaux, 1843).

[Anon.] *De l'influence de la démocratie dans les questions du libre-échange et de l'octroi* (Lyon, 1847).
[Anon.] *Mémoire des manufacturiers de coton de Paris* (Paris, 1817).
[Anon.] *Mémoire sur la prohibition des mousselines* (Paris, 1816).
[Anon.] *Observations à Messieurs les députés contre les articles 59 et suivants du titre 6 de la loi sur les douanes* (Paris, 1816).
[Anon.] *Observations sur la question des sucres* (Valenciennes, 1839).
[Anon.] *Paroles d'un négociant* (Paris, 1834).
[Anon.] *Le Pour et le contre* (Paris, 1817).
[Anon.] *Pétition des manufacturiers, banquiers, négociants et commerçants de la place de Paris* (Paris, 1827).
[Anon.] *Pétition des propriétaires de vignes et des négociants en vins du département des Bouches du Rhône* (Marseille, 1829).
[Anon.] *Pétition du commerce de Nantes à MM. les membres de la chambre des députés* (Nantes, 1831).
[Anon.] *Pétition du commerce du Havre à la chambre des députés contre l'établissement projeté des entrepôts intérieurs* (Le Havre, 1831).
[Anon.] *Pétition par les propriétaires du vignoble blanc des coteaux de la Loire* (Paris, 1828).
[Anon.] *Questions sur les prohibitions* (Paris, 1817).
[Anon.] *Réflexions sur l'article 61 du projet de loi de budget de 1816* (Paris, 1816).
[Anon.] *Réflexions sur les articles 58, 59, 61, 62 et 63 du projet de loi sur le budget de 1816* (Paris, 1816).
Arlès-Dufour, François-Barthélémy and André Dervieu, *Un mot sur les fabriques étrangères de soieries* (Lyon, 1834).
Association Belge pour la Liberté Commerciale, *Congrès des économistes de Bruxelles* (Brussels, 1847).
Association pour la Défense du Travail National, *Examen des théories du libre-échange et des résultats du système protecteur* (Paris, 1847).
Réunion annuelle du comité central: séance du 17 janvier 1848 (Paris, 1848).
Association pour la Défense du Travail National de Mulhouse *Association pour la Défense du Travail National, formée à Mulhouse le 4 novembre 1846* (Mulhouse, 1848).
Enquête industrielle dans les départements de l'Est (Mulhouse, 1848).
Première publication (Mulhouse, 1846).
Réunion du 11 novembre 1848 (Mulhouse, 1848).
Association pour la Liberté des Échanges, *Banquet offert à Richard Cobden* (Paris,1846).
Cinquième séance publique (Paris, 1847).
Déclaration (Paris, 1846).
Deuxième séance publique (Paris, 1846).
Première séance publique (Paris, 1846).
Subsistances publiques: la vie à bon marché (Paris, [1848]).
Association pour la Liberté des Échanges de Bordeaux, *Fondation de la société, 23 février 1846: Manifeste* (Bordeaux, 1846).
Association pour la Liberté des Échanges de Lyon, *Liberté des échanges: association lyonnaise* (Lyon, 1846).

Liberté des échanges: le libre-échange à Lyon (Lyon, 1847).
Association de Nantes pour la Défense du Travail National, *Réforme commerciale* (Nantes, [1847]).
Audouin, Xavier, *Du commerce maritime, de son influence sur la richesse et la force des États* (Paris, [1800]).
[Audouin, Xavier], *Quelques idées sur les prohibitions commerciales* (Paris, 1816).
Balzac, Honoré de, *La Comédie humaine*, ed. Pierre-Georges Castex, 11 vols. (Paris, 1978).
Barrault, Emile (ed.), *Religion saint-simonienne: recueil des prédications*, 2 vols. (Paris, 1832).
Bastiat, Frédéric, *Ce qu'on voit et ce qu'on ne voit pas* (Paris, 1850).
Cobden et la Ligue (Paris, 1845).
Œuvres complètes de Frédéric Bastiat, ed. Prosper Paillotet and Robert de Fontenay, 2nd edn, 6 vols. (Paris, 1862–4).
Protectionisme et communisme (Paris, 1849).
Réflexions sur les pétitions de Bordeaux, Le Havre et Lyon concernant les douanes (Mont-de-Marsan, 1834).
Sophismes économiques (Paris, 1846).
Bénard, M., *De la liberté du commerce* (Arras, 1834).
Bentham, Jeremy, *Observations on the Restrictive and Prohibitory Commercial System*, ed. John Bowring (London, 1821).
Béranger, Pierre-Jean de, *Chansons nouvelles et dernières* (Paris, 1833).
Bigot de Morogues, Pierre, *Du paupérisme, de la mendicité, et des moyens d'en prévenir les funestes effets* (Paris, 1834).
Blanc, Louis, *Organisation du travail*, 2nd edn (Paris, 1841).
Blanqui, Adolphe, *Algérie: Rapport sur la situation économique de nos possessions dans le nord de l'Afrique* (Paris, 1840).
Cours d'économie industrielle, 3 vols. (Paris, 1837–9).
Précis d'économie politique (Paris, 1826).
Voyage d'un jeune français en Angleterre et en Ecosse (Paris, 1824).
Bonald, Louis de, *Œuvres complètes de M. de Bonald*, ed. Abbé Migne, 3 vols. (Paris, 1864).
Bonaparte, Napoléon-Louis, *Analyse de la question des sucres* (Paris, 1842).
Des idées napoléoniennes (Paris, 1839).
Extinction du paupérisme (Paris, 1844).
Boucher de Perthes, Jacques, *Opinion de M. Christophe sur les prohibitions et la liberté du commerce*, 2nd edn (Paris, 1831).
Petit Glossaire; traduction de quelques mots financiers; esquisses de mœurs administratives, 2 vols. (Paris, 1835).
Bowring, John, *Details of the Arrest, Imprisonment and Liberation of an Englishman by the Bourbon Government of France* (London, 1823).
Buckingham, James S., *Discours préliminaire prononcé à l'Athénée à l'occasion d'un cours sur les Indes orientales*, trans. Benjamin Laroche (Paris, 1830).
Buret, Eugène, *De la misère des classes laborieuses en Angleterre et en France*, 2 vols. (Paris, 1840).

Cabet, Etienne, *Voyage en Icarie* (Paris and Geneva, 1979).
Carey, Henry, *Commerce, Christianity and Civilization versus British Free Trade* (Philadelphia, Pa., 1876).
Letters to the President on the Foreign and Domestic Policy of the Union (Philadelphia, Pa., 1858).
Chambre de Commerce de Bordeaux, *Des intérêts maritimes et de la protection* (Bordeaux, 1847).
Chambre de Commerce de Dunkerque, *Lettre sur la question du libre-échange* (Dunkerque, 1847).
Chambre de Commerce de Nantes, *Un dernier mot sur les entrepôts intérieurs* (Nantes, 1831).
Chambre de Commerce de Rouen, *Mémoire sur la nécessité de maintenir le système prohibitif et sur les inconvénients d'un traité de commerce avec l'Angleterre* (Rouen, 1814).
Chambre de Commerce de Strasbourg, *Pétition aux fins de l'établissement du transit général par la France et subsidiairement du transit de l'Allemagne en Suisse* (Strasbourg, 1817).
Chambre de Commerce de Toulouse, *Lettre sur la question du libre-échange* (Toulouse, 1847).
Chambre Consultative des Arts et Manufactures de Bar-le-Duc, *Délibérations* (Bar-le-Duc, [1846]).
Chapelle, Victor, *Pétition adressées à MM: les membres de la chambre des députés relativement à la filature du lin* (Paris, [1841]).
Chaptal, Jean-Antoine, *De l'industrie française* (Paris, 1819).
Des douanes et des prohibitions (Philadelphia, Pa., 1819).
Chateaubriand, François-René de, *Mémoires d'outre-tombe*, 12 vols. (Paris, 1849–50).
Chedeaux, Pierre-Joseph, *Lettre sur le transit et l'entrepôt* (Paris, 1828).
Chevalier, Michel, *Cours d'économie politique*, 3 vols. (Paris, 1842–50).
Examen du système commercial connu sous le nom de système protecteur (Paris, 1852).
Lettres sur l'Amérique du Nord, 2 vols. (Paris, 1836).
Système de la Méditerranée (Paris, 1832).
Cobbett, William, *Rural Rides*, 3rd edn, 2 vols. (London, 1885).
Cobden, Richard, *The European Diaries of Richard Cobden, 1846–1849*, ed. Miles Taylor (Aldershot, 1994).
Comité des Lins, *Compte-rendu* (Paris, 1845).
Des modifications de tarif réclamés par la filature du lin et la fabrication des toiles en France (Paris, [1838]).
Réclamations de l'industrie française des toiles de lin et de chanvre (Paris, 1842).
Résumé de la question des fils et des toiles de lin et de chanvre (Paris, [1838]).
Commission d'Agriculture de Draguignan, *Libre-échange: défense du travail national* (Draguignan, 1847).
Commission Commerciale de Bordeaux, *Adresse des négociants de Bordeaux aux chambres législatives* (Bordeaux, 1834).

Congrès Agricole, *Protection du travail national* (Amiens, 1846).
Considérant, Victor, *De la politique générale et du rôle de la France en Europe* (Paris, 1840).
Projet de loi sur les sucres: un enseignement donné au pays (Paris, 1840).
Constant, Benjamin, *Commentaire sur l'ouvrage de Filangieri*, 2 vols. (Paris, 1822–4).
Écrits politiques, ed. Marcel Gauchet (Paris, 1997).
Coquelin, Charles, *Essai sur la filature mécanique de lin et de chanvre* (Paris, 1840).
(ed.), *Dictionnaire d'économie politique* (Paris, 1854).
Coudert, François, *Recueil d'économie politique* (Bordeaux, 1833).
Defitte, Xavier and Ernest Feray, *Nécessité d'une prompte et efficace modification à notre tarif de douanes, relativement aux fils et aux toiles de lin et de chanvre* (Corbeil, 1838).
Delaunay, Jean-Baptiste, *Lettre à M. Tanneguy Duchâtel* (Le Havre, 1834).
Dollfus, Jean, *Communication sur l'opportunité d'une réforme dans le système protecteur des douanes* (Mulhouse, 1851).
Droz, Joseph, *Économie politique, ou principes de la science des richesses* (Paris, 1829).
Dubuc, Jean-Baptiste, *Le Pour et le contre sur un objet de grande discorde et d'importance majeure* (London, 1784).
Duchâtel, Tanneguy, *La Charité dans ses rapports avec l'état moral et le bien-être des classes inférieures* (Paris, 1829).
[Duchâtel, Tanneguy], *Mémoire sur le système actuel des douanes* (Paris, 1829).
Ducoudray-Bourgault, Henry, *Réflexions d'un ancien commerçant sur l'industrie agricole, commerciale et manufacturière et particulièrement sur l'ouvrage récemment publié par M. de Dombasle* (Nantes, 1834).
Dupin, Charles, *Appel au bon sens* (Paris, 1843).
Défense du système protecteur de la production française et de l'industrie nationale (Paris, 1836).
Effets de l'enseignement populaire sur les prospérités de la France (Paris, 1826).
Faits et calculs (Paris, 1837).
Forces commerciales et productives de la France, 2 vols. (Paris, 1827).
Mémoire adressé par le conseil des délégués des colonies aux ministres du roi sur la question des sucres (Paris, 1842).
Observations exposées au Conseil Général d'Agriculture (Paris, 1842).
Le Petit Commerçant (Paris, 1828).
Tableau des intérêts de la France (Paris, 1836).
La Vérité des faits sur les cultures comparées des colonies et de la métropole (Paris, 1842).
Voyages dans la Grande-Bretagne, 5 vols. (Paris, 1821–4).
Estancelin, Louis, *De l'importation en France des fils et tissus de lin et de chanvre d'Angleterre* (Paris, 1842).
Faucher, Léon, *Études sur l'Angleterre*, 2 vols. (Paris, 1845).
Léon Faucher [correspondence and parliamentary speeches], 2 vols. (Paris, 1867).
L'Union du midi (Paris, 1842).

Feray, Ernest, *Réponse sur les négociations commerciales ouvertes entre la France et l'Angleterre* (Paris, 1839).
Ferrier, François, *De l'enquête commerciale* (Paris and Lille, 1829).
De l'entrepôt de Paris: second mémoire (Paris and Lille, 1828).
Du gouvernement considéré dans ses rapports avec le commerce (Paris, 1805).
Du gouvernement dans ses rapports avec le commerce, 2nd edn (Paris, 1821).
Du gouvernement dans ses rapports avec le commerce: de l'administration commerciale opposée aux économistes du 19e siècle, 3rd edn (Paris, 1822).
Du système maritime et commercial de l'Angleterre au XIXe siècle (Paris, 1829).
Mémoire sur la demande d'un entrepôt de denrées coloniales à Paris (Paris and Lille, 1819).
Fichte, Johann Gottlieb, *L'État commercial fermé*, trans. Jean Gibelin (Paris, 1940).
Fiévée, Joseph and François Ferrier, *Correspondance de Joseph Fiévée et de François Ferrier (1803–1837)*, ed. Etienne Hofmann (Bern and Paris, 1994).
Flaubert, Gustave, *Correspondance*, ed. Jean Bruneau, 4 vols. (Paris, 1991–7).
Dictionnaire des idées reçues: édition diplomatique des trois manuscrits de Rouen, ed. Léa Laminiti (Naples and Paris, 1966).
[Fonfrède, Henri], *Observations à l'appui des réclamations du commerce de Bordeaux sur le privilège colonial et sur la surtaxe des sucres étrangers* (Bordeaux, 1832).
Fonfrède, Henri, *La Liberté protège mieux que la prohibition* (Paris, 1835).
Œuvres de Henri Fonfrède, ed. Charles-Alcée Campan, 10 vols. (Bordeaux, 1844–7).
Frères, Adam et al., *Prohibition des produits des fabriques étrangères, répression de la fraude* (Paris, 1814).
Ganilh, Charles, *Théorie de l'économie politique fondée sur les faits résultant des statistiques de la France et de l'Angleterre*, 2 vols. (Paris, 1815).
Garnier, Joseph, *Eléments de l'économie politique* (Paris, 1846).
Goethe, Johann Wolfgang, *Gedenkausgabe der Werke, Briefe und Gespräche*, ed. Ernst Beutler, 27 vols. (Zurich, 1949–77).
Goldenberg, Gustave, *Libre-échange et protection* (Paris, 1847).
Grar, Edouard, *Question des sucres* (Valenciennes, 1843).
Guépin, Ange, *Traité d'économie sociale* (Paris, 1833).
Guillemot, Jean-Baptiste, *Esquisse au sujet de l'association des propriétaires de vignes* (Dijon, 1833).
Hantute, *Du libre-échange* (Paris, 1847).
Harcourt, Eugène d', *Discours en faveur de la liberté du commerce* (Paris, 1846).
Hauterive, Alexandre d', *De l'état de la France à la fin de l'an VIII* (Paris, [1800]).
Eléments d'économie politique (Paris, 1817).
Hecquet d'Orval, E., *Quelques mots contre le libre-échange* (Abbeville, 1848).
Heine, Heinrich, *The Complete Poems of Heinrich Heine*, trans. Hal Draper (Boston, Mass., 1982).
[Hervé, Etienne], *Pétition des propriétaires de vignes du département de la Gironde et mémoire à l'appui* (Bordeaux, 1828).
Homon, Charles, *Question des lins et des chanvres* (Morlaix, 1842).

Huerne de Pommeuse, Louis-François, *Des colonies agricoles et de leurs avantages* (Paris, 1832).

Hugo, Victor, *Œuvres complètes*, 18 vols. (Paris, 1967–71).

Humann, Jean-Georges and Saum l'Aîné and Charles-Henri Schattenmann, *Du transit d'Alsace* (Paris, 1818).

[Humann, Jean-Georges and Saum l'Aîné and Charles-Henri Schattenmann], *Encore un mot du transit d'Alsace* (Paris, 1818).

Quelques observations présentées à la chambre des députés en faveur du transit d'Alsace (Paris, 1818).

Jaenger, Pierre-Paul, *Mémoire sur le libre-échange* (Colmar, 1847).

Jaurès, Jean, *A qui profite le protectionnisme?*, ed. Igor Martinache (Paris, 2012).

Koechlin, Nicolas, *Réplique aux délégués de la Chambre de Commerce de Mulhouse* (Paris, 1835).

Lamartine, Alphonse de, *Discours de M. de Lamartine à la réunion publique de l'association pour la liberté des échanges à Marseille* (Paris, 1847).

Lamennais, Félicité de, *Le Livre du peuple*, 2nd edn (Paris, 1838).

Lamothe, Auguste de, *De l'abolition des droits de douane sur les houilles étrangères et des effets de cette mesure sur l'avenir industriel de la France* (Clermont-Ferrand, 1834).

[Laroche, Benjamin and Thomas Perronet Thompson], *Contre-enquête, par l'homme aux quarante écus* (Paris, 1834).

Larréguy, François, *Des entrepôts intérieurs d'après le droit commun et l'intérêt général* (Paris, 1829).

Lebaillif, Jean-Jacques, *Essai sur la question de la liberté du commerce entre tous les peuples* (Falaise, [1834]).

Lebastier, Jules, *Défense du travail national* (Paris, 1847).

Ledru-Rollin, Alexandre, *De la décadence de l'Angleterre*, 2 vols. (Paris, 1850).

Le Mesl, Pierre-Marie, *Mémoire sur la nécessité de prohiber l'importation des fils de lin de provenances étrangères* (Saint-Brieuc, 1838).

Lestiboudois, Thémistocle, *Des colonies sucrières et des sucreries indigènes* (Lille, 1839).

Économie pratique des nations (Paris, 1847).

List, Friedrich, *Das nationale System der politischen Ökonomie* (Baden-Baden, 2008).

Outlines of American Political Economy/Grundriß der amerikanischen politischen Ökonomie (Wiesbaden, 1996).

Schriften, Reden, Briefe, ed. Erwin von Beckerath, Karl Goeser, Friedrich Lenz et al., 10 vols. (Berlin, 1927–35).

Le Système national d'économie politique, trans. Henri Richelot (Paris, 1851).

Louvet, Charles, *Dialogue sur la liberté du commerce* (Saumur, 1834).

Maître, Charles, *Richard Cobden* (Paris, 1846).

Marcet, Jane, *Entretiens sur l'économie politique dégagée de ses abstractions* (Paris, 1825).

Marx, Karl, *The Class Struggles in France, 1848–1850*, trans. Henry Kuhn (New York, 1924).

Discours sur la question du libre-échange (Brussels, 1848), reprinted in *Misère de la philosophie* (Paris, 1908), pp. 273–300.

Mathieu de Dombasle, Christophe-Joseph-Alexandre, *De l'avenir de l'Algérie* (Paris, 1838).
De l'impôt sur le sucre indigène: nouvelles considérations (Nancy, 1837).
Des intérêts respectifs du midi et du nord dans les questions de douanes (Paris, 1834).
Du sucre indigène (Nancy, 1835).
Question des sucres (Nancy, 1840).
Question des sucres: conséquences du système adopté (Nancy, 1839).
La Question des sucres en 1843 (Nancy, 1843).
Questions des sucres: nouvelles considérations (Nancy, 1838).
Méline, Jules, *Le Retour à la terre et la surproduction industrielle* (Paris, 1905).
Michelet, Jules, *Le Peuple*, 3rd edn (Paris, 1846).
Voyage en Angleterre, ed. Jean-François Durand (Arles, 2005).
Mill, John Stuart, *Autobiography* (London, 1989).
Mimerel, Auguste, *Du paupérisme dans ses rapports avec l'industrie en France et en Angleterre* (Lille, [1842]).
Molinari Gustave de, *Histoire du tarif*, 2 vols. (Paris, 1847).
Moret de Moy, *Misère des classes laborieuses et ses causes, démontrées par les faits, par l'abandon de l'intérêt agricole, et notamment de l'industrie des lins* (Saint-Quentin, 1840).
Morlot, Charles, *La Comédie du libre échange: dialogues sur la liberté commerciale* (Le Havre, 1847).
Nollet, Ponce, *Libre-échange, apologie du Cobden de Rheims* (Épernay, 1847).
Pautet, Jules, *Manuel d'économie politique* (Paris, 1835).
Pochard, F., *Exposé de la situation critique du commerce à Paris* (Paris, 1827).
Proudhon, Pierre-Joseph, *Système des contradictions économiques ou philosophie de la misère*, 2 vols. (Paris, 1846).
Pryme, George, *Autobiographic Recollections*, ed. Alicia Bayne (Cambridge, 1870).
Quinet, Edgar, *Allemagne et Italie* (Paris, 1836).
Raynal, Guillaume-Thomas, *Histoire philosophique et politique des établissements et du commerce des Européens, vol. I, books I–V*, ed. Anthony Strugnell, Andrew Brown, Cecil Courtney et al. (Paris, 2010).
Reybaud, Louis, *Jérôme Paturot à la recherche d'une position sociale*, 4th edn (Paris, 1846).
Richelot, Henri, *L'Association douanière allemande* (Paris, 1845).
Rodet, D.-L., *Questions commerciales* (Paris, 1828).
Rossi, Pelegrino, *Cours d'économie politique*, 2 vols. (Paris, 1840–1).
Rubichon, Maurice, *De l'Angleterre*, 2nd edn, 2 vols. (Paris, 1817–19).
Saint-Chamans, Auguste de, *L'Anti-romantique* (Paris, 1816).
Du système d'impôt fondé sur les principes de l'économie politique (Paris, 1820).
Nouvel Essai sur la richesse des nations (Paris, 1824).
Le Petit-Fils de l'homme aux quarante écus (Paris, 1823).
Saint-Ferréol, *Exposition du système des douanes en France* (Marseille, 1835).
Say, Jean-Baptiste, *Catéchisme d'économie politique* (Paris, 1815).
Cours complet d'économie politique pratique, 6 vols. (Paris, 1828–9).

De l'Angleterre et des Anglais, 2nd edn (Paris, 1816).
Mélanges et correspondance d'économie politique, ed. Charles Comte (Paris, 1833).
Œuvres Diverses, ed. Charles Comte, Eugène Daire and Horace Say (Paris, 1848).
Traité d'économie politique, 2 vols. (Paris, 1803).
Traité d'économie politique, 2nd edn, 2 vols. (Paris, 1814).

Schlegel, August von, *Sur le système continental et ses rapports avec la Suède* (Hamburg, 1813).

Senior, Nassau William, *Conversations with M. Thiers, M. Guizot, and Other Distinguished Persons, during the Second Empire*, 2 vols. (Edinburgh, 1878).

Smith, Adam, *The Wealth of Nations: Books IV–V*, ed. Andrew Skinner (London, 1999).

Société d'Agriculture de l'Ain, *Opinion et vote de la société d'agriculture de l'Ain sur la question du libre-échange* (Bourg-en-Bresse, 1847).

Société d'Agriculture de l'Aisne, *Rapport de M. Bauchart sur la question du libre-échange, au point de vue agricole* (Saint-Quentin, 1848).

Société d'Agriculture de l'Ariège, *Du libre-échange en matière d'agriculture* (Foix, 1847).

Société d'Agriculture de l'Aube, *Rapport sur la théorie du libre-échange* (Paris, 1847).

Société d'Agriculture du Calvados, *Le Libre-échange apprécié par l'agriculture à sa juste valeur* (Caen, 1847).

Société d'Agriculture de la Haute-Garonne, *Question du libre-échange: rapport à la société d'agriculture de Haute-Garonne* (Toulouse, 1847).

Société d'Agriculture de la Haute-Saône, *État de l'industrie agricole en France, ce qu'elle doit redouter de la concurrence étrangère* (Vesoul, 1847).

Staël, Germaine de, *Considérations sur la révolution française* (Paris, 1983).

Stendhal, *Mémoires d'un touriste*, ed. Victor Del Litto, 3 vols. (Paris, 1981).

Thiers, Adolphe, *De la propriété*, ed. Comité Central de l'Association pour la Défense du Travail National (Paris, 1848).
Discours prononcé par M. Thiers, le jour de sa réception à l'Académie Française (Paris, 1834).
Discours sur le régime commercial de la France (Paris, 1851).
Law: encyclopédie progressive (Paris, 1826).
Les Pyrénées et le midi de la France (Paris, 1823).
Speech of Mr Thiers on the Commercial Policy of France and in Opposition to the Introduction of Free Trade in France, trans M. de Saint-Felix (London, 1852).

Tocqueville, Alexis de, *De la démocratie en Amérique*, 14th edn, 2 vols. (Paris, 1864).
Œuvres complètes, 18 vols. (Paris, 1951–83).
Textes économiques: anthologie critique, ed. Jean-Louis Benoît and Eric Keslassy (Paris, 2005).

Union Vinicole, *Assemblée générale des délégués des départements* (Bordeaux, 1843).

Viénot de Vaublanc, Vincent, *Du commerce de la France* (Paris, 1822).
Du commerce maritime (Paris, 1828).

Du commerce de la France: examen des états de M. le directeur général des douanes (Paris, 1824).
Rivalité de la France et de l'Angleterre (Paris, [1803]).
Villeneuve-Bargemont, Alban de, *Économie politique chrétienne, ou recherches sur la nature et les causes du paupérisme en France et en Europe*, 3 vols. (Paris, 1834).
Villermé, Louis-René, *Tableau de l'état physique et moral des ouvriers*, 2 vols. (Paris, 1840).
Wolowski, Louis, *Cours de législation industrielle*, 3 vols. (Paris, 1840–4).

Secondary sources

Adelman, Jeremy, 'An Age of Imperial Revolutions', *American Historical Review*, 113 (2) (2008): 319–40.
Aldenhoff-Hübinger, Rita, *Agrarpolitik und Protektionismus: Deutschland und Frankreich im Vergleich, 1879–1914* (Göttingen, 2002).
Alexander, Robert, 'Benjamin Constant as a Second Restoration Politician', in Helena Rosenblatt (ed.), *The Cambridge Companion to Constant* (Cambridge, 2009), pp. 146–71.
Rewriting the French Revolutionary Tradition: Liberal Opposition and the Fall of the Bourbon Monarchy (Cambridge, 2003).
Allix, Edgar, 'Jean-Baptiste Say et les origines de l'industrialisme', *Revue d'économie politique*, 24 (4) (1910): 303–13 and 24 (5) (1910): 341–63.
Almodovar, António and Pedro Teixeira, '"Catholic in Its Faith, Catholic in Its Manner of Conceiving Science": French Catholic Political Economy in the 1830s', *European Journal of the History of Economic Thought*, 19 (2) (2012): 197–225.
Amé, Léon, *Études sur les tarifs de douanes et sur les traités de commerce*, 2 vols. (Paris, 1876).
Anderson, Benedict, *Imagined Communities: Reflections on the Origins and Spread of Nationalism*, 2nd edn (London, 1991).
Armitage, David, *Foundations of Modern International Thought* (Cambridge, 2013).
'Globalizing Jeremy Bentham', *History of Political Thought*, 32 (1) (2011): 63–82.
Armitage David and Sanjay Subrahmanyam (eds.), *The Age of Global Revolutions in Global Context* (Basingstoke, 2009).
Auerbach, Jeffrey, *The Great Exhibition of 1851: A Nation on Display* (New Haven, Conn., 1999).
Bairoch, Paul, *Commerce extérieur et développement économique de l'Europe au XIXe siècle* (Paris, 1976).
Barbier, Frédéric, 'The Publishing Industry and Printed Output in Nineteenth-Century France', in Kenneth Carpenter (ed.), *Books and Society in History* (New York, 1983), pp. 199–230.
Baslé, Maurice and Alain Gélédan, 'Frédéric Bastiat, 1801–1850: théoricien et militant du libre-échange', in Yves Breton and Michel Lutfalla (eds.), *L'Économie politique en France au XIXe siècle* (Paris, 1991), pp. 83–110.
Baubérot, Jean and Séverine Mathieu, *Religion, modernité et culture au Royaume-Uni et en France, 1800–1914* (Paris, 2002).

Bayly, Christopher A., '"Archaic" and "Modern" Globalization in the Eurasian and African arena, c. 1750–1850', in Anthony G. Hopkins (ed.), *Globalization in World History* (London, 2002), pp. 47–73.

The Birth of the Modern World, 1780–1914: Global Connections and Comparisons (Oxford, 2004).

Recovering Liberties: Indian Thought in the Age of Liberalism and Empire (Cambridge, 2011).

Belko, William S., *The Triumph of the Antebellum Free Trade Movement* (Gainesville, Fla., 2012).

Bell, David, *The Cult of the Nation in France: Inventing Nationalism, 1680–1800* (Cambridge, Mass., 2001).

Bell, Duncan, *The Idea of Greater Britain: Empire and the Future of World Order* (Princeton, NJ, 2007).

Bellanger, Claude, Jacques Godechot, Pierre Guiral and Fernand Terrou (eds.), *Histoire générale de la presse française*, 5 vols. (Paris, 1969–76).

Bellos, David, 'Le Marché du livre à l'époque romantique: recherches et problèmes', *Revue française d'histoire du livre*, 20 (3) (1978): 647–59.

Benot, Yves, *La Démence coloniale sous Napoléon* (Paris, 1992).

Bensel, Richard F., *The Political Economy of American Industrialization* (Cambridge, 2000).

Bensimon, Fabrice, 'British Workers in France, 1815–1848', *Past and Present*, 213 (2011): 147–89.

Bertier de Sauvigny, Guillaume, 'Liberalism, Nationalism and Socialism: The Birth of Three Words', *Review of Politics*, 32 (2) (1970): 147–66.

Biagini, Eugenio, *Liberty, Retrenchment and Reform: Popular Liberalism in the Age of Gladstone, 1860–1880* (Cambridge, 1992).

Blackburn, Robin, *The Overthrow of Colonial Slavery* (London, 1988).

Boizard, E. and H. Tardieu, *Histoire de la législation des sucres (1664–1891)* (Paris, 1891).

Bolado, Elsa and Lluis Argemi, 'Jean-Antoine Chaptal: From Chemistry to Political Economy', *The European Journal of the History of Economic Thought*, 12 (2) (2005): 215–39.

Bordas, Jean, *Les Directeurs généraux des douanes: l'administration et la politique douanière, 1801–1939* (Paris, 2004).

Boscher, John F., *The Single Duty Project* (London, 1964).

Bots, Hans and Françoise Waquet, *La République des lettres* (Paris, 1997).

Bourguinat, Nicolas, *Les Grains du désordre: l'État face aux violences frumentaires dans la première moitié du XIXe siècle* (Paris, 2002).

Bourloton, Edgar, Gaston Cougny and Adolphe Robert (eds.), *Dictionnaire des parlementaires français*, 5 vols. (Paris, 1889–91).

Boyé, Michel, *La Douane de Bordeaux: un lieu, des hommes* (Bordeaux, 1999).

Bradley, Margaret and Fernand Perrin, 'Charles Dupin's Visits to the British Isles, 1816–1824', *Technology and Culture*, 32 (1) (1991): 47–68.

Braudel, Fernand and Ernest Labrousse (eds.), *Histoire économique et sociale de la France*, 4 vols. (Paris, 1977–93).

Breton, Yves, 'Les Économistes français et les écoles historiques allemandes: rencontre entre l'économie politique et l'histoire?', *Histoire, Économie et Société*, 7 (3) (1988): 399–417.

Breuilly, John, 'On the Principle of Nationality', in Gareth Stedman Jones and Gregory Claeys (eds.), *The Cambridge History of Nineteenth-Century Political Thought* (Cambridge, 2011),pp. 77–109.

Brière, Jean-François, *Haïti et la France, 1804–1848: le rêve brisé* (Paris, 2008).

Broder, Albert, *L'Économie française au XIXe siècle* (Paris, 1993).

Brown, Lucy, *The Board of Trade and the Free-Trade Movement, 1830–1842* (London, 1958).

Bullen, Roger, *Palmerston, Guizot and the Collapse of the Entente Cordiale* (London, 1974).

Burns, Arthur and Joanna Innes (eds.), *Rethinking the Age of Reform: Britain, 1780–1850* (Cambridge, 2003).

Bury, John and Robert Tombs, *Adolphe Thiers, 1797–1877: A Political Life* (London, 1986).

Butel, Paul, 'Crise et mutation de l'activité économique à Bordeaux sous le Consulat et l'Empire', *Revue d'Histoire Moderne et Contemporaine*, 17 (3) (1970): 540–58.

Les Dynasties bordelaises (Paris, 1991).

Histoire des Antilles françaises, XVIIe–XXe siècles (Paris, 2002).

'Succès et déclin du commerce colonial français de la Révolution à la Restauration', *Revue Économique*, 40 (6) (1989): 1079–96.

Cadier-Rey, Gabrielle, 'Bordeaux et le libre-échange sous le Second Empire' (unpublished doctoral thesis, University of Bordeaux III, 1972).

Cahen, Georges, 'L'Économie sociale chrétienne et la colonisation agricole sous la Restauration et la Monarchie de Juillet', *Revue d'Économie Politique*, 17 (6) (1903): 511–46.

Canton-Debat, Jacques, 'Un homme d'affaire lyonnais: Arlès-Dufour (1797–1872)' (unpublished Ph.D. dissertation, University of Lyon II, 2000).

Carpenter, Kenneth, *The Dissemination of the Wealth of Nations in French and in France, 1776–1843* (New York, 2002).

Casanova, Pascale, *La République mondiale des lettres* (Paris, 1999).

Cavignac, Jean, *Les Vingt-Cinq Familles: les négociants à Bordeaux sous Louis-Philippe* (Bordeaux, 1985).

Charles, Albert, *La Révolution de 1848 et la Seconde République à Bordeaux* (Bordeaux, 1945).

Chartier, Roger, *Les Origines culturelles de la Révolution française*, 2nd edn (Paris, 2000).

Chassagne, Serge, *Le Coton et ses patrons: France, 1760–1840* (Paris, 1991).

Cheney, Paul, *Revolutionary Commerce: Globalization and the French Monarchy* (Cambridge, Mass., 2010).

Christen, Carol and François Vatin (eds.), *Charles Dupin (1784–1873): ingénieur, savant, économiste, pédagogue et parlementaire du premier au second empire* (Rennes, 2009).

Clark, Christopher, 'After 1848: The European Revolution in Government', *Transactions of the Royal Historical Society*, 6th series, 22 (2012): 171–97.

Clinquart, Jean, *L'Administration des douanes sous le Consulat et l'Empire* (Neuilly-sur-Seine, 1979).

L'Administration des douanes sous la Restauration et la Monarchie de Juillet (Neuilly-sur-Seine, 1981).

Clout, Hugh D., *Agriculture in France on the Eve of the Railway Age* (London, 1980).

Collingham, Hugh A. C., *The July Monarchy: A Political History of France, 1830–1848* (London, 1988).

Conrad, Sebastian, *Globalisation and the Nation in Imperial Germany* (Cambridge, 2010).

Courteault, Henri, 'La Formation commerciale d'un jeune bordelais il y a cent ans', *Revue Philomatique de Bordeaux*, 26 (1923): 62–70.

Courtois, Alphonse, *Notice sur la vie et les travaux de Michel Chevalier* (Paris, 1889).

Crouzet, François, 'Les Conséquences économiques de la Révolution: à propos d'un inédit de Sir Francis d'Ivernois', *Annales Historiques de la Révolution Française*, 168 (1962): 182–217 and 169 (1962): 336–62.

L'Économie britannique et le blocus continental, 1806–1813, 2nd edn (Paris, 1987).

'Essai de construction d'un indice annuel de la production industrielle française au dix-neuvième siècle', *Annales: Économies, Sociétés, Civilisations*, 25 (1) (1970): 56–99.

La Guerre économique franco-anglaise au XVIIIe siècle (Paris, 2008).

'The Historiography of French Economic Growth in the Nineteenth Century', *Economic History Review*, new series, 56 (2) (2003): 215–42.

'Wars, Blockade and Economic Change in Europe, 1792–1815', *Journal of Economic History*, 24 (4) (1964): 567–88.

Cubitt, Geoffrey, 'The Political Uses of Seventeenth-Century English History in Restoration France', *Historical Journal*, 50 (1) (2007): 73–95.

Cuvillier, Armand, *Un journal d'ouvriers: L'Atelier, 1840–1850* (Paris, 1954).

Daget, Serge, *Répertoire des expéditions négrières françaises à la traite illégale: 1814–1850* (Nantes, 1988).

Darnton, Robert, *The Forbidden Best-Sellers of Pre-Revolutionary France* (New York, 1996).

Darriulat, Philippe, *Les Patriotes: la gauche républicaine et la nation, 1830–1870* (Paris, 2001).

Daudin, Guillaume, *Commerce et prospérité: la France au XVIIIe siècle* (Paris, 2005).

Daunton, Martin, *Trusting Leviathan: The Politics of Taxation in Britain, 1799–1914* (Cambridge, 2001).

Davis, John R., *Britain and the German Zollverein, 1848–1866* (Basingstoke, 1997).

Davis, Ralph, 'The Rise of Protection in England, 1689–1786', *Economic History Review*, 19 (2) (1966): 306–17.

Delalande, Nicolas, *Les Batailles de l'impôt: consentement et résistances de 1789 à nos jours* (Paris, 2011).

Delattre, Frédéric, 'Pierre-Auguste Mimerel', *Mémoires de la Société d'Émulation de Roubaix*, 35 (1961): 81–5.

Démier, Francis, 'Adolphe Blanqui: la leçon anglaise d'un économiste libéral français', in Sylvie Aprile and Fabrice Bensimon (eds.), *La France et l'Angleterre au XIXe siècle* (Paris, 2006), pp. 49–67.

'Nation, marché et développement dans la France de la Restauration' (unpublished doctoral thesis, University of Paris X, 1991).

Derainne, Pierre-Jacques, 'Le Travail, les migrations et les conflits en France: représentations et attitudes sociales sous la Monarchie de Juillet et la Seconde République' (unpublished doctoral thesis, University of Bourgogne, 1999).

Deschamps, Henry-Thierry, *La Belgique devant la France de Juillet* (Paris, 1956).

Digeon, Claude, *La Crise allemande de la pensée française, 1870–1914*, 2nd edn (Paris, 1992).

Dijn, Annelien de, *French Political Thought from Montesquieu to Tocqueville: Liberty in a Levelled Society?* (Cambridge, 2008).

Donaghay, Marie, 'Exchange of Products of the Soil and Industrial Goods in the Anglo-French Commercial Treaty of 1786', *Journal of European Economic History*, 19 (2) (1990): 377–401.

Donato, Clorinda, 'Benjamin Constant and the *Commentaire sur l'ouvrage de Filangieri*: Notes for an Intercultural Reading', *Historical Reflections – Réflexions Historiques*, 28 (3) (2002): 439–54.

Dormois, Jean-Pierre, *La Défense du travail national? L'Incidence du protectionnisme sur l'industrie en Europe (1870–1914)* (Paris, 2009).

Drescher, Seymour, 'British Way, French Way: Opinion Building and Revolution in the Second French Slave Emancipation', *American Historical Review*, 96 (3) (1991): 709–34.

Abolition: A History of Slavery and Anti-Slavery (Cambridge, 2009).

Drolet, Michael, 'Industry, Class and Society: A Historiographic Reinterpretation of Michel Chevalier', *English Historical Review*, 123 (504) (2008): 1229–71.

Dubois, Laurent, *Avengers of the New World: The Story of the Haitian Revolution* (Cambridge, Mass., 2004).

Dumke, Rolf H., *German Unification in the Nineteenth Century: The Political Economy of the Zollverein* (Munich, 1994).

Dunham, Arthur, *The Anglo-French Treaty of Commerce and the Industrial Revolution in France* (Ann Arbor, Mich., 1930).

Dupuch, Robert, 'Le Parti libéral à Bordeaux et dans la Gironde sous la deuxième Restauration', *Revue Philomathique de Bordeaux*, 5 (1902): 21–31, 77–86, 172–88.

Duroselle, Jean-Baptiste, *Les Débuts du catholicisme social en France (1822–1870)* (Paris, 1951).

'Michel Chevalier et le libre-échange avant 1860', *Bulletin de la Société d'Histoire Moderne*, 2nd series, 5 (1956): 2–5.

Ellis, Geoffrey J., *Napoleon's Continental Blockade: The Case of Alsace* (Oxford, 1981).

Faccarello, Gilbert and Philippe Steiner (eds.), *La Pensée économique pendant la Révolution française 1789–1799* (Grenoble, 1990).

Feret, Edouard, *Statistique de la Gironde*, 3 vols. (Bordeaux, 1874–89).

Findlay, Ronald and Kevin H. O'Rourke, *Power and Plenty: Trade, War, and the World Economy in the Second Millenium* (Princeton, NJ, 2009).

Finer, Samuel E., 'The Transmission of Benthamite Ideas, 1820–50', in Gillian Sutherland (ed.), *Studies in the Growth of Nineteenth-Century Government* (London, 1972), pp. 11–32.

Forsyth, Murray, 'The Old European States System: Gentz versus Hauterive', *Historical Journal*, 23 (3) (1980): 521–38.

Fox, Edward W., *History in Geographic Perspective: The Other France* (New York, 1972).

Furet, François, *La Gauche et la Révolution au XIXe siècle: Edgar Quinet et la question du jacobinisme* (Paris, 1986).

La Révolution de Turgot à Jules Ferry, 1770–1880, 2 vols. (Paris, 1988).

Furner, Mary O. and Barry Supple (eds.), *The State and Economic Knowledge* (Cambridge, 1990).

Gallagher, John and Ronald Robinson, 'The Imperialism of Free Trade', *Economic History Review*, new series, 6 (1) (1953): 1–15.

Gambles, Anna, *Protection and Politics: Conservative Economic Discourse* (London, 1999).

Gavignaud-Fontaine, Geneviève, *Les Catholiques et l'économie sociale en France: XIXe–XXe siècles* (Paris, 2011).

Gehrig, Hans, *Friedrich List und Deutschlands politisch-ökonomosiche Einheit* (Leipzig, 1956).

Gehring, Paul, *Friedrich List: Jugend und Reifejahre, 1789–1825* (Tübingen, 1964).

Gélédan, Alain, 'Paul Cauwès, un nationaliste pour l'état régulateur', in Yves Breton and Michel Lutfalla (eds.), *L'Économie politique en France au XIXe siècle* (Paris, 1991), pp. 335–51.

Gellner, Ernest, *Nations and Nationalism*, 2nd edn (Oxford, 2006).

Gille, Bertand, *Recherches sur la formation de la grande entreprise capitaliste, 1815–1848* (Paris, 1959).

Goblot, Jean-Jacques, *La Jeune France libérale: Le Globe et son groupe littéraire, 1824–1830* (Paris, 1995).

Godechot, Jacques, 'Nation, patrie, nationalisme et patriotisme', *Annales de l'Histoire de la Révolution Française*, 206 (1971): 481–501.

Golob, Eugen O., *The Méline Tariff: French Agriculture and Nationalist Economic Policy* (New York, 1944).

Gonnet, Paul, 'Esquisse de la crise économique en France de 1827 à 1832', *Revue d'Histoire Économique et Sociale*, 33 (3) (1955): 249–91.

Goswami, Manu, 'From Swadeshi to Swaraj: Nation, Economy, Territory in Colonial South Asia', *Comparative Studies in Society and History*, 40 (4) (1998): 609–36.

Goujon, Bertrand, *Monarchies post-révolutionnaires* (Paris, 2012).

Green, Abigail, 'Representing Germany? The Zollverein at the World Exhibitions, 1851–1862', *Journal of Modern History*, 75 (4) (2003): 836–63.

Grimmer-Solem, Erik, *The Rise of Historical Economics and Social Reform in Germany, 1864–1894* (Oxford and New York, 2003).

Gueslin, André, *L'Invention de l'économie sociale en France: le XIXe siècle français* (Paris, 1987).

Guiral, Pierre, *Adolphe Thiers, ou de la nécessité en politique* (Paris, 1986).

Gunn, John A. W., *When the French Tried to Be British: Party, Opposition and the Quest for Civil Disagreement, 1814–1848* (Montreal, 2009).

Guyot, Raymond, *La Première Entente Cordiale* (Paris, 1926).

Hahn, Hans-Werner, *Geschichte des deutschen Zollverein* (Göttingen, 1984).

Hahn, Hans-Werner and Marko Kreutzmann (eds.), *Der deutsche Zollverein: Ökonomie und Nation im 19 Jahrhundert* (Cologne, 2012).

Harismendy, Patrick (ed.), *La France des années 1830 et l'esprit de réforme* (Rennes, 2006).

Harpaz, Ephraïm, 'Le Censeur européen: histoire d'un journal industrialiste', *Revue d'Histoire Économique et Sociale*, 37 (2) (1959): 185–219 and 37 (3) (1959): 328–57.

Harte, Negley B., 'The Rise of Protection and the English Linen Trade, 1690–1790', in Negley B. Harte and Kenneth G. Ponting (eds.), *Textile History and Economic History* (Manchester, 1973), pp. 74–112.

Hau, Michel and Nicolas Stoskopf, *Les Dynasties alsaciennes: du XVIIe siècle à nos jours* (Paris, 2005).

Haynes, Christine, *Lost Illusions: The Politics of Publishing in Nineteenth-Century France* (Cambridge, Mass., 2010).

Hazareesingh, Sudhir, *The Legend of Napoleon* (London, 2004).

Heckscher, Eli, *The Continental System: An Economic Interpretation* (Oxford, 1922).

Hémardinquer, Jean-Jacques, 'Henri Fonfrède ou l'homme du midi révolté (1827–1838)', *Annales du Midi*, 88 (1976): 451–64.

Henderson, William O., *Friedrich List: Economist and Visionary* (London, 1983).

'Friedrich List and the French Protectionists', *Zeitschrift für die gesamte Staatswissenschaft*, 138 (2) (1982): 262–75.

'Friedrich List and the Social Question', *Journal of European Economic History*, 10 (3) (1981): 697–708.

'Introduction', in Friedrich List, *The Natural System of Political Economy*, trans. William O. Henderson (London, 1983), pp. 17–25.

The Zollverein, 3rd edn (London, 1984).

Hilsheimer, Jürgen, *Interessengruppen und Zollpolitik in Frankreich: die Auseinandersetzungen um die Aufstellung des Zollstarifs von 1892* (Heidelberg, 1973).

Hilton, Boyd, *The Age of Atonement: The Influence of Evangelicalism on Social and Economic Thought* (Oxford, 1988).

Corn, Cash and Commerce: The Economic Policies of the Tory Governments, 1815–1830 (Oxford, 1977).

Hirsch, Jean-Pierre, *Les Deux rêves du commerce: entreprise et institution dans la région lilloise (1780–1860)* (Paris, 1991).

Ho, Hai Qang, *Contribution à l'histoire économique de l'"île de La Réunion, 1642–1848* (Paris, 1998).

Hobsbawm, Eric, *Nations and Nationalism since 1780: Programme, Myth, Reality*, 2nd edn (Cambridge, 1992).

Hont, Istvan, *The Jealousy of Trade: International Competition and the Nation-State in Historical Perspective* (Cambridge, Mass., 2005).

'The "Rich Country-Poor Country" Debate Revisited: The Irish Origin and French Reception of the Hume Paradox', in Carl Wennerlind and Margaret Schabas (eds.), *David Hume's Political Economy* (London, 2008), pp. 243–323.

Horn, Jeff, *The Path Not Taken: French Industrialization in the Age of Revolution, 1750–1830* (Cambridge, Mass., 2006).

Howe, Anthony, 'Free Trade and Global Order: The Rise and Fall of a Victorian Vision', in Duncan Bell (ed.), *Victorian Visions of Global Order* (Cambridge, 2007), pp. 26–46.

Free Trade and Liberal England (Oxford, 1997).

'Re-forging Britons: Cobden and France', in Sylvie Aprile and Fabrice Bensimon (eds.), *La France et l'Angleterre au XIXe siècle* (Paris, 2006), pp. 89–104.

Huzzey, Richard, 'Free Trade, Free Labour, and Slave Sugar in Victorian Britain', *Historical Journal*, 53 (2) (2010): 359–79.

Iliasu, Asaana, 'The Cobden-Chevalier Commercial Treaty of 1860', *Historical Journal*, 14 (1) (1971): 67–98.

Irwin, Douglas, *Against the Tide: An Intellectual History of Free Trade* (Princeton, NJ, 1996)

Jaume, Lucien, *L'Individu effacé, ou le paradoxe du libéralisme français* (Paris, 1997).

Jennings, Jeremy, 'Constitutional Liberalism in France: From Benjamin Constant to Alexis de Tocqueville', in Gareth Stedman Jones and Gregory Claeys (eds.), *The Cambridge History of Nineteenth-Century Political Thought* (Cambridge, 2011), pp. 349–73.

'The Debate about Luxury in Eighteenth- and Nineteenth-Century French Thought', *Journal of the History of Ideas*, 68 (1) (2007): 79–105.

'Nationalist Ideas in the Early Years of the July Monarchy: Armand Carrel and *Le National*', *History of Political Thought*, 12 (3) (1991): 497–514.

Revolution and the Republic: A History of Political Thought in France since the Eighteenth Century (Oxford, 2011).

Jennings, Lawrence C., *French Anti-Slavery: The Movement for the Abolition of Slavery in France, 1802–1848* (Cambridge, 2000).

Jouvenel, Bertrand de, *Napoléon et l'économie dirigée* (Brussels and Paris, 1942).

Kaiser, Wolfram, 'Cultural Transfers of Free Trade at the World Exhibitions, 1851–1862', *Journal of Modern History*, 77 (3) (2005): 563–90.

Kapila, Shruti, 'Global Intellectual History and the Indian Political', in Darrin M. McMahon and Samuel Moyn (eds.), *Rethinking Modern European Intellectual History* (Oxford, 2014), pp. 253–74.

Kaplan, Steven L., *Bread, Politics and Political Economy in the Reign of Louis XV*, 2 vols. (The Hague, 1976).

Kedourie, Elie, *Nationalism*, 4th edn (Oxford, 1993).

Kent, Sherman, *The Election of 1827 in France* (Cambridge, Mass., 1975).

Kiestra, Paul, *The Politics of Slave Trade Suppression in Britain and France, 1814–1848* (Basingstoke, 2000).
Kindleberger, Charles P., 'The Rise of Free Trade in Western Europe, 1820–75', *Journal of Economic History*, 35 (1) (1975): 20–55.
Kluge, Friedrich (ed.), *Etymologisches Wörterbuch der deutschen Sprache* (Berlin, 1967).
Knittel, Fabien, 'L'Europe agronomique de C. J. A. Mathieu de Dombasle', *Revue d'Histoire Moderne et Contemporaine*, 57 (1) (2010): 119–38.
'Mathieu de Dombasle: agronomie et innovation' (unpublished doctoral thesis, University of Nancy II, 2007).
Kwass, Michael, 'The Global Underground: Smuggling, Rebellion, and the Origins of the French Revolution', in Suzanne Desan, Lynn Hunt and William M. Nelson (eds.), *The French Revolution in Global Perspective* (Ithaca, NY, 2013), pp. 15–31.
Kymlicka, Will, *Politics in the Vernacular: Nationalism, Multiculturalism and Citizenship* (Oxford, 2001).
Labrousse, Ernest, *La Crise de l'économie française à la fin de l'Ancien Régime* (Paris, 1943).
'How Revolutions Are Born 1789–1830–1848', in François Crouzet, William H. Chaloner and Walter M. Stern (eds.), *Essays in European Economic History, 1789–1914* (London, 1969), pp. 1–14.
Lachiver, Michel, *Vins, vignes et vignerons français*, 2nd edn (Paris, 1997).
Laquièze, Alain, *Les Origines du régime parlementaire en France (1814–1848)* (Paris, 2002).
Larrère, Catherine, *L'Invention de l'économie au XVIIIe siècle: du droit naturel à la physiocratie* (Paris, 1992).
Lebovics, Herman, *The Alliance of Iron and Wheat in the Third French Republic, 1860–1914: Origins of the New Conservatism* (Baton Rouge, La., 1988).
Lemercier, Claire, *Un si discret pouvoir: aux origines de la chambre de commerce de Paris, 1803–1853* (Paris, 2003).
Lepler, Jessica M., *The Many Panics of 1837: People, Politics, and the Creation of a Transatlantic Financial Crisis* (Cambridge, 2013).
Leuilliot, Paul, *L'Alsace au début du XIXe siècle*, 3 vols. (Paris, 1959).
Le Van-Lemesle, Lucette, 'Les Économistes français et l'usage des modèles étrangers', *Revue d'Histoire du XIXe Siècle*, 23 (2001): 73–86.
'Guillaumin, éditeur d'économie politique, 1801–1864', *Revue d'Économie Politique*, 95 (2) (1985): 134–49.
Le Juste ou le riche: l'enseigement de la l'économie politique, 1815–1950 (Paris, 2004).
Levasseur, Ernest, *Histoire du commerce de la France*, 2 vols. (Paris, 1911–12).
Lévêque, Pierre, *Une société provinciale: la Bourgogne sous la Monarchie de Juillet* (Paris, 1983).
Lévy-Leboyer, Maurice, *Les Banques européennes et l'industrialisation internationale dans la première moitié du XIXe siècle* (Paris, 1964).
Liesse, André, 'Un professeur d'économie politique sous la Restauration: Jean-Baptiste Say, au Conservatoire des Arts et Métiers', *Journal des Économistes*, 5th series, 44 (1901): 3–22, 161–74.

Liu, Tessie P., *The Weaver's Knot: The Contradictions of Class Struggle and Family Solidarity in Western France, 1750–1914* (Ithaca, NY, 1994).

Livesey, James, 'Agrarian Ideology and Commercial Republicanism in the French Revolution', *Past and Present*, 157 (1997): 94–121.

Livet, Georges and Raymond Oberlé (eds.), *Histoire de Mulhouse des origines à nos jours* (Strasbourg, 1977).

Lutfalla, Michel, 'Aux origines du libéralisme économique en France: le *Journal des Économistes*, analyse de la première série, 1841–1853', *Revue d'Histoire Économique et Sociale*, 50 (4) (1972): 494–517.

Lyons, Martyn, 'Les Best-sellers', in Roger Chartier and Henri-Jean Martin (eds.), *Histoire de l'édition française*, 2nd edn, 4 vols. (Paris, 1989–91), vol. III, pp. 409–37.

Mackensen, Lutz (ed.), *Ursprung der Wörter* (Wiesbaden, 1998).

Magnusson, Lars, *Mercantilism: The Shaping of an Economic Language* (London, 1994).

The Tradition of Free Trade (London, 2004).

Marçot, Jean-Louis, *Comment est née l'Algérie française (1830–1850)? la belle Utopie* (Paris, 2012).

Marquant, Robert, *Thiers et le Baron Cotta: étude sur la collaboration de Thiers à la Gazette d'Augsbourg* (Paris, 1959).

Marsh, Peter T., *Bargaining on Europe: Britain and the First Common Market* (New Haven, Conn., 1999).

Marzagalli, Silvia, 'Le Négoce maritime et la rupture révolutionnaire: un ancien débat revisité', *Annales Historiques de la Révolution Française*, 352 (2008): 184–207.

Maunier, René, 'Les Économistes protectionnistes en France de 1815 à 1848', *Revue Internationale de Sociologie*, 19 (3) (1911): 485–514.

McClelland, Charles E., *The German Historians and England: A Study in Nineteenth-Century Views* (Cambridge, 1971).

McCord, Norman, *The Anti-Corn Law League, 1838–1846* (London, 1958).

Meyssonnier, Simone, *La Balance et l'horloge: la genèse de la pensée libérale en France au XVIIIe siècle* (Paris, 1989).

Minard, Philippe, *État et industrie: la fortune du colbertisme dans la France des Lumières* (Paris, 1998).

Minart, Gérard, *Frédéric Bastiat (1801–1850): le croisé du libre-échange* (Paris and Dunkirk, 2004).

Morey, Philip, 'Through French Eyes: Victorian Cities in the Eighteen-Forties Viewed by Léon Faucher', forthcoming in *Historical Research*.

Morgan, Kenneth, 'Mercantilism and the British Empire, 1688–1815', in Patrick O'Brien and Donald Winch (eds.), *The Political Economy of British Historical Experience, 1688–1914* (Oxford, 2002), pp. 165–92.

Morieux, Renaud, 'Diplomacy from Below and Belonging: Fishermen and Cross-Channel Relations in the Eighteenth Century', *Past and Present*, 202 (2009): 83–125.

Moyn, Samuel and Andrew Sartori, 'Approaches to Global Intellectual History', in Samuel Moyn and Andrew Sartori (eds.), *Global Intellectual History* (New York, 2013), pp. 3–30.

Murphy, Orville T., 'Du Pont de Nemours and the Anglo-French Commercial Treaty of 1786', *Economic History Review*, new series, 19 (3) (1966): 569–80.

Nakhimovsky, Isaac, *The Closed Commercial State: Perpetual Peace and Commercial Society from Rousseau to Fichte* (Princeton, NJ, 2011).

Napoli, Paolo, *Naissance de la police moderne* (Paris, 2003).

Newman, Edgar L., 'What the Crowd Wanted in the French Revolution of 1830', in John Merriman (ed.), *1830 in France* (New York, 1975), pp. 17–40.

Nye, John V., 'Guerre, commerce, guerre commerciale', *Annales ESC*, 47 (3) (1992): 613–32.

'The Myth of Free-Trade Britain and Fortress France: Tariffs and Trade in the Nineteenth Century', *Journal of Economic History*, 51 (1) (1991): 23–46.

War, Wine, and Taxes: The Political Economy of Anglo-French Trade, 1689–1900 (Princeton, NJ, 2007).

O'Brien, Patrick, 'Path Dependency, or Why Britain Became an Industrialized and Urbanized Economy Long before France, *Economic History Review*, new series, 49 (2) (1996): 213–49.

O'Brien, Patrick and Cağlar Keyder, *Economic Growth in Britain and France, 1780–1914: Two Paths to the Twentieth Century* (London, 1978).

O'Rourke, Kevin H., 'The Worldwide Economic Impact of the French Revolutionary and Napoleonic Wars', *Journal of Global History*, 1 (1) (2006): 123–49.

O'Rourke, Kevin H. and Jeffrey G. Williamson, *Globalization and History: The Evolution of a Nineteenth-Century Atlantic Economy* (Cambridge, Mass., 1999).

'When Did Globalization Begin?', *European Review of Economic History*, 6 (1) (2002): 23–50.

Osterhammel, Jürgen, *The Transformation of the World: A Global History of the Nineteenth Century*, trans. Patrick Camiller (Princeton, NJ, 2014).

Ott, Florence, *La Société Industrielle de Mulhouse, 1826–1876: ses membres, son action, ses réseaux* (Strasbourg, 1999).

Paillère, Fernand, *La Lutte en Gironde pour l'amélioration des échanges entre les nations, 1842–1937* (Bordeaux, 1937).

Parry, Jon, *The Politics of Patriotism: English Liberalism, National Identity and Europe, 1830–1886* (Cambridge, 2006).

Perrot, Jean-Claude, *Une histoire intellectuelle de l'économie politique, XVIIe–XVIIIe siècles* (Paris, 1992).

Petiteau, Nathalie, *Lendemains d'Empire: les soldats de Napoléon dans la France du XIXe siècle* (Paris, 2003).

Pfeifer, Wolfgang (ed.), *Etymologisches Wörterbuch des Deutschen*, 2 vols. (Berlin, 1993).

Piat, Jean, *Quand Mimerel gouvernait la France* (Roubaix, 1992).

Pickering, Paul A. and Alex Tyrrell, *The People's Bread: A History of the Anti-Corn Law League* (London, 2000).

Pilbeam, Pamela, 'The Economic Crisis of 1827–1832 and the 1830 Revolution in Provincial France', *Historical Journal*, 32 (2) (1989): 319–38.

Pinkney, David, *The French Revolution of 1830* (Princeton, NJ, 1972).

Pitts, Jennifer, 'Constant's Thought on Slavery and Empire', in Helena Rosenblatt (ed.), *The Cambridge Companion to Constant* (Cambridge, 2009), pp. 115–45.
A Turn to Empire: The Rise of Imperial Liberalism in Britain and France (Princeton, NJ, 2005).
Plack, Noelle, *Common Land, Wine and the French Revolution: Rural Society and Economy in Southern France, c.1789–1820* (Farnham, 2009).
Pollard, Sidney, *Peaceful Conquest: The Industrialisation of Europe* (Oxford, 1981).
Price, Roger, *The French Second Empire: An Anatomy of Political Power* (Cambridge, 2001).
Procacci, Giovanna, *Gouverner la misère: la question sociale en France, 1789–1848* (Paris, 1993).
Puymège, Gérard de, *Chauvin, le soldat-laboureur* (Paris, 1993).
Rader, Daniel L., *The Journalists and the July Revolution: The Role of the Political Press in the Overthrow of the Bourbon Restoration* (The Hague, 1973).
Ratcliffe, Barrie M., 'Great Britain and Tariff Reform in France, 1831–1836', in William H. Chaloner and Barrie M. Ratcliffe (eds.), *Trade and Transport: Essays in Economic History in Honour of T. S. William* (Manchester, 1977), pp. 98–135.
'The Tariff Reform Campaign in France, 1831–1836', *Journal of European Economic History*, 7 (1) (1978): 61–138.
Ravix, Joël, 'Le Libre-échange et le protectionnisme en France', in Yves Breton and Michel Lutfalla (eds.), *L'Économie politique en France au XIXᵉ siècle* (Paris, 1991), pp. 485–523.
Reddy, William M., *The Rise of a Market Culture: The Textile Trade and French Society* (Cambridge and Paris, 1984).
Régent, Frédéric, *La France et ses esclaves: de la colonisation aux abolitions* (Paris, 2007).
Reinert, Sophus, *Translating Empire: Emulation and the Origins of Political Economy* (Cambridge, Mass., 2011).
Resnick, Daniel P., *The White Terror and the Political Reaction after Waterloo* (Cambridge, Mass., 1966).
Rey, Alain (ed.), *Dictionnaire historique de la langue française*, 2 vols. (Paris, 1993).
Rimmer, William G., *Marshalls of Leeds: Flax Spinners, 1788–1886* (Cambridge, 1960).
Robert, Alasdair, *America's First Great Depression: Economic Crisis and Political Disorder after the Panic of 1837* (Ithaca, NY, 2012).
Rodgers, Daniel T., *Atlantic Crossings: Social Politics in a Progressive Age* (Cambridge, Mass., 1998).
Røge, Pernille, 'Political Economy and the Reinvention of France's Colonial System, 1756–1802' (unpublished Ph.D. thesis, University of Cambridge, 2010).
Romani, Roberto, *National Character and Public Spirit in Britain and France* (Cambridge, 2002).
'Political Economy and Other Idioms: French Views on English Development, 1815–1848', *European Journal of the History of Economic Thought*, 9 (3) (2002): 359–83.
Rosanvallon, Pierre, *Le Moment Guizot* (Paris, 1985).

La Monarchie impossible: les Chartes de 1814 et 1830 (Paris, 1994).
La Société des égaux (Paris, 2011).
Rothschild, Emma, 'An Alarming Commercial Crisis in Eighteenth-Century Angoulême: Sentiments in Economic History', *Economic History Review*, new series, 51 (2) (1998): 268–93.
Economic Sentiments: Adam Smith, Condorcet, and the Enlightenment (Cambridge, Mass., 2001).
The Inner Life of Empires: An Eighteenth-Century History (Princeton, NJ, 2011).
'Language and Empire, c. 1800', *Historical Research*, 78 (200) (2005): 208–29.
'Political Economy', in Gareth Stedman Jones and Gregory Claeys (eds.), *The Cambridge History of Nineteenth-Century Political Thought* (Cambridge, 2011), pp. 748–79.
Sage, Elizabeth M., *A Dubious Science: Political Economy and the Social Question in Nineteenth-Century France* (New York, 2009).
Sartori, Andrew, 'Global Intellectual History and the History of Political Economy', in Samuel Moyn and Andrew Sartori (eds.), *Global Intellectual History* (New York, 2013), pp. 110–33.
Schafmeister, Klaus, *Entstehung und Entwicklung des Systems der politischen Ökonomie bei Friedrich List: eine Rekonstruktionsanalyse seiner Beiträge zur wirtschaftlichen Entwicklung in Württemberg 1806–1823 und Pennsylvania 1806–1835* (St Katharinen, 1995).
Schnerb, Robert, 'La Politique fiscale de Thiers', *Revue Historique*, 201 (1949): 186–211, and 202 (1949): 184–220.
Schonhardt-Bailey, Cheryl, *From the Corn Laws to Free Trade: Interests, Ideas, and Institutions in Historical Perspective* (Cambridge, Mass., 2006).
Schoorl, Evert, *Jean-Baptiste Say: Revolutionary, Entrepreneur, Economist* (London, 2013).
Schui, Florian, *Early Debates about Industry: Voltaire and His Contemporaries* (London, 2007).
Schurman, Paul, 'Fénelon on Luxury, War and Trade', *History of European Ideas*, 38 (2) (2012): 179–99.
Schyler, Guy, *Guestier: souvenirs et documents* (Bordeaux, 1993).
Semmel, Bernard, *The Rise of Free Trade Imperialism: Classical Political Economy, the Empire of Free Trade and Imperialism, 1750–1850* (Cambridge, 1970).
Shionoya, Yuichi (ed.), *The German Historical School: The Historical and Ethical Approach to Economics* (London, 2001).
Shovlin, John, *The Political Economy of Virtue: Luxury, Patriotism, and the Origins of the French Revolution* (Ithaca, NY, 2006).
Sibalis, Michael D., 'Corporatism after the Corporations: The Debate on Restoring the Guilds under Napoleon I and the Restoration', *French Historical Studies*, 15 (4) (1988): 718–30.
Simpson, James, *Creating Wine: The Emergence of a World Industry, 1840–1914* (Princeton, NJ, 2011).
Smith, Michael S., *Tariff Reform in France, 1860–1900: The Politics of Economic Interests* (Ithaca, NY, 1980).

Sonenscher, Michael, *Before the Deluge: Public Debt, Inequality, and the Intellectual Origins of the French Revolution* (Princeton, NJ, 2007).
Sprietsma, Cargill, *Lamartine et Théophile Foisset* (Paris, 1936).
Staum, Martin S., 'French Lecturers in Political Economy, 1815–1848: Varieties of Liberalism', *History of Political Economy*, 30 (1) (1998): 95–120.
Stedman Jones, Gareth, *An End to Poverty? A Historical Debate* (London, 2004).
'*Industrie*, Pauperism, and the Hanoverian State: The Genesis and Political Context of the Original Debate about the "Industrial Revolution" in England and France, 1815–1840', Centre for History and Economics, working paper (Cambridge, 1997).
Languages of Class: Studies in English Working Class History 1832–1982 (Cambridge, 1983).
'National Bankruptcy and Social Revolution: European Observers on Britain, 1813–1844', in Patrick O'Brien and Donald Winch (eds.), *The Political Economy of British Historical Experience, 1688–1914* (Oxford, 2002), pp. 61–92.
Steiner, Philippe, 'French Political Economy, Industrialism and Social Change', in George Stathakis and Gianni Vaggi (eds.), *Economic Development and Social Change: Historical Roots and Modern Perspectives* (London, 2006), pp. 232–56.
'Introduction: l'économie politique comme science de la modernité', in Jean-Baptiste Say, *Cours d'économie politique et autres essais*, ed. Philippe Steiner (Paris, 1996), pp. 9–46.
'J.-B. Say et les colonies ou comment se débarrasser d'un héritage intempestif', *Cahiers d'Économie Politique*, 27 (1996): 153–73.
'Jean-Baptiste Say et l'enseignement de l'économie politique en France, 1816–1832', *Économies et Sociétés: Cahiers de l'ISMÉA, série PE*, 20 (1986): 63–95.
Sullivan, Anthony T., *Thomas-Robert Bugeaud: France and Algeria, 1784–1849: Politics, Power, and the Good Society* (Hamden, Conn., 1983).
Szporluk, Roman, *Communism and Nationalism: Karl Marx versus Friedrich List* (Oxford, 1988).
Tarrade, Jean, *Le Commerce colonial de la France à la fin de l'Ancien régime: l'évolution du régime de 'l'exclusif' de 1763 à 1789*, 2 vols. (Paris, 1972).
'La Révolution et le commerce colonial: le régime de l'exclusif de 1789 à 1800', in Comité pour l'Histoire Économique et Financière de la France, *État, finances et économie pendant la Révolution francaise* (Paris, 1991), pp. 553–64.
Terjanian, Anoush F., *Commerce and Its Discontents in Eighteenth-Century French Political Thought* (Cambridge, 2013).
Tiano, André, *Alban de Villeneuve-Bargemont (1784–1850): le précurseur de l'État social ou un grand notable bien ordinaire?* (Nîmes, 1993).
Todd, David, 'Before Free Trade: Commercial Discourse and Politics in Early Nineteenth-Century France', in Martin Daunton and Frank Trentmann (eds.), *Worlds of Political Economy: Knowledge and Power in the Nineteenth and Twentieth Centuries* (Basingstoke, 2004), pp. 47–68.

'A French Imperial Meridian, 1814–1870', *Past and Present*, 210 (2011): 155–86.
'John Bowring and the Global Dissemination of Free Trade', *Historical Journal*, 51 (2) (2008): 373–97.
'La Nation, la liberté et les colonies dans la pensée économique de Charles Dupin', in Carole Christen and François Vatin (eds.), *Charles Dupin (1784–1873): ingénieur, savant, économiste, pédagogue et parlementaire du premier au second empire* (Rennes, 2009), pp. 177–89.
'Remembering and Restoring the Economic Old Regime: France and Its Colonies, 1815–1830', in Alan Forrest, Karen Hagemann and Michael Rowe (eds.), *War, Demobilization and Memory: The Legacy of War in the Era of Atlantic Revolutions* (Basingstoke, forthcoming).
'Resituer l'expédition d'Alger dans l'histoire de l'impérialisme français: problèmes de périodisation et perspectives trans-impériales', forthcoming in *Revue d'Histoire Moderne et Contemporaine*.
'Transnational Projects of Empire in France, c. 1815–c.1870', forthcoming in *Modern Intellectual History*.
Tombs, Robert and Isabelle Tombs, *That Sweet Enemy: The French and the British from the Sun King to the Present* (London, 2006).
Torp, Cornelius, *Die Herausforderung der Globalisierung: Wirtschaft und Politik in Deutschland, 1860–1914* (Göttingen, 2005).
Toutain, Jean-Claude, 'Les Structures du commerce extérieur de la France, 1789–1970', in Maurice Lévy-Leboyer (ed.), *La Position internationale de la France: aspects économiques et financiers, XIX*e*–XX*e *siècles* (Paris, 1977), pp. 53–74.
Trentmann, Frank, *Free Trade Nation: Commerce, Consumption and Civil Society in Modern Britain* (Oxford, 2008).
Tribe, Keith, *Strategies of Economic Order: German Economic Discourse, 1750–1950* (Cambridge, 1995).
Tudesq, André-Jean, 'Les Débuts de la monarchie de juillet', in Louis Desgraves and Georges Dupeux (eds.), *Bordeaux au XIX*e *siècle, Histoire de Bordeaux*, VI (Bordeaux, 1969), pp. 61–82.
Les Grands Notables en France, 1840–1849, 2 vols. (Paris, 1964).
'La Restauration: renaissance et déceptions', in Louis Desgraves and Georges Dupeux (eds.), *Bordeaux au XIX*e *siècle, Histoire de Bordeaux*, VI (Bordeaux, 1969), pp. 35–59.
Turner, Michael J., 'The "Bonaparte of Free Trade" and the Anti-Corn Law League', *Historical Journal*, 41 (4) (1998): 1011–34.
Tyrrell, Alex, '"La Ligue française", the Anti-Corn Law League and the Campaign for Economic Liberalism in France during the Last Days of the July Monarchy', in Anthony Howe and Simon Morgan (eds.), *Rethinking Nineteenth-Century Liberalism: Richard Cobden Bicentenary Essays* (Aldershot, 2006), pp. 99–116.
Vardi, Liana, *The Physiocrats and the World of Enlightenment* (Cambridge, 2012).
Verley, Patrick, 'Essor et déclin des industries du luxe et du demi-luxe au XIXe siècle', in Jacques Marseille (ed.), *Le Luxe en France: du siècle des 'Lumières' à nos jours* (Paris, 1999), pp. 107–23.

Villermé, Louis, *L'Agriculture française: Mathieu de Dombasle, sa vie, ses œuvres, son influence* (Paris, 1864).
Wahnich, Sophie, *L'Impossible citoyen: l'étranger dans le discours de la Révolution française* (Paris, 1997).
Walch, Jean, *Michel Chevalier, économiste saint-simonien* (Paris, 1975).
Walton, Whitney, 'Political Economists and Specialized Industrialization during the French Second Republic, 1848–1852', *French History*, 3 (3) (1988): 293–311.
Waresquiel, Emmanuel de and Benoit Yvert, *Histoire de la Restauration, 1814–1830: naissance de la France moderne* (Paris, 1996).
Wendler, Eugen, *Friedrich List: politische Wirkungsgeschichte des Vordenkers der europäischen Integration* (Munich, 1989).
(ed.), *'Die Vereinigung des europäischen Kontinents': Friedrich List, gesamteuropäischen Wirkungsgeschichte seines ökonomischen Denkens* (Stuttgart, 1996).
Werner, Michael and Bénédicte Zimmerman, 'Beyond Comparison: *Histoire Croisée* and the Challenge of Reflexivity', *History and Theory*, 45 (1) (2006): 30–50.
Whatmore, Richard, *Against Empire: Geneva, Britain and France in the Eighteenth Century* (New Haven, Conn., 2012).
'The Politics of Political Economy in France from Rousseau to Constant', in Mark Bevir and Frank Trentmann (eds.), *Markets in Historical Context: Ideas and Politics in the Modern World* (Cambridge, 2004), pp. 46–69.
Republicanism and the French Revolution: An Intellectual History of Jean-Baptiste Say's Political Economy (Oxford, 2000).
Whiteman, Jeremy J., 'Trade and the Regeneration of France, 1789–1791: Liberalism, Protectionism and the Commercial Policy of the Constituent Assembly', *European History Quarterly*, 31 (2) (2001): 171–204.
Wilson, Bee, 'Counter-revolutionary Thought', in Gareth Stedman Jones and Gregory Claeys (eds.), *The Cambridge History of Nineteenth-Century Political Thought* (Cambridge, 2011), pp. 9–38.
Winch, Donald, *Riches and Poverty: An Intellectual History of Political Economy in Britain, 1750–1834* (Cambridge, 1996).
Wealth and Life: Essays on the Intellectual History of Political Economy in Britain, 1848–1914 (Cambridge, 2009).
Woolf, Stuart J., *Napoleon's Integration of Europe* (London, 1991).
Yuichi Shionoya (ed.), *The German Historical School: The Historical and Ethical Approach to Economics* (London, 2001).

Index

Abbeville, 65, 92, 203
Académie des Sciences Morales et Politiques, 150, 151, 183
Agenais, 68
Aisne, 174, 203, 210
Alençon, 135
Alexandria, 235
Algeria, 16, 84, 93, 132, 137, 173, 177, 179, 185, 227, 233, 235
Alsace, 16, 32, 40, 43, 78, 87, 94, 135, 148, 165, 168
America, 46, 169, 175
Amiens, 33, 136, 203
Amsterdam, 42, 43
Angers, 108
Anglophilia, 14, 57, 84, 97, 102, 111, 207, 230
Anglophobia, 12, 14, 17, 107, 160, 201, 205–8, 217, 218, 219, 221, 231, 234
Angoulême, 108
Anti-Corn Law League, 2, 3, 4, 9, 105, 121, 155, 183, 190, 191, 193, 197, 213
Antilles, 155, 173, 178
Antwerp, 42, 43, 143
Ardennes, 203
Argout, Antoine Maurice Apollinaire d', 95, 101
Arlès-Dufour, François-Barthélémy, 120
Armentières, 202, 203
Arras, 119, 135
Asia, 27, 46, 176
Association pour la défense du travail national, 9, 138, 190, 213, 222, 225
  creation of, 201–4
  and the protection of agriculture, 210
  and the protection of workers, 217–18
Association pour la Liberté des Echanges, 190, 191, 199, 221, 222
  in Bordeaux, 193–94
  national organization of, 195–96
  and political liberalism, 200
Ateliers Nationaux, 221, 222
Athénée, 59, 60, 63
Aude, 203
Audouin, Xavier, 37–38
autarky, 8, 131, 233
Avesnes, 176, 202

balance of trade, 12, 27, 31, 36, 37, 48, 60, 61, 77, 81, 93, 125, 126, 154
Balzac, Honoré de, 92, 167
Barbet, Henri, 168
Bar-le-Duc, 135, 203, 209
Barrot, Odilon, 174
Basel, 32
Bas-Rhin, 43, 78, 87, 165
Bastiat, Frédéric, 3, 4, 190, 195, 208, 212, 218, 230, 236
  on Anglo-French divergence, 183
  early years, 191–92
  on Fonfrède, 119
  and *Le libre-échange*, 197
  on protectionist propaganda, 207
  on the radical left and protectionism, 219, 221
Bayonne, 26, 64, 121
Beaune, 80, 81, 120, 121
beet-sugar industry, 17, 18, 130, 156, 171, 173, 176, 177, 180, 183, 202
Belfast, 157
Belgium, 23, 35, 39, 89, 137, 151, 157, 167, 170, 185
  commercial negotiations with, 155, 161–62, 167
Bengal, 47
Bentham, Jeremy, 25, 63, 98, 99, 101, 102
Béranger, Pierre-Jean de, 93
Berryer, Pierre-Antoine, 224
Besançon, 66
Bigot de Morogues, Pierre, 133
Birmingham, 131
Blanc, Louis, 187, 218
Blanqui, Adolphe, 25, 55, 57, 63–64, 140, 185, 196, 201
Board of Trade, 63, 91, 98, 100, 126, 159
Bolbec, 136

Bonald, Louis de, 11, 54, 133, 194
on Christian manners vs commerce, 48
on Saint-Chamans, 49
Bonaparte, Louis-Napoléon, 152, 156, 226, 232
on the sugar question, 180
Bordeaux, 15, 38, 42, 57, 66, 74, 75, 81, 87, 90, 92, 94, 102, 106–7, 109, 113, 114, 119, 120, 121, 127, 135, 172, 179, 186, 192–94, 195, 197, 200, 201, 209, 222, 237
and the *Adresse* on commercial liberty, 109–12
and liberalism, 103–4
and mercantile jealousy, 42
and warehousing privileges, 42, 70, 103
Boucher de Perthes, Jacques, 92, 93
Bouches-du-Rhône, 38, 79
Boulogne, 109, 135, 143
Bourbon (Réunion), 40, 46, 179
Bourbon Restoration, 6, 68, 80, 115, 123
and commercial reconstruction, 21
and reactionary economic policy, 22, 55
and revival of colonial trade, 40–41
Bourgogne, Jean-Baptiste, 38
Bourienne, Louis, 47
Bowring, John, 4, 91, 112, 117, 118, 126, 128, 135, 138, 143, 150, 159, 205, 236
in Bordeaux, 106–8
in Burgundy and Languedoc, 120
early life, 97–98
impact of his tours, 108
influences newspapers, 102, 108
motives, 98–99
on the propagation of ideas, 99–100
in the south-east, 100–1
Boyer-Fonfrède, Jean-Baptiste, 67
Braudel, Fernand, 8
Brazil, 47
Bresson, Henri, 166
Brest, 108
Britain, 3, 6, 9, 14, 15, 26, 31, 47, 48, 53, 55, 63, 73, 78, 85, 89, 100, 126, 128, 150, 158, 193, 196, 200, 209, 210, 213, 217, 219, 221, 223, 234
and adoption of free trade, 1, 2, 4, 5, 8, 13, 60, 123, 136, 146, 155, 159, 183, 188, 191, 192, 195, 198, 201, 204, 205, 208, 209, 226, 227, 230, 237
commercial instability, 138, 169
commercial negotiations with, 33, 97, 160, 161, 167
commercial reforms, 56, 62, 72, 83–85, 96, 116
convergence with, 10, 89, 91, 97, 107
divergence from, 189, 191, 232
as an economic model, 13, 21, 171, 184, 193, 223, 231
economic supremacy of, 24, 50, 56, 84, 108, 160, 215
economic warfare against, 6, 20, 23, 28
and mercantile jealousy, 23, 25, 28–30, 33, 53, 56, 63, 78, 107, 116, 127, 131, 145, 153, 175, 202, 205
social conditions in, 11, 17, 36, 47, 96, 124, 132, 147, 169, 170, 205, 210
Brittany, 14, 157, 161
Broglie, Victor de, 102
Brussels, 69, 199
Buchez, Philippe, 186, 217, 220
Bugeaud, Thomas Robert, 177
Bureau du Commerce et des Colonies, 35, 83
Buret, Eugène, 169
Burgundy, 76, 80, 81, 87, 92, 115, 119, 120
Burke, Edmund, 27, 110, 133

Cabet, Etienne, 11, 187, 216
Caen, 108
Calais, 135
Campan, Charles-Alcée, 69, 185
Canada, 4
Carcassonne, 121, 136, 203
Carey, Henry, 4, 30
Carey, Matthew, 30
Caribbean (the), 21, 156, 172
Caudelec-les-Elebeuf, 203
centralization, 66, 72, 74, 80, 96, 110, 116
Châlons, 121
Champagne, 81, 115, 120
Chaptal, Jean-Antoine, 30, 52, 77, 144, 149, 151
Charleville, 203
Charter (of 1814), 11, 28, 36, 51, 71, 78, 89
Charter (of 1830), 143
Chateaubriand, François-René de, 13
Chedeaux, Pierre-Joseph, 71
Cheney, Paul, 27
Cherbourg, 179
Chevalier, Michel, 191, 220, 227, 232, 235
adheres to free trade, 225
on commercial and political liberty, 226–27
hostile to *laissez-faire*, 183
China, 99, 169, 237
Clermont-Ferrand, 134
Cobbett, William, 3
Cobden, Richard, 13, 16, 105, 192, 208, 218, 232
on the Association pour la Liberté Des Échanges, 201
Cochinchina, 232
Code civil, 37, 144, 170, 180
Colbert, Jean-Baptiste, 7, 144, 151, 153
Colmar, 39
colonial trade, 6, 7, 22, 23, 27, 40–41, 43, 50, 156, 178

colonies, 40, 41, 44, 47, 49, 50, 71, 84, 105, 132, 155, 157, 172, 176
colonization, 16, 25, 62
Comité pour la Défense du Travail National, 156, 170, 193
commercial treaty of 1786, 6, 23, 33, 85, 126, 136, 205, 207
commercial treaty of 1860, 228, 232, 234
Comte, Charles, 58, 62, 72, 92, 150, 192
Conseil Supérieur de Commerce, 95, 100, 134, 136, 137, 160
Conservatoire des Arts et Métiers, 60, 61, 63, 183
Considérant, Victor, 187, 219
Constant, Benjamin, 11, 23, 35, 41, 48, 67, 68, 78, 92, 111, 229
  on Britain, 47, 52
  Commentaire sur l'ouvrage de Filangieri, 51–54
  on commerce and liberty, 50–51
  on French corn laws, 47
Consulate, 23, 30
Continental Blockade, 6, 15, 22, 23, 25, 26, 29, 32, 35, 43, 66, 68, 71, 84, 161, 171, 175, 215
Continental System, 21, 23, 24, 28, 36, 40, 126, 130, 144, 147, 163
Convention, 67, 223
Coquelin, Charles, 184
Corn Laws, 4, 21, 53, 96, 146, 171, 191, 195, 205, 210, 216, 221, 223
corn laws (French), 21, 46, 52, 96
Corne, Augustin, 182
Cornet d'Incourt, Charles, 34
Côte d'Or, 80, 120
Côtes-du-Nord, 160
cotton industry, 33, 73, 94, 127, 135, 136, 145, 157, 160, 164, 168, 208
cotton textiles, 19, 21, 22, 32, 34, 36–39, 47, 78, 100, 101, 107, 118, 127, 135, 164, 165, 223
Coudroy, Félix, 194
Crimea, 78, 113
Cromwell, Oliver, 24
Cry, 121
Cuba, 47
Cunin-Gridaine, Laurent, 178, 212
customs administration, 11, 25, 27, 32, 34–36, 39, 93, 95, 187
customs legislation, 23, 34, 47–48, 95, 101, 119, 125, 140, 147, 161, 213, 222

Daumier, Honoré, 224
Decazes, Élie, 133
Defitte, Xavier, 159
Delacroix, Eugène, 91
Delaunay, Jean-Baptiste, 120
Delille, Jacques, 133
Dieppe, 179
Dijon, 119
Disraeli, Benjamin, 99
Dockès, Lazare, 39
Dollfus, Jean, 165, 222, 224
Doubs, 165
Draguignan, 39, 211
Dresden, 150
Droz, Joseph, 64
Duchâtel, Tanneguy, 82–83, 97, 99, 117, 138, 173, 195
Ducos, Théodore, 110, 133
Duffour-Dubergier, Pierre-Lodi, 193
Dufour, Aristide, 114
Dundee, 157
Dunkirk, 136, 210
Dunoyer, Charles, 58, 62, 72, 92, 185, 192
Dupérier de Larsan, Armand, 113
Dupin, Charles, 57, 63, 68, 70, 72, 73, 75, 77, 92, 124, 141, 149, 150, 151, 186, 198, 230
  on Britain, 63
  on prohibitions, 65
  propagator of industrialist ideas, 64–65
  on the protection of agriculture, 96
  on the protection of workers, 144–45
  on the protective system, 142–44
  on the sugar question, 178–79
Dupont de Nemours, Pierre Samuel, 61
Dussumier-Fonbrune, Antoine, 34
Dutot, Nicolas, 27

economic nationalism, 11, 124, 140, 154, 188, 190
  and pauperism, 123, 141
  strands of, 155–56
économistes, 18, 26, 54, 56, 196
Egypt, 210
Elberfeld, 71
Elbeuf, 203
empire, 16–17, 21, 40, 50, 234
England. *See* Britain
Epernay, 121
Eure, 203
exclusif, 16, 21, 23, 27, 37, 40, 41, 178

Faucher, Léon, 161, 162, 163, 170, 196, 200, 206
Fénelon, François, 25
Feray, Ernest, 159
Ferme Générale, 35, 65
Ferrier, François, 28, 31, 32, 35, 47, 49, 54, 56, 61, 81, 83, 87, 92, 101, 116, 127, 133, 155, 215
  on British commercial reforms, 84–85
  and mercantile jealousy, 25–27
  on warehouses, 42, 71
Fichte, Johann Gottlieb, 12, 50, 53, 124
Fiévée, Joseph, 27, 31, 85
Filangieri, Gaetano, 51–52

First Empire, 2, 27, 110, 123, 160, 223
Flanders, 14, 127, 157
Flaubert, Gustave, 91, 232
Foisset, Théophile, 80–82, 92, 120
Fonfrède, Henri, 18, 57, 66, 74, 76, 80, 86, 88, 96, 103, 110, 112, 118, 122, 133, 140, 192, 194, 229
  on Britain, 72, 116
  on colonization, 172
  early life and personality, 67
  on economic despotism, 115–17
  impact of his articles, 69, 73, 74, 117
  on industrialism, 69, 73
  on political economy, 73, 116
  posthumous edition of his works, 185–86
  on statistics, 68
  on the sugar question, 105–6, 173, 174
  on warehouses, 72, 104
Fourier, Charles, 111, 186
Freihandel, 1, 3, 12
Fréville, Jean-Baptiste de, 97
Furet, François, 10, 229

Galiani, Ferdinando, 52
Galos, Henri, 111, 141
Ganilh, Charles, 30
Ganneron, Auguste, 96
Garnier, Joseph, 183
Gazel, Albert, 218
Geneva, 59
Genoa, 26, 143
Gentz, Friedrich, 24
George Eden, Earl of Auckland, 100
Germany, 5, 7, 23, 43, 48, 78, 127, 150, 151, 152, 157, 165, 169, 198, 208, 236, 237
  as an economic model, 124, 214–15, 233, 234
  economic unification of, 145–47, 152
  exchanges of ideas with France, 12, 154
Giacomini, Gaspard, 39
Girard, Philippe de, 161
Girardin, Saint-Marc de, 147
Gironde, 19, 34, 38, 66, 67, 68, 70, 80, 86, 87, 96, 118, 185, 190, 222, 224
  and liberalism, 103
  and winegrowers' petitions, 76–77, 79, 112–14
Girondin (faction), 30, 68, 113, 116, 230
Glasgow, 63
globalization, 1, 2, 5, 7, 9, 11, 13, 19, 46, 55, 123, 124, 155, 228, 234
  acceleration, 234–35
  intellectual history of, 235–37
Goethe, Johann Wolfgang von, 12, 92
Grandin, Victor, 202, 206
Granville, 179
Grenoble, 135
Gréterin, Théodore, 95
Guadeloupe, 40, 179
Guépin, Ange, 186
Guestier, Pierre-François, 111, 112
Guillaumin, Gilbert-Urbain, 184, 197
Guizot, François, 74, 82, 110, 150, 162, 163, 168, 174, 180, 190, 195, 201, 230
  on free trade, 212

Hadol, 166, 167
Haiti, 21, 23, 41, 46, 50
Hamburg, 152, 237
Harcourt, Eugène d', 195, 200, 206
Haute-Marne, 203
Hauterive, Alexandre d', 28, 37, 215
  on Britain and mercantile jealousy, 24–25
  on commercial causes of the Revolution, 22
Haute-Saône, 165
Haute-Vienne, 203
Haut-Rhin, 32, 38, 39, 43, 164, 165
Hébert, Jacques, 37
Heine, Heinrich, 157
Hérault, 224
Hervé, Etienne, 77, 113
Hogendorp, Dirk van, 25
Hovyn de Tranchère, Jules, 223, 224
Huerne de Pommeuse, Louis-François, 132
Hugo, Victor, 91, 224
Hume, David, 2
Hundred Days, 26, 33, 34, 41
Hungary, 15
Huskisson, William, 63

imperialism, 16, 24, 99
India, 14, 47, 62, 73, 127, 145, 153, 160, 175, 205, 237
Indochina, 233
Indre-et-Loire, 77
industrialism, 62, 69, 70, 74, 92, 104, 149, 151, 164, 165, 185, 204, 217, 229, 230
industrialization, 3, 9, 14, 104, 110, 171, 231
inquiry
  on commercial legislation, 78, 83
  on prohibitions, 121, 134–37, 165
Ionian islands, 143
Ireland, 78, 153
Italy, 23, 59, 148, 198

Jacobinism, 10, 204
Japan, 15
Jaubert, Hippolyte François, 141
Jaurès, Jean, 233
Jay, Antoine, 96
jealousy, 16, 63, 101, 128, 129, 134, 145, 146

industrialist, 127, 151, 154, 155, 156, 171, 177, 204, 220, 231, 236
and liberalism, 154
mercantile, 11, 14, 23, 24, 25, 28, 31, 32, 39, 40, 50, 52, 53, 56, 60, 66, 71, 77, 84, 155, 158, 230
and reactionary royalism, 32, 34, 45–46
July Monarchy, 89, 90, 92, 96, 126, 133, 144, 155, 160, 232

Koechlin, Ferdinand, 164
Koechlin, Nicolas, 165
Kolb-Bernard, Charles, 202
Kreveld, 71

La Rochelle, 108, 109
Labrousse, Ernest, 8
laissez-faire, 6, 7, 23, 50, 53, 54, 71, 110, 184, 229
Lamartine, Alphonse de, 80, 81, 92, 206, 224
on commercial liberty, 142
on *libre-échange*, 199
on the sugar question, 174, 182
Lamennais, Félicité de, 111, 197, 224
Lancashire, 128, 192
Landes, 191, 221
Languedoc, 68, 115, 120
Latin America, 55, 237
Law, John, 125
Le Cannet, 39
Le Havre, 103, 108, 109, 119, 120, 135, 149, 179, 198, 199, 209, 235
Le Libre-échange, 3, 19, 190, 200, 214
contents of, 198
creation of, 197
Le Moniteur Industriel, 19, 190, 208, 218
contents of, 204–7
creation of, 204
on the protection of agriculture, 210
Le Puy, 134
Lebeuf, Louis, 202, 206, 214
Ledru-Rollin, Alexandre, 225
Leeds, 157
Leipzig, 150
Leroux, Pierre, 217
Lestiboudois, Thémistocle, 176, 215
Levant (the), 55
liberalism, 16, 54, 57, 72, 74, 90, 91, 96, 103, 110, 119, 125, 132, 175, 188, 191, 209, 214, 219, 220, 227, 230, 231
and Anglo-French divergence, 6, 190
in Bordeaux, 103
in Britain, 188, 230
commercial, 13, 14, 56, 114, 120, 122, 147, 185, 191, 196, 229
in France, 11, 90, 125, 190, 223
and industrialism, 69
and nationalism, 231
and protectionism in France, 5–9
Librairie administration, 18, 30, 37, 58
libre-échange, 5, 91, 119, 190, 194, 201, 202, 204, 206, 207, 208, 210, 211, 214, 218, 219, 220, 225, 226, 227, 230, 232, 237
as completion of the 1789 Revolution, 193, 195–97
limited enthusiasm for, 199–200
origins of the phrase, 1, 3, 197–98
rejected by the radical left, 216–17
Liguria, 26
Lille, 65, 135, 136, 137, 166, 202, 203, 218
Limoges, 135, 203
linen question, 14, 155, 156–61, 163, 184
Lisieux, 163
List, Friedrich, 12, 13, 15, 92, 125, 155, 214, 219, 230, 236
on Adam Smith, 148
his admiration for France, 147–49
and Adolphe Thiers, 147, 152
on the linen question, 159, 161
National System of Political Economy, 152–53
natural system of political economy, 150–51
on political economy, 150, 152
on the sugar question, 178
Loire, 203
Loire-Inférieure, 37, 38, 203
London, 59, 63, 97, 109, 171, 187, 192, 197, 206, 222, 225
Lorient, 108, 179
Lorraine, 18, 81, 124, 129, 233
Louis, Joseph Dominique, 97
Louis-Philippe, 87, 94, 102, 107, 125, 162
Louviers, 136, 203
luxury, 7, 9, 22, 49, 53, 55, 85, 96, 133
Lyon, 38, 73, 94, 100, 101, 102, 106, 113, 117, 119, 120, 121, 129, 131, 135, 136, 148, 199, 209, 218

Mably, Gabriel de, 185
Mâcon, 119, 121
Madagascar, 25
Maistre, Joseph de, 194
Malthus, Thomas Robert, 58, 82
Manchester, 131, 192, 197, 208
Manuel, Jacques-Antoine, 46, 52
Marcet, Jane, 64, 119
Marne, 210
Marseille, 38, 42, 119, 120, 121, 135, 179, 199, 209
Martignac, Jean-Baptiste de, 75
Martinique, 40, 178, 179
Marx, Karl, 26, 90
on *libre-échange*, 220

Mathieu de Dombasle, Christophe-Joseph-Alexandre, 18, 124, 155, 169, 180, 213, 219, 230, 233
on colonization, 175
defends self-sufficiency, 129–31
on German self-sufficiency, 146
on liberty and nationality, 133
on political economy and liberalism, 131
on the sugar question, 175–76
Méline, Jules, 233
Melon, Jean-François, 27
mercantile system, 23, 25, 37, 48, 49, 50, 73, 85, 130, 151, 231
mercantilism, 7, 48, 50
mercantilist, 1, 11, 55, 61, 70
Methuen treaty of 1703, 78, 107
Metternich, Klemens von, 148
Metz, 71, 203
Meurthe, 130, 165
Meuse, 203
Mexico, 232
Michelet, Jules, 17, 92
Midlands, 128
Mill, James, 58
Mill, John Stuart, 58, 90
Mimerel, Auguste, 124, 134, 155, 190, 206, 231
and Association pour la Défense du Travail National, 202
on Britain's commercial instability, 138, 169
and Comité pour la Défense du Travail National, 167
on pauperism, 168–70
on political economy, 213
on solidarity between producers, 137–38
Ministry of Commerce, 35, 75, 86, 95, 129, 166
Molé, Louis-Mathieu, 78, 162, 174
Montagnard, 68, 116, 231
Montbron, Joseph de, 47
Mont-de-Marsan, 119
Montesquieu, Charles Secondat de, 7, 27, 74, 77, 185, 196
Montpellier, 121
Moravia, 78
Morgan de Belloy, Adrien Marie, 44
Morlaix, 108
Moselle, 203
Mouvement, 90, 101, 103, 106, 140, 141, 142, 165
Mulhouse, 38, 94, 135, 203, 208, 218, 222
and Association pour la défense du travail national, 202, 208, 222
and Comité de l'industrie cotonnière de l'Est, 164–67
Nantes, 38, 42, 103, 108, 109, 134, 135, 179, 203, 210
Napoleon, 6, 18, 23, 27, 28, 29, 32, 41, 47, 68, 80, 81, 125, 136, 142, 144, 151, 153, 161, 179, 180, 182, 231
national labour, 4, 5, 9, 15, 18, 168, 170, 189, 194, 198, 216, 221, 237
Navigation Acts, 24, 42
Necker, Jacques, 24, 52, 144
Netherlands, 43, 78
Neufchâteau, François de, 144
Nevers, 134
New York, 59
Nice, 39
Nièvre, 127
Nîmes, 199
Niort, 135
Nord, 19, 38, 168, 174, 176, 181, 210, 215, 221
Normandy, 14, 85, 134, 135, 157, 163, 168, 202, 221
North Africa, 16, 84, 85, 155, 172, 175, 177, 179
North America, 55
Nuremberg, 71

Odessa, 47
Odier, Antoine, 202
Oise, 210
Old Regime, 7, 17, 21, 23, 32, 35, 40, 43, 46, 81, 154, 184, 189
Orléans, 135
Orne, 160

Paris, 9, 15, 18, 36, 37, 38, 43, 45, 59, 70–72, 80, 82, 95, 96, 102, 103, 108, 109, 114, 118, 121, 125, 129, 133, 141, 149, 162, 166, 168, 173, 179, 181, 183, 186, 195, 196, 197, 201, 202, 211, 213, 218, 221, 224, 231, 232, 235
Paschoud, Jean-Jacques, 59
Pas-de-Calais, 174, 210
Passy, Hippolyte, 141
pauperism, 5, 8, 11, 122, 123, 129, 132–33, 141, 169, 171, 177, 213, 230
Peace of Amiens, 21
Peel, Robert, 191, 195, 205, 211
Perier, Casimir, 95, 97, 100
Périgord, 177
Physiocrats, 5, 7, 18, 22, 25, 26, 28, 49, 52, 54, 56, 205
Picardy, 86, 157, 161, 168, 202
Piedmont, 39
Plouëc, 160
Poland, 78, 85
Polignac, Jules de, 83, 87
Portugal, 41, 78, 89, 107, 116, 153

prohibitive system, 22, 32, 33, 36, 47, 55, 56, 62, 64, 65, 72, 75, 77, 78, 80, 82, 86, 88, 91, 93, 97, 100, 106, 115, 125, 127, 173, 187, 199
protectionism, 2, 3–5, 8, 16, 94, 115, 137, 191, 219, 220, 221, 233, 234, 237
and Anglophobia, 12, 231
and economic development, 9–10, 235
and empire, 16
and exchanges of ideas with Germany, 12
and legacy of the 1789 Revolution, 204, 207, 227
and liberalism, 231
protectionnisme, 2, 4, 137
protectionniste, 4, 145, 186, 192
protective system, 4, 85, 86, 106, 110, 113, 115, 141, 146, 165, 199, 207, 208, 209, 211, 212, 214, 223, 226
Proudhon, Pierre-Joseph, 11, 219
Prussia, 78
Pryme, George, 4
public debt, 7, 53, 72, 86

Quesnay, François, 2, 6
Quinet, Edgar, 14, 225

Raynal, Guillaume Thomas, 2, 40
re-exportation, 41–43, 71, 95. *See also* transit *and* warehouses
Reims, 121
Remscheid, 71
Rennes, 135
republicanism, 10, 15, 87, 105, 215, 221, 230, 231, 232, 233
Résistance, 90, 95, 101, 103, 106, 111, 120, 140, 141, 142
Rethel, 135
Revolution of 1789, 10, 17, 20–22, 23, 27, 34, 37, 40, 85, 96, 111, 142, 191, 193, 195–97, 201, 207, 223, 225, 227, 229, 230, 232
Revolution of 1830, 7, 11, 17, 87, 91, 92, 96, 115, 123, 136, 149, 229
economic causes of, 56
and liberalism in France, 89–91
Revolution of 1848, 216, 220, 221, 223
Reybaud, Louis, 137
Rhineland, 26
Rhône (department), 38
Ricardo, David, 58, 61, 64, 127
Richard, Charles, 37, 44
Robespierre, Maximilien de, 50
Rochefort, 108
romanticism, 91–92
Rome, 26, 221
Rossi, Pelegrino, 183
Roubaix, 19, 124, 134, 136, 137, 139, 202, 203
Rouen, 85, 108, 135, 166, 168, 179, 202, 203
Rousseau, Jean-Jacques, 53, 185, 196
Roville, 129
Rubichon, Maurice, 29–30, 48, 133
Russia, 46, 78, 85, 127, 210

Saint-Brieuc, 108
Saint-Chamans, Auguste de, 49, 52, 61, 81, 92, 127, 133, 155
Saint-Cricq, Pierre de, 35, 39, 45, 56, 76, 81, 85, 86, 95, 100, 101, 102, 116, 141, 143, 186
on British commercial reforms, 83–84
his influence on Thiers, 127
on liberty of commerce, 75
on prohibitions, 78–79
on protection, 107
Saint-Dizier, 203
Saint-Domingue. *See* Haiti
Sainte-Beuve, Pierre-Henri, 223, 224
Saint-Etienne, 203
Saint-Louis de Montferrand, 67
Saint-Malo, 108, 179
Saint-Quentin, 86, 136, 166, 203
Saint-Simon, Henri de, 106, 111
Sand, George, 217
Saumur, 119, 135
Saxony, 85
Say, Jean-Baptiste, 16, 18, 25, 28, 36, 37, 41, 44, 53, 56, 64, 70, 71, 74, 77, 79, 81, 82, 88, 101, 119, 125, 127, 130, 149, 151, 161, 170, 192, 213, 218, 227, 229
on Britain, 29, 62
on colonization, 62
and the dissemination of political economy, 57–61
on free trade, 31, 60, 61
on statistics, 68
Schlegel, August von, 24
Schoelcher, Victor, 225
science of commerce, 7, 77
Second Empire, 2, 175, 228, 232
Second Republic, 220
Sedan, 136, 203
Seine (department), 38
Seine-et-Marne, 202
Seine-Inférieure, 135, 202, 203
self-sufficiency, 12, 15, 18, 49, 85, 125, 134, 135, 138, 145, 146, 151, 155, 156, 162, 163, 164, 171, 175, 177, 180, 182, 188, 205, 220, 225, 230, 231, 233
Silesia, 157
silk industry, 9, 78, 85, 99, 100, 127, 162
silk workers, 9, 129, 131, 209

Simonde de Sismondi, Jean-Charles, 30, 104, 169, 219
Sinclair, John, 129
slave trade, 40, 41, 45, 89
slavery, 23, 25, 40, 41, 46, 50, 87, 156, 170, 171, 175, 177, 179, 205
Smith, Adam, 1, 5, 6, 25, 26, 27, 28, 31, 37, 40, 44, 48, 49, 54, 60, 62, 64, 77, 96, 110, 127, 130, 132, 149, 161, 192, 205
Smith-Stanley, Early of Derby, 225
smuggling, 22, 32–34, 36, 39, 42, 44, 51, 64, 66, 93
socialists, 11, 104, 169, 186–88, 216–17, 218, 220, 221, 225, 231
Somme, 34, 174, 203, 210
Soult, Hector-Napoléon, 142
South Africa, 113, 120
South America, 64
South Asia, 55
South Carolina, 14, 102
Southampton, 63
South-East Asia, 55
Spain, 35, 46, 64, 78, 85, 89, 98, 116, 192, 199, 205
Staël, Germaine de, 23–24, 52, 72, 92, 102, 185
statistics, 64, 68, 76, 112, 165, 215
Stendhal (Henri Beyle), 11, 92
Strasbourg, 43, 45, 66, 148
Stuttgart, 148, 152
sugar question, 105, 155, 171–72, 173–74, 175, 178, 181, 184, 187
Sweden, 64, 127
Switzerland, 32, 43, 48, 59, 78, 148, 165, 208

Talleyrand-Périgord, Charles-Maurice de, 22, 97
Terror, 30, 37, 68, 123, 204
Thaër, Albrecht, 129
Thierry, Augustin, 72
Thiers, Adolphe, 11, 92, 101, 108, 112, 116, 117, 120, 124, 138, 141, 152, 155, 162, 174, 183, 191, 212, 220, 225, 228, 230, 232
  on France's commercial system, 223–24
  on the linen question, 159
  on the sugar question, 177
  on the 'veritable science' of economics, 126–29
  on the Zollverein, 147
Third Republic, 11, 232
Thompson, Thomas Perronet, 3, 140, 229
  assists Bowring in France, 139–40
Thomson, Charles Poulett, 98, 103
Tocqueville, Alexis de, 14, 16, 90, 182, 230
  on free trade, 213
Torquemada, Tomás de, 66
Toulon, 143, 235
Toulouse, 109, 121, 186, 209
Tourcoing, 137, 202, 203
Tours, 135
Trafalgar, 23
transit, 18, 97
  across Alsace, 43–45
transnational intellectual history, 5, 13, 235
travail national, 4, 5, 237
Troyes, 33, 121, 203
Turgot, Anne-Robert-Jacques, 2, 6, 53, 96, 196

Ukraine, 46
ultra-royaliste, 34, 37, 44, 45, 46, 49, 52, 74, 76, 79, 83, 86, 95, 132
United States of America, 4, 14, 30, 47, 59, 103, 127, 148, 149, 150, 155, 198, 209, 210, 213, 237
  as an economic model, 15, 224, 233, 234
universal exhibition of 1851, 222, 227

Valenciennes, 135, 176, 202
Var, 39, 211
Vaublanc, Vincent de, 52, 61, 127, 155
  on British commercial reforms, 56, 84
  on colonial trade, 50
Véron de Forbonnais, François, 27
vexations, 17, 66, 93
Vidal, François, 218, 225
Vienna, 93
Villèle, Joseph de, 45, 51, 70, 75, 78, 85, 116, 148
  on grain imports, 46
  on prohibitions, 47
Villeneuve-Bargemont, Alban de, 130, 132, 169, 213, 230
Villermé, Louis-René, 168
Villiers, George, 97, 98, 99, 106, 107, 128
Vimoutiers, 160
Vire, 135
Voltaire (François-Marie Arouet), 49, 139, 196
Vosges, 165

Wales, 128
warehouses, 18, 42, 70–72, 74, 83, 95, 97, 99, 103
West Indies, 42, 55
Westphalia, 71
Whatmore, Richard, 57
White Terror, 33, 38, 50
William Wentworth-Fitzwilliam, Earl of Fitzwilliam, 4
wine industry, 9, 18, 57, 76, 78, 80, 82, 93, 99, 102, 112, 127, 162, 184, 219, 224

winegrowers, 9, 18, 19, 70, 76, 82, 83, 85, 86, 87, 88, 93, 102, 121, 185, 192
  petitions by, 77–78, 79, 80–82, 112–14
Wittemberg, 152
Wolowski, Louis, 183, 197, 200
Wurttemberg, 148
Wustemberg, Jacques-Henri, 141

Yvetot, 136

Zollverein, 14, 15, 120, 124, 145–47, 215

IDEAS IN CONTEXT

Edited by

DAVID ARMITAGE, RICHARD BOURKE, JENNIFER PITTS and JOHN ROBERTSON

1. RICHARD RORTY, J. B. SCHNEEWIND and QUENTIN SKINNER (eds.)
Philosophy in History
Essays in the Historiography of Philosophy
PB 978 0 521 27330 5

2. J. G. A. POCOCK
Virtue, Commerce and History
Essays on Political Thought and History, Chiefly in the Eighteenth Century
PB 978 0 521 27660 3

3. M. M. GOLDSMITH
Private Vices, Public Benefits
Bernard Mandeville's Social and Political Thought
HB 978 0 521 30036 0

4. ANTHONY PAGDEN (ed.)
The Languages of Political Theory in Early Modern Europe
PB 978 0 521 38666 1

5. DAVID SUMMERS
The Judgment of Sense
Renaissance Naturalism and the Rise of Aesthetics
PB 978 0 521 38631 9

6. LAURENCE DICKEY
Hegel: Religion, Economics and the Politics of Spirit, 1770–1807
PB 978 0 521 38912 9

7. MARGO TODD
Christian Humanism and the Puritan Social Order
PB 978 0 521 89228 5

8. LYNN SUMIDA JOY
Gassendi the Atomist
Advocate of History in an Age of Science
PB 978 0 521 52239 7

9. EDMUND LEITES (ed.)
Conscience and Casuistry in Early Modern Europe
PB 978 0 521 52020 1

10. WOLF LEPENIES
Between Literature and Science: The Rise of Sociology
PB 978 0 521 33810 3

11. TERENCE BALL, JAMES FARR AND RUSSELL L. HANSON (eds.)
Political Innovation and Conceptual Change
PB 978 0 521 35978 8

12. GERD GIGERENZER ET AL.
The Empire of Chance
How Probability Changed Science and Everyday Life
PB 978 0 521 39838 1

13. PETER NOVICK
That Noble Dream
The 'objectivity question' and the American Historical Profession
HB 978 0 521 34328 2
PB 978 0 521 35745 6

14. DAVID LIEBERMAN
The Province of Legislation Determined
Legal Theory in Eighteenth-Century Britain
PB 978 0 521 52854 2

15. DANIEL PICK
Faces of Degeneration
A European Disorder, c. 1848–c. 1918
PB 978 0 521 45753 8

16. KEITH BAKER
Inventing the French Revolution
Essays on French Political Culture in the Eighteenth Century
PB 978 0 521 38578 7

17. IAN HACKING
The Taming of Chance
HB 978 0 521 38014 0
PB 978 0 521 38884 9

18. GISELA BOCK, QUENTIN SKINNER and MAURIZIO VIROLI (eds.)
Machiavelli and Republicanism
PB 978 0 521 43589 5

19. DOROTHY ROSS
The Origins of American Social Science
PB 978 0 521 42836 1

20. KLAUS CHRISTIAN KOHNKE
The Rise of Neo-Kantianism
German Academic Philosophy between Idealism and Positivism
HB 978 0 521 37336 4

21. IAN MACLEAN
Interpretation and Meaning in the Renaissance
The Case of Law
HB 978 0 521 41546 0
PB 978 0 521 02027 5

22. MAURIZIO VIROLI
From Politics to Reason of State
The Acquisition and Transformation of the Language of Politics 1250–1600
HB 978 0 521 41493 7
PB 978 0 521 67343 3

23. MARTIN VAN GELDEREN
The Political Thought of the Dutch Revolt 1555–1590
HB 978 0 521 39204 4
PB 978 0 521 89163 9

24. NICHOLAS PHILLIPSON AND QUENTIN SKINNER (eds.)
Political Discourse in Early Modern Britain
HB 978 0 521 39242 6

25. JAMES TULLY
An Approach to Political Philosophy: Locke in Contexts
HB 978 0 521 43060 9
PB 978 0 521 43638 0

26. RICHARD TUCK
Philosophy and Government 1572–1651
PB 978 0 521 43885 8

27. RICHARD YEO
Defining Science
William Whewell, Natural Knowledge and Public Debate in Early Victorian Britain
HB 978 0 521 43182 8
PB 978 0 521 54116 9

28. MARTIN WARNKE
The Court Artist
On the Ancestry of the Modern Artist
HB 978 0 521 36375 4

29. PETER N. MILLER
Defining the Common Good
Empire, Religion and Philosophy in Eighteenth-Century Britain
HB 978 0 521 44259 6
PB 978 0 521 61712 3

30. CHRISTOPHER J. BERRY
The Idea of Luxury
A Conceptual and Historical Investigation
PB 978 0 521 46691 2

31. E. J. HUNDERT
The Enlightenment's 'Fable'
Bernard Mandeville and the Discovery of Society
HB 978 0 521 46082 8
PB 978 0 521 61942 4

32. JULIA STAPLETON
Englishness and the Study of Politics
The Social and Political Thought of Ernest Barker
HB 978 0 521 46125 2
PB 978 0 521 02444 0

33. KEITH TRIBE
Strategies of Economic Order
German Economic Discourse, 1750–1950
HB 978 0 521 46291 4
PB 978 0 521 61943 1

34. SACHIKO KUSUKAWA
The Transformation of Natural Philosophy
The Case of Philip Melanchthon
HB 978 0 521 47347 7
PB 978 0 521 03046 5

35. DAVID ARMITAGE, ARMAND HIMY AND QUENTIN SKINNER (eds.)
Milton and Republicanism
HB 978 521 55178 6
PB 978 0 521 64648 2

36. MARKKU PELTONEN
Classical Humanism and Republicanism in English Political Thought
1570–1640
HB 978 0 521 49695 7
PB 978 0 521 61716 1

37. PHILIP IRONSIDE
The Social and Political Thought of Bertrand Russell
The Development of an Aristocratic Liberalism
HB 978 0 521 47383 5
PB 978 0 521 02476 1

38. NANCY CARTWRIGHT, JORDI CAT, LOLA FLECK AND THOMAS E. UEBEL
Otto Neurath: Philosophy between Science and Politics
HB 978 0 521 45174 1

39. DONALD WINCH
Riches and Poverty
An Intellectual History of Political Economy in Britain, 1750–1834
PB 978 0 521 55920 1

40. JENNIFER PLATT
A History of Sociological Research Methods in America
HB 978 0 521 44173 5
PB 978 0 521 64649 9

41. KNUD HAAKONSSEN (ed.)
Enlightenment and Religion
Rational Dissent in Eighteenth-Century Britain
HB 978 0 521 56060 3
PB 978 0 521 02987 2

42. G. E. R. LLOYD
Adversaries and Authorities
Investigations into Ancient Greek and Chinese Science
HB 978 0 521 55331 5
PB 978 0 521 55695 8

43. ROLF LINDNER
The Reportage of Urban Culture
Robert Park and the Chicago School
HB 978 0 521 44052 3
PB 978 0 521 02653 6

44. ANNABEL BRETT
Liberty, Right and Nature
Individual Rights in Later Scholastic Thought
HB 978 0 521 56239 3
PB 978 0 521 54340 8

45. STEWART J. BROWN (ed.)
William Robertson and the Expansion of Empire
HB 978 0 521 57083 1

46. HELENA ROSENBLATT
Rousseau and Geneva
From the First Discourse to the Social Contract, 1749–1762
HB 978 0 521 57004 6
PB 978 0 521 03395 4

47. DAVID RUNCIMAN
Pluralism and the Personality of the State
HB 978 0 521 55191 5
PB 978 0 521 02263 7

48. ANNABEL PATTERSON
Early Modern Liberalism
HB 978 0 521 59260 4
PB 978 0 521 02631 4

49. DAVID WEINSTEIN
Equal Freedom and Utility
Herbert Spencer's Liberal Utilitarianism
HB 978 0 521 62264 6
PB 978 0 521 02686 4

50. YUN LEE TOO AND NIALL LIVINGSTONE (eds.)
Pedagogy and Power
Rhetorics of Classical Learning
HB 978 0 521 59435 6
PB 978 0 521 03801 0

51. REVIEL NETZ
The Shaping of Deduction in Greek Mathematics
A Study in Cognitive History
HB 978 0 521 62279 0
PB 978 0 521 54120 6

52. MARY S. MORGAN AND MARGARET MORRISON (eds.)
Models as Mediators
Perspectives in Natural and Social Science
HB 978 0 521 65097 7
PB 978 0 521 65571 2

53. JOEL MICHELL
Measurement in Psychology
A Critical History of a Methodological Concept
HB 978 0 521 62120 5
PB 978 0 521 02151 7

54. RICHARD A. PRIMUS
The American Language of Rights
HB 978 0 521 65250 6
PB 978 0 521 61621 8

55. ROBERT ALUN JONES
The Development of Durkheim's Social Realism
HB 978 0 521 65045 8
PB 978 0 521 02210 1

56. ANNE MCLAREN
Political Culture in the Reign of Elizabeth I
Queen and Commonwealth 1558–1585
HB 978 0 521 65144 8
PB 978 0 521 02483 9

57. JAMES HANKINS (ed.)
Renaissance Civic Humanism
Reappraisals and Reflections
HB 978 0 521 78090 2
PB 978 0 521 54807 6

58. T.J. HOCHSTRASSER
Natural Law Theories in the Early Enlightenment
HB 978 0 521 66193 5
PB 978 0 521 02787 8

59. DAVID ARMITAGE
The Ideological Origins of the British Empire
HB 978 0 521 59081 5
PB 978 0 521 78978 3

60. IAN HUNTER
Rival Enlightenments
Civil and Metaphysical Philosophy in Early Modern Germany
HB 978 0 521 79265 3
PB 978 0 521 02549 2

61. DARIO CASTIGLIONE AND IAIN HAMPSHER-MONK (eds.)
The History of Political Thought in National Context
HB 978 0 521 78234 0

62. IAN MACLEAN
Logic, Signs and Nature in the Renaissance
The Case of Learned Medicine
HB 978 0 521 80648 0

63. PETER MACK
Elizabethan Rhetoric
Theory and Practice
HB 978 0 521 812924
PB 978 0 521 02099 2

64. GEOFFREY LLOYD
The Ambitions of Curiosity
Understanding the World in Ancient Greece and China
HB 978 0 521 81542 0
PB 978 0 521 89461 6

65. MARKKU PELTONEN
The Duel in Early Modern England
Civility, Politeness and Honour
HB 978 0 521 82062 2
PB 978 0 521 02520 1

66. ADAM SUTCLIFFE
Judaism and Enlightenment
HB 978 0 521 82015 8
PB 978 0 521 67232 0

67. ANDREW FITZMAURICE
Humanism and America
An Intellectual History of English Colonisation, 1500–1625
HB 978 0 521 82225 1

68. PIERRE FORCE
Self-Interest before Adam Smith
A Genealogy of Economic Science
HB 978 0 521 83060 7
PB 978 0 521 03619 1

69. ERIC NELSON
The Greek Tradition in Republican Thought
HB 978 0 521 83545 9
PB 978 0 521 02428 0

70. HARRO HOPFL
Jesuit Political Thought
The Society of Jesus and the state, c. 1540–1640
HB 978 0 521 83779 8

71. MIKAEL HORNQVIST
Machiavelli and Empire
HB 978 0 521 83945 7

72. DAVID COLCLOUGH
Freedom of Speech in Early Stuart England
HB 978 0 521 84748 3

73. JOHN ROBERTSON
The Case for the Enlightenment
Scotland and Naples 1680–1760
HB 978 0 521 84787 2
PB 978 0 521 03572 9

74. DANIEL CAREY
Locke, Shaftesbury, and Hutcheson
Contesting Diversity in the Enlightenment and Beyond
HB 978 0 521 84502 1

75. ALAN CROMARTIE
The Constitutionalist Revolution
An Essay on the History of England, 1450–1642
HB 978 0 521 78269 2

76. HANNAH DAWSON
Locke, Language and Early-Modern Philosophy
HB 978 0 521 85271 5

77. CONAL CONDREN, STEPHEN GAUKROGER AND IAN HUNTER (eds.)
The Philosopher in Early Modern Europe
The Nature of a Contested Identity
HB 978 0 521 86646 0

78. ANGUS GOWLAND
The Worlds of Renaissance Melancholy
Robert Burton in Context
HB 978 0 521 86768 9

79. PETER STACEY
Roman Monarchy and the Renaissance Prince
HB 978 0 521 86989 8

80. RHODRI LEWIS
Language, Mind and Nature
Artificial Languages in England from Bacon to Locke
HB 978 0 521 874750

81. DAVID LEOPOLD
The Young Karl Marx
German Philosophy, Modern Politics, and Human Flourishing
HB 978 0 521 87477 9

82. JON PARKIN
Taming the Leviathan
The Reception of the Political and Religious Ideas of Thomas Hobbes in England 1640–1700
HB 978 0 521 87735 0

83. D WEINSTEIN
Utilitarianism and the New Liberalism
HB 978 0 521 87528 8

84. LUCY DELAP
The Feminist Avant-Garde
Transatlantic Encounters of the Early Twentieth Century
HB 978 0 521 87651 3

85. BORIS WISEMAN
Lévi-Strauss, Anthropology and Aesthetics
HB 978 0 521 87529 5

86. DUNCAN BELL (ed.)
Victorian Visions of Global Order
Empire and International Relations in Nineteenth-Century Political Thought
HB 978 0 521 88292 7

87. IAN HUNTER
The Secularisation of the Confessional State
The Political Thought of Christian Thomasius
HB 978 0 521 88055 8

88. CHRISTIAN J EMDEN
Friedrich Nietzsche and the Politics of History
HB 978 0 521 88056 5

89. ANNELIEN DE DIJN
French Political thought from Montesquieu to Tocqueville
Liberty in a Levelled Society?
HB 978 0 521 87788 6

90. PETER GARNSEY
Thinking About Propety
From Antiquity to the Age of Revolution
HB 978 0 521 87677 3
PB 978 0 521 70023 8

91. PENELOPE DEUTSCHER
The Philosophy of Simone de Beauvoir
Ambiguity, Conversion, Resistance
HB 978 0 521 88520 1

92. HELENA ROSENBLATT
Liberal Values
Benjamin Constant and the Politics of Religion
HB 978 0 521 89825 6

93. JAMES TULLY
Public Philosophy in a New Key
Volume 1: Democracy and Civic Freedom
HB 978 0 521 44961 8
PB 978 0 521 72879 9

94. JAMES TULLY
Public Philosophy in a New Key
Volume 2: Imperialism and Civic Freedom
HB 978 0 521 44966 3
PB 978 0 521 72880 5

95. DONALD WINCH
Wealth and Life
Essays on the Intellectual History of Political Economy in Britain, 1848–1914
HB 978 0 521 88753 3
PB 978 0 521 71539 3

96. FONNA FORMAN-BARZILAI
Adam Smith and the Circles of Sympathy
Cosmopolitanism and Moral Theory
HB 978 0 521 76112 3

97. GREGORY CLAEYS
Imperial Sceptics
British Critics of Empire 1850–1920
HB 978 0 521 19954 4

98. EDWARD BARING
The Young Derrida and French Philosophy, 1945–1968
HB 978 1 107 00967 7

99. CAROL PAL
Republic of Women
Rethinking the Republic of Letters in the Seventeenth Century
HB 978 1 107 01821 1

100. C. A. BAYLY
Recovering Liberties
Indian Thought in the Age of Liberalism and Empire
HB 978 1 107 01383 4
PB 978 1 107 60147 5

101. FELICITY GREEN
Montaigne and the Life of Freedom
HB 978 1 107 02439 7

102. JOSHUA DERMAN
Max Weber in Politics and Social Thought
From Charisma to Canonizaion
HB 978 1 107 02588 2

103. RAINER FORST
(translated by Ciaran Cronin)
Toleration in Conflict
Past and Present
HB 978 0 521 88577 5

104. SOPHIE READ
Eucharist and the Poetic Imagination in Early Modern England
HB 978 1 107 03273 6

105. MARTIN RUEHL
The Italian Renaissance in the German Historical Imagination 1860–1930
HB 978 1 107 03699 4

106. GEORGIOS VAROUXAKIS
Liberty Abroad
J. S. Mill on International Relations
HB 9781107039148

107. ANDREW FITZMAURICE
Sovereignty, Property and Empire, 1500–2000
HB 978 1 107 07649 5

108. BENJAMIN STRAUMANN
Roman Law in the State of Nature
The Classical Foundations of Hugo Grotius' Natural Law
HB 978 1 107 09290 7

109. LIISI KEEDUS
The Crisis of German Historicism
The Early Political Thought of Hannah Arendt and Leo Strauss
HB 978 1 107 09303 4

110. EMMANUELLE DE CHAMPS
Enlightenment and Utility
Bentham in French, Bentham in France
HB 978 1 107 09867 1

111. ANNA PLASSART
The Scottish Enlightenment and the French Revolution
HB 978 1 107 09176 4

112. DAVID TODD
Free Trade and its Enemies in France, 1814–1851
HB 978 1 107 03693 2